Real Estate Investment

Colin A. Jones · Edward Trevillion

Real Estate Investment

Theory and Practice

palgrave
macmillan

Colin A. Jones
Heriot-Watt University
Edinburgh, UK

Edward Trevillion
Heriot-Watt University
Edinburgh, UK

ISBN 978-3-031-00967-9 ISBN 978-3-031-00968-6 (eBook)
https://doi.org/10.1007/978-3-031-00968-6

Cover illustration: I Wei Huang/shutterstock.com

This Palgrave Macmillan imprint is published by the registered company Springer Nature Switzerland AG
The registered company address is: Gewerbestrasse 11, 6330 Cham, Switzerland

Preface

The inspiration for this book came from updating Will Fraser's text, '*Principles of Property Investment and Pricing*', the last edition of which was published in 1993. Much has changed to the property market context since that popular textbook was the mainstay of teaching of real estate investment. Colin was a colleague of Will's and both of us have used the book for our teaching over the years. This new book reflects the growing globalisation of real estate investment, information availability and benchmarking, the rethinking of pensions, the rise of sustainability issues and technological change since the publication of Will's book.

The book also draws on our teaching of the subject over the years. The book comprises a combination of the essentials of how real estate markets work with the consequences for investment decisions. It explains theories of portfolio construction and how they relate to real estate. There is also a chapter on the management of real estate portfolios. The book ends with the continuing challenges for real estate investment.

We wish to thank colleagues and former colleagues as well as PhD students who have contributed to our research and thinking that is distilled in the book. Notable mentions include Neil Dunse, Alan Gardiner, Stewart Cowe, Nicola Livingstone, Tunbosun Oyedokun and Allison Orr.

We also wish to acknowledge the support of the Investment Property Forum (IPF) and MSCI Real Capital Analytics for some of the statistics and charts published in the book. Parts of the book are also based on research financially supported by the IPF.

Colin A. Jones
Heriot-Watt University
Edinburgh, UK

Edward Trevillion
Heriot-Watt University
Edinburgh, UK

Contents

List of Figures

List of Tables

Part I

The Real Estate Sector

Introduction 1

Introduction

In this chapter, some essential building blocks to understanding real estate investment decisions are set out. It begins with the essential nature of investment and an introduction to the factors influencing motivations. The chapter then focuses on property investment and its specific qualities distinguishing between the 'direct' purchase of real estate and assets that are 'indirectly' linked as their returns are derived from the property market. The significance of real estate investment relative to other types of investments is also explained as well as the differences in the way they are bought and sold. Because of these differences information on the property market is less transparent than for other types of investments. The chapter explains that the implications are that real estate trends are based on indices constructed by private organisations.

The next sections of the chapter consider the basics of how the real estate market works. First, the economics of the determination of the rent of individual properties is set out. Second, the inter-relationships between the demand for space, investment and development are considered via a graphical model. Finally, the structure of the book is given with brief outlines of each chapter. The structure of the chapter is as follows:

- What do we mean by investment?
- Property as an investment
- The financial environment
- Property indices and performance measurement
- User demand and the determination of rental value
- Property market dynamics
- Book structure

C. A. Jones and E. Trevillion, *Real Estate Investment*,
https://doi.org/10.1007/978-3-031-00968-6_1

What Do We Mean by Investment?

Investment may be defined as *the act of laying out money now in order to receive financial recompense in the future.* An investor investing money does so in the hope of earning more money in the future and this is true regardless of the type of investment. It involves two elements: a money outlay and future money receipts either in the form of a flow of income and/or capital sums in the future (e.g. an increase in the market price of the asset when it is sold to another party).

At the root of wealth creation is the concept of cash flow and the time value of money. Importantly, however, future receipts *may or may not be guaranteed.* Some investments do more than just yield a financial benefit for the owner. For example, an entrepreneur who invests capital in setting up a business may appreciate the raised profile linked with creating employment in a community. Financial investments, such as company shares and bonds, however, are regarded as pure forms of investments because the investor has, in the main, no interest other than in the future income they generate. A share, as its name implies, is a share in the capital of a company and entitles the owner to a requisite proportion of any of its profits. A bond holder is entitled to receive a periodic stream of income over time. Investors in these financial assets exchange a known amount of money in return for expected future receipts of money.

Ideally for many investors the aim of investment is to produce a maximum return for the minimum financial outlay with minimum risk. All of these aspects will be discussed as we go through the book, but it really is all about finding an investment that provides the best value for money and investors must continually compromise between risk and return depending on their own investment strategies. Importantly, however, we must be able to evaluate whether the proposed investment (which could have far reaching financial implications) is wealth creating. By wealth creating we mean whether the value created by the decision to invest is higher than the cost of the decision.

Many financial investments are assets that can be bought and sold at any time. These assets are marketable securities as the selling investor can always find another investor who is willing to acquire the asset and the entitlement of the future income. The price paid may not be the same as the one the seller paid. This is either due to a change in market conditions or the expected amount of money the investment will pay in the future. If the resale price is higher than the price paid to acquire the asset, then the investor has made a capital return (also called capital growth). All investors are aiming to achieve this outcome.

However, it may not always happen. When the price paid at the end of the holding period is less than the price originally paid then the investment has made a capital loss. Investors must weigh up the potential of an investment not to produce the expected capital growth or income streams. The chance of a loss either in capital or income occurring is the risk associated with an investment. Typical investors aim to maximise the return on their money invested while minimising the risk of losing it.

Investors do not have unlimited capital and financial decisions to invest will only be reached after the investor has logically undertaken a comparison of the cost and return associated with alternative investments. This decision would be taken after a consideration of several factors which include:

- Risk
- The investor's view on the value of money today compared with income in the future
- Liquidity (effectively the ease with which the asset could be re-sold)
- Marketability and transaction coasts
- Ease of management
- Real value of capital investment and returns with inflation over time.

These concepts are fleshed out in more detail in Chapter 2. Financial investments usually have a market price and an expected pattern of future cash flows. It is easy enough to compare the market prices of alternative investments. But this does not tell the investor how much return the investments will yield for the capital spent. An alternative, and more meaningful, way of comparing different investments is to examine their expected cash flows relative to their cost. This is true of both financial investments and property investments.

In addition to price and return, investors are interested in the certainty of earning a surplus over the price they pay. In this context, risk represents the likelihood of receiving more or less income than expected. It is a hugely important aspect of investment and has attracted a great deal more attention post the global financial crisis (GFC) from 2007, which came about partly because of insufficient attention to risk. Investors do not like risk. In principle they would prefer more secure income patterns than more uncertain income patterns and there are many circumstances where they would prefer a secure income over uncertain higher returns.

Property as an Investment

Property is unusual in that some investors acquire it purely for the financial returns it may generate while other investors buy it because it provides additional benefits. For example, a homeowner buys a house as somewhere to live. It functions as a consumer good since they occupy the space but at the same time it acts as an investment because a rise in house prices may generate a future capital growth.

Business or commercial property also has a dual function. It is an important factor of production. Without factories, offices, shops and leisure facilities the productive activities of business would not be possible. However, over the last two hundred years, commercial property has been transformed from a 'social institution' to a financial asset and its value now reflects both its importance as a factor of production and its value as an investment medium. This process has happened not least because of the increasing involvement of financial institutions in the investment process. In Western countries, it occurred as a response to the rapid socio-economic changes and rising inflation that occurred during the nineteenth century. A growing middle class (and a concomitant growth in middle-class savings), with concerns almost exclusively relating to financial return rather than non-monetary factors, resulted in savings being channelled into property sectors.

As a pure investment, the owner of a property can let the space out to a tenant(s) in return for a rental income. The return to direct property investment usually takes the form of both rental income and capital growth, and the risks depend on the type of property, its location, the lease terms attached to it and the quality of tenant. However, real estate investment has radically changed over the last 30 to 40 years with the introduction of new indirect forms. In this context, property investments can be split into two broad categories:

- Direct investment which is the ownership of the physical asset and its legal interests. It includes investors who buy land and buildings for owner occupation and those for whom it is a pure investment as they intend to let the occupation right to another party.
- Indirect investment is a 'paper' asset backed by property returns. Shares in companies that own property are an example of an indirect real estate investment. Mortgages and loans to property owners are debt based indirect property investments.

The return and risk attributes of different types of direct and indirect property investments are examined later in the book.

Inevitably, because business property is such an important factor of production its performance is closely linked to the overall performance of a nation's economy. In different ways, this is true of both the occupier (rental) and investment markets. This dual susceptibility has been amply demonstrated in the aftermath of the GFC when a double whammy of poor economic performance and the lack of available credit significantly affected the performance of both the investment and occupier markets.

The significance of real estate as an investment can be illustrated by the following statistics from the UK. By the end of 2018 the Investment Property Forum estimates there was around £951bn of commercial property in the UK, not including residential property. Of this £512bn was property held as an investment mainly by institutions and overseas investors, with the rest owner occupied. Property owned for investment purposes is referred to as investment stock or the investable universe throughout this book. The total values of each of the main UK commercial property classes or sectors (excluding residential, farmland and woodlands) are given in Fig. 1.1, broken down by both total stock and investable stock. Offices are the largest sector in the investment stock, representing 43% of total holdings. This weighting compares with the 31% offices in the total stock of UK real estate (investable and non-investable sock), demonstrating the popularity of offices. Retail property is also an important investment sector representing 32%

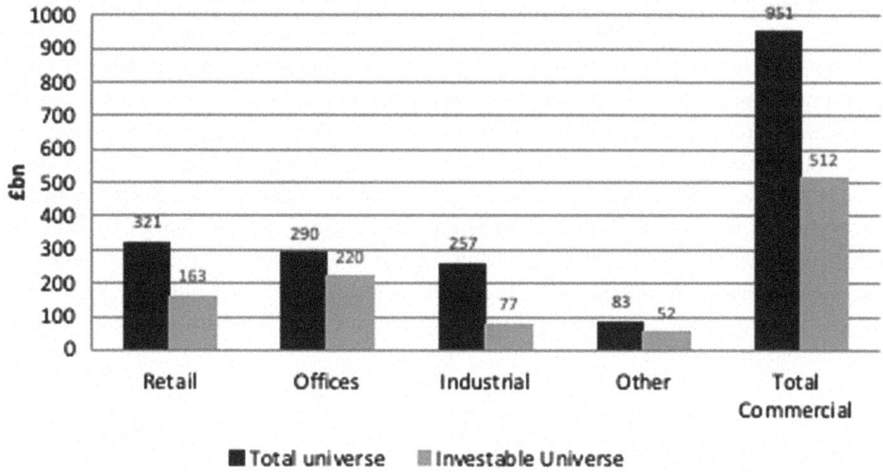

Fig. 1.1 The value of the UK commercial property universe (£bn) by property sector at the end of 2018 (*Source* Authors construct derived from Investment Property Forum [2020])

of the investment stock at the end of 2018. Of the 'other' sector two thirds is represented by hotels and leisure property.

In comparison, the total stock of residential property in the UK has been estimated at £6.7 trillion at the end of 2018, of which the private-rented sector (PRS) investment universe was valued at around £1.2trillion, significantly higher than the commercial property universe. While this book is mainly about commercial property as an investment class, readers should note the importance of residential property in investment portfolios in some countries and there will be some discussion of investment in this asset class later in the book.

In the UK, institutional investment in the PRS has historically been low, although there is growing interest. Some institutions are now investing significant sums in purpose built residential properties to rent, known as 'Build to Rent' (BTR), and student housing. At the end of 2018 institutional involvement in the residential sector stood at £35bn, mainly in BTR.

The Financial Environment

Shares in companies can be in private or public companies. Private companies, such as frequently football clubs, for example, can issue shares. Owners of these investments who wish to sell will need to seek out potential buyers through private channels. There is no marketplace for these shares so investments in a private company are therefore potentially very illiquid, reducing their marketability and price. Indeed, the prices are not publicly available and need to be negotiated between parties.

Companies whose shares are transacted on a stock exchange are known as publicly quoted or simply public companies. To be eligible to be quoted on a stock exchange a company needs to meet a set of criteria and initially issue a prospectus to potential investors. Shares in these companies and bonds as financial investments are then traded on stock markets with the amount of transactions and market prices published.

A stock exchange has benefits to investors and companies by offering a transparent market for shares. It ultimately reduces the cost of capital finance to industry and provides active information to allow investment decisions and future predictions to be made. A stock exchange can provide a large amount of long-term capital finance to industry and a wide range of securities for investors to choose from. In detail its main characteristics include:

- Potentially many buyers and sellers of assets
- No barriers to entry/exit for investors
- Information to investors available at little or no cost
- Low transaction and management costs
- It enables investors a platform to sell their investments if they choose and there a high turnover potential
- Assets are very liquid as transactions and payments can occur quickly
- Exchanges are often regulated by government
- Prices respond to new information quickly and generally efficiently.

There are now more than 60 countries in the world with stock exchanges. Two of the most important are London (LSE) and New York. They provide a platform for the buying and selling of shares in a fair and (not always) orderly way. The dealing in the LSE is not confined to UK securities but it is also a major centre for dealing in overseas securities and bonds. It operates, as do most stock exchanges, as a primary market where companies sell new securities (see earlier), fulfilling an economic function of raising money for industry and as a secondary market where investors can release their investment capital by selling their securities to a new buyer. The exchange prices of these securities depend on the flows of demand and supply at the time of the sale. Fluctuations in security prices can generate capital gains and losses for investors. An efficient secondary market is needed because investors like to know that there is a place they can go and sell shares quickly, cheaply and at the going rate. The LSE also co-ordinates the exchange of government and public authority bonds.

Besides the LSE in the UK, there is the AIM (Alternative Investment Market) share exchange for small and medium sized companies that do not meet the criteria to join it. More broadly financial markets which may be defined as *any mechanism for trading financial assets or claims*. There are a range of such markets that include:

- Capital markets (stock markets and bond markets)
- Commodity markets

Table 1.1 Lenders, borrowers and markets

	Relationship between lenders and borrowers		
Lenders	Financial intermediaries	Financial markets	Borrowers
Individuals	Banks	Interbank	Individuals
Companies	Insurance companies	Stock exchange	Companies
		Money markets	Central government
		Bond markets	Municipalities
		Foreign exchange markets	Public corporations

- The money market (short-term debt financing and investment)
- Derivatives markets (which provide instruments for the management of financial risk (see later in the book)
- Insurance markets
- Foreign exchange markets
- Futures and options markets.

Financial markets are a way of bringing together borrowers and lenders. A framework between borrowers and lenders is outlined in Table 1.1.

For financial markets, the point at which lenders and borrowers come together is in the markets themselves whether in a stock exchange, money market, bond market, interbank or foreign exchange markets.

Despite the huge investment potential, there is no sophisticated market for property transactions like those for financial products, except where property is bound up in listed property companies and investment trusts (indirect property noted earlier). For direct property, the barriers to entry are significant linked both to the nature of the market and the variability in the characteristics of individual buildings. As Chapter 4 details real estate is not homogeneous, it comes in large lot sizes with high unit costs, is illiquid, involves high transaction costs and investment requires a significant amount of specialist management costs. It is important to appreciate these barriers if property market dynamics are to be understood. They are discussed at length in the book and are a constant theme as the book progresses.

Although there is no property market similar to those financial markets described above, the relationship between borrowers and lenders of capital is not so different in principle within real estate markets. Sources of capital for investment need to be matched with borrowers to enable real estate development and investment to take place.

Property Indices and Performance Measurement

Where the information on prices in other financial markets is openly displayed and monitored on an hour-by-hour basis, the flow of information on property

Table 1.2 Indexing total returns

Year	1	2	3	4	5	6	7	8	9	10
Total return (%)		8.6	4.2	5.9	5	−7.6	−4.5	7.5	22.9	13
Indexed to year 1	100	108.6	113.1	119.8	125.7	116.1	110.9	119.3	146.6	165.7

transactions relies on agent contacts and the trade press. The property market has historically suffered from severe information constraints. Secrecy and misinforming the market are not an uncommon profit-generating technique in the property market. This results in a reluctance by private sector organisations to openly publish the information they collect. This information gap is often met by providers of property indices at the national and international level although this comes at a cost. It is therefore useful to explain the basics of property indices as they are referred to throughout the book.

An index expresses data relative to a given base value. So, for price-based indices, for example, the index takes the new price and expresses it as a function of earlier prices as follows:

$$\text{New price} * 100/\text{Base year price} \tag{1.1}$$

This allows us to compare numbers without emphasising the units to which they refer and is exampled in Table 1.2, which indexes a hypothetical property return series over a time frame of 10 years.

In the property market, indices are commonly used as estimates of market activity and to benchmark the performance of property against the performance of other investment media. They are used as measures of volatility and market return of property assets. Used in this manner, indices are fundamental aids that enable investors to make informed decisions when they are constructing multi-asset portfolios.

Property indices can be differentiated by the techniques used to collect data and compile the series. The two main types are appraisal-based and transaction-based indices:

Appraisal-based indices are common in the commercial property market where information on transaction prices is scarce. These indices are based on valuations because properties are sold infrequently. They are constructed by valuing the estimated market prices for a sample of properties owned by major investors. They are conducted on a regular basis for a given period, say a month, quarter or a year. The valuations are aggregated into one measure. This single figure is then transformed into an index by dividing it by the value in the base year and multiplying by 100 as in Eq. 1.1.

The frequency of the valuations generally reflects the size of the sample. For example, the UK MSCI property indices (see below) the larger the sample then the less frequent the index observation. In the case of MSCI an annual index is based on a sample larger than that used to construct their monthly and quarterly series. The monthly index is based on a sample of unitised funds, which require monthly valuations. It represents a market movement index while the annual index is a performance measurement index. These indices are useful as property information is scarce but can be misleading in extremis when the market is suffering a severe downturn.

Transaction-based indices are more common in the residential rather than the commercial market because more information on property transaction prices is available. Their application is discussed in detail in Chapter 12, and these indices can be constructed in a number of ways:

- Averaging transaction prices in a given time period.
- Using statistical modelling that assumes that property values depend on the nature of individual attributes. The price of a standardised property can then be estimated by feeding in its characteristics to the statistical price model.
- Applying a repeat sales method where the construction of this type of index is based on calculating the price change that occurs when properties are sold more than once in a specific period.

MSCI/IPD is by far the largest UK property index provider and is now used as the industry standard. It is appraisal-based and provides data in the form of a single composite measure for all-property and for the four broad property types—residential, offices, industrial units and shops, although these sectors are being continually extended. There are three principal published UK indices: annual, quarterly and monthly (see above). MSCI also publishes equivalent indices in other countries. In the United States, the NCREIF Property Index (NPI) is the primary index, and it is also an appraisal-based.

User Demand and the Determination of Rental Value

An important concept is in the understanding of the economics of the commercial real estate sector that of rent as a surplus. Tenants compete with other firms to rent a particular property. The rent a prospective tenant is prepared to pay is based on the profitability of carrying on a business activity in the property. The funds available for rent will be the difference between the revenue that can be generated and the cost of the other factors of production including wages and any raw materials. A firm will also have to make an allowance for (normal) profit.

The amount of rent paid for the use of a property, namely the rental value, will depend on competition from firms each of whom will be calculating how much rent they are prepared to pay based on their evaluation of the surplus generated. Competition will not only achieve higher rents but also mean that the property is allocated to the most profitable use of the interested firms.

The rental value of a property will change over time according to changes in the expected surplus of revenue over cost of firms who wish to occupy it. However, rising rents generally may have a negative impact on some firms seeking commercial property if their company finances cannot justify paying the additional asking levels. The flow of firms seeking property, namely market demand, may be reduced. The degree to which demand varies with a change in rent is known as the price elasticity of demand for property. The more responsive the number of firms occupying premises are to changes in rent the more the market is deemed to be elastic.

There is no substitute for land and property in a general sense, neither are the major categories of property close substitutes for each other, an office is not a substitute for a shop. Although a factory office or shop in one area might seem to be a close substitute for a similar property in another area, the importance of location to property is a fundamental reason for the perception the property in general has a very inelastic demand, i.e. the percentage change in quantity demanded is smaller than that in price. The concept of demand elasticity helps to explain the large disparities in rental value between similar shops in different parts of the market.

In seeking to explain rental values, it is the demand to lease property that is relevant, but we must acknowledge owner occupation as the alternative means of occupation. Thus, the cost of availability of owner-occupied premises will tend to affect the demand for rented accommodation. The elasticity of demand also depends on its cost as a proportion of total factor costs. So, the higher the rent becomes as a proportion of business cost, the more elastic/responsive will be occupation demand.

Property Market Dynamics

The real estate market overall can be represented by three overlapping sectors:

- Occupation/use
- Investment
- Development.

The duality of commercial property as a consumption and investment good results in complex relationships between the occupier and investment sectors, and also the development sector.

Demand and supply **flows** determine the exchange price of interests. Occupation demand flow relates to firms seeking property to rent or own. The occupation supply is premises available on the market from existing property that is empty, or about to become available, plus new property coming on the market for the first time. The interaction of these flows determines rent levels. Similarly, the supply flow of new and second-hand properties available for purchase interacts with demand from investors to establish capital values. The flow of newly developed properties and demolitions ultimately changes the stock.

The price/rent of property in the letting or occupation sector is demand led as without occupation demand a property has no value. Occupiers require commercial property as a factor of production, and the amount they need is determined by their scale of output, which in turn is driven by the state of the economy. Demand for commercial property therefore depends on the ability of the occupier to produce goods and services and it is a derived demand from its (expected) level of output. It is this demand for space which drives the whole real estate sector; occupation demand generates value that is the basis for investment demand. An imbalance between occupation demand and supply impacts on development flows: for example, excess demand for space leads to rising rents and makes development more viable. Increased development results in an increase in the stock. It is these relationships that are at the heart of the representation in Fig. 1.2.

These flows in the real estate system, shown in Fig. 1.2, interact through the linkages between segments through market signals. The core and subsidiary loops are marked with a B, indicating that they are balancing and marked with a + or – depending on whether the market impacts are positive or negative.

The core real estate circle or loop centres on occupation supply/demand interaction leading to rent levels that eventually influence new supply. Occupier demand supported by the state of the economy impacts on the demand for space and then on the rental levels in the marketplace. If firms' revenues grow with positive economic growth tenants are likely to be able to make greater profits and be prepared

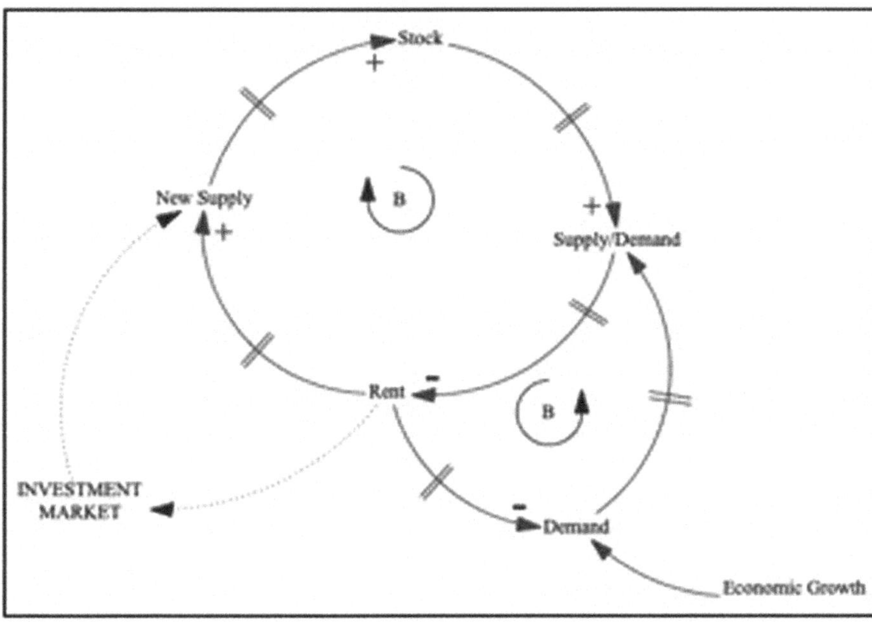

Fig. 1.2 The real estate circle

to pay higher rents while the opposite occurs in a downturn. Actual rent levels will depend on the balance between demand and supply.

The dynamics of this feedback loop start as the supply/demand balance impacts on rent and then demand. It can be seen more precisely as the interaction between the amount of vacant floor space available and the desired take up rate by occupiers. If desired take up is more than vacancies, then rents will rise and choke off some demand. If the reverse is true and vacancies are greater than tenants looking for property then rents fall, potentially stimulating more demand.

The model has a subsidiary loop that notes explicitly the role of investment. Rents feed through to both investment demand and influence the potential of new construction. In the case of investment demand, rental growth will push up capital values, which will also positively impact on investment demand. Rising investment demand will encourage the building of new developments as a means of meeting the demand. On the other hand, falling rents will have the reverse impacts. These investment processes will also depend on the availability of finance.

These market processes do not happen instantaneously and take time. The supply of new properties is unable to adjust immediately to changes in demand. New development may depend on the supply of the right kind of land in the right place and be subject to planning restrictions. In addition, there can be changes in the use of existing buildings in response to changing demand but again properties will take time to be adapted and potentially refurbished. Overall, there are a host of potential delays within the feedback loops indicated in Fig. 1.2 by breaks in lines by II. The volatility in demand relative to supply and the price changes it generates can give rise to real estate cycles as outlined in Chapter 3.

The nature of these processes outlined above demonstrate the complexities of the property market system, and they are discussed in detail as the book progresses. It is further complicated by the fact that at various points in history real estate markets have suffered from irrationality. The structure of the book in this regard is discussed in the next section.

Book Structure

The subject of the book is investment in the real estate sector, a not insignificant part of the wider investment community, and the benefits it offers investors compared with other asset classes. The primary aim is to provide an overview of real estate investment and it is aimed primarily at students of the subject. It also provides a useful refresher for property professionals, providing them with a different, and sometimes new view of how the property market really works. It mainly concerns itself with the commercial property market. However, it recognises that in some countries there are large investors in the residential sector and an increasing interest in it in others such as the UK.

Each chapter of the book starts with learning aims and ends with summaries and expected learning outcomes. As noted, it is aimed at students and explains the various aspects of real estate investment in as simple terms as possible, without losing sight of the important issues surrounding this important investment medium. An important part of the book examines developing real estate paradigms and the challenges and opportunities arising from these new ways of thinking and operation. The final part of the book examines possible areas of future work that might be used in an academic environment for dissertation topics or new research programmes. At the same time, this will highlight for property professionals the way that the industry is changing.

The book is in three parts, each part providing a progressively more detailed view of the market and how it functions. The first part looks at the nature of the real estate sector and the principles of investment in broad terms. It then moves on to look at real estate investment in much more depth adding more theoretical material especially around portfolio theory, market efficiency and asset pricing. The third part of the book asks what of the future and outlines developing paradigms in the real estate sector. The final part of the book draws the work together and suggests areas for future work. The following sub-sections outline the contents of each book chapter in detail.

Chapter 2 Principles of Investment

This chapter focuses on the principles of investment. It looks at basic concepts underpinning investment decision-making and begins by defining risk and return and explains the use of yields (the most used method of valuing investments). The concept of 'value' itself varies dependent on the investor and its purpose, and so the chapter distinguishes between price, value and worth. Investing in risky assets as opposed to risk-free assets implies that an investor expects to be compensated by higher return. This compensation is often referred to as a risk premium, and the chapter delves into the principles of how this might be calculated for real estate investment.

The chapter sets out the Discounted Cash Flow (DCF) approach to estimating value which allows an assessment of an investment based on the ideas of the time value of money and which enables an investor to price an investment by examining its expected future stream of returns. DCF is an essential investment tool, and the chapter explains it in detail.

The final topics of the chapter are gearing and maturation. These are key processes in the real estate market that influence returns. The former is particularly important in short-term variations in returns while the latter is a long-term influence on investment.

Chapter 3 The Macroeconomy and Real Estate Cycles

There is a clear link between the performance of the macroeconomy and the real estate market. An increase in national manufacturing output brings a rise in demand for factories. Similarly greater output of services in the economy leads to more offices. The switch to a services-based economy in many developed countries has been reflected in a growth of offices and a decline in factories. Rising real wages also brings higher consumer spending and feeds through to an expansion in the number of shops and leisure real estate space. Overall economic growth generates a rise in demand for different types of property.

In this context, the chapter explores the close link between the macroeconomy and real estate cycles. The dynamic nature of the real estate market is explained by reference to underlying economic forces and the incidence of cycles. The fundamental economic determinants of real estate change are considered and their links to development activity. The significance of cycles to real estate markets is demonstrated through documented examples in an international history.

From this base a model of the cycle of commercial property development, distinct from the business cycle, is set out. Commercial real estate cycles are supported and indeed can be generated by credit availability. Variability in finance per se and changes to gearing can generate real estate cycles through their impact on yields. Changing sentiment and liberal lending by banks can support increasing investment funds into real estate that can lead to falling yields. It can occur without expectations of rental growth/supply shortages or time lags. In this context, there is a discussion of how real estate cycles can be generated by the availability of investment funds alone, based on the real estate boom of the 2000s. The final section of the chapter considers the role of sentiment influencing the repetition of cycles and the failure of forecasting.

Chapter 4 Characteristics of Real Estate Investment

The focus of this chapter is the nature and logic of real estate investment. It begins by distinguishing direct and indirect real estate investment. Direct investment being the ownership of the physical asset while indirect investment in real estate is the ownership of paper assets backed by property. A further differentiation is then made between assets that can be bought and sold relatively easily on a stock market (listed) and those that are marketed individually say through a market broker.

The chapter then examines the principal forms of real estate sectors that constitute the investment market, and their financial characteristics, noting the importance of legal interests. The characteristics of these investments are compared with those of stock market assets, and this leads to a comparison of the operation of real estate markets with the stock market and the fundamentally different characteristics of the former.

A more in-depth comparative analysis recaps the definition and use of yields and considers the yields of real estate assets relative to stock market assets, especially the gap between gilt and property yields in different countries. There then follows a section on the wider logic of holding real estate including its role as a hedge against inflation, and as a diversification tool in a multi-asset portfolio. The next section examines the underlying factors influencing residential investment and the growing interest in this sector as an investment medium in the UK. Finally, the chapter considers alternative forms of real estate assets including specialised privates sector business accommodation and infrastructure and service property.

Chapter 5 Investors

This chapter is concerned with the owners of commercial property who let space out to a tenant in return for a rental income rather than owner occupiers. The chapter sets the current property investment market in an historical context because as the market adapted and developed so too did the nature and range of investors and their impact on the overall structure of the marketplace. The nature of real estate assets and investors have radically changed over time with the emergence, particularly, of new types of funds investing in the sector and the chapter chronicles the evolution of investment in real estate and the different mechanisms utilised by investors. The chapter reviews a spectrum of investors and their various reasons for investing or not investing in real estate. In doing so, it revisits the characteristics of real estate relative to other asset classes and with it the motives for investing in commercial real estate. The chapter also examines their choice of real estate investments and why.

It examines the types of financial institutions investing in property and their investment priorities. A distinction can be made between direct and indirect investors in real estate. As noted in Chapter 4, direct investment can be seen as the purchase of individual assets, whereas indirect investment is the purchase of a share or a unit in a fund or company that then invests in real estate. This distinction in practice is blurred because in one sense nearly all the investors considered are collective schemes whereby individuals buy into a fund that then invests in real estate on their behalf. Further some of these investments not only purchase individual properties but also participate in collective investment arrangements.

The chapter ends with a case study of hedge fund involvement in the property market, specifically the purchase of entire housing associations in Germany and the purchase of distressed debt associated with portfolios of properties from the banks following the GFC.

Chapter 6 Market Efficiency and Asset Pricing

The chapter builds on the theory of pricing examined in Chapter 2 which examined the concept of value and the use of DCF models to distinguish between price, value and worth. The process of determining market prices cannot be analysed without investigating how efficient a market is at reflecting price and price movements. Market efficiency is defined as the degree to which market prices reflect all available relevant information. It can have a significant bearing on how the prices of assets are established. In this context, the chapter examines market efficiency as it applies to the property market and the implications that information inefficiency has on the investment decision-making process.

The chapter begins by examining the efficient market hypothesis (EMH). It describes ways to test the information efficiency of the property market and looks at irrational behaviour in the marketplace, an important marker of how well it is at handling information. In this context, a major factor affecting whether the EMH is sufficient to describe markets is the extent to which investor behaviour impacts on the market overall. The chapter therefore examines rational and irrational behaviour in the marketplace.

It revisits the issue of mispricing of property assets and the part that valuations and their accuracy plays. The chapter examines the consequences of overoptimism, a symptom of irrational behaviour and how irrational behaviour can impact on the stability of property markets, and can result in severe financial penalties.

To underline theory the chapter undertakes a case study which analyses the UK property market during and after the GFC of 2007–2008 as an example of irrational behaviour in commercial property markets.

Chapter 7 Portfolio Theory and Property in a Multi-Asset Portfolio

Most of the commercial properties held as an investment are wrapped up in funds, large and small, held by financial institutions, property companies, REITs and high net worth individuals. Because of this no study of commercial property investment is complete without an examination of the benefits and characteristics of holding property in these bundles of investments or portfolios. The importance of this aspect of property investment is reflected in two chapters in this book devoted to portfolio theory and portfolio management, the first of these in Chapter 7.

In Chapter 2, we discussed how to measure the risk and return characteristics of property investments. Risk was defined as the potential variation in returns in the future but noted that it can be gauged by what has happened to a particular investment in the past. We also examined how investors evaluate individual assets by comparing the expected returns from a range of probable outcomes with the risk attached to the investment. In this chapter, we apply the concepts of risk and return to combinations of investments.

Combining assets that react differently under certain economic and financial conditions can reduce a portfolio's risk and portfolio theory can help the investor to decide which combinations of investments give the best return for the risk involved. In this context, the chapter outlines the components of risk in a portfolio and how risk can be reduced by diversification. The chapter then goes on to examine the application of Modern Portfolio Theory (MPT) to property and the development of MPT in recent decades. The fundamental principle of MPT is that the risk return attributes of individual investments are important not so much independently but in the way they contribute to the risk and return of the portfolio overall.

The chapter then looks at the Capital Asset Pricing Model (CAPM0 as a way of assessing returns as a function of market risk). Like MPT, the model was developed with financial markets in mind but has been adapted for use for property markets with some reservations. The chapter finishes by reprising the case for real estate in multi-asset portfolios, and the practicalities of building and holding real estate in real estate only and multi-asset portfolios.

Chapter 8 Property Portfolio Management

The second part of the book's consideration of portfolio theory and management adopts a broader perspective and examines the overall investment strategies used by investors when constructing and managing a portfolio. The chapter examines the investment process including the choice of portfolio (fund) assets, how these choices match the preferences of potential investors, the ongoing monitoring of performance. In particular, it considers how portfolio performance is judged against certain reference behaviours in the form of benchmarking. The chapter also looks at important elements of monitoring and managing performance including the use of indices.

The starting point is that an investment strategy should be shaped by the objectives of the portfolio. An investor or fund manager can only set these objectives after determining certain characteristics about the investment preferences of the investor(s). For instance, the investment objectives need to reflect the required risk and return of the investor(s), details of their existing wealth, their tax position, liquidity requirements and future liabilities. Only, after these objectives are established can an investment strategy and relevant policies be devised, and a suitable monitoring programme constituted.

The chapter begins by defining some useful fund management terms. It then outlines aspects of the investment and finance decision in general and decision-making processes in more detail including portfolio construction and strategy. An important element of the chapter is that devoted to portfolio monitoring which includes a section on benchmarking and the use of forecasts to anticipate the potential success of future strategies.

Chapter 9 The Internationalisation of Property Investment

The organisation of economic activity, and with it commercial property markets, has become increasingly global and integrated over the last three decades. Despite trends in some regions towards nationalism and fragmentation, markets are much more integrated compared to the early 1990s.

For much of the twentieth century international property markets were fragmented with mature (established) markets limited to Europe, North America and British Commonwealth countries on the Pacific Rim. Even in these countries there was no real harmonisation of market practices apart from countries where legal systems mirrored those of the UK. The globalisation of financial and property markets really only developed towards the end of the twentieth century and was driven by socio, economic and political changes worldwide.

It can argued that the globe has become more democratic, and there is no doubt that this has led to greater harmonisation in general. However, the real game-changer towards internalisation has been the move to economic neo-liberalism and global capitalism, irrespective of whether governments are considered democratic or not. It has led to the recognition or acceptance that this economic approach had the potential for providing greater market efficiency compared to strict command economies.

Chapter 9 aims to provide an analysis of this internationalisation process. It undertakes an in-depth analysis of investment issues relating to the ownership, management, valuation, development and acquisition of property in international real estate markets. Specifically, it includes: an examination of international property investment markets and the globalisation processes, and the consequences. It also encompasses an analysis of the economic drivers of international property cycles, a discussion of market maturity and market transparency, and an outline of the practical aspects of owning and trading in international properties. In doing so it includes a brief look at the variations in lease structures and valuation methodologies.

As part of the discussion of market maturity, the chapter finishes with a number of case studies to analyse some emerging markets in Eastern Europe and Asia and separately to examine the characteristics of global cities. It also undertakes a separate case study relating to BREXIT in the context of the impact of political risk and nationalism on segmentation.

Chapter 10 State Intervention and Implications for Investment

Real estate markets operate within a framework set by government and to some extent by supra-national ones working in concert. Government regulations therefore can be seen as a series of tiers of control by local city governments through to international treaties. In each case the rules they set have ramifications for the operation of real estate markets.

Chapter 10 looks at these layers of intervention and the influence of the removal of regulation. It begins by examining the potential impact of land use planning, noting variations between countries and even between regions/states of a country. Whereas planning acts primarily by controlling new development and shaping urban travel patterns, there are wider consequences for real estate market values and investment.

Climate change is inevitably focusing the minds of governments around the world. As a result, there is an increasing policy emphasis on the energy use of real estate. Governments are seeking ways to impose greener standards for existing and new buildings, and nudge tenants and investors to address these issues by recognising the importance of energy use. The chapter chronicles the various government approaches to this issue and the real estate market's response.

The chapter also reviews the role of government regulation in the housing market through residential rent controls and the associated security of tenure for tenants. Regulation can also extend to the nature of commercial real estate leases. The market impacts of types of rent controls are examined.

The consequences of the removal of regulation are then considered using examples. In the residential sector, the removal of rent controls in the UK is shown to ultimately revive the private-rented sector. However, it also explains why the revival took some time to happen. The chapter also reflects on the impact that the worldwide deregulation of the banks had on lending and its contribution to the commercial real estate boom of the 2000s.

Finally, the chapter assesses the role of international banking regulations to control lending to real estate via a series of Basel Accords. It provides an historical review of their development from 1988 and explains how they were tightened as a response to the banking crisis following the GFC.

Chapter 11 Investment Consequences of Changing Occupier Needs and Obsolescence

The chapter focuses on how changing occupier needs are framed by the state of technology and demonstrates how technological advances lead to new built forms in the different sectors. In particular, the emergence of these new forms is shown to replace traditional buildings causing obsolescence in the existing stock. The chapter reveals how no real estate sector is immune from obsolescence and that in turn there are consequences for investment decisions and the composition of portfolios.

It defines and examines the causes of obsolescence. In this context, it outlines how new environmental standards encouraged by a new green agenda seeking a zero-carbon future is promoting greener buildings and a new 'green label' for buildings that meet the requisite environmental standards. While there is no one definition of a green building and there are a range of voluntary accreditation green label systems around the world, there are potentially equivalent obsolescence consequences for investors.

Changing occupier needs are highlighted in the retail sector where for example the impact of online sales on retailing is only the latest of a long line of changes that have impacted on the retail sector with consequences for investment. Many of these changes were brought about by the growth of car usage and led to new retail forms and locations and the chapter examines this process of change and considers the response of large investors.

Finally, the chapter looks at the investment consequences of technological change in the office and warehousing sector, in particular as a result of the improvement in ICT applications.

Chapter 12 Real Estate Opportunities and Challenges

Real estate markets are constantly subject to change and change inevitably offers opportunities and challenges to investors. The motivations for changing the way real estate investment are undertaken and the way the market operates have often been shaped and stimulated by external macroeconomic forces, what is happening in the stock market, and facilitated by technological advances. This chapter reviews the decades of change in the commercial real estate market since the turn of the millennium and the challenges and opportunities presented by this change.

Some of the challenges and opportunities examined have spun out of the GFC and the need to re-examine risk assessment and valuations, but some, such as those relating to pension reform had been developing before the GFC. The chapter looks at these in detail but also examines some of the structural consequences of the GFC, the usefulness of transaction-based indices to monitor performance and the potential for using sustainable valuations, and their possible mitigating effects on bubbles when assessing new loans for property investment. It also looks at the opportunities arising from the use of AI and other new technology as well as examining the need to include behaviour in our models of the market.

Finally, the chapter examines the emergence of alternative real estate assets to the traditional sectors and considers different ways of generating return from property. Alternative assets are an eclectic collection of asset types that can be divided into two types: operational entities or trade related properties and social infrastructure. Both types involve the operation and management of a specialist real estate form. The chapter examines these in some detail and considers how technological change is creating substantial upheaval in the ownership and use of the industrial, office and retail real estate sectors, and driving innovation in the way property is used and paid for.

Chapter 13 Future Research and Dissertations

The final part of the book briefly reviews potential future research and student dissertation topics.

Readings

Fraser, W. D. (1993) *Principles of Property Investment and Pricing*. 2nd Edition. Palgrave, Macmillan, London. ISBN 0333716922.

Gough, L. (2011) *How the Stock Market Really Works*. 5th Edition. Financial Times, Prentice Hall, London. ISBN 9780273743552 (pbk.).

Investment Property Forum (2020) *The Size and Structure of the UK Commercial Property Market*. IPF, London.

Jones, C., Cowe, S. and Trevillion, E. (2018) *Property Boom and Banking Bust: The Role of Commercial Lending in the Bankruptcy of Banks*. Wiley-Blackwell, Chichester. ISBN-13 978-1119219255.

Principles of Investment

2

Introduction

This chapter looks at basic concepts underpinning investment decision-making. It begins by defining risk and return and explains the use of yields. Yields are the most commonly used method of valuing investments. The concept of 'value' itself varies dependent on the investor and its purpose, and so the chapter distinguishes between price, value and worth.

Investing in risky assets as opposed to risk-free assets implies that an investor expects to be compensated by higher return. This compensation is often referred to as a risk premium, and the chapter delves into the principles of how this might be calculated for real estate investment.

Assessing an investment also requires a balance between returns now and in the future. Or more precisely the choice between returns in the short term versus the long term. This task can be achieved by reference to a technique called Discounted Cash Flow (DCF). This discounting approach also enables an investor to price an investment by examining its expected future stream of returns. DCF is an essential investment tool and the chapter explains it in detail.

The final topics of the chapter are gearing and maturation. These are key processes in the real estate market that influence returns. The former is particularly important in short-term variations in returns while the latter is a long-term influence on investment. The chapter covers the following topics:

- Defining risk and return
- Yields
- Risk premium
- Yields and capital values
- Price, value and worth

C. A. Jones and E. Trevillion, *Real Estate Investment*,
https://doi.org/10.1007/978-3-031-00968-6_2

- Theory of pricing— discounted cash flow framework
- Gearing and the role of debt
- Maturation

Defining Risk and Return

Return at its simplest is the income generated from owning an investment. However, the return from owning an individual property asset is not exclusively the income generated from the rent received from the tenant. There is also the potential of capital gain from any increase in value. Return from a property therefore has two components—rent received and any change in capital value. The latter could be negative.

This division of return between income and capital change applies also to buying company shares. Owning a share entitles an investor to a share of the profits in the form of a dividend paid usually every six months. Share ownership also entitles the investor to the opportunity to make a capital gain if the shares rise in value (although they may also fall).

The possibility that capital values of properties or shares may fall in value reveals the risk associated with investment. It is also possible that rental income and dividends may fall in the future adding to the potential risk.

Risk is therefore the potential variation in returns in the future, but it can be gauged by what has happened to a particular investment in the past. The risk can be quantified by calculating the standard deviation of past returns around the mean or average return. The greater the variation then the larger the standard deviation and the higher the risk.

The formula for the standard deviation is as follows:

$$\sigma = \frac{1}{n}\sqrt{}(\text{rent}_i - \mu)^2$$

where:

σ = standard deviation
rent_i = rent in year i
μ = mean rent
n = number of years in calculation

Yields

At its simplest, investors choose between investments based on which gives value for money in terms of returns. In theory, this involves comparing the capital values of different properties with their likely returns, particularly the current rental income. The problem is that it is difficult to compare properties that are very different in terms of size or value. The issue is resolved using yields.

Yields address the problem by standardising for the different capital values of individual properties. The (initial) yield is calculated as:

$$\frac{\text{net rental income}}{\text{capital value}} * 100$$

It tells an investor the value for money of a property by expressing the initial rent as a percentage of its capital value. It enables investors to compare in a consistent way a range of real estate assets. In some countries, for example the United States, these are termed capitalisation rates.

Using yields to compare assets is not just used in real estate. They are also applied in the stock market to compare the value for money of individual shares and bonds. To calculate the yield of a share, you replace net rental income with dividend. Similarly, for a bond you replace it with the interest payment. The basic generic yield model is then:

$$\frac{\text{net initial income}}{\text{capital value}} * 100$$

By comparing yields, it is possible to assess which of two investments is more expensive based on their current or initial rental income.

The yield itself is also linked to what an investor expects to happen to the rent of the property, i.e. how much rental growth is anticipated in the future. The yields of two properties may have different yields simply because one has the potential for greater rental growth. An investor may accept/take a low-initial yield to purchase an asset if it is expected to generate growth in future income.

The yield an investor pays for an asset therefore reflects the anticipated return over time. In addition, an investor in real estate and shares would expect a return greater than simply putting money in the bank or buying a government bond as he/she is taking a risk. On the other hand, a government bond gives (in theory at least) a fixed risk-free rate of interest that does not change.

There is a spectrum of yields for different investment (types) reflecting the degree of potential rental growth. As noted above, investors accept lower yields for investments that are expected to grow in value. Alternatively, if the expected return is to stay constant, investors would need to be compensated by a higher-initial return, i.e. yield. In both cases, the yield reflects the potential income growth and the investor's required rate of return.

These ideas can be expressed in the following simple equation:

$$k = r - g \tag{2.1}$$

where:

k = current income yield

r = required rate of return
g = expected rental growth

Using this formula, it can be seen that a fixed income investment would mean $g = 0$ and so the yield equals the required rate of return. An example of a fixed income investment is a bond issued by a government or company. For investments that incorporate income growth potential, the greater the anticipated growth the lower the yield will be.

The analysis above presents the essentials within the framework of Eq. 2.1. The reality is more complex. The formula can be extended to take account of the length of rent reviews within lease terms. Expected rental growth then changes in steps, say every three years, when a rent review occurs. Anticipated future income can also be deflated by the influence of depreciation of the value of the asset. These impacts can be included in a more detailed formula for the equation above. Nevertheless, the essence of Eq. 2.1 remains.

Risk Premium

The required rate of return for a risky asset needs some further amplification. As noted above, it must be at least the return from putting your money in the bank (or buying a bond) because you are taking a risk. To recap, risk is defined by the potential variation in returns. The required rate of return for a risky asset is therefore higher than that achieved by buying a government bond. In particular, the required return can be broken down into the return from risk-free investment plus a risk premium.

If the risk premium was 3% and the risk-free return was 2%, then the investor would require a 5% return on that particular investment. The nature of a risk premium is wider than being purely derived from potential variations in returns and depends on other related aspects of the asset or asset class. Real estate is generally deemed to have a higher risk premium than blue chip shares because of the imperfections or characteristics of the real estate market.

The source of the additional risk premium for real estate assets has a number of elements. Real estate is deemed to have higher transactions and management costs, lower liquidity and marketability and poorer market data. All of these could affect market value. It is a long list highlighted in Chapter 1. In other words, the premium is based on the weak efficiency of real estate markets and the nature of property as an investment (see also Chapter 6).

The conventional traditional rule of thumb assumption was that this risk premium meant that the required rate of return on property was 2% over the risk-free rate as in the example above. However, there are several reasons for querying this rate. It is very difficult to estimate from market data, but studies have put the long run average figure as higher, the order of 3%.

Part of the estimation problem is that the risk premium is likely to vary with the characteristics of an individual property or property type or real estate sector and indicative differential risk premiums relate to not only real estate sector, lease type, tenant covenant and building, but also to the location of a property. Location is an important risk factor both in terms of where a property is within in a city and also which city. A prime location say in a city centre may be deemed a very safe investment because demand will always ensure that its value is maintained. Properties in a small provincial centre may have a high risk premium because there are few transactions in the city. It could be difficult to find a purchaser if an investor chose to sell and as a result the value would be lessened. In contrast, an investment in a capital or global city would almost certainly be much more easily sold and so maintain its value.

There are studies that have also shown that the risk premium varies with the state of the real estate market. Some of the components of the risk premium should logically vary with market conditions. For example, the issues of liquidity and marketability disappear during a long real estate boom because properties are easily sold. The size of the risk premium is therefore likely to vary with point in the market cycle.

More generally, the risk premium is partly based on expectations for income growth that in turn depend on the real estate cycle, inflation, uncertainty and other factors. A long period of high inflation, for example in the 1970s in Western economies, may also influence real estate risk premiums. During years of sustained inflation, the ability for properties to maintain their value is likely to counterbalance any concerns about liquidity, marketability, transactions costs and management. It has been argued that in these circumstances, real estate could have a negative risk premium. The argument for a negative risk premium is extended by real estate having arguably its own distinct cycle return making it a good portfolio diversifier (see Chapter 7).

Market sentiment is also an important influence on the size of the risk premium. Real estate may be seen in a favourable or unfavourable light relative to other investments such as shares. To give two counter examples, real estate was viewed unfavourably as an asset class during the 1990s only for the reverse to happen in the first part of the 2000s. In the first of these decades, company shares were consistently generating high returns relative to real estate, only for the market to collapse around the millennium. Disillusion in stock market investment led to a reappraisal downwards of the real estate risk premium.

One further influence on the risk premium is the uncertainty about future income caused by potential obsolescence linked to technological change. Obsolescence in this way leads to the depreciation of rental values. Technological change tends to happen in waves. Examples include the impacts on real estate of information communications technology and the growth of personal computers or the online sales revolution. In both cases, these developments led to a reappraisal of the demand for property, depreciation of values and the risks to real estate, albeit limited to specific sectors.

The influence of obsolescence on the risk premium can be summarised by, first, adapting Eq. 2.1 to:

$$k = rf + \mathrm{RP} - g \tag{2.2}$$

where:

k = current income yield (as before)
rf = risk free rate of return
RP = risk premium
g = expected rental growth (as before)

Rearranging this equation gives:

$$\mathrm{RP} = k + g - rf \tag{2.3}$$

This can be modified to accommodate potential obsolescence by including a term for the depreciation in rental value from that of a new property (Eq. 2.4).

$$\mathrm{RP} = k + g_N - rf - d \tag{2.4}$$

where:

g_N = expected annual rental growth of new properties
d = expected annual depreciation

Expected annual depreciation is taken as a negative number in the equation. In this way, potential depreciation increases the risk premium.

As noted earlier, the required rate of return for an investor is composed of the risk premium plus the risk-free rate of return. This risk-free component is seen as the return from investing in government securities as their returns are guaranteed. In particular, the risk-free rate is generally taken by industry to be the redemption yield on long-dated (ten-year) government bonds. These are known as gilts in the UK.

The main reason for the choice of long-dated gilts is that they are seen as a close substitute for real estate for the long-term investor. There is also a close relationship between the yields of these bonds and real estate over time. The market in long-dated gilts is larger than that for short-dated gilts, and demand is less speculative, so redemption yields are stable. They are also believed to provide a better indication of the costs of long-term borrowing by a private investor.

Nevertheless, there is an argument that long-dated gilts are not risk-free as their returns can be diminished by inflation. To resolve this problem, there is a robust case for using index-linked gilts instead. Indeed, one recent study found that in Australia, the UK and the United States, there was a stronger relationship between yields (capitalisation rates) of real estate and index-linked bonds.

It should be remembered that this long run risk-free rate of return is not necessarily constant. The yields on government bonds move with changes to interest/bank base rates. Higher interest rates lead to a higher-required return from bonds resulting in higher yields on these assets and vice versa. These rates are determined by governments by reference to national macroeconomic factors.

Yields and Capital Values

From the analysis so far, yields are dependent on the rate of interest/risk-free rate of return, expected rental growth and the risk premium attributed to the property. The yield an investor is prepared to accept for the rental income generated by a property is also linked to the comparative return from alternative investments—primarily shares and government bonds.

The level of yields is important for the determination of capital values. Yields (or capitalisation rates) are used to monitor the performance of the commercial property market. A key point to remember is that the price investors are prepared to pay for a property is determined by the yield that they want. A change in the yield brought about by changes to these underlying variables results in a change in price/capital value.

It is important to stress the causal relationships in this yield model. It is the yield required by the investor that is the driver of the capital value. In the formula above, assuming initial rental income does not change, then a change in required yield determines the capital value of a property. The higher the yield an investor requires then the lower the capital value he/she is prepared to pay, and vice versa. Similarly, if the required yields in general rise, then the capital values as a whole fall. For example, if the required yield by investors generally rises from 5 to 6%, capital values fall by 16.6% (try out some hypothetical numbers to show this). A small change in yields has a large impact on capital values.

Price, Value and Worth

So far, the chapter has looked at the relationship between yields and capital values in general. However, it is important to note that there is a distinction between a value to one investor and to another that is the basis for why property transactions occur. In particular, it is useful to distinguish the difference between the **price, value and worth** of an investment.

In simple terms, '**worth**' is a specific investor's perception of the capital sum which they would be prepared to pay (or accept) for the stream of benefits which they expect to be produced by the investment. An investor can derive this capital sum by using a discounted cash framework explained in the next section.

'*Price*' is the actual observable exchange price in the open market. '*Value*' is an estimate of this price that would be achieved if the property were to be put on the market for sale. Put another way: worth can be expressed as the value in use and is crucial to understanding why there is a market.

In particular, the following relationships hold in an open and free market. There will be no transaction if:

Value in use/worth (vendor) > value in use (potential purchaser)

Price > value in use (purchaser)

These principles are fundamentally important when considering the purchase/sale decision, as is the way in which each of these interests is valued. There is a potential clear distinction between the worth of a property to a user and the market price/value.

Theory of Pricing—Discounted Cash Flow Framework

Investment, as noted, involves spending a capital sum to receive a stream or flow of income payments over time into the future, potentially stretching into decades. A question for the potential investor is what price to pay for this future income or alternatively does the quoted sale price make financial sense.

A key issue is how to balance expenditure now with income in the future. Money payable or receivable at different points of time has a different value. A £1 receivable today is not the same thing as a £1 receivable a year from now; it has a different time value. This is quite separate from changing values brought about by inflation (deflation) where future pounds will not represent the same purchasing power as today.

It is also separate from risk and the knowledge that £1 today is safer because you have it in your pocket now and you don't know what a year will bring. Both of these issues, inflation and risk, are highly important and have to be dealt with, but even in an inflation and risk-free world, there is a time value of money, and this is our immediate concern.

A £1 today has a different value from a £1 one year from now because the £1 today can be consumed immediately and we get this benefit now or it can be invested and earn interest. If invested, then a year from now we will have not only the original £1 but also the accumulated interest. In other words, you need some compensation for delaying expenditure.

It can be seen in a simple example: how much would you need to be compensated for in a year's time to lock £100 away, say in a bank, now to get a higher income in a year's time. Put another way, the answer can be seen as the required return on your investment from the £100, as discussed earlier. If the answer is £2 and you invest £100 to receive £102 in a year's time, then your required annual rate of return is 2%. This sum in generic terms is calculated as 100 multiplied by $(1 + r)$.

Extending the logic beyond one year, the investor requires a further 2% compensation in the following year and the one after. These observations provide the basis for a 'Discounted Cash Flow (DCF) approach' to pricing investments. In doing so, instead of looking at how much more income in the future we require, 'discounting' is the reverse approach. It permits a value to be allocated to future income in terms of what it is worth today.

The weighting of future income flows to the present day again uses an annual discount rate that is defined as the required rate of return. Whereas in the analysis above, future-required income in year 1 is calculated by multiplying the original sum by $(1 + r)$ now the task is in reverse. It takes the sum to be received in a year's time and divides by $(1 + r)$.

Beginning with year 1, the discounted value of say £100 in that year back to year 0 is £100 divided by $1 + r$. If r is 2%, then $1 + r = 1.02$ and the discounted value of the £100 is just over £98. In other words, the receipt of £100 in a year's time is currently worth £98. This figure can be seen as the present value of £100 in a year. The name comes from the fact that it enables future income to be discounted back to its value at the present time.

This framework permits an analysis that does not just think in terms of income returns one year ahead but multiple years into the future. The discounted value of £100 in two years' time is £96.1, and £94.2 after three years and so on. The present value of £100 two years in advance is calculated by dividing by $(1 + r)^2$, i.e. $(1.02)^2$ in our example. Similarly, the present value for income received three years hence is derived by dividing the sum by $(1 + r)^3$ and so on.

The DCF framework can be presented in Eq. 2.5 for the specific case of an asset that generates an income of £100 per year forever:

$$\mathrm{PV} = \frac{100}{(1+r)} + \frac{100}{(1+r)^2} + \frac{100}{(1+r)^3} + \cdots \tag{2.5}$$

where:

PV = the present value of the asset
r = discount rate

Using this formula and applying a 2% discount rate, then Eq. 2.5 becomes:

$$\mathrm{PV} = 98 + 96.1 + 94.2 + \cdots \tag{2.6}$$

This equation does not take into account the initial outlay or price paid. To take this into account, the cost has to be subtracted to give what is known as the net present value (NPV) of an investment (Eq. 2.7):

$$\mathrm{NPV} = -P_0 + \frac{100}{(1+r)} + \frac{100}{(1+r)^2} + \frac{100}{(1+r)^3} + \cdots \tag{2.7}$$

If the NPV is positive, then the investment is worthwhile, but if negative then the decision would be not to invest.

This DCF approach can be applied to different types of periods so it could be based on years, quarters and even months. The future cash flows also do not need to be constant and can vary from one year to the next. A generalised form of the framework for present value is:

$$\mathrm{PV} = \frac{R_1}{(1+r)} + \frac{R_2}{(1+r)^2} + \frac{R_3}{(1+r)^3} + \cdots \tag{2.8}$$

where:

PV = the present value of the asset
R_t = the amount of income receivable at the end of time period t
r = discount rate

The PV can be either the marker price P_p of the asset or its worth to an individual investor. The difference relates to the discount rate applied. In the case of **worth,** then the discount rate is the target rate of return for that individual investor. If the PV equals *price* then r is the 'market' or average discount rate.

To summarise, the DCF framework explicitly outlines how investors exchange their present capital for future income and capital. The present value of the income streams generated by an investment is the sum of the present values of the individual cash flows in each period into the future as shown in Eq. 2.8. These cash flows vary dependent on the nature of the individual asset.

Within the framework, investors can assess how risky or variable are the income flows. For bonds the income flows are constant as in Eq. 2.5. The income flows of shares are based on the annual dividends paid by the company. In theory, these vary from one year to the next, but many companies try to avoid lowering dividends. The nature of the future income of a real estate investment depends on rent review timings, so rental income is unchanged between these reviews.

All of these three asset classes generate regular income in the form of interest payments, dividends or rental payments. However, the degree of susceptibility to inflation varies. Bonds as fixed income investments are most likely to lose their real value (not index-linked ones). Dividends and rental payments are likely to increase in line with inflation, albeit with a potential lag until the next rent review in the case risk of real estate.

The income from government bonds is the most secure. On the other hand, dividends are dependent on company profits that are in turn subject to the macroeconomic cycle. Real estate rents too are influenced by the national economy but are to a degree sheltered from any volatility by the existence of rent reviews.

Investors can apply the DCF framework taking into account of the timing and security of income flows. The higher the risk of non-payment of income, for example through rent voids, then the higher the return required by an investor. The required rate of return is the risk-free rate of return plus the appropriate risk premium as discussed earlier.

The example presented in Eq. 2.5 could be a government bond with a guaranteed £100 income per year, so the 2% return applied is implicitly taken to be the risk-free rate. For a real estate asset with three-year rent reviews, the pattern of annual income would be very different. The annual income would remain the same for the first three years followed by a new rent agreed for the next three years. Assuming an average 3% risk premium, the required annual rate of return would be 5%. This required rate again repeats itself in all subsequent years as in Eq. 2.9.

$$PV = \frac{R}{(1.05)} + \frac{R}{(1.05)^2} + \frac{R}{(1.05)^3} + \frac{R_4}{(1.05)^4} + \frac{R_4}{(1.05)^5} \cdots \tag{2.9}$$

Gearing, Risk and Returns

An important dimension of investment is the relationship between gearing, risk and return. The concept of gearing, called leverage in the United States, is basically using other people's money to invest and make a profit. To be more precise, it is borrowing other people's money to invest. This section examines what difference it makes to risk and return to an investor if a proportion of the investment capital is borrowed.

To get some insight into this, we compare two investment alternatives:

a. buy a house outright for £300,000
b. buy the same house with a 95% mortgage on an interest-only basis

Buying a house outright should be a safe investment as in most countries house prices keep pace with inflation in the long term, and if an owner-occupier you live 'rent free'. Buying the same house with a mortgage, the nature of the investment is rather different.

This latter investment involves borrowing money from a bank at a fixed or variable rate of interest, covering 95% of its original value. If house price inflation is 2% per year, then the house is worth £331,224 in five years' time. Given that the investor only paid a deposit of £15,000, the investment is now worth £31, 224 plus the original sum, even though annual house price inflation has been only modest. In other words, the investor has more than doubled the capital in the five years. However, the investor will have to pay interest on the mortgage. While an interest only mortgage at an annual rate of 3% would cost say £20,250 over the period, it can be set against the rent that would have been paid by the owner as a tenant. Alternatively, the property could be rented out to cover the mortgage costs.

The potential long-term financial benefits given that house prices tend to keep pace with inflation are clear. However, there is a risk as it is possible that there is a sudden short-term downturn in the housing market and house prices fall 10%. The impact is severe if it happens just after purchase. If for some reason the investor was required to sell the house (perhaps because they had become unemployed) during the downturn, it would only be worth £270,000. The investor will have lost all the capital invested in the house and still owe the bank £15,000.

These investment alternatives illustrate the difference between an ungeared investment, buying the house outright, and a geared investment, buying with a mortgage. Buying a house outright is a very safe investment and even if house prices fall by 10%, the investor only loses 10% of their capital. Buying a house with a mortgage provides the opportunity to make a high percentage return on capital. But there is also greater risk as a downturn linked to the macroeconomy could bring a severe capital loss. The nature of the risk depends on the volatility of the housing market and the macroeconomic cycle.

Two types of gearing can be distinguished—income and capital. The housing market example relates to capital gearing, namely the percentage of the capital involved in an investment that has been borrowed. Income gearing measures the percentage of trading profits accounted for by interest payments. There are no formal definitions of gearing but they can be defined by the following ratios:

$$\text{Income Gearing} = \frac{\text{interest paid}}{\text{trading profit}} \times 100$$

and

$$\text{Capital Gearing} = \frac{\text{debt capital}}{\text{total capital}} \times 100$$

Debt capital is borrowed capital and equity is the investor's own capital. Debt and equity capital added together is total capital. The following notional numerical example allows us to highlight the relationship between risk and return and debt and equity, as well as using these gearing ratios.

Gearing a Notional Example

Consider an investor who has £5 m of their own (equity) capital. The investor borrows a further £5 m to set up a business. The rate of interest on the loan is 5%. In terms of the definitions noted above, equity capital equals 50% and debt capital equals 50%, so capital gearing is 50%. The investor pays £250,000 in annual interest on the debt capital.

In the first year, the business makes a net profit of £750,000. Net profit is calculated after costs of salaries, rent, heating, lighting, property tax, etc., are accounted for. But the business also must pay interest charges of £250,000. The income gearing is 33%. The return on equity capital of £5 m is £500 k. The percentage return is therefore 10% on equity capital.

In the second year of operation the economy begins to boom and net trading profits rise to £1.25 m. Interest rates do not change so interest charges remain at £250 k so income gearing falls to 20%. Equity profit increases to £1 m, and the percentage return on equity capital rises to 20%.

In year 3, inflation associated with the economic boom leads to higher interest rates and the state of economy starts to deteriorate. From the business perspective, interest rates rise to 10% and the wages of the business go up, while consumer demand falls leading to reduced turnover. These changes, clearly have an impact on the finances of the business.

Interest costs are now £500 k while net trading profits have fallen to £500 k because of reduced turnover and increased wages. As a consequence, there are nil equity earnings, and the business is just about breaking even. The income gearing is now 100%. The return on equity capital is zero.

So, what do we learn? The debt capital owned by the bank is a relatively secure/stable investment, and it **must** be paid as it is a contractual obligation. Equity earnings, as represented by the net trading profits are **more volatile and riskier**. The risk arises from the variability of the macroeconomy and rising interest rates. The business could have reduced its interest rate risk by locking into a longer-term fixed rate when setting up rather than opting for a variable rate loan from the bank. But in doing so, it would have increased initial interest charges.

Gearing is also a factor in influencing risk and return. To explore this **influence,** it is useful to revisit year 2 when net trading profit was £1.25 m on £10 m total capital and there were £250 k interest charges. With equity capital of £5 m, these figures generate a capital gearing of 50% and an equity return of 20%. This equity return is entirely dependent on the amount borrowed.

If instead of borrowing £5 m the investor had borrowed £7.5 m, then the capital gearing would increase to 75%. With borrowing now £7.5 m interest charges rise to £375 k, the net profit is now less at £1.125 m. However, this net profit is generated from only £2.5 m equity capital and the equity return has risen to 45%. In other words, equity return has more than doubled, from 20 to 45%, because of borrowing more and having a higher capital gearing.

Similarly, the financial numbers can be reworked for year 3 with this higher capital gearing. Originally when the capital gearing was 50%, net profit was zero on £10 m total capital with £500 k interest charges. The equity return was zero. If the capital gearing was 75%, borrowing of £7.5 m brings interest charges of £750 k with the rise in interest rates in that year. The net profit of zero at 50% gearing becomes minus £250 k with 75% gearing.

In this example when the economy is booming, a higher-geared investment generates high returns on equity capital, but the reverse happens as the economy turns down. Increasing the gearing means that in year 3 the business goes from breakeven to a loss. In fact, the investor has lost 10% of their original capital.

Essentially if an investor is highly capital geared, then when real estate market conditions are favourable, high returns can be generated. These conditions can occur when the economy or the respective market sector is growing while at the same time interest rates are relatively low. However, the investor's position changes dramatically when the economy/market turns down as the macro effect is magnified in the reverse direction. Gearing brings higher risk but also the potential for higher returns than simply using just equity capital. The importance of gearing is seen in two examples.

Real World Examples

In the UK, the private rented housing sector expanded dramatically in the decade up to the global financial crisis (GFC). This phenomenon was facilitated by the availability of mortgages from banks with high loan-to-value ratios, a house price boom and relatively low interest rates. Rents of housing also rose because of the expansion of the student population, high immigration into the country and a large number of young professionals who could not afford to buy a home because of the high house prices.

Private landlords were highly geared with mortgages that were as high as 95% of the house price value. The high gearing together with rising rents and capital values enabled landlords to make high returns in beneficial economic circumstances. These profits were, in the main, reinvested in more property and the sector grew by 40% in less than a decade.

The GFC and the subsequent recession brought an end to this rapid growth. The associated banking crisis brought an end to easy credit and the required deposits rose for house buyers. Furthermore, the recession increased unemployment and dampened the potential for rents to rise. Given that private landlords were highly **geared,** and many had mortgages that had short-term interest rate reviews pending, the prognosis for the sector was very negative. While many landlords were forced to leave the business, the sector overall had a soft landing because the government chose to significantly lower interest rates to counter the recession.

The role of capital gearing is a central element of the underlying processes within commercial property booms and busts. Some property companies/investors buy during the upturn by borrowing a high percentage of the capital from a bank. This enables them to make high profits/returns as capital and rental values rise. It encourages them to buy more property and others to buy too on the same basis. This 'speculation' contributes to pushing up prices/capital values as investors chase a finite number of properties.

But once the economy turns, some of these highly geared investors, especially those who bought at the top of the market, will see the value of their assets fall to less than they paid for them. More importantly they could lose all their capital they have invested, for example if they had borrowed 70% of the property value just at the peak and prices fall by 35%.

In addition, market rents may fall impacting the rental income of new properties. The implications are that income gearing becomes less than 100%, with income less than interest payments to banks. Indeed, the rental income from the property may become much less than the interest payments on the debt and the owner may be forced to sell.

The impact of gearing in the UK commercial property boom and bust of the 2000s can be seen from comparing Tables 2.1 and 2.2 taken from Jones et al. (2018). In the first table 80% gearing gives you a return of 204% in the boom years, 2004–2006 while capital values rose on average 40.7%. In comparison 40% gearing, namely borrowing 40% of the value of the purchase, brought returns on average of 67.9%.

Table 2.1 Indicative capital returns in the UK over the period 2004–2006 with different gearing ratios

Capital gearing ratio	0%	20%	40%	60%	80%
Return on capital	40.7%	50.9%	67.9%	101.8%	203.7%

Table 2.2 Indicative capital losses in the UK over the period 2006–2008 with different gearing ratios

Capital gearing ratio	0%	20%	40%	60%	80%
Return on capital	−42.4%	−53.0%	−70.7%	−100%	−100%

Once the economy turns investors, especially those who bought at top of market, see the value of assets fall, maybe to less than they paid for them. The position is exacerbated by borrowing, i.e. gearing. When the bust came after the GFC, capital values fell on average 42.4%. Those investors who had borrowed 60% of the funds at the top of the boom lost all their capital.

The Maturation Process

A key underlying influence on investment is financial maturation. It can be seen in the process of buying a house. In the example above, the house bought increases in value from £300,000 to £331,224 over five years but the mortgage debt of £285,000 is unchanged. As house prices rise in line with inflation, the size of the loan to be repaid stays the same. As inflation rises, the value of the loan sum falls in real terms while the value of the house rises. The result is that the value of the investor's share will rise from 5% simply because of house price inflation. In addition, the long-term rise in incomes on average tends to reduce the proportion of household income accounted for by mortgage repayments.

More generally if a purchaser of commercial property relies on debt funding, over time the real value of the outstanding debt decreases even with only modest long-term inflation. At the same time, property prices or rents also rise over the long term in line with incomes. Consequently, there can be a widening difference between the outstanding real debt against property bought in the past and debt on new building or recently acquired or renovated stock with a loan.

This maturation process is common to all property in which purchasers incur debt, including owner-occupiers as well as owners of rental property. The process essentially enables mortgagors to increase their equity (share of the capital) in their home over time.

It is also significant for owners of portfolios of rental properties, comprising long-standing and new investments. This phenomenon is especially useful for housing portfolios. Through cost/rent pooling within a portfolio, landlords can take advantage of this maturation process by the averaging of debt across new and old housing. Rent setting can also reflect the relative attractiveness of homes, with attractive older properties in a portfolio generating surpluses to cross-subsidise the purchase of newer housing.

In other words, financial maturation is more effective the larger and more diverse the portfolio of rental properties. In countries in which rental housing is owned predominantly by small 'Mum and Dad' investors and/or small-scale social housing agencies (e.g. Australia and the UK), the potential for reaping the benefits of financial maturation is much less.

Theoretically, financial maturation can benefit social housing landlords in the long-term as eventually the rents necessary to cover costs will begin to fall, enabling 'cost renting'. In these circumstances, there is no need of ongoing subsidies from the state, as in the Netherlands. Maturation in principle enables social housing in the long term to compete with private landlords on equivalent terms without subsidy.

Summary

The chapter has examined the basic concepts underpinning investment decision-making. It has defined risk and return and explained the use of yields. The components of return from real estate comprise rental income and any change in capital value. For comparison, owning shares provides parallel elements of return in terms of dividend payments and any rise or fall in capital values.

A yield is the most commonly used method of valuing investments. They are a way of comparing the attractiveness of potential investments and standardise for the size or value of a property. Yields can also be applied to compare stock market investments. They express current net income of investments as a percentage of their capital value. Investors can then decide, based on comparative yields, which is the best value for money. The concept of 'value' itself varies dependent on the investor and its purpose, and so the chapter distinguishes between price, value and worth.

'Worth' relates to a view of what a specific investor is prepared to pay or accept for a stream of financial benefits over time. 'Price' is the actual exchange value observed in the open market. 'Value' is an estimate of this price that would be received if the property were to be put on the market. Market transactions are dependent on differences in the value of worth (or use) to investors.

The determination of the appropriate yield is partly based on the expected growth in future income. A lower-initial yield is acceptable if income is anticipated to rise. A higher yield would be required if no income growth was expected.

Risk can be defined as the potential variation in these returns. Given that the future is unknown, risk is estimated by reference to returns in previous years. Greater expected variation means higher risk. The standard deviation of past returns is a way of measuring risk. Investing in risky assets as opposed to risk-free assets implies that an investor expects to be compensated by higher return. This compensation is often referred to as a risk premium, and the chapter has outlined the principles of how this might be calculated for real estate investment.

The required return can be decomposed into two elements—the return from risk-free investment plus a risk premium. Real estate is regarded as having a higher risk premium than blue chip shares because of the imperfections or characteristics of the real estate market compared to the stock market. These imperfections encompass higher transactions and management costs, lower liquidity and marketability and poorer information in the real estate market.

The risk-free element of a required return is generally taken by the real estate industry to be the redemption yield on long-dated (ten-year) government bonds. Nevertheless, technically long-dated gilts are not risk-free as their returns can be reduced by inflation. Index-linked gilts offer a more logical alternative. In either case, the long-run risk-free rate of return moves with changes to interest/bank base rates.

The long run average risk premium is likely to be the order of 3% but it varies with individual property characteristics and lease type. Location is an important contributor to an individual property's risk premium, both in terms of whether it is at a prime locality within a city and the size of the city. The scale of the risk premium also varies with point in a market cycle.

Market sentiment is also a factor in influencing the risk premium. Inflationary periods are likely to offer a positive perspective on real estate investment contributing to a low-risk premium. Similarly, there are periods when the relative returns performance of shares can bring a negative or positive view on real estate affecting the risk premium accordingly. Technological change can further lead to a periodic rethink in the risk premium for particular real estate sectors. The most recent example is the growth of online retail sales having a detrimental impact on shopping centres.

Assessing an investment also requires a balance between returns now and in the future. Or more precisely, the choice between returns in the short term versus the long term. This task can be achieved by reference to a technique called Discounted Cash Flow (DCF). This discounting approach also enables an investor to price an investment by examining its expected future stream of returns. The DCF approach provides a framework to price investments. It provides a present value to be allocated to future income in different periods. The approach can be applied to different types of periods so it could be based on years, quarters and even months and can take into account the timing and security of income flows. The discount rate applied takes into account the level of risk and so is a combination of the risk-free rate of return plus the appropriate risk premium.

The sum of the present values of the incomes to be received in each future individual period is the overall present value of the investment. The initial cost of buying the investment can be incorporated by subtracting it from the present value to give the NPV of the investment. A positive NPV means the investment is worthwhile to the investor. DCF is an essential investment tool.

The chapter examines the concept of gearing in detail. Gearing refers to the relationship, or ratio, of a company's debt-to-equity. It shows the extent to which a firm's operations are funded by debt. It can have a critical role in boosting investment returns but also brings potential great risk. It essentially involves borrowing capital to invest.

There are two types of gearing—income and capital. When the economy is booming, and interest rates are relatively low, a geared investment generates high returns on equity capital, but the reverse happens as the economy turns down. The financial benefits of a geared investor's position changes dramatically when the market turns down as the macro effect is magnified in the opposite direction. Gearing incorporates higher investment risk but also the possibility of higher returns compared to simply using just equity capital.

Capital gearing was an important force in the commercial property boom of the 2000s and the bust following the GFC. Investors bought during the upturn by borrowing a high percentage of the capital from a bank, enabling high returns as capital and rental values rose. When the bust came after the GFC, capital values fell on average 42.4% in the UK. Those investors who had borrowed 60% of the funds at the top of the boom lost all their capital.

Financial maturation is the basis by which owner-occupiers acquire a greater share of equity in their home. It arises because over time house prices in general rise with inflation while the mortgage debt remains constant, falling in real terms. The same process applies to the purchase of commercial property that depends on debt finance. As well as market values increasing over time so rising rents or incomes make it easier to pay mortgage repayments even if interest rates rise. It has a long-term consequence for investment.

Learning Outcomes

Having completed this chapter, the reader should be able to:

- Understand that the return from real estate arises from rental income and any change in capital value. Capital values may fall so return can be negative.
- Recognise that risk can be defined as the potential variation in returns, with the greater the variation meaning higher risk.
- Understand that yields express current net income as a percentage of their capital value of an asset and that low-initial yields imply expected future growth in incomes. Also, that yields change with interest rates. Higher yields lead to a general fall in capital values.
- Appreciate that the required return from a risky investment has two components: the return from risk-free investment plus a risk premium and that real estate has a high-risk premium because of the imperfections or characteristics of the real estate market compared to the stock market.
- Comprehend that the long run average risk premium is the order of 3% but that it is difficult to quantify, and varies substantially with individual properties, locations, and over time through a market cycle.

- Discuss the factors that can lead to changes in the risk premium for particular real estate sectors.
- Be aware that the redemption yield on long-dated (ten-year) government bonds is normally taken as the risk-free rate of return.
- Understand the distinction between the price, value and worth of an investment. The 'worth' of a property will vary to individual investors whereas price is determined by the market.
- Appreciate that DCF provides a framework to price investments by calculating the present values of incomes expected to be received at different points in the future and that the net present value of an investment can be calculated by subtracting the initial cost from the overall present value. A positive NPV means the investment is worthwhile to the investor.
- Comprehend that the discount rate applied in a DCF analysis is a combination of the risk-free rate of return plus the appropriate risk premium.
- Understand that gearing can boost investment returns but also increase risks.
- Appreciate that here are two types of gearing—income and capital. During a boom, a geared investment generates high returns on equity capital but the opposite; even losses occur when the economy turns down.
- Comprehend that financial maturation benefits investors over time because capital values rise with inflation while any mortgage debt remains constant, falling in real terms. At the same time as capital values increase, rising rents or incomes make it easier to pay mortgage repayments even if interest rates go up.

Readings

Fraser, W. D. (1993) *Principles of Property Investment and Pricing*. 2nd Edition. Palgrave, Macmillan, London. ISBN 0333716922.

Jones, C., Cowe, S. and Trevillion, E. (2018) *Property Boom and Banking Bust: The Role of Commercial Lending in the Bankruptcy of Banks*. Wiley-Blackwell, Chichester. ISBN-13 978-1119219255

RICS, Royal Institution of Chartered Surveyors (1997) *Calculation of Worth: An IPF/RICS Information Paper*. RICS, London.

Macroeconomy and Real Estate Cycles

3

Introduction

In this chapter, the dynamic nature of the real estate market is explained by reference to underlying economic forces and the incidence of cycles. The fundamental economic determinants of real estate change are considered and their links to development activity. The significance of cycles to real estate markets is demonstrated through documented examples in an international history.

From this base, a stages model of the cycle of commercial property development, distinct from the business cycle, is set out. The building and timing of skyscrapers is then shown to fit into development cycles. The following section discusses how real estate cycles can be generated by the availability of investment funds alone. This section is based on the real estate boom of the 2000s. In the final section, the chapter considers the role of sentiment influencing the repetition of cycles and the failure of forecasting. The chapter covers the following topics:

- Role of real estate in the economy
- International history of cycles
- Commercial real estate cycles and development time lags
- Skyscrapers and development cycles
- Availability of finance and investment cycles
- Forecasting and cycles

Role of Real Estate in the Economy

There is a clear link between the performance of the macroeconomy and the real estate market. An increase in national manufacturing output brings a rise in demand for factories. Similarly greater output of services in the economy leads to

C. A. Jones and E. Trevillion, *Real Estate Investment* ,
https://doi.org/10.1007/978-3-031-00968-6_3

more offices. The switch to a services-based economy in many developed countries has been reflected in a growth of offices and a decline in factories. Rising real wages also brings higher consumer spending and feeds through to an expansion in the number of shops and leisure real estate space. Overall economic growth generates a rise in demand for different types of property.

Property can be seen as a factor of production and a crucial input to industrial production. For example, services output is dependent on the availability of offices of the right quality in the right location and at the right price. Commercial property also contributes to the quality of life by providing social infrastructure in terms of shops and leisure facilities. From this perspective, the availability of property is a prerequisite for economic growth.

The close relationships between real estate and the economy therefore operate in two ways. Demand for real estate is influenced by the state of the economy but weak supply can constrain economic growth. From a real estate perspective, the core of the real estate market is the existence of occupational demand. No demand for real estate space then there is no market.

Given that the economy is cyclical, it means that the real estate market is subject to booms and downturns. As an economy grows, there could be shortages of property as demand increases, and as a result rent would rise. Alternatively economic recession could see demand fall away leading to vacancies in the market. With demand less than supply rents could fall.

Economic cycles are therefore reflected in rental cycles. From Eq. 2.1, these rental cycles feed through to yields and hence to capital values. Expectations of rising rents in an upturn result in falling yields and higher capital values. Similarly, as demand subsides with an economic downturn it leads to lower rents, and potentially expected negative rental growth. Investors then require higher yields resulting in lower capital values.

Development activity is also linked to the business cycle. To take an individual example, a factory owner faced with rising demand can choose to meet this by building a new factory. More generally, development may not be undertaken on a bespoke basis by the subsequent occupier but by a developer anticipating a growth in demand with an upturn in the cycle. In this case, development is undertaken on a speculative basis in anticipation of finding an occupier.

Development in this way on a speculative basis is dependent on perceived viability. It is in turn based on expected capital values and the cost of borrowing, namely interest rates. Technological change can also have an influence on development activity. As noted in Chapter 2, obsolescence can lead to buildings becoming unfit for modern requirements, and in need of replacement.

While technological change and obsolescence can be seen as long-term influences on the real estate market, their principal impacts tend to occur over relatively short periods or waves. As a result, the (re)development consequences tend to be encompassed within real estate cycles.

International History of Cycles

Real estate cycles embrace change in rents, capital values and development activity with usually a clear link to the macroeconomic cycle. Cycles can be traced back into history in many countries since the industrial revolution. The amplitude of these cycles varies, related to the causes and the local circumstances. In many cases, real estate cycles are linked to individual cities and the underpinnings of local commerce.

Perhaps the first clear short-term cycle was the New York office market in the 1920s. The property development boom in the city occurred against a backdrop of increasing economic vitality. America recovered relatively quickly from a recession following the First World War and in 1921, the economy entered a period of prosperity with rising growth, productivity and profits. New York for the first time became the leading international banking centre in the world as Europe sought to cope with the debts from that war. The boom came to a sudden end with the Wall Street Crash of late 1929 and banks beginning to fail.

A similar post-war property boom occurred in London after the Second World War. The rebuilding of the national economy coincided with a shortage of offices. Few offices had been built during the previous two decades. First, in the 1930s because of the depressed macroeconomy and then because of World War II and subsequent building material shortages. The growing demand meant rising rents and capital values, and development was very profitable. The development boom was supported by the availability of many potential sites because of bombing during the war.

Fast forward a decade, New York experienced a development boom between 1967 and 1973. London too experienced a boom in commercial property prices in the early 1970s. Property booms then occurred in many countries during the 1980s. In London, for example, it is estimated that new development during the 1980s boom contributed a net addition of nearly 30% to the office stock of the central area. This development boom was partly driven by the need to replace offices unable to cope with the heavy cabling demands of ICT at that time.

Again, there are strong similarities in New York with a development boom that reached its height in 1986–87. Both cities were consolidating their positions as the world's leading financial centres over this decade. Together these cities captured much of the expansion of international financial services in the 1980s.

These property booms in London and New York can be seen within a wider international picture of real estate cycles. Dehesh and Pugh report on a series of Japanese property cycles from the early 1950s through to the early 1990s as shown in Fig. 3.1 (as indicated by commercial land prices). The amplitudes of these cycles are very large because of the land constraints in Japan creating more volatility but the cycles themselves follow parallel booms and busts in other industrialised countries. Specifically, there were booms in the late 1950s, early 1970s and the latter half of the 1980s. Over this period, Japan was establishing itself as an industrialised economy. Latterly in the 1980s that property boom was partly driven by the emergence of Tokyo as a world financial centre.

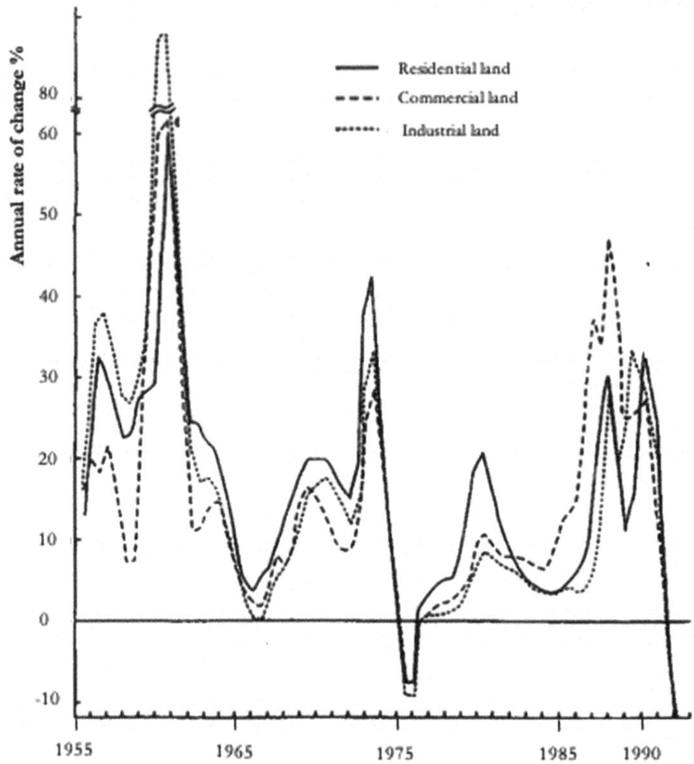

Fig. 3.1 The annual rates of change in land values in six Japanese cities 1951–1991 (*Source* Dehesh and Pugh (1998))

Barras in 2007 identified three global office cycles since the 1980s, beginning with the speculative boom of the late 1980s, followed by a more subdued upturn in the late 1990s and another speculative-driven boom in the mid-2000s. The scale of the real estate cycles in the 2000s is presented in Fig. 3.2 that on the one hand shows there are commonalities across countries but also differences in the amplitudes. Ireland saw the largest increases in the boom followed by the UK. The boom across the European Union was lower primarily because of the negative trend in Germany over the period. The peak of the cycles is 2007 except for the UK that is earlier.

These examples of property cycles illustrate the intertwining of real estate markets and the (local) economy. The examples have focused on offices as they have a clearer cycle, but real estate cycles are not simply confined to this sector. The timescales of the cycles also demonstrate that booms (and busts) do not occur continuously but there are gaps, sometimes of decades. The variability in the amplitude of cycles suggest there are local factors at work. In the next section, the chapter

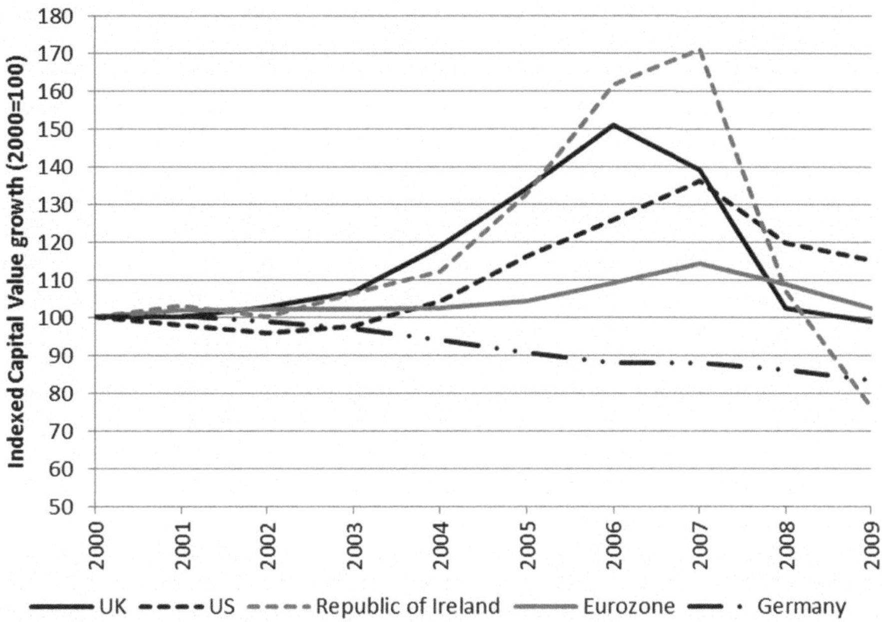

Fig. 3.2 International perspective on real estate cycles in the 2000s (*Source* Jones et al. (2018))

examines more closely the dynamic relationships between cycles, the economy and financing.

Commercial Real Estate Cycles and Development Time Lags

The demand for commercial and industrial real estate is dependent on the economy. At one level, given the existence of business cycles, it is inevitable that there are commercial real estate cycles. However, it is also clear that real estate cycles, as outlined above, have their own distinct characteristics, reflecting the nature of property and market dynamics. These cycles may arise from the potential time lags in development activity as the real estate market responds to macroeconomic cycles. Variability in the availability of finance through the banking system with stage in the economic cycle can also be a factor.

Development activity is influenced by the macroeconomy in a number of ways. Fundamentally, as noted above, the state of the economy influences the demand for space. A growing/declining economy leads to rising/falling demand respectively. In terms of development, this can influence viability by changing the rents and hence capital values of buildings on completion. Rising or falling values thereby expand or stop construction activity. In fact, these changes may only be expectations but could still be sufficient to influence the rate of development to be completed in the future.

Changing capital/rental values can also influence the development time period. If capital values are rising, the rate of development may be sped up to ensure that the finished development is able to achieve a high price. On the other hand, if capital/rental values are falling it may make sense to slow the development process down if possible. In this way, immediate expenditure is reduced while delaying completion will give time for capital values to rise later.

Other macroeconomic factors include interest rates. The cost of borrowing capital is a crucial variable in determining financial viability and the level of development activity. Higher interest rates have a double impact. First, the increased cost of borrowing by investors will mean that they require a higher yield when purchasing a completed development. It results in lower capital values in the market, and a reduction in development profitability. Second, higher interest rates raise the cost of loan finance for developers, increasing costs as a whole and reducing viability.

High interest rates are linked to high inflation. High inflation tends to impinge on construction costs through labour and raw material costs. If these costs are rising, then they dampen development viability.

In practice strong/weak economic growth, the level of interest rates and inflation are all related so individual impacts of these variables may not be isolated. Nevertheless, the viability of a potential development will be dependent on macroeconomic prospects and the consequences for the real estate market. Expected development viability has to accommodate the time delays necessary to complete a project.

These time delays are important because history shows that changes in the supply of real estate tend to lag changes in demand. Speculative property developers tend to be inherently conservative as they wish to be confident that there will be a tenant/owner for their completed buildings. They tend to respond to demand rather than anticipate it. If demand rises developers therefore initially respond slowly and then there is the construction process which also adds to the delay in the supply response.

In addition, there are supply constraints on new urban development that a real estate company need to resolve, even once the decision to proceed has been taken. Land assembly may be complicated and long-winded, especially in cities, and there are planning requirements to be met. Existing properties may need to be demolished and underlying difficult soil conditions may have to be addressed. Overall, it means that there are often many years between the rise in demand and the completion of buildings to meet the demand. These time lags are the basis for the classic cycle that is set out in the case study at the end of the chapter that was developed by Barras in 1994. It is summarised in (Fig. 3.3).

Skyscrapers and Development Cycles

As capital values rise through the real estate boom, the expected profits from development become greater. It encourages not only more development but more

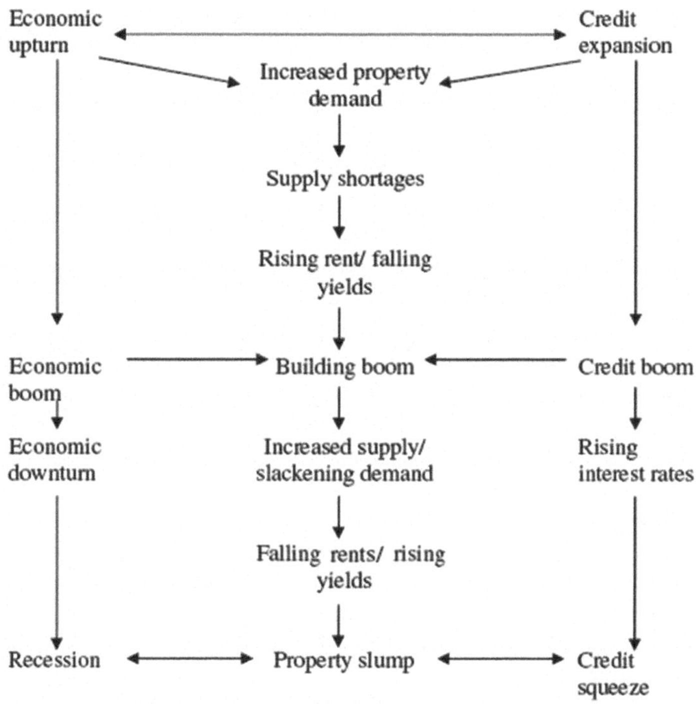

Fig. 3.3 A stylised commercial estate cycle based on development time lags (*Source* Barras (1994))

grandiose projects, including higher and higher skyscrapers. Typically, towards the end of the boom the highest buildings are conceived and initiated. The finance for building such large projects is also normally only available near the peak of a real estate boom, thereby enabling the development to happen.

Given the scale of these projects, there are often planning obstacles and public objections. In addition, the size of the project can mean that the developments can take a long time to complete, in some cases in time for the next real estate boom.

The first example of such a skyscraper is the Empire State Building in New York. As noted earlier, the city experienced a real estate boom in the 1920s. During this period, the number of storeys in new developments kept increasing. The Empire State Building was the culmination of this trend with 102 storeys that made it the world's highest building.

It was conceived in the late 1920s at the end of the boom. Indeed, building work did not start on it until after the Wall Street Crash that abruptly brought the real estate boom to an end. The result was that the building opened in 1931 coinciding with the Great Depression, and as a result most of its office space lay empty for some years.

It remained the highest building in the world until the opening of the twin towers of the World Trade Center in 1970. While this latter building was completed during a real estate boom, it was conceived earlier as a subsidised urban regeneration project to revitalise lower Manhattan. It does not fit into a market development cycle.

In London, the development boom from the mid-1950s saw the first tall buildings started towards the end of this period. A 34-storey office block, Centre Point, was constructed from 1963 to 1966. The initial plans for the Nat West Tower were also formulated in the early 1960s but it was not begun until 1971 and completed in 1980. This tower of 42 storeys (now called Tower 42) was the first skyscraper in the square mile of the City of London. It was also the tallest building in the City district for 30 years, until it was surpassed by the Heron Tower (see below) in 2011.

The subsequent 1980s development boom did not produce a building to rival the height of this building in the City itself. However, One Canada Square at Canary Wharf in the dockland area of the city was completed in 1991. At 50 storeys it became the highest building in Britain. The scheme was formulated in 1985 at the height of the 1980s boom and construction began in 1988 just as the market cycle was turning.

The building was completed in November 1990. Despite inducements to attract tenants, the market downturn meant that it was difficult to attract tenants. With only one floor occupied Olympia and York, the developer, went into administration/liquidation in May 1992. It was unable to service its debts.

The boom of the 2000s in London was not associated with significant development but it did generate two significant skyscrapers. First, the skyscraper popularly known as Heron Tower was built between 2007 and 2011. At the time of completion, it was the highest building in the City of London.

The tower had originally received planning permission in 2002 but construction was delayed until just before the GFC when funding was made available. By the time the tower was completed, the economy was still in a weak state and it was some years before it was fully let.

Heron Tower was soon superseded by the Shard as the highest building in the City of London in 2012. The 72-storey tower had originally been conceived in 2000 and received planning permission in 2003. However, the finance to build it was only put in place in late 2007 and demolition of the previous building started the following year. On completion, the building had few tenants and given the state of the economy it was not until October 2017 that it was fully let.

These examples are not exhaustive, but they emphasise the role of development lags and at a micro-level the consequences for individual projects. Most were started at the later stages of a real estate boom as finance became available and were then completed in the aftershock of a bust. The immediate impact was a lack of occupation demand and vacant space for years.

Availability of Finance and Investment Cycles

So far commercial real estate cycles have been explained in reference to development time lags and changes in rental and capital values. But as Fig. 3.2 indicates, the role of credit availability is an important factor in influencing capital values and the nature of the cycle. In fact, variability in finance per se and changes to gearing can generate real estate cycles through their impact on yields without recourse to time lags.

Put another way, changes in property yields over time can contribute to cycles without rental change brought about by supply shortages. The required rate of return underpinning yield levels can bring change partly determined by other national factors. In particular, there can be revisions to the risk-free rate of return/interest rates and the risk premium associated with real estate. The risk premium is aligned to investment sentiment towards real estate that in turn can be dependent on stock market returns and the share price cycle (see Chapter 2).

The real estate boom in the UK of the 2000s is illustrative of how changes in yields can underpin a cycle. During the early half of that decade, capital values rise faster than rents. In this period, it was primarily falling yields driving rising capital values while rental growth is modest. In contrast during the 1980s boom, capital values were being pushed by rental value growth. The relative impacts of yield change and rental growth on capital values in the two decades is shown in Fig. (3.4).

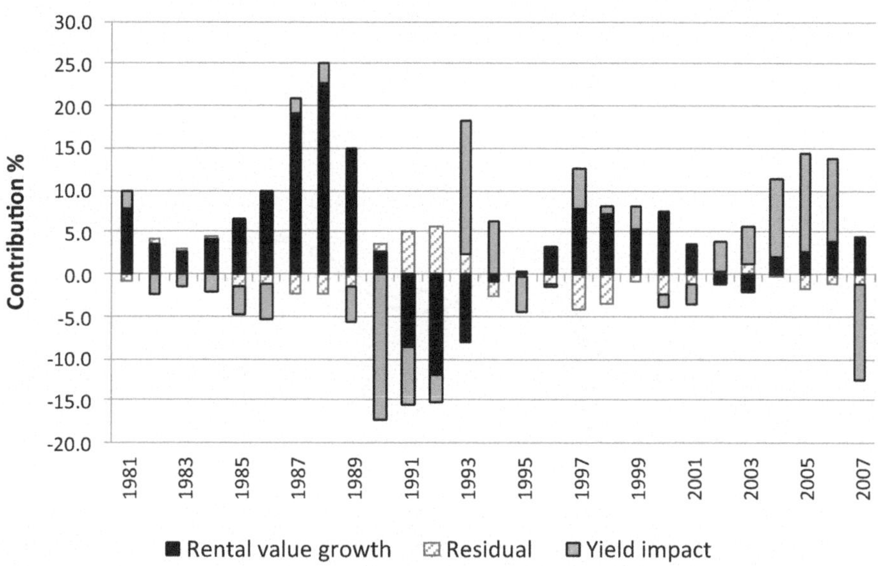

Fig. 3.4 Relative contributions of changes in UK Rents and Yields to capital value growth, 1981–2007 (*Source* Jones et al. (2018))

The impact of yield falls in the 2000s and its distinctiveness from past cycles can also be seen in Fig. 3.5. The figure also demonstrates the scale of the cycle of that decade that cannot be explained by rental growth or development lags. The question is then why yields fell spawning the real estate boom. The answer lies in a more positive view towards real estate investment buoyed by a negative reappraisal of the returns from stock market investment. The stock market had lost some of its gloss with share prices falling from the collapse of the dot com bubble around the millennium.

The result is a vast flow of funds into real estate as Fig. 3.6 shows. The expansion of investment funds into the UK real estate market was supported by banks lending money to purchasers. Bank lending terms became more generous as the boom progressed, and the number of transactions increased to a peak in 2006 as Fig. 3.7 records. In the process, the amount of lending by banks rose to historically high levels as Fig. 3.8 denotes.

The weight of money buying property expanded dramatically while the commercial real estate stock remained broadly static. It inevitably led to higher and higher capital values as demand increased but supply did not. The result was that the property boom of the 2000s generated dramatic returns.

These returns were magnified by the liberal lending policies of banks offering higher and higher loan-to-value ratios. It enabled investors to become more heavily geared and encouraged/enabled them to pay more for individual properties. High returns were achieved by the substantial gearing in a rising market as considered in Chapter 2. These returns attracted more investors prepared to accept even lower yields and capital values kept rising.

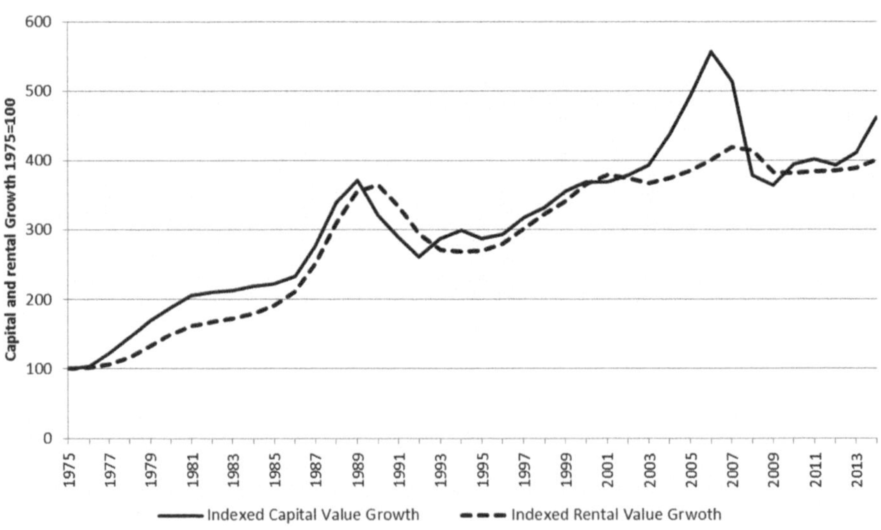

Fig. 3.5 Changes in UK real and capital values 1975–2013 (*Source* Jones et al. (2018))

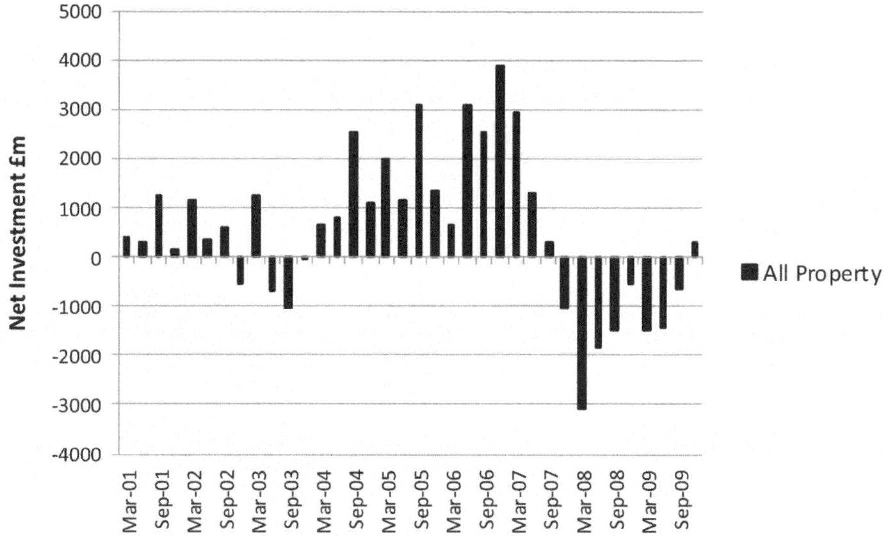

Fig. 3.6 Net Investment into the UK real estate market 2001–2009 (*Source* Jones et al. (2018))

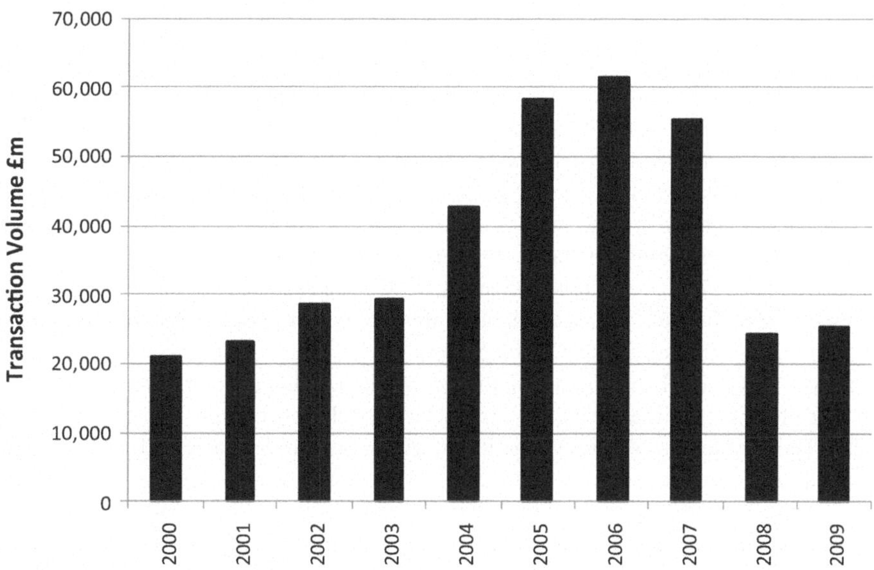

Fig. 3.7 Annual UK commercial real estate transactions 2000–2009 (*Source* Jones et al. (2018))

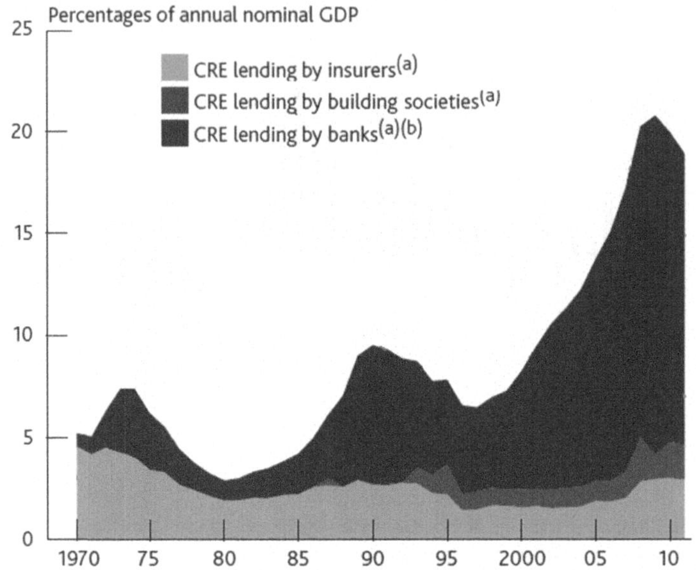

Fig. 3.8 Commercial real estate lending in the UK 1970–2012 (*Source* Jones et al. (2018))

The property boom comes to an abrupt end with the GFC that brought a liquidity and an existential crisis for major banks. The funding of the boom had been based on mortgage-backed securities. The interest from these loans were parcelled up and used as the basis for the sale of bonds. The revenue generated from the sale of the bonds, usually to other banks, could then be used to issue more loans.

This practice, known as wholesale funding, occurred on a global basis and removed the constraints on banks from a simple reliance on domestic saving. It supported banks' desire to lend extensively on the perceived lucrative lending for commercial real estate. The use began to unravel with the sub-prime lending crisis in the housing market of the United States.

It was discovered that many of these mortgage-backed bonds were supported by worthless sub-prime mortgages issued to people who could not afford to pay them. The problem was that no one knew which bonds were affected, so all bonds were tainted. But the real problem came when these bonds were due to mature and a bank had to pay the holders their money back. Normally the bank would effectively reissue them to pay the original bond holders. However, no one had any confidence to buy them leaving banks with a large gap in their finances.

The result was that banks from 2007 were not in a position to issue many loans and there was a sudden famine of investment finance. Investment into the real estate market falls away dramatically as shown in Fig. 3.5 from 2007. In parallel, Fig. 3.6 demonstrates that the number of transactions nose dives as the deals frenzy of the boom ends. The consequence, reported in Fig. 3.4 is a substantial rise in yields and a fall in capital values, even though rental growth continues in the short term.

Forecasting and Cycles

At the centre of the UK 2000s commercial real estate boom was the willingness of banks to fund investment deals without any concern that the bonanza might not continue. The focus of banks was entirely on growth and return with no reference to downside risk. This issue encompasses not just the banks but also the property professionals who were advising the banks, developers and investors.

It incorporates the failure of commercial property market forecasting. Despite the long evidence of cycles, real estate industry forecasts are essentially backward-looking. They are little more than the extrapolation of trends combined with industry sentiment that always has a positive gloss. Downturns are not predicted. It is probable in the 2000s that the prolonged period of economic growth from the 1990s reinforced these perspectives.

There is a broader question of the amnesia about real estate cycles by key players. As reported earlier, there is a continuing history of real estate cycles while the previous sections explain how they can occur. A fundamental issue is therefore why is there such a repetition of cycles when real estate decisions could take into account time lags and market fundamentals? Conventional economics assumes rational behaviour, and in a sense the replication of the excesses of property cycles is irrational. There is a failure to learn from experience. These failures can be attributed not just to real estate professionals, banks and forecasters, but developers too.

First, development is instigated based on expected profitability as discussed earlier. In undertaking these calculations, developers use current values or expected values of completed buildings derived from trends continuing. These values are used to calculate the price to be paid for land. In a development boom, the use of unsustainable property values in financial appraisals feeds unrealistic bids for land values.

If a developer does not accept this industry view, then they will be outbid by the others and forced out of the market. The consequences are that development activity is ultimately too "high" and unsustainable. In turn it means that the downturn, or more likely slump, is greater.

Why do developers act in this way? There are a few potential reasons including:

- Developers in one boom go bankrupt and do not participate in the next
- Successful developers who do survive a property slump may attribute their success to their entrepreneurial skills and continue to operate in the same way.

Banks use the valuations and development appraisals presented to them by real estate companies to assess loans but as we have seen it is irrational to use these without caution. However, historically bank staff are driven by targets and bonuses linked to making loans, but staff do not suffer any losses personally. Remuneration in this way does not reflect an appropriate balance between risk and reward for banks. If the property company defaults on the loan when the bust arrives, bank employees can point to the fact that most banks were involved in losses and that they were shared across the board.

These incentives encourage excess lending. In the repercussions following the GFC and the subsequent real estate bust, the bad debts of the bankrupt property companies led to large banking losses. The result was the collapse of banking systems in many Western countries that were ultimately to be rescued by government support.

Summary

The chapter has examined the dynamic nature of the real estate market and its relationship to underlying economic forces. It has considered the fundamental economic determinants of real estate change and their links to development activity.

The demand for property is a derived demand. The level of economic activity will ultimately impact on the demand for shops, offices and industrial units. There is therefore a close relationship with the macroeconomy, and real estate supply constraints can slow economic growth.

The cyclical nature of the macroeconomy gives rise, to a degree, to an equivalent cyclicity in real estate market rents and capital values. However, a real estate cycle differs first because capital values are partly dependent on expectations about the future, notably rental change.

Expectations about the implications of the business cycle for the real estate market also feed into development activity. Much commercial property development is undertaken on a speculative basis and is dependent on the anticipated viability on completion of the project.

The profitability of development is not only dependent on expected capital values but also the cost of construction and borrowing, namely interest rates. Waves of technological change may also impact development activity by increasing the value of modern properties and severely reducing those of old buildings. Given these underlying influences on development, it tends to have its own distinctive cycle.

However, real estate cycles more generally too have their own distinct characteristics distinct from national economic cycles. One potential reason is time lags in development activity as the real estate market responds to the macroeconomic cycle. These time lags relate to the development period and the slowness of new supply to respond to macroeconomic change. There are also supply constraints caused by the need to assemble land plots together in cities, planning processes and in some cases difficult soil conditions.

The chapter has set out a stylised real estate cycle based on these time lags. The dynamics of the cycle looks at the interaction between changes in occupation demand through the economic cycle and the lagged supply response. It is conceived as a series of stages in which first the slowness of supply to an economic upturn leads to rents and capital rising fast. Eventually development responds but the delays in new supply ultimately mean that a real estate bust arrives. As the economic downturn arrives so does a substantial amount of new supply, leaving too many properties on the real estate market.

As a result, when the next business upturn occurs, there is sufficient supply available. There is no requirement for a wave of new development and so a speculative boom occurs every second business cycle. However, it is important to remember that while the stylised cycle does explain instances of cycles in the real world, it is not definitive.

As capital values rise through the real estate boom, the expected profits from development become greater. It encourages not only more development but more grandiose projects, including higher and higher skyscrapers. Typically, towards the end of the boom the highest buildings are conceived and initiated. The finance for building such large projects is also normally only available near the peak of a real estate boom, thereby enabling the development to happen.

Given the scale of these projects, there are often planning obstacles and public objections. In addition, the size of the project can mean that the developments can take a long time to complete, in some cases in time for the next real estate boom.

Real estate cycles can be charted back in time in many countries. However, although there may be common timings the amplitude of cycles varies implying local as well as worldwide influences.

The building of high skyscrapers can be seen within the context of development cycles. The Empire State Building in New York, for example, was planned towards the peak of the 1920s property boom in the city. By the time construction started the boom was over and on completion much of space in the building lay empty for years. There are similar examples in London such as Canary Wharf, again started on the cusp of a downturn and completed in the early 1990s when there was virtually no demand for its space. As a result, the developer went bankrupt.

Commercial real estate cycles are also supported and indeed can be generated by credit availability. Variability in finance per se and changes to gearing can generate real estate cycles through their impact on yields. Changing sentiment and liberal lending by banks can support increasing investment funds into real estate that can lead to falling yields. It can occur without expectations of rental growth/supply shortages or time lags.

A good example of this is in the period in the run up to the GFC of 2007/2008. Purchases by highly geared investors with increased funding provided by banks led to higher and higher capital values as demand increased but supply did not. The high returns attracted more investors prepared to accept even lower yields and capital values kept rising.

The GFC brought the investment frenzy to a close as banks turned off their lending tap. The collapse of the international mortgage-backed bonds market led to the inability of banks to lend to investors, and a dearth of investment finance. As a result, investment into the real estate market plummets, and the number of transactions collapses. The outcome was a substantial rise in yields and a fall in capital values even though rental growth was largely unaffected in the short term.

A critical issue about the existence of cycles is that participants seem to believe that there will be no end to the associated boom. Despite the long record of real estate cycles' property professionals, banks, developers and investors seem oblivious to the risks and the inevitability of the pain of the downturn.

Part of the problem is the failure of commercial real estate market forecasting to be little more than extrapolations of market trends. Developers use current values or expected values based on trends continuing. Developers who are not prepared to accept this industry view are outbid and forced out of the market.

Banks exacerbate the boom pressures by using targets and bonuses linked to making loans, and as a result, can encourage excess lending.

Learning Outcomes

Having completed this chapter, the reader should be able to:

- Understand the relationship between the demand for commercial real estate and the level of economic activity.
- Understand why real estate supply constraints can slow economic growth.
- Appreciate why real estate cycles differ from macroeconomic cycles.
- Explain why development activity is related to business and real estate cycles.
- Understand the basic macroeconomic variables that underpin the profitability of development.
- Appreciate that technological change may drive development activity.
- Be aware that there is a long history of international real estate cycles that can be charted back in time in many countries.
- Note that there have been three global office cycles identified since the 1980s through to the speculative-driven boom in the mid-2000s.
- Understand that local factors as well as global influences affect the timing and shape of real estate cycles.
- Explain how and why development time lags can generate a real estate cycle and only happen every second business cycle by using a stylised stages model.
- Appreciate the importance of finance to the underpinnings of commercial real estate cycles and understand how this drove the real estate boom and bust of the 2000s.
- Understand why real estate professionals, banks, developers and investors have ignored forecasting a downturn and its associated financial losses.

Case Study *The 'Classic' Commercial Real Estate Cycle*

This view of the dynamics of real estate cycles supposes that a business cycle upturn leads to an increase in demand for real estate and a shortage of commercial property. As economic growth continues, commercial property demand strengthens and restricted supply causes rents and property values to rise. This in turn improves the expected profitability of development. This triggers a wave of development.

If economic growth perpetuates, this is often associated with a credit boom. In particular, the banks continue to fund development that is more speculative and with more relaxed terms. Meanwhile the lack of actual new completions continues to push commercial rents and capital values up because of the time lags in the development process.

The whole process can be seen through a simplified stylised 'model' of the real world that highlights the role of time lags. Following Barras, it is seen as a series of stages through the commercial real estate cycle from boom to bust.

Stage 1

The starting point is a strong business upturn. It coincides with shortages in the available supply of real estate after a period of low development activity in the previous business cycle. As a result, rents and capital values begin to rise increasing development viability. However, developers are reluctant to address the shortages through speculative development. They are unsure if the increases in values are sustainable and hold back from responding.

Stage 2

As economic momentum grows, there is strengthening demand while supply is still restricted because of the lack of new development. It leads to a sharp rise in rents and capital values, increasing the profitability of development even more. As a result, a wave of new development eventually starts in response to the business upturn.

Stage 3

As the business cycle upturn continues at a pace, it is supported by expansion of credit from banks. At this stage, the upturn could become an economic boom. With the development wave still to generate any completed buildings, real estate values continue to rise. The response is a second and much larger wave of speculative development activity supported by generous funding terms from banks.

Stage 4

A major building boom is now underway. Although some of the space from the first wave of development may now be available, it does not meet the real estate demands generated by the expanding economy. Construction and development time lags continue to mean that rents and capital are rising.

Stage 5
The macroeconomic boom begins to 'overheat' as excess demand creates high inflation. The result is a tightening of monetary policy including a rise in interest rates. As a result, the business cycle downturns. Meanwhile the bulk of the new building in the second wave of development is nearing completion.

Stage 6
As the economic boom subsides, the demand for real estate space also weakens. However, because of development time lags, the new supply from the building boom reaches its zenith. This peak flow of completions is now available for let but its arrival coincides with falling demand for space. The result is vacant floor space leading to falling rents and capital values.

Stage 7
With the economy moving downwards, possibly towards recession, the demand for space also experiences a marked decline stifled by the high interest rates. It exacerbates the already excess supply in the commercial real estate and amplifies the fall in rents and capital values.

Aftermath
The high real estate vacancy rates contribute to a credit squeeze facing real estate development companies. These companies have to pay high interest payments on their loans from banks with the rise in interest rates. At the same time, many companies are holding unlet buildings with no rental income.

There are potentially widespread bankruptcies of development companies. The properties of these companies are then taken by the banks as their creditors. Forced sales by banks to recoup their losses may lead to depressed commercial property values. This market outcome can be described as a 'slump' with a large overhang of empty properties.

The scale of the surplus stock means that there is sufficient supply to meet the growth in occupation demand emanating from the next business upturn. The next business cycle therefore does not create a development surge, and so a speculative boom occurs every second business cycle.

This stylised real estate cycle based on the role of time lags is illustrative rather than a definitive statement that describes all such booms and busts. Not all development cycles will follow this path. However, it usefully brings together the interaction between economic, credit and development cycles as shown in Figure 3.3. It also demonstrates the potential that development time lags have for destabilising the real estate market. Earlier in the chapter, an alternative perspective on real estate cycles is presented.

Reading

Dehesh, A. and Pugh, C. (1998) *Property Cycles in a Global Economy*, Paper presented to the RICS Cutting Edge Conference, September, De Montfort University, Leicester. ISBN 0 - 8 5 4 0 6 - 9 4 6 -1.

Barras, R. (1994) Property and the economic cycle: building cycles revisited, *Journal of Property Research,* 11, 183–197.

Barras, R. (2009) *Building Cycles: Growth and Instability*, Wiley-Blackwell, Oxford.

Jones, C., Cowe, S. and Trevillion, E. (2018) *Property Boom and Banking Bust: The Role of Commercial Lending in the Bankruptcy of Banks*. Wiley-Blackwell, Chichester. ISBN-13 978–1,119,219,255.

Scott, P. (1996) *The Property Masters*, Spon, London.

Part II

Real Estate Investment

Characteristics of Real Estate Investment

4

Introduction

The focus of this chapter is the nature and logic of real estate investment. It begins by distinguishing real estate assets per se with assets that invest in real estate. A further differentiation is then made between assets that can be bought and sold relatively easily on a stock market and those that are marketed individually say through a market broker. The next part of the chapter examines the principal forms of real estate investments noting the importance of legal interests. The characteristics of these investments are compared with those of stock market assets, and this leads to a comparison of the operation of real estate markets with the stock market.

A more in-depth comparative analysis then considers the yields of real estate assets relative to stock market assets, especially the gap between gilt and property yields in different countries. There then follows a section on the wider logic of holding real estate including its role as a hedge against inflation, and as a diversification tool in a multi-asset portfolio. The final sections of the chapter examine underlying factors influencing residential investment and alternative forms of real estate assets. The chapter covers the following topics:

- Indirect versus direct real estate investment
- Listed and unlisted investments
- Types of investment in terms of land use and legal title – freehold, types of leases
- Characteristics of real estate investments relative to stock market securities
- Comparison of real estate markets and stock markets
- Investment spectrum and yield gap
- Wider logic of real estate investment
- Residential as an investment class
- Characteristics of 'alternative' investments

C. A. Jones and E. Trevillion, *Real Estate Investment*,
https://doi.org/10.1007/978-3-031-00968-6_4

Indirect versus Direct Real Estate Investment

Real estate investments can be split into two broad categories:

- *Direct investment* is the ownership of the physical asset. It includes investments bought for owner occupation and those that are let or intend to be let to a tenant for occupation. The latter investments receive an income in the form of rent. Owner-occupiers receive the benefits of occupying the premises, and in some countries are taxed on the notional rent they should be paying themselves.
- *Indirect investment* is a paper asset backed by property. These paper assets can be issued by owners. There are a range of such owners that are discussed in detail in Chapter 5. For now, it is useful to note that such assets include shares in real estate companies and units in investment trusts. These can be described as indirect real estate **equity** investments as their return is based on the changing values of properties held in a portfolio. Indirect-based investments can also take the form of the holding of mortgages and loans secured against individual real estate values. The income from these investments is in the form of regular repayments of the **debt** borrowed.

Listed and Unlisted Investments

The distinction between listed and unlisted investments relates to whether assets can be bought and sold on a stock market. As we noted in Chapter 1, a stock market is a market where different types of financial investments are traded including shares in companies and bonds. Listed assets are available to be exchanged quickly on a stock market with the most recent price publicly available to buyers and sellers.

Such assets, as noted above, are paper assets backed by real estate values. These listed assets can take the form of equity interests, shares in a company or trust holding an investment portfolio of real estate properties. Alternatively, the assets can take the form of bonds issued by a public company to raise capital. The investment advantage of these shares or bonds is that they can not only be bought and sold relatively easily but also with low transaction costs.

Direct investment through the purchase of a property, or a share of one, has the disadvantage that it lacks the liquidity benefits of a stock market asset. Ownership of mortgages and loans that are not listed on a stock exchange are in a similar position. The sale of these assets would need to be undertaken through a specialist broker or estate agent, and it could be time-consuming. However, there are benefits that are discussed below.

Types of Real Estate Investment

Real estate investments can be distinguished by the legal interest applicable and type of property. The existence of leases as set out in Chapter 1 is the basis for real estate as an investment. The owner of a property can let it to a tenant to generate a rental income for a fixed period as set out in the lease. Within a lease, there can be rent reviews when the rent will usually be reset at market value or adjusted for inflation. Rental income is fixed in nominal terms between reviews.

The income and risk characteristics of direct property investment varies and can have the characteristics of both a fixed income and an equity investment. Between reviews, rental income is fixed in nominal terms, so property has the income characteristics of conventional bonds. The longer the review period the more it can be characterised as a fixed income producing asset. The existence of regular rent reviews to market value is important to ensure that income rises (or falls) in line with the economy and inflation. The existence of frequent rent reviews in this way means that real estate can be characterised as an equity investment.

The shorter the length of the lease or the period between rent reviews then the more quickly rents will adjust to the real economy, and the more the property is an equity investment. Lease lengths vary between countries and property type. Leases of commercial property in mainland Europe have been historically short. In France, leases are either 3, 6 or 9 years while in Germany they are 5 to 10 years. In North America, leases are also typically 5 to 10 years (Chapter 9 reviews the nature and form of international leases in much more detail).

In the UK, until relatively recently leases of prime commercial properties were 25 years with five years upward only rent reviews. Leases are now usually between 5 and 15 years with the average length of a lease for a commercial property in the UK around 9 years, depending on the sector. Three or five years rent reviews are also now the norm.

Leases can offer the opportunity for tenants to end the lease, sometimes on given dates specified at the outset. This arrangement is known as a break clause. Break clauses are not universally available across countries and very often they are subject to negotiation. Leases can be assigned to a different tenant as an alternative.

If there is a long period between rent reviews or no rent reviews within a lease, then ownership of the property is equivalent to investing in a fixed income bond. The tenant is unlikely to leave or not pay the rent because of the financial benefits. At the same time, the tenant who holds this lease has an equity interest in the property, representing the gap between the rent paid and the rental value of the property. If it is large, then it could be worthwhile subletting the property to generate an income stream.

These examples show that the nature of the income received from investing directly in property varies with leases and can have the characteristics of both fixed income and equity investments. The precise balance depends on the lease arrangements. Shorter rent review or lease periods mean that the investment is more of an equity investment. These characteristics are beneficial to investors during periods of strong economic growth and rising rents. When rents are declining, a longer period between rent reviews can also be attractive to an investor, as the income is protected from falling.

The types of leases vary with real estate sector, as does the nature of income generation over time. The real estate sectors that constitute the investment market, and their financial characteristics, vary from country to country. The most commonly held sectors for investment purposes are:

- ***Farmland***. Private individuals, and family companies and trusts dominate the ownership of farmland. Owners may farm the land themselves or employ managers or let the property to tenants. Institutional investors in the UK are not major holders of agricultural land as legislation means that tenants not only have security of tenure but the right to bequeath his/her tenancy to family. This means that owners may be unable to gain vacant possession for generations. This reduces the likelihood of vacant possession for the investor.
- ***Woodlands***. This type of investment property usually involves the freehold occupation of land where the income is only gained from the felling of the timber. It is a very long-term investment and was encouraged in the UK by tax incentives. However, the removal of this tax break has led to a decline in the amount of woodland held for investment purposes.
- ***Shops***. Most retail units in large shopping centres are tenanted. Shops have been popular with large investors because rental growth has historically been supported by the growth in real incomes. Popular locations have also historically benefitted from a low risk of long-term vacancy and subsequent income voids but online sales have become a major threat.
- ***Offices***. Large office blocks are also generally tenanted. Offices have seen a continuing rise in occupier demand over decades because of the growth of services. However, offices can suffer from obsolescence caused by technological advances.
- ***Industrial Units***. Owner occupation is the more common tenure of industrial units. The sector has been less attractive to investors because it has been historically vulnerable to vacancies during economic downturns, although investment demand is now more popular.
- ***Logistics Warehousing.*** The changing nature of the distribution of goods has seen a significant expansion of this sector. However, units are again mainly owner-occupied.
- ***Residential Property.*** In many countries, the dominant housing tenure is owner-occupied. Housing can also be provided by the state directly or indirectly through subsidies to private providers for low-income households. In many countries, this is called social or public housing or affordable housing. In addition, there is usually also an unsubsidised private-rented sector where leases and rent review periods are very short, potentially less than a year. Much of this housing is provided by small private investors although there are countries where large investors exist such as the United States (see later in the chapter). The precise tenure structure varies across countries reflecting historical housing development, taxation differences and the accepted role of the state. In the

last decade, institutions have become increasingly interested in this sector as an investment class (the so-called Build to Rent sector discussed later in the chapter).

Overall, the income growth of real estate investments depends on the economic performance of these individual sectors and the lease structure of the individual asset. It is also a function of the characteristics of individual properties including their location and quality.

Characteristics of Real Estate Investments Relative to Stock Market Securities

These latter characteristics of property can be distinguished as follows:

- ***Location.*** No two properties are the same simply because each has a unique location. Two identical office blocks side by side still have different locational characteristics. One may be closer to the rail station, the other to the bus station. The further apart the more the potential for rental income differences. Equivalent office blocks in different cities almost certainly have different rents.
- ***Heterogeneity.*** It is not just location that differentiates real estate assets. By its very nature, individual properties are inherently different. Two nearby farms may have very different levels of fertility and income potential that is reflected in their comparative rental values as explained in Chapter 1. More generally properties in a real estate sector can differ by size, construction, design and quality of tenant. All these factors will influence the rental value of a property.
- ***Lumpy.*** Property comes in large lot sizes with high unit costs. Direct property investment normally means ownership of a whole building. As a result, real estate investors require large amounts of capital. In turn it means that if an investor wanted to hold a diversified real estate portfolio, then the size of the investment fund needs to be substantial. A consequence of the high unit value of property is that borrowing is important.
- ***Long-Term Nature of the Holding.*** Pure land is totally durable, and buildings and other capital improvements also have a relatively long life compared to other goods. Over time buildings can deteriorate and investors must expect repair and refurbishment costs, so depreciation occurs in the value of their asset. Depreciation therefore can arise simply from the deterioration of buildings over time because of wear and tear, and the effects of the elements.

  But rental value may also be affected by functional obsolescence that depreciates rental values and may even make a building redundant. This issue can occur because of advances say in information and communications technologies, so that buildings find it difficult or impossible to adapt to the requirements of property occupiers. Similarly changing market conditions or transport infrastructure developments may make the location of a building no longer attractive to occupiers.

- ***Immobility.*** Once a property is fixed at a given location. You cannot move property from an area of low demand to an area of high demand.
- ***Management.*** Property as an investment medium requires a continuing relationship with a tenant. There is potentially a significant amount of specialist management and administration. The day-to-day obligations include maintenance/repairs, rent collection, rent reviews and lease negotiations. This adds to the costs of holding this type of asset as investors either must employ their own specialists or the services of a property management practice. Some property management obligations can lead to opportunities, for example refurbishment, redevelopment and extensions that can add value to a property. The management/rationalisation of leases and rent reviews can also affect income and thus value.
- ***Government Intervention.*** Real estate is subject to a range of potential government regulation that are discussed in detail in Chapter 10. Land use planning and environmental controls together with building regulations are all essential components of a modern economy. In most countries, there are regulations governing private housing and commercial landlords encompassing tenants' rights, leases and rent increases.
- ***Taxation.*** Real estate taxation can have important ramifications for investment decisions. There are considerable variations between countries. Capital gains and transfer taxes influence the cost of trading and transactions activity. A reduction in transfer tax can increase market transactions and potentially lead to rising capital values as the savings to the investor enable a higher bid price for a property. The ownership of a household's main residence can be exempt from capital gains tax as in the UK, thereby encouraging home ownership. Inheritance tax obligations may lead people to restructure their family's investment portfolios to minimise tax payments.

  The minimisation of the payment of taxation is a key influence on the devising and structuring of investment vehicles (see below). The application of differential tax (incentives) can also shape the nature of real estate investment. As noted above woodland in the UK has in the past benefitted. Lower taxation rules in particular locations can encourage economic activity in these areas and hence new development. An example would be an enterprise zone.

  Many countries offer tax relief on mortgage interest payments on real estate loans, especially to purchase housing. In this way mortgage repayments are reduced making the cost of purchase of a house cheaper. With no equivalent benefits to be a residential tenant, it means that owner occupation has a more favourable tax treatment. In addition, while landlords pay tax on the rental income from their tenants, owner-occupiers usually do not pay the equivalent tax on the notional rent to themselves. These differences have contributed to the attractiveness of owning a home in many countries rather than renting.

Comparison with Stock Market Investments

Investments in the stock market are arguably more homogeneous than real estate. All standard shares offer the same legal interest in a company, with a share in the distributed profits through dividends. Standard bonds also provide a fixed income return whether issued by a government or a company. Two shares in the same company or two gilts of a particular issue are homogeneous unlike necessarily ownership of two office blocks in the same city centre.

It does not mean all shares or bonds are the same. Shares in a very established growing company, sometimes described as 'blue chip' are more expensive than those in a firm that is in a declining sector of the economy. The latter could have weak economic prospects and be riskier. The expected dividend growth of the former would be greater resulting in a higher share price.

Similarly, bonds issued by a government of a Western economy are seen as a very safe investment. In comparison, the future income from a bond issued by a private company is inevitably less secure, and so is riskier. An investor needs to be compensated for the extra risk by paying less for the same promised income stream.

These differences in potential income growth and risk are also to be found in real estate investments. But there are other differences between real estate and stock market investments. As noted above, real estate requires management whereas ownership of a bond or a share can be regarded as a passive form of investment. For most investors, there is no management input beyond the decisions to buy and sell. Share and bond ownership can also be achieved with much smaller amounts of capital.

Comparison of Real Estate and Stock Markets

The differences between real estate and stock market assets also encompass the characteristics of the markets in which they are traded. These can be detailed as follows:

- There is no central marketplace for real estate assets unlike the stock market where shares and bonds are traded normally via computer screens. In contrast, properties are bought and sold and let through agents who market them on websites. The market is much less transparent and less efficient because there is no one database where transactions are recorded.

  Whereas prices of shares (and dividends) and bonds are publicly, and immediately available details of real estate transactions take time to emerge and require research. In some countries, there are specialist companies that collect this information on transactions, both new tenancies and sales, from agents and then sell it.

  Even with ready information on real estate transactions, some further analysis is required to account for the complexities of each asset in terms of the legal interest including lease structures and tenancy covenant. Location is also important for evaluating future income. It also means that information on one transaction does not provide an exact proxy for the likely rent or selling price of another property. In practice, the price/rent for a real estate investment is the product of negotiation between the seller and one or more buyers for unique properties in local markets.

- Given that property is complex and not sold as frequently as shares and bonds, then the monitoring of a real estate investment portfolio necessitates periodic valuations of individual properties. Such valuations can be undertaken monthly, but normally quarterly. Real estate valuations are less volatile than prices on the stock market, so comparison of the performance of asset types is difficult.
- The complexity of the financial arrangements of real estate investments with different legal interests results in transactions being lengthy and costly. Real estate assets are therefore illiquid, and it can take 3–6 months to buy and sell a property. The time that it takes to realise the cash tied up in a property asset is significantly longer than the time it takes to sell equities and gilts. The revenue from a sale of a stock market investment can be received almost immediately.
- High transaction costs inhibit sales activity and market participants from responding rapidly to changing conditions. The illiquidity and transaction costs also increase the gross return required by real estate investors.

Investment Spectrum and Yield Gaps

In Chapter 2, it was explained that the required returns from real estate investment is subject to a greater risk premium than blue chip shares and long-dated gilts. The chapter also noted that the value of a real estate investment is partly determined by reference to the returns from investments on the stock market. It is possible to think in terms of an investment spectrum of different types of assets each with their own characteristics that are competing for investment funds. A wide range of potential assets was set out in Chapter 1. This section considers the place of freehold real estate in the investment spectrum of shares and gilts, and the implications for its pricing and comparative yields.

The relative merits of these investments reflected are in what investors are prepared to pay for them. Although some investors have different priorities, and hence value investments differently, a market view can be seen in the relative yields of different investments. It is useful at this point to recap on the definition of a yield as more precisely the initial income yield of an investment, expressed formally as,

$$\frac{\text{net initial income}}{\text{capital value}} * 100$$

From Chapter 2, it can be shown that the determinants of a yield can be encapsulated by the following simple equation:

$$k=r-g \tag{4.1}$$

where:
k = current income yield
r = required rate of return
g = expected rental growth

From this formula, it can be that the spectrum of different types of investments exhibit a range of yields for different investment (types) mirroring their characteristics.

Investors accept lower yields (initial return) for investments that are expected to grow in value such as shares or freehold property. But if the expected return is constant or expected to fall, then on the flip side investors require to be compensated by a higher-initial yield. As noted in Chapter 2, the greater the anticipated growth of equity investments the lower the yield is. Following this logic with the income return from normal bonds fixed their yields are generally higher than equity investments to account for the lack of potential income growth.

The picture is a little more complicated than this when potential changes to the macroeconomy are considered. If inflation is expected to fall, then the value of a fixed income bond will increase in real terms and this real rise will be reflected in a lower-initial yield. Similarly, if inflation is expected to rise, the reverse will happen and investors require an even higher-initial yield to compensate for the expected fall in real value of payments.

This variation in gilt yields with inflation indicates that they are not fully risk-free (see Chapter 2). For this reason, index-linked gilts were introduced in the UK in 1983 although much later in 1997 in the United States. These gilts have their income adjusted in line with inflation, and are therefore, in theory at least, risk-free.

The macroeconomy has equivalent impacts on equity yields. Expected lower inflation could also signal less income growth for shares and real estate leading to higher yields for these investments. The reverse is also true. Furthermore, if the economy is booming, then company profits/dividends and rents would be anticipated to rise leading to lower yields. On the other hand, if a recession is seen as imminent with lower returns on the horizon, then yields will rise. However, these cyclical impacts on returns to real estate will be moderated by the stability brought about by leases and rent reviews.

The foregoing analysis suggests that there should be a difference or gap between gilt and real estate yields. In general, real estate yields are lower than the yields on bonds because of the potential growth in returns. The actual size of the gap depends on the macroeconomy. In low inflationary periods, the gap should be low because real estate yields are relatively high while gilt yields are relatively low in historic terms. The reverse is true with high inflation: real estate yields are lower

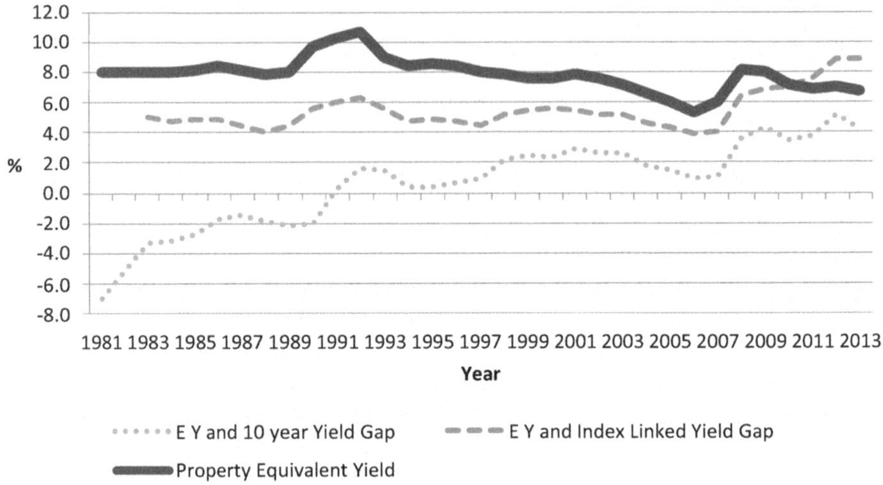

Fig. 4.1 UK Yield Gap Trends on annual basis 1983–2013 (*Source* Jones et al. [2015])

than average because of the expected large rise in rents while gilt yields are high because interest payments will fall substantially in real terms.

Inflation is not the only influence on yields. When a government has a policy of high interest rates then the gap relationship could be changed on its head. High interest rates mean that gilt yields are high, and they also dampen demand for real estate. With low rental growth expectations, real estate yields will be high but not necessarily as high as gilt yields. Figure 4.1 demonstrates how these macroeconomic influences have been reflected in the yield gaps in the UK between 1981 and 2013. The real estate yield gap with 10-year gilts is negative from the early 1980s through to 1991 because interest rates were very high and there were low rental growth expectations. However, the gap was subsequently marginally positive during an era of falling inflation.

Interestingly the UK yield gap with index-linked gilts is consistently positive, and between 4 and 6% until the GFC. A similar picture is found in the United States shown in Fig. 4.2, although the ten-year yield gap is higher between 2 and 4% after 1990. The index-linked gilt yield is also higher (and always positive). The time series for Australia given in Fig. 4.3 is shorter but broadly consistent with the other two countries albeit more stable.

The real estate **equivalent yields** (EY) presented in these graphs is different from initial yields. They are a further way of comparing investments and Chapter 5 examines behaviour of initial yields in the context of market behaviour.

An equivalent yield can be seen as the internal rate of return (IRR) of a property's cash flow (see Chapter 2) assuming a rise to estimated rental value at the next rent review but with no further rental growth. It is called the capitalisation rate in the United States and other countries. There are parallel yields that can be calculated for bonds and shares. It is analogous to a bond's **gross redemption**

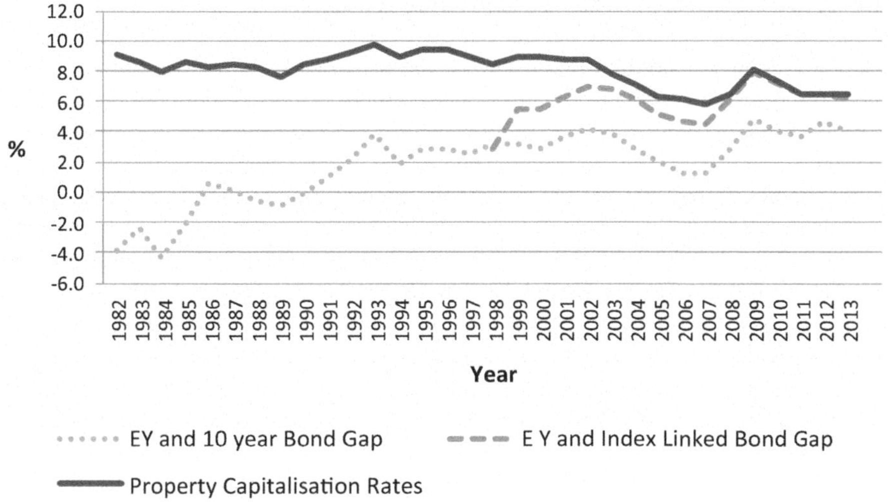

Fig. 4.2 US Yield Gap Trends on annual basis 1981–2013 (*Source* Jones et al. [2015])

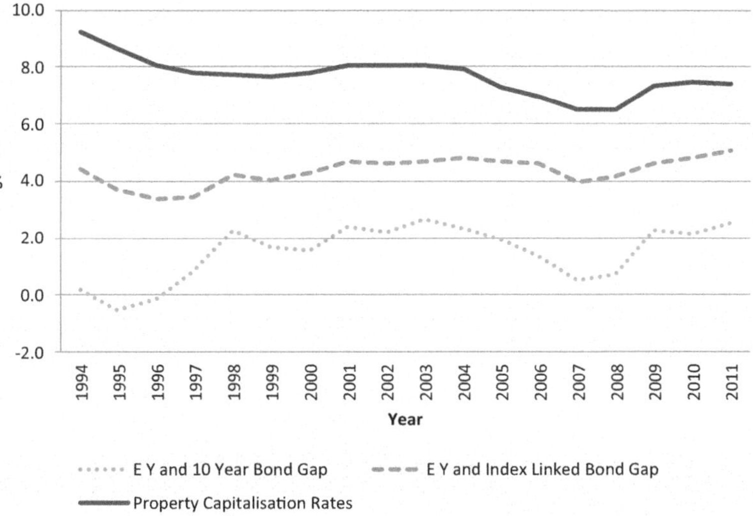

Fig. 4.3 Australian Yield Gap Trends on annual basis 1994–2011 (*Source* Jones et al. [2015])

yield which is calculated by working out its IRR encompassing its future interest payments and its final repayment of capital sum (if applicable). The corresponding statistic for a share is its holding period return.

The Wider Logic of Real Estate Investment

A key argument for holding real estate is that it is a hedge against inflation, especially for property in prime locations where there is excess demand. The value of property in the long run is deemed to keep pace with inflation even though as Chapter 3 notes, there are clear real estate cycles when values fall. In other words, the real value of property is seen as stable in the long run, even increasing in value.

The impact of the cyclical nature of the real estate market activity is demonstrated in Fig. 4.4. It gives the average variation in total returns, capital growth and income return over the period 1971 to 2016 of UK prime property. It clearly shows the cyclical nature of total returns and capital growth, but it also shows an important feature of the property market, namely the constancy of income returns. Over the forty or so years covered, including three cycles, income returns were in the range 4.3 to 7.7% per annum averaging 6.2% per annum over the period.

These results stem from the ability of leases to maintain income through economic bad times providing landlords can keep tenants in place and the income stream holds. However, in recent years technological change has threatened this traditional role with commercial property suffering from obsolescence or excess supply, with consequences for rents and capital values.

Investing in real estate as noted above can be undertaken directly in individual properties or indirectly on the stock market. Real estate stock market investments take the form of property company shares or bonds. The two alternatives have different attributes and relative attractions. Stock market investments have the benefit of liquidity and low transaction costs, and in the case of shares the benefits of a diversified portfolio of assets supporting the income. Direct investment has the

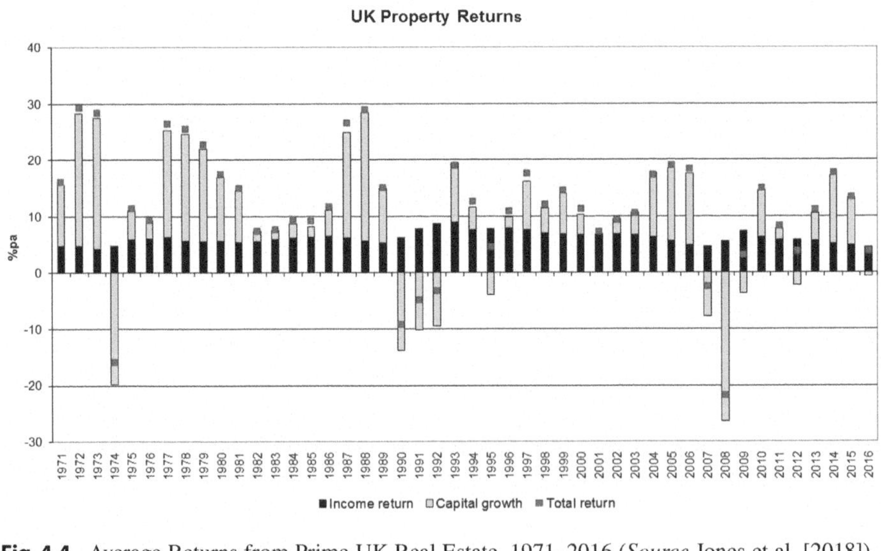

Fig. 4.4 Average Returns from Prime UK Real Estate, 1971–2016 (*Source* Jones et al. [2018])

Table 4.1 Correlation Coefficients between UK Asset Classes for Average Total Returns, 1971 to 2016

Asset correlation of direct property	UK Property	Gilts	Equities
UK Property	1.0	0.03	0.27

Source Derived data from MSCI 2016 and Barclays Annual Equity Gilt Study 2016

attraction of control and management of the asset enabling an investor to add value to it over time.

The returns from indirect real estate investments also tend to reflect the stock market as a whole in the short term. This phenomenon negates one of the attractions of investing in real estate, namely the potential to enhance the diversification benefits of a portfolio including shares and bonds. The essential argument is that the existence of real estate rent reviews generates a different cycle of returns than shares and bonds, as Fig. 4.4 demonstrates.

The consequences can be seen in the correlations between the average returns of asset classes shown in Table 4.1. It can be argued that one of the strengths of commercial property is that returns have an element of counter cyclicality. The result is that there are very relative low correlation coefficients compared with bonds and equities. However, it is useful to note a word of caution about the statistics in Table 4.1 as property returns are based on valuations while those for shares and bonds are derived from actual prices. Valuations tend to smooth out cycles.

The low correlations presented in Table 4.1 are therefore overestimates. The problem is that it is difficult to estimate adjusted real estate returns that de-smooth valuation-based returns. There are different statistical approaches to address the problem and as result they do not fully produce one convincing answer. The issue is ultimately which approach to de-smoothing is correct, but there is no way of knowing which is right.

Residential as an Investment Class

Historically, large investors have viewed the characteristics of residential investment as less favourable than commercial property because:

- Of high investment transaction costs linked to the small-scale nature of individual residential assets
- Residential returns comprise a significant capital element that cannot be realised without selling properties with vacant possession
- There are intensive management and maintenance responsibilities
- There is high tenant turnover adding to costs
- There are potential reputational problems through, for example, evictions

- The sale of properties with tenants may be difficult making such investments illiquid and difficult to value. Traditionally in the UK properties with a tenant in situ are sold at a discount
- There is potential political risk through restrictive rent controls

On the positive side, there are long run capital returns associated with housing with vacant possession and the returns from the short leases associated with the sector may offer portfolio diversification.

For these reasons globally most residential investment has been owned by small individual investors although there are large-scale investors in Europe and the United States. In Britain, the majority of landlords are private individuals and couples. This ownership structure is a long-standing position going back more than a century. A sudden rise in the UK's private-rented sector (PRS) since the millennium has reinforced this phenomenon. Small investors were attracted to 'buy to let' in which landlords buy properties with a mortgage, supported by a long housing price boom. Many of these landlords see their involvement as a secondary activity rather than their primary source of income.

The picture in the UK has parallels around the world. Small-to-medium-sized landlords, perhaps holding property portfolios in double figures, are cost-competitive relative to larger ones over wide portions of the rental housing stock. These landlords can flexibly invest their own time and do not have high overheads. In particular, such enterprises hold significant cost advantages over larger landlords within the heterogeneous, often old and scattered stock of properties that comprise most of the private rental stock. Overall, there are limited management economies of scale to private landlordism given the range and location of housing in the sector.

Large-scale investors across the world are normally confined to a segment of the private-rented sector. They generally own and manage large, standardised apartment blocks for young, middle-and low-income households. Typically, they hold a large block of tenanted properties as one unit. In the United States, most of the stock owned by large landlords usually takes the form of communities of 200 or more small apartments in urban areas. In this segment of the market, large-scale investors can have a competitive edge in terms of marketing/branding, quality control and creating distinctive and cost-effective rental products. The 'deep' rented markets in cities, given the local scale of size (and demand for) of the PRS, also minimise investment risk and enable purpose-built large-scale developments for private renting.

In the UK, after decades, when large investors sold off their rental stock, new interest emerged in the early 1990s following the removal of rent controls and tax incentives offered by the government. In many ways, this proved a false dawn and this investment stock was eventually sold off. However, since the millennium there has been a surge in large investors providing purpose-built multi-storey blocks of student housing. Specialist operators have multiple student residential blocks in many city centre locations. Large investors have been able to prosper due to their new accommodation offering a better quality of accommodation encompassing en-suite facilities compared to the older flats provided by small landlords. They also offer a tailored and distinctive service package for students.

There has also been an increasing movement towards investors building custom-built large blocks to rent in cities, following the model in the United States, and supported by subsidies from central government. This phenomenon is known collectively as 'build to rent' (BTR). The aim is to introduce mass-produced rental housing for middle market tenants such as younger office workers. These developments are, generally speaking, not aimed at the lower end of the market but increasingly opportunities are being examined for encompassing affordable rents into larger BTR schemes.

The investors in BTR are focused on the potential long-term cash flow potential from the net rental stream that offers better returns than government bonds. BTR developments are expected to generate take-up of flats by tenants that is faster than for owner-occupied blocks. It is envisaged that there is a long-term demand for such flats as owner occupation is increasingly more difficult to access and there is a consequent growth of long-term renters. Long-term tenants will be promoted by high management standards, services and de facto security of tenure. Schemes aim to promote a lifestyle choice of inner city living incorporating community facilities. These schemes are not restricted to flatted development but are now also encompassing a range of housing types including low density developments.

Characteristics of Alternative Investments

The growing interest by large investors in the residential sector in the UK is part of a much wider trend of considering alternative real estate investments beyond the traditional asset types. In the process, it begs a question about what is real estate? At one level, 'alternative' can encompass asset classes that are not the traditional property types listed at the beginning of the chapter. A useful classification is given in Table 4.2 that includes some specialist segments of traditional assets such as student housing and serviced offices offering space and facilities on a short-term basis.

The potential list of alternative real estate assets is long and diverse. Table 4.2 distinguishes between alternative investments based on specialist private business functions and those whose returns derive from providing specialised infrastructure services. It is useful to compare the predictability and security of the underlying revenue stream of these heterogeneous assets with the fundamentals of traditional real estate.

Traditional real estate assets are essentially dependent on future income streams linked to the performance of a property sector and location. There is a degree of contractual certainty given by leases and rent reviews. There is some specific risk associated with the failure of a tenant's business, but a new tenant can resolve this

Table 4.2 A Comparison of Traditional and Alternative Real Estate Asset Classes

Traditional	Alternative	
	Specialised Private Business	Infrastructure/Service
Farmland Industrial Offices Residential Shops Woodland	Hotels and leisure Student Accommodation Self-storage Medical Practices Care Homes Pubs and Bars Cinemas and Bowling Alleys Serviced Offices Data Centres Airports Car parks	Medical facilities (Hospitals) Education Facilities (Schools/Colleges and Universities) Energy Public facilities (Museums, Courts and Libraries)

temporary void. However, by choosing good tenant covenants, and prime locations and properties this risk can be minimised. The choice of business function is flexible and not dependent on the structure of the building.

As an asset class infrastructure investment is drawn together by the observation that they have a very predictable underlying revenue stream that is often public sector-backed, typically agreed at the outset on a long-term contract and often with built-in inflation protection. From an investor's perspective, the emphasis is on investing in an investment where revenue is subject to predictable demand and is not reliant on short-term economic cycles. As an investment class, its potential is driven less by operator skill but by long-term economic growth, technological progress and climate change. By comparison with traditional assets, risk is relatively low and returns predictable over the economic life of the asset.

Specialised businesses are backed by a specific real estate asset but unlike traditional real estate, the returns are more dependent on the operation of the business carried out within the building. Investors expect returns, say from a hotel, that are based on the tenant's performance through a contract and therefore the business component of the future income flows is critical. However, in choosing to invest they are also doing so with regard to the covenant of the operator and the property/location. They are not hybrid assets but real estate assets where there is heightened operational risk and specialist skills needed to manage them. As with normal real estate investments, the exit or terminal value at the end of the contract is the building itself on eventual resale.

These alternative assets have lower transaction volumes and so less liquidity, at least compared to commercial real estate. As a result, there is limited market information on their transactions and therefore less transparency. On the other hand, they may have diversification advantages by being subject to different macro trends in the economy and demographics. There are other positive pull factors such as the search for greater potential returns, the rise in the importance of the leisure sector, and a shift in public infrastructure funding models. The discussion of investment in these types of assets is extended in Chapter 12.

Summary

The focus of this chapter has been the nature and logic of real estate investment. It has distinguished real estate assets per se with other asset types that invest in real estate. In this context, real estate assets can be differentiated between direct and indirect investment. Direct ownership includes investments that are owner-occupied and those that are let to a tenant. Indirect investment is a paper certificate that entitles the owner to an income supported by a portfolio of properties.

Returns from these indirect real estate equity investments derive from the changing value of properties. Indirect real estate investments also take the form of the holding of mortgages and loans secured against individual real estate values. Indirect investments may be bought and sold cheaply and quickly on a stock market with prices readily available.

Direct investment in property lacks these liquidity benefits. It takes the form of legal interests in individual properties. Typically, an owner receives rent from a tenant over a period as set out in the lease, although the rent can be reset at a rent review date. Between reviews, rental income is fixed like that of a bond but with regular rent reviews to market value, real estate can be characterised as an equity investment. The briefer the period between reviews the more property is an equity investment. Lease lengths of commercial property typically vary between 5 and 10 years.

Very long periods between rent reviews result in property ownership being equivalent to an investment in a fixed income bond. The tenant then has an equity interest and may have an opportunity to sublet the property and make a profit.

The most common real estate investment sectors are farmland, woodlands, shops, offices, industrial units, logistics warehousing and residential property. The returns from these real estate investment asset classes depend on the economic performance of the individual sectors and the lease structure of the individual asset. Returns also relate to the attributes of individual properties encompassing their location and quality.

Direct property has some key attributes that differentiate it from other investment classes. It is tied to a specific location, the asset class is heterogeneous, lumpy, generally held longer term, involves significant management, has different taxation attributes and is subject to government intervention.

In this context, stock market investments can be viewed as more homogeneous than real estate ones. However, the value of shares in different companies or bonds issued by different companies depend on the prospects of the company. Equivalent differences in potential growth or risk are also applicable to real estate investments. But real estate investment requires management whereas ownership of a bond or a share can be regarded as passive.

There is no formal real estate market with properties bought, sold or let through agents who market them individually. As a result, the market is much less transparent and less efficient than the stock market. The complexity of real estate assets also means that market information on real estate transactions requires analysis and interpretation of the potential value of other properties. Further as property transactions occur less frequently than shares and bonds, monitoring of a real estate investment portfolio necessitates periodic valuations of individual properties.

Real estate assets are illiquid, as it can take 3–6 months to buy and sell a property. Transactions are also expensive inhibiting market activity.

There is an investment spectrum of shares, gilts and real estate with their relative yields reflecting their different characteristics, and in particular their anticipated future returns. Investors accept lower yields (initial return) for assets that are expected to grow in value. Similarly, if the expected return is constant or expected to fall, then investors require to be compensated by a higher-initial yield. Inflation in the macroeconomy will influence these expectations about future returns, and hence required initial yields. Inflation reduces the future real value of income from government bonds so that they are not risk-free. To counter this issue, index-linked gilts were introduced.

Logically real estate yields are lower than the yields on bonds because of the potential growth in returns. The actual size of the gap varies with inflation and interest rates. High interest rates mean that gilt yields are high while at the same pushing real estate yields up because of low expected rental growth. Nevertheless, while real estate yields are high, they are not necessarily as high as gilt yields.

Times series of the yield gaps for the UK, the United States and Australia show these macroeconomic influences. The yield gap with 10-year gilts in the UK was negative from the early 1980s through to 1991 because interest rates were very high but is subsequently marginally positive during an era of falling inflation. The same occurs in the United States. In contrast, the yield gap with index-linked gilts is consistently positive in all countries.

A key argument for holding real estate is that it is a hedge against inflation, especially for property in prime locations where there is excess demand. The argument is seen to apply despite the existence of cycles when values fall. Part of the reason is that leases help to maintain income through economic bad times providing landlords can keep tenants in place.

Investing indirectly in real estate through property company shares or bonds has the benefit of liquidity and low transaction costs. However, direct investment has the attraction of control and management of the asset enabling an investor to add value to it over time. Direct investment also has the potential to enhance the diversification benefits through the existence of real estate rent reviews generating a different cycle of returns than shares and bonds.

Traditionally, large investors have preferred to invest in commercial property rather than housing. There are a wide range of reasons, encompassing the intensive management requirements and high tenant turnover. As a result, around the world much residential investment is owned by small individual investors. Small-to-medium-sized landlords are generally cost-competitive relative to larger ones, as there are limited management economies of scale.

Since the millennium in the UK, there has been a surge in large investors providing purpose-built multi-storey blocks of student housing. There has also been a move towards investors building custom-built large blocks to rent in cities, supported by subsidies from central government, known collectively as BTR.

There is a growing interest by large investors in alternative real estate investments beyond traditional assets. The potential list of alternative real estate assets is related to specialist private business functions and those whose returns derive from providing specialised infrastructure services. Whereas traditional real estate assets are fundamentally dependent on future income streams linked to the performance of a property sector and location returns from alternative investments are linked more to individual performance.

Infrastructure investment has a very predictable underlying revenue stream that is often public sector-backed, typically agreed at the outset on a long-term contract. Investment in specialised businesses is supported by a specific real estate asset and returns are dependent on the operation of the business. These alternative assets are less liquid and lack transparency, but they may have diversification advantages by generating different patterns of income flows over time.

Learning Outcomes

Having completed this chapter, the reader should be able to:

- Distinguish between listed and unlisted investments
- Appreciate the broad investment attributes of property
- Understand the characteristics of property investment relative to other investments, and how lease terms can shape these characteristics
- Appreciate the distinctiveness (and imperfections) of the real estate market and its implications for investment
- Understand the reasons for the differences in yields between government bonds and real estate
- Be aware of the potential diversification benefits of real estate investment
- Have an awareness of the differential attraction of residential tenancies as an investment class for large and small investors
- Be conscious of the recent BTR growth in the UK and the reasons why
- Note the growing popularity of investment in alternative forms of real estate offering infrastructure services or occupied by specialist businesses

Reading

Barclays Bank (2016) *Annual Equity Gilt Study*, Barclays Bank, London.

Fraser, W. D. (1993). *Principles of Property Investment and Pricing*. 2nd Edition. Palgrave, Macmillan, London. ISBN 0333716922.

Gough, L. (2011). *How the Stock Market really Works*. 5th Edition. Financial Times, Prentice Hall. London. ISBN 9780273743552 (pbk.).

Investment Property Forum (2017) *Understanding UK Commercial Property Investments: A Guide for Financial Advisers,* IPF, London.

Jones, C., Dunse, N. and Cutsforth, K. (2015) The changing relationships between government bond yields and capitalisation rates, *Journal of European Real Estate Research*, 8, 2, 153–171.

Jones, C., Cowe, S. and Trevillion E. (2018) *Property Boom and Banking Bust: The Role of Commercial Lending in the Bankruptcy of Banks*. Wiley-Blackwell, Chichester. ISBN-13 978-1119219255.

MSCI (2016) *Annual Digest*, MSCI, London.

Investors 5

Introduction

We have noted in earlier chapters that real estate is an unusual commodity as the legal interests of ownership and use can be split. This chapter is concerned with the owners of commercial property who let space out to a tenant in return for a rental income. To address this task, it is necessary to consider a broad range of investors and their motives. In particular, this chapter reviews a spectrum of investors and their various reasons for investing or not investing in real estate. In doing so, it revisits the characteristics of real estate relative to other asset classes. This chapter also examines their choice of real estate investments and why.

As noted in Chapter 4, a distinction can be made between direct and indirect investors in real estate. Direct investment can be seen as the purchase of individual assets, whereas indirect investment is the purchase of a share or a unit in a fund or company that then invests in real estate. This distinction in practice is blurred because in one sense nearly all the investors considered are collective schemes whereby individuals buy into a fund that then invests in real estate on their behalf. Further some of these investments not only purchase individual properties but also participate in collective investment arrangements.

The nature of real estate assets and investors has radically changed over time with the emergence, particularly, of new types of funds investing in the sector. This chapter chronicles the evolution of investment in real estate and the different mechanisms utilised by investors. It considers the following:

- The history of commercial real estate investment
- Types of financial institutions and investment priorities
- Real estate investment trusts (REITs)
- Property companies
- Investment and unit trusts
- Limited partnerships etc.

C. A. Jones and E. Trevillion, *Real Estate Investment* ,
https://doi.org/10.1007/978-3-031-00968-6_5

- Private equity and hedge funds
- Exchange traded funds

History of Commercial Real Estate Investment

In the UK property really began the transition from social institution to financial asset over the twenty years from 1850 to 1870, with many of the trends later mirrored globally. Environmental pressures resulting from a. growing national economy increased the demand for new commercial and residential buildings. This economic growth, the concomitant increase in the accumulation of capital and the size of companies that were accommodated also increased the average scale of building projects. A major factor that contributed to the structural change at this time was a growing middleclass. It led to a growth in middleclass savings with concerns almost exclusively relating to financial return rather than non-monetary factors. In addition, there was an expansion in property companies and indirect investment in property, a growth in the property investment market per se and with it the development of market intermediaries.

Insurance companies began to take an increasingly active role in the urban property market during this period. There had been little direct investment before 1870, but there began to be a switch in funds from Government stock to mortgages. One of the earliest companies to become involved in property was Standard Life Assurance Company. It appears to have made a direct investment in land, *as a hedge against inflation*, as early as 1852. Other institutional players included *The British Empire Mutual Life Assurance Company* and *Royal Exchange Assurance*.

These factors contributed to the changing nature of property investment and financing and the commodifying of commercial property. The changes had brought new actors to the game and while these actors were not yet dominating the play, they were influencing the market structurally through their direct involvement in property and involvement in short term finance.

Links between the investment market and real estate continued to strengthen over the late 1800s to the immediate pre-World War I period. There was extensive involvement by the insurance companies in the property market regarding low yielding secure investments and there was a move towards a more active investment policy on the part of a few companies. Direct investment in property offered a means of placing money at substantially higher yields than could be obtained on bonds or mortgages, and during this period the proportion of insurance company funds invested in land, property and ground rents nearly doubled.

In the 1890s, the Royal Exchange Assurance, the National Provident Institution and the Clerical Medical and General Life Assurance Society began to purchase freehold ground rents and began to invest in buildings per se by the early 1900s. Some of Clerical Medical's early property investment deals involved cooperation with potential tenants using techniques that were to develop during the interwar years.

An initial high-profile example of the changing nature of the market in the United States was the Park Row Building in New York, with 29 storeys in 1899. It was then the tallest building in the world and built by an investor on a speculative basis with a view to letting out office suites to different tenants. A further notable example, cited in Chapter 3, is the Empire State Building opened in 1931.

Although many features of the modern property market, per se, existed in one form or another by the end of World War I, the interwar period was to have the greatest impact on the structural development and behaviour of the property investment market. Many basic features of Britain's modern property investment market appeared in the years 1914 to 1939. These included:

- The growth of intermediaries
- Securitisation of investment property
- Development of funding links between funding institutions and property

The growth of multiple retailers, together with the associated development of nationally based property market intermediaries were particularly important. This created the conditions required to persuade institutional investors to undertake a substantial volume of direct property investment.

Despite the major changes in attitude during this period, investment property still constituted a virtually fixed interest asset since it was still subject to long lease fixed rents. Property activity increased, however, because it offered a yield of around 2% higher than bonds and offered more stability than equities in the generally unstable economic conditions of the 1920s and 1930s.

The final transition to a commercial property market occurred in the post-war period up to the early 1970s. Strong demand pressures, particularly in the early part of this period, resulted from the destruction of commercial space during World War II and the pent-up demand for space from before the war. This trend was supported by macroeconomic growth and the expansion in services with rising demand for retail and office space. The emergence of inflation in the 1960s brought increased interest in commercial real estate investment as a hedge against inflation.s The rampant inflation of the 1970 further enhanced the position of commercial real estate investment with the associated good rental growth prospects.

The growth of inflation from the 1960s wrought a reappraisal of financial investment models. Inflation was rising to such an extent that no-one could ignore its consequences in portfolio construction. Up until this point institutional fund managers had predominantly invested in fixed interest securities. But as inflation increased, so did interest rates, and with increasing interest rates came falling bond prices. There was a general move into equities that encompassed not just company shares but also commercial real estate. It was encouraged by the shortening of lease lengths on shops and offices in the UK that saw the introduction of rent review periods every five years. These shorter review timescales were also stimulated by inflation. Commercial real estate became more akin to real assets than fixed interest bonds. With these features financial institutions began investing both in direct property and in property companies.

Table 5.1 Structure of UK Real Estate Portfolios (%) of Financial Institutions 1950–2009

	Offices	Retail	Industrial	Residential	Other
1950	36	40	4	13	6
1960	41	47	6	6	-
1970	64	30	6	-	1
1981	54	27	15	-	4
1985	51	34	12	-	3
1990	52	35	12	-	2
1995	39	46	13	1	3
2000	35	47	14	1	3
2005	31	50	15	-	3
2009	31	50	15	1	1

Source Jones (2013)

In the UK, high street shops were initially the most popular type of investment by financial institutions as Table 5.1 indicates. Following successive office development booms of the 1950s through to the 1970s, offices became their most popular type of investment in the 1960s. However, their hegemony in institutional portfolios was dented by the emergence of obsolescence problems in the 1980s with the beginnings of the ICT revolution. Unable to cope with the heavy cabling demands of ICT at that time many offices suffered obsolescence. It led to the depreciation of rental and capital values and provided a major challenge to investing in offices.

From 1994 retailing regained its position as the largest component of institutional portfolios. The attractiveness of the sector at that time focused high street shops as an investment and was based on two key pillars. First, rental income (growth) was supported by the long-term rise in real incomes/consumer expenditure. Second, the supply of high street shops was constrained by the urban fabric limiting development activity to the benefit of existing shops. However, the nature of investment in the retailing sector has changed dramatically, arguably even before the 1990s. The issues raised by the transformation of retailing are set out in Chapter 11.

Types of Financial institutions and Investment Priorities

The main equity investors in the real estate market is financial institutions and property companies. Increasingly in Western economies there are also overseas real estate investors of different forms including sovereign wealth funds as well as different types of investment funds. A sovereign wealth fund is a state-owned investment vehicle. It invests monies derived from a country's resources, such as oil, to provide long-term benefits to its citizens.

Financial institutions are more strictly defined as non-bank financial institutions and encompass general insurance and life assurance companies as well as pension funds. Other financial institutions such as high/main street clearing banks, merchant banks, building societies/mortgage banks, finance houses and foreign banks almost exclusively invest in loans, including construction development loans and mortgages. As a result, these latter institutions are not considered here.

This section now focuses on the economics of each of the non-bank financial institutions in turn with the implications for real estate investment. It distinguishes between general insurance companies, life assurance funds and pension funds.

General Insurance

General insurance companies sometimes referred to as houses charge short term premiums to provide insurance cover against the loss from the occurrence of uncertain events. The premiums are calculated based on the sum insured and the probability of loss. The unpredictability of the amount and timings of claims introduce a significant element of uncertainty to their business.

People pay regular premiums to these companies, often monthly, to insure themselves against potential losses that may occur, albeit very infrequently. Such insurance may cover car accidents, losses from a break in, weather damage to houses, travel problems, health issues, marine difficulties, professional indemnity and so on. Essentially such insurance can cover every aspect of life.

The insurance companies therefore have a regular income but irregular pay outs. To some extent, it can pool the income to cover insurance pay outs. In addition, rather than simply putting this income in the bank and waiting to pay out claims, when necessary, the insurance companies invest the cash in income generating assets. But prudent managers of these general insurance companies need to invest funds in such a way as to ensure that these assets are liquid, or easily liquidated assets, and are greater than expected liabilities.

Nevertheless, liabilities can be unexpected and excessively high, for example, because of extreme weather events including hurricanes, extensive fires and flooding in unlikely places. To some extent, these events may average themselves out over a period of years but to ensure credibility insurance companies need to pay out promptly when they occur.

The implications are that insurers require to pursue a matching principle. This dictates that the nature of expected liabilities should match the nature of the assets. For example, if their liabilities are short term and uncertain in nature, they will purchase short term and liquid assets. Gilts and shares provide a degree of liquidity in this regard, even though they are low yielding investments in the short term.

The lack of liquidity makes direct property an unfavourable short term investment medium. But real estate investment has a role for general insurance companies in terms of helping to grow its capital base. Customers need to be sure that if they make an insurance claim the company can afford to pay out. To ensure credibility, the amount of insurance business a company can deal with is constrained by the size of its capital base, thereby giving reassurance to its customers. The capital base constrains new business, so it is important for a company to expand it via investments.

In addition to safeguarding that insurance companies can meet their obligations to customers they are usually subject to controls by governments. In the European Union, for example, this is known as the 'Minimum Capital Requirement'. Under this Directive an annual capital requirement is set so that an insurance company can pay out any claims over the following 12 months with a 99.5% probability. Overall, the portfolios of assets held by insurance companies are designed to ensure high liquidity but also capital growth, with real estate investment tied to the latter.

Life Assurance

Life assurance provides a fundamentally different function to the public than general insurance businesses. These funds deal with paying out a lump sum/benefits when events that are certain occur, for example, death or when a person reaches a specified age. The only uncertainty may be when these events occur. However, while the life expectancy of individual policy holders may vary averages are very stable.

The essential financial model of life assurance is that the funds are long-term saving schemes very often for income during retirement or a lump sum on death. The funds collect regular and predictable premiums over many years until policies mature and benefits are payable. Typically, these products take the form of endowment policies that promise a capital sum/benefits at a specified date plus life assurance if death occurs prior to this date. In some countries, save for retirement schemes are known as pension insurance contracts, as, for example, in Denmark and France. In the United States, 'individual retirement accounts' are offered by banks and investment companies. The maturation dates of these contracts are given at the start, and the statistical probability of death rates also provide certainty, so funds have reasonable sureness about the amount and timing of liabilities.

As the outgoing and incoming flows to life funds are predictable and relatively stable, liquidity is not a significant issue in investment strategies. The business task is that funds need to be invested in assets that will generate sufficient capital to meet the promised pay outs to policy holders. In practical terms, it means that life funds must ensure returns on their investments that keep pace with inflation while minimising risk. In particular, the investment strategy is to match payment liabilities to asset values and incomes. At its simplest fixed sum liabilities tend to be matched to fixed income investments of a similar duration. In this way gilts, corporate bonds or mortgages should mature in the same year as the fixed sum liabilities. But most policies are aimed at meeting inflation proofed sums, known as 'stated or defined benefits', and require to be matched by equity investments in the long run. The portfolios of life funds are therefore comprised of shares and to some extent real estate to provide long-term growth, with fixed investments added to give stability and security.

In recent decades, newer forms of policies, such as unit linked assurance, unit linked pension funds and unit trusts have emerged as part of the product range. In these products, assurers typically also offer pension provision. In some cases, life assurance companies manage the investments for other institutions such as small pension funds, perhaps of the entire workforce of a company. These managed assets are usually referred to as 'segregated funds' (although the term has different meanings in various parts of the world). Assurance companies also offer policies to individual pensions where (typically) self-employed people can buy into a pension plan. These pensions can be tailored to providing income or capital growth, depending on investors' wishes. The investment implications of these new unit linked 'defined contribution' policies are considered in Chapter 12.

Pension Funds

A further form of institutional investor are private pension funds. These are normally company-based pension funds that began in the nineteenth century in the United States and expanded significantly in the immediate post World War II period across developed economies. The essential objective is for regular payments by both individual employees and the employer to be paid into the company's pension fund to offer pensions on retirement. Historically, these pensions have been linked to an employee's final salary and their years of membership. Normally payments by employers and employees into pension plans get preferential tax treatment.

The pension funds of large companies have sufficiently large assets to independently provide investment services internally without recourse to external fund managers. Smaller pension funds may use external management in the form of life assurance companies (see above).

The liabilities of pension funds are traditionally to pay pensions that are linked to employees' final salaries. Employees pay into the scheme potentially for all their working life (they may transfer to different schemes with change of employment), for the order of forty years. In return, they often receive life cover while working and often a lump sum on retirement followed by a pension. It means that investments by the pension fund need to generate capital growth to keep pace with any inflation and the potential rise in incomes over time.

Pension funds begin what can be called an 'accrual' phase as they gain contributing members while none or few have yet to receive benefits so initially there are inflows and no outflows. Even as the funds mature often inflows meet outflows and outflows are predictable, and so liquidity is not that essential. It enables pension funds to pursue growth and high return investments at the expense of security. A reasonable degree of stability is obtained by holding a good proportion of funds as gilts and other fixed interest investments.

In most countries, the investment returns of pension funds have tax breaks. For example, in the UK pension fund investment is exempt from capital gains and income tax on approved investments. These approved investments include shares quoted on a stock exchange, governments and corporate bonds, cash and real estate. It means that pension funds are more likely to invest directly in real estate rather than buying shares in a property company because in the latter dividends are paid after tax.

Recently private pension schemes have moved towards an alternative approach whereby members receive a pension based on the sums that have been paid in, and how these contributions are invested. These are called 'defined contribution' schemes (see Chapter 12 where these schemes are examined in more depth). The reason is that defined benefit schemes are seen as risky to employers and increasingly expensive to provide. If the investments in the pension fund are not sufficient to pay the promised pension under 'stated or defined benefits' schemes, then the shortfall would have to be made up by the employer. To avoid this risk defined contributions schemes have been introduced that mirror the plans offered by life assurance companies. The implications for real estate investment are considered in Chapter 12.

A Worldwide Perspective on Pension Funding

Given the scale of pension funds and pension plans administered by life assurance companies together they have vast sums available for investment. As a result, they are the largest investors in equities worldwide and hold substantial real estate investments. In fact, OECD estimates that retirement savings plans have assets of more than USD 50 trillion worldwide at the end of 2019. These pension assets were overwhelmingly accumulated in pension funds, gathering accounting for USD 32 trillion of assets.

In absolute terms, the largest pension funds are in in Canada and the United States in North America, the Netherlands, Switzerland and the UK in Europe and in Australia and Japan. In relative terms there are large differences between countries. Comparing the amount of pension assets to the size of the economy, measured by the GDP presents a better picture of the relative importance of retirement savings plans in a country. If the size of the economy is controlled for then the Netherlands tops the ranking in 2019 with pension fund assets worth 191% of GDP (see Fig. 5.1), followed by Iceland (168%) and Switzerland 142%, although if all retirement assets are taken into account Denmark tops the ranking with total assets of 220% of GDP. There are also many countries, both developed and developing, that have minimal retirement savings plans. However, the long-term global trend is for the expansion of these plans.

In some countries, employers may be legally obliged to offer retirement savings plans and to automatically enrol employees. Also, some employees are obliged to join a private pension plan. In addition, some countries apply minimum mandatory contributions from employees and employers.

Investments held by these funds are predominantly shares and fixed interest investments (see below). The proportions vary by country with some countries showing a high proportion of portfolios in bonds because of the lack of other

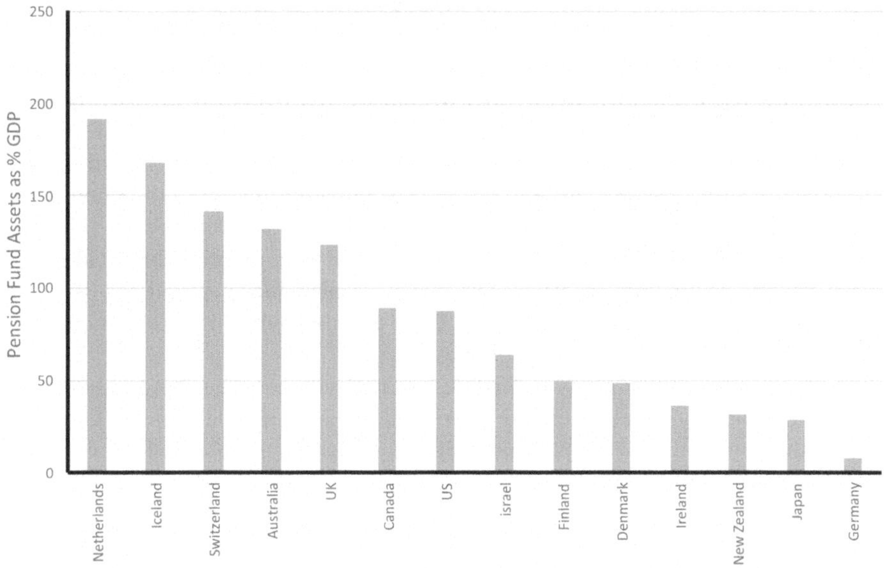

Fig. 5.1 Pension Fund Assets as a Proportion of a Country's GDP (2019)

investments available. In some cases, regulations require a high proportion of assets to be held as bonds, for example, Israel where at least 30% of assets must be in government bonds.

In many countries, the proportion of assets in the form of direct real estate is relatively small, less than 10%. Exact figures are difficult to decipher because of investments in joint or collective funds that may invest in real estate. There are some exceptions to this low percentage, including 35% in Switzerland, 37% in Canada and 41% in Germany. Many governments also limit investment in real estate. It is not permitted, for example, in Hong Kong, Japan (except for the Mutual Aid Associations) and Thailand. On the other hand, indirect investments in real estate in these countries are allowed through bonds and shares of property companies, or real estate investment trusts.

Real Estate Investment Trusts (REITs)

A REIT is a specific form of company that owns real estate, and many started life as a normal property company. The similarity is that investors buy units or shares in the trust to acquire income from or provide financing for all forms of real estate. The key difference compared to a property company is that a REIT is a tax transparent investment vehicle, which means that it does not pay tax. Instead, unit holders pay personal tax on the income distributed from the REIT and the tax applicable is based on their own income and circumstances. This essential feature means that investors do not have to pay double taxation, i.e. they only pay tax once on their individual investment income with the REIT itself exempt from tax on its profits.

They are usually traded on a stock exchange like shares, but there are private REITs and public non-listed ones. REITs are therefore a form of indirect investment in real estate. The attractions of listed REITs are that they are liquid assets with returns that are tax free, as well as enabling investors to benefit from diversification by buying into funds that own a portfolio of properties.

These are equity REITs where it owns or operates income-producing real estate. These are the main type of REIT but there are also mortgage REITs in some countries that provide mortgage finance. There are also hybrid REITs that combine the activities of equity and mortgage ones.

The specific rules that apply to REITs vary between countries but to qualify for the tax transparency benefit there are restrictive rules on their activities. These vary from country to country. In the United States to qualify to be a REIT a company must meet the following criteria:

- Invest at least 75% of its total assets in real estate
- Derive at least 75% of its gross income from rents from real property, interest on mortgages financing real property or from sales of real estate
- Pay at least 90% of its taxable income in the form of shareholder dividends

There are also rules about the nature of the shareholders encompassing the minimum number of and the percentage ownership by individuals. The fundamental regulations controlling UK REITs are the same as the United States. A REIT has to distribute 90% of its rental income in dividends. A REIT must have at least 75% of gross assets used in the rental business and at least 75% of the UK REITs profits must be earned in its qualifying rental business. In addition, it must own at least three properties with no one property accounting for more than 40% of the value of the REIT assets. Property development is permitted subject to constraints including the property is not sold within three years of completion. A REIT must be quoted on a stock exchange.

The concept of REITS began in the United States in the 1960s and there are now more than 200 with more than $3 trillion of assets. The idea was slow to catch on in other countries. Their equivalents in Australia, originally known as Listed Property Trusts (LPTs), have existed since 1970.

In Europe, equivalent tax transparent structures were established in 1969 in the Netherlands (FBIs) but the 2000s saw finally growing interest and enabling national legislation. France and Belgium introduced REITs in 2003, known as SIICs (Société d'Investissement Immobilier Cotée) and SOCAFI, respectively. In January 2007, REITs were introduced in the UK and immediately all of the largest commercial property companies converted. Germany and Italy (SIIQS) similarly introduced REITs in 2007. REITs spread across Asia in the first half of the 2000s from Japan through Singapore, Hong Kong, Malaysia, Taiwan, South Korea and Thailand. The investment rules applicable vary by country.

Originally designed to attract small investors REITs now attract institutional investors. Very often a REIT specialises in a particular segment of the real estate market such as shopping centres or warehouses. Indeed, there is a trend towards specialist REITs. In general, they tend to own prime commercial real estate equivalent to those types of properties bought by institutions, or specialist uses.

Residential REITs are found around the world including Canada, Japan, the United States and Thailand but not all countries have REITs that invest in housing. In Germany, they are specifically excluded by the government regulations. REITS in Australia do not undertake residential investment by choice because it is deemed there is no investment demand.

Property Companies

REITS can be viewed as a specific type of property company that necessarily has a focus on investment given the regulations they have to adhere to. But there are property companies whose activities embrace investment and development or focus on trading. The latter could be companies that buy large real estate portfolios and essentially asset strip, as a means to make a profit. The former encompass regional companies that specialise in development but in some cases retain completed assets within their portfolio. Many property companies have been users of debt from banks and listed companies have the ability to raise further capital through a stock exchange.

In the main REITs concentrate on investing in the highest grade or prime properties, and this makes them attractive to financial institutions to invest in. Unlisted property companies (i.e. not on a stock exchange) include private property companies, family trusts and funds of high net worth individuals. Many of these private investors focus on lower grade, 'secondary' or 'tertiary' properties. These real estate companies range significantly in size although there is also a myriad of small local companies that only own small properties in secondary locations.

Investment and Unit Trusts

Investment and unit trusts are traditional forms of collective investment funds. They can be defined as follows:

- **Investment trusts.** These are limited liability companies set up for the purpose of investing in other companies and whose assets consist almost entirely of shares in other companies. The return to investors is in the form of a dividend and capital gains or losses from the sale of their shares. The size of an investment trust fund is fixed. New money in the investment trust can only come from a rights issue or from borrowing.
- **Unit trusts** are legal trusts in which the money and the investments are held by trustees acting on behalf of the unit holders. If investors wish to invest in the

trust, then the fund manager creates new units to meet demand. This increases the size of the fund which is why unit trusts are also known as 'open ended' funds. The investors buy units at a price determined by the fund managers, which is usually based on the underlying market value of the portfolio at the time of the purchase. If the investor wishes to realise his/her capital then the manager buys back the units, and the trust shrinks in size.

While both have a trust structure, they are very different animals. Investment trusts like REITS are closed funds and so their capital base is fixed. Unit trusts are open ended, so the size of the fund is determined by the scale of investment funds flowing in and out.

Historically unit trusts had been one of the most successful forms of products available to retail or individual investors in equities. These have been a popular means of investment for small investors since their introduction in the 1930s. The property equivalent, however, was not as well received by the market, although existing in some countries for decades. Part of the problem was how such funds, known as APUTS (authorised property unit trusts) in the UK are valued, and how often they are assessed. Whereas the value of unit trusts specialising in shares are valued by market prices instantly property funds' performance is based on valuations that can be infrequent and can be prone to over or under valuation.

These unit trusts became very popular in the UK following the bursting of the dot com bubble at the beginning of the millennium. There was a renewed attractiveness of commercial real estate as an investment asset class as equities lost their lustre. It was also because property investment became more available to small investors as real estate unit trusts became more accessible and attractive. The number of property funds, known as retail funds, offered to small investors increased dramatically, from only 5 in 2003 to 34 by the end of 2007. This trend was supported by the real estate boom over this period. Small investors had indirect access to property investments with some (relatively small) minimum investment requirements. These funds are sold to individual investors through dealers and independent financial advisors.

By 2006 purchases of these investments had reached a record annual figure of £3.6bn or 3% of the total assets of UK investment funds. By the end of 2007, the total funds under management in retail property funds had reached £12.5bn. However, these unit linked funds can also face a weight of requests from investors to withdraw cash when conditions become unfavourable. The real estate bust following the global financial crisis brought just such a huge outflow of funds. The 21-month period from the second quarter of 2007 saw more than £2.8bn flows out of these specialist real estate funds.

As a result, the value of these retail funds fell rapidly so every new deal completed was at a new, lower, valued benchmark. The requirement to generate cash and maintain liquidity levels linked to the overall value of the funds led to the need to sell real estate assets in a falling market. These liquidity problems and forced sales in a downturn are not unique to such funds in the UK, but ubiquitous to open-ended funds. The same issues have occurred in Germany, the Netherlands and Australia, amongst others.

Limited Partnerships (LPs)

As the name implies, a LP is a partnership formed between at least two investors as a means of collective ownership. There must be a general partner with the other partners then defined as limited partners. The general partner is usually the manager of the partnership, namely the one making the investment decisions. The limited partners are therefore passive investors; that do not 'influence' decisions, and so in return, are granted limited liability. This limited liability is equivalent to any losses being capped at the amount they have invested in the partnership. In contrast, the general partner has unlimited liability for the debts and obligations of the partnership if things go wrong. However, the general partner is usually a special purpose vehicle with negligible assets to protect against any adversities.

LPs had been around for more than a century before they began to be applied to real estate investment in the 1990s. The real estate assets of an LP are acquired and held by the general partner acting on behalf of the partnership. Each LP is funded by capital from its partners together with any borrowings from third parties. Any loans can be secured against the partnership's assets.

A crucial attraction of LPs is the payment of tax by partners. In the UK, the taxes paid on income profits and capital gains by a partner are the same as if the investor had invested directly in the assets. Institutions are the most dominant group of investors in these LPs, so few risks are taken with the portfolio. Gearing ratios also tend to be conservative in terms of the loan-to-value (LTV) borrowing ratio, the total loan divided by the total value of the assets. The level of gearing can also influence the level of transaction taxes if an investor chooses to sell its share. In addition, an investor who wishes to sell needs to find a purchaser, and this may include negotiation of the price.

LPs with large memberships face potential conflicts about how the funds should be run; some looking to the longer term, some with shorter term horizons; some wishing higher levels of gearing, some wishing lower and so on. An alternative is to invest jointly with a small number of partners that know, trust and understand each other. It could be a life fund partnering another life fund, or a pension fund that may have worked together before or at least understand their modus operandi. These can be called investment 'clubs' and often, but not exclusively, are conducted between two partners. A formal entity may be established (such as a limited partnership) but mostly these deals are merely conducted informally between the two parties. The formal arrangements encompass legal documentation that sets the details on how the venture is to be run, which party is to manage the asset and so on.

Private Equity and Hedge Funds

An equity or hedge fund is a fluid term in the sense it includes a heterogeneous range of investment strategies. It is fundamentally a pooled investment fund that aggregates capital from multiple investors like a limited partnership but one that is open ended. A hedge fund issues a prospectus, sometimes called an offering memorandum, that provides potential investors with information about it, including the investment and diversification strategy, invested asset types and gearing/debt limits.

Investors can invest and withdraw capital periodically based on the fund's net asset value, although restrictions on withdrawals were imposed in the aftermath of the global financial crisis. While hedge funds are subject to less regulations than financial institutions, they are subject to restrictions on their investors. Usually investors are financial institutions, sovereign wealth funds or individuals of high net worth. Hedge funds are also required to provide accurate information to potential investors and have strategies in place to manage risk. They are arguably less risky than some investment vehicles because of the use of hedging techniques, but they are willing to take on more risk and their gearing is not generally capped by regulators.

The phrase 'to hedge a bet' first appeared in 1672 in the coffee houses of London, where brokers bet on the movement of equity stakes in the Bank of England and other companies. Investors who owned shares could offset the possibility of future losses by hedging, for example, by betting in advance on the stock's downward movement. However, hedge funds in the modern sense can trace their history back to the 1920s, although the term only came into use after World War II.

They often start originally as a group of people coming together to invest in a market (and raise funds to do so). Ultimately, the fund is opened up to others. Since the early 1990s the number of hedge funds has increased significantly, attracting greater funds from institutional investors, who now account for more than half of their invested capital. Hedge funds invest in the whole range of potential assets including real estate.

Hedge funds have variable strategies to investing in real estate. Some invest heavily in publicly traded stock of existing real estate companies, principally REITs. Investment in these types of hedge fund permits risk diversification. However, many hedge funds invest in broad terms in discounted/under-priced or underperforming properties or distressed debt. Their business model is short term with a view to selling during an upswing in a market, as the case studies at the end of the chapter illustrate.

Exchange Traded Funds (ETF)

An ETF is an open-ended pooled investment fund. It normally provides an opportunity for investors to track an index. They can track the performance of a specific stock market index, industry sector or asset. Shares in a fund can be bought and sold on a stock exchange. ETFs hold a portfolio of stocks and bonds that match the index the fund is tracking. There are specialist funds that track the price of a commodity, say gold or oil. Real estate ETFs track a specific investment index.

Most ETFs are located in the United States but they are growing fast around the world. They are a passive way of investing and investors do not need large amounts of capital. Particular attractions of ETFs are that they are transparent and can easily be liquidated at low cost. However, while shares in these funds can readily sold, it can mean that in a period of outflow of funds the share price is below the notional (net) value of the assets.

The Size and Structure of UK Investment Markets

The intricacies of the types of investors revealed in the chapter show that financial institutions invest in REITs, ETFs and hedge funds as well as limited partnerships. At the same time, life assurance companies can manage segregated funds for pension funds and other private investors. There is an interwoven web of direct and indirect investment that means that it is difficult to assess the relative significance of different types of investors, with the potential for double counting. In addition, there are identification issues regarding international investment: large institutions in say the UK or the United States can manage funds derived from another country based on their expertise.

Perspective on this last issue is given by the following statistics for 2019. The asset management industry in the United States is the largest in the world with the equivalent of £31.9 trillion worth of assets. However, it's services are primarily for a domestic market. The European asset management industry encompasses £27.3 trillion of assets servicing a more worldwide clientele. The largest centre outside these localities is Japan with control of £4.4 trillion of assets. The UK dominates European asset management with a 37% share, more than the combined total of France (18%), Germany (10%) and Switzerland (8%).

According to the Investment Association investment funds in the UK managed some £8.5 trillion worth of assets in 2019. The assets of UK private equity and hedge funds managed in that year totalled £650 billion, while the figure for ETFs was £33 billion. The figure for commercial real estate assets (investable stock) at the end of 2018 was £525 billion.

Focusing only on UK institutional investment it amounted to almost £4 trillion of investment funds. Some 65% of these funds are accounted for by pension funds and 35% managed on a pooled basis. Institutional investment in 2019 was split 35/65 per cent between pooled and segregated funds. The investment split by asset type is given in Table 5.2. Equities and fixed income investments account for more than three quarters of the total with real estate comprising just over 6%.

These figures vary by type of institution as suggested above. The aggregate portfolio of UK corporate pension funds had 46% in fixed income assets compared with 33% in equities. This is consistent with the worldwide pattern noted earlier. The figures are similar to the average in Table 5.2 reflecting the dominance of

Table 5.2 The breakdown of UK institutional investment by asset class in 2019

Asset Class	Percentage of Total Funds
Equities	35
Fixed Income	42.4
Cash/Money Market	9.5
Real Estate	6.1
Other	6.9

Source Derived data from Investment Association (2020)

pension fund investment. Insurance companies in contrast had a higher proportion of fixed income assets, with a percentage around 55%.

The proportion of fixed income assets held by financial institutions has grown since the 1980s with the decline in inflation reducing the imperative for capital growth. The proportion of direct real estate investment is consistently low across all investor types and has fallen over recent decades. In contrast 'other' alternative investments have seen long-term growth.

The aggregate picture of the ownership of commercial real estate in the UK in 2018, as estimated by the Investment Property Forum, is given in Table 5.3. The combination of pension funds and insurance funds with collective schemes (including limited partnerships) means that a third of all commercial real estate is held directly by UK financial institutions. Overseas equivalents account for a further 13% of the commercial stock, bringing the total of institutional investment to 46%. Listed property companies and REITS, most of whose shares are owned by financial institutions represent 14% of the stock. With the 4% of the stock owned by foreign REITs, it can be argued that institutional investment owns almost two thirds of the commercial real estate stock.

Table 5.3 also demonstrates the significance of overseas investment, amounting to 31% of the whole of the UK commercial real estate stock. In fact, 6% is owned by sovereign wealth funds and foreign governments (see Chapter 9).

Table 5.3 The Ownership of the UK Commercial Property Stock by Investor Type in 2018

Investor Type	Percentage
Insurance Direct & Funds	9
Pension Funds	8
Unlisted & Collective Schemes	16
Listed Companies & REITs	14
Private Companies	11
Estates & Charities	4
Private Investors	3
Other Owners	4
Overseas Investors	31

Source Derived data from Investment Property Forum (2020)

Much of this investment by sovereign wealth funds is held in central London offices and retail units. Indeed, most of central London real estate is now owned by foreign investors. These figures illustrate that distinct sectors of the real estate market are attractive to different types of investors as noted earlier. It also explains why Fig. 1.1 based on all investment and Table 5.1, focusing on UK financial institutions, present different perspectives on real estate investment in the UK.

Summary

Investment in real estate by financial institutions was mainly in the form of mortgages until after World War II and even the 1950s.

A post-war real estate boom together with the emergence of inflation in the 1960s stimulated interest in commercial real estate investment as a hedge against inflation. This interest was consolidated with the unbridled inflation of the 1970s. The rise in real estate investment was paralleled by an equivalent shift into equities from a previous focus on fixed interest investments.

The focus of real estate investment by financial institutions in the UK has ebbed and flowed over the decades. Initially, high street shops were the most popular asset class, but they were replaced by offices in the 1960s. However, as problems of obsolescence emerged in the 1980s shops and retail centres recovered their hegemony in institutional portfolios.

General insurance companies provide insurance cover against the loss of events that might occur from the occurrence of uncertain events linked to, for example, accidents or damages to property. The income of these companies is in the form of regular premiums but their potential claims and pay outs are irregular.

To maximise profits insurance, companies invest their income from premiums while ensuring it is possible to liquidate assets quickly to pay claims as they occur. Gilts and shares offer suitable liquidity but direct ownership of property is unattractive because of the time necessary to sell. However, real estate investment can support general insurance companies to enable them to expand their capital base. The capital resources of a company are of twofold importance. First, it offers reassurance to customers in convincing them that claims will be met. Second, government regulations normally require a minimum capital requirement to safeguard customers.

The financial basis of life assurance is that people contribute into long-term saving schemes to derive an income during retirement or a lump sum on death. Regular contributions provide a steady income stream to a life assurance company and pay outs or liabilities can be predicted.

While liquidity is not such an issue, the fund has to ensure that the returns from the assets invested are sufficient to meet the promised pay outs to policy holders. Investments must match payment liabilities, and comprise a combination of fixed income assets, equities, and to a lesser extent real estate. In some cases, life assurance companies manage 'segregated funds' for other institutions such as small pension funds.

Traditionally pay outs have been in the form of 'defined benefits' whereby the broad principles of the sums are known from the outset. Today pension plans offered by life assurance companies are unit linked with pay outs coupled to the performance of the investments placed by the fund not to initial promises.

Company based pension funds normally encompass payments by employers and employees into pension plans. Employees pay into the scheme(s) for the order of forty years, and in return receive, life cover, a lump sum on retirement followed by a pension based on final salary. These schemes are described as 'defined benefits'.

Since the millennium there has been a shift in the approach to providing pensions. Increasingly, members of schemes receive a pension based on the sums that have been paid in, and how effective these contributions are invested. These are called 'defined contribution schemes'.

Pension funds worldwide are the largest investors in equities and hold substantial real estate investments.

The investment strategies of pension schemes are often regulated by governments. The proportion of assets held in real estate directly in different countries is generally quite low with some governments limiting investment in this asset class. However, such restrictions do not bar investment in shares of property companies, or real estate investment trusts.

A REIT is a tax transparent investment vehicle that does not pay tax. Unit holders still have to pay personal tax on the income received from an investment in a REIT. They are normally traded on a stock exchange like shares, but there are private REITs and public non-listed ones. REITs provide a form of indirect investment in real estate.

Equity REITs that own or operate income-producing real estate are the main type of REIT but there are also mortgage REITs in some countries that provide mortgage finance. To qualify for the benefits of tax transparency there are restrictive rules on their activities that differ from country to country. In the main, the regulations cover a minimum proportion of assets and income from real estate and that virtually all taxable income should be paid as dividends. There are also rules covering the breakdown of their asset portfolio and the nature of activities undertaken.

In January 2007, REITs were introduced in the UK and immediately all the largest commercial property companies converted. They often specialise in a particular segment of the real estate. In general, they tend to own prime commercial real estate equivalent to those types of properties bought by institutions, or specialist uses. Residential REITs exist in some parts of the world but not everywhere.

The activities of other types of property companies can also involve development and trading. In some cases, companies buy large real estate portfolios and essentially asset strip, as a way of making a profit. Some are developers and traders of the completed buildings. Many property companies seek to fund their activities through borrowing from banks. Private companies tend to focus on the ownership and management of lower grade properties than REITs.

Other ways of investing collectively and indirectly in real estate are through investment and unit trusts. Investment trusts are limited liability companies whose total assets are fixed like REITs, but comprise almost entirely of shares in other companies. As such returns take the form of any dividend and capital gains or losses from the sale of their shares. Unit trusts are very different creatures, set up as legal trusts the fund managers establish new units to meet demand. They are therefore 'open ended' funds and investors buy or sell units at a price determined by the fund managers.

Unit trusts had been very successful way of small investors have access to equities. The real estate equivalent has been less successful partly because the performance of their assets is based on valuations that can be infrequent and can be prone to over or under valuation. The number of these 'retail' property funds expanded substantially post the dot com bubble supported by the real estate boom of the 2000s. When the real estate bust came after the global financial crisis, it saw a dramatic reverse and a huge outflow of funds, and a fire sale of the assets held by these funds.

LPs are a further form of collective ownership involving a general partner/manager with other passive partners having limited liability. They began to be applied to real estate investment in the 1990s with financial institutions as the mainstay investors. Each LP is funded by capital from its partners together with any borrowings from third parties. An alternative to forming a LP are investment clubs with as low as two partners.

An equity or hedge fund is an open-ended investment vehicle with many investors. Investors choose to buy into a hedge fund based on its published strategy, including its policy on diversification, asset classes and gearing/debt limits. Investors endow and withdraw capital periodically based on the fund's net asset value. Hedge funds invest in the whole range of potential assets including real estate.

Some hedge funds invest heavily in publicly traded stock while others focus on distressed or under-priced assets. Examples of the latter regarding real state include the purchase of newly privatised housing portfolios in Germany and collections of bad debts held by European banks following the global financial crisis.

Exchange traded funds (ETFs) are open-ended pooled investment funds with shares exchanged on a stock exchange. They normally track an index. There are specialist funds that can track a real estate investment index. They offer a passive form of investing that are transparent, and shares can be bought and sold at low cost, albeit the share price may be deflated below the notional (net) value of the assets.

Overall, there are a range of investors with different priorities and motivations for holding real estate. In addition, there is an inter-related and tangled network of investors, that encompasses indirect and direct investment in real estate. Furthermore, life assurance companies can manage segregated funds for pension funds and other private investors. Some 65% of UK institutional investment in 2019 was in segregated funds. Fund managers can apply their expertise to manage funds that emanate from elsewhere in the world. The European asset management industry, especially that in the UK, has a global customer base.

In 2019, the aggregate portfolio of UK pension funds comprised 46% in fixed income assets together with 33% in equities, and real estate was just over 6%. In comparison, insurance companies had 55% of fixed income assets reflecting their different business model. Over recent decades the proportion of direct real estate investment by pension funds has fallen and other types of assets become more popular.

Nevertheless, a third of all British commercial real estate in 2018 was held directly by UK financial institutions. If overseas investors and REITs are included as institutional investors, then the total rises to two thirds of the commercial real estate stock. Foreign investors have become a major force with much of central London real estate now owned by foreign investors. More generally, ownership patterns, in terms of the characteristics of investors, are segmented by the type and location of real estate.

Learning Outcomes

Having completed this chapter, the reader should be able to:

- Appreciate the history of the ownership of real estate as an investment class.
- Know that there is a spectrum of investors with various reasons for holding real estate.
- Understand that real estate can be held directly or indirectly through pooled investment vehicles.
- Understand the business model of general insurance companies and why they invest primarily in liquid assets to quickly pay claims as they occur
- Comprehend the financial basis of life assurance whereby people contribute into long-term saving schemes to derive an income during retirement or a lump sum on death.
- Recognise that the investments of pension funds have to match payment liabilities
- Recognise the difference between defined benefit and defined contribution and that defined benefit pension plans have increasingly been replaced by unit linked or defined contributions schemes.
- Appreciate that a REIT is a tax transparent real estate investment vehicle, that means that it does not pay tax and that there are restrictive rules on their activities that differ from country to country.

- Know that other types of property companies can be involved in development and trading as well as investment, and usually focus on lower grade properties than REITs.
- Apprehend that investment trusts are limited liability companies whose total assets are fixed like REITs and comprise almost entirely of shares in other companies.
- Note that unit trusts are open-ended funds that enable investors to buy or sell units at a price determined by the fund managers and the impact this had during the GFC.
- Understand that LPs are a type of collective ownership involving a general partner/manager with other passive partners having limited liability.
- Recognise that an equity or hedge fund is an open-ended investment vehicle with many investors. Hedge fund investors do so based on a published strategy and endow or withdraw capital periodically based on the fund's net asset value.
- Be aware that ETFs are open-ended pooled investment funds that track specific indexes with their shares exchanged on a stock exchange.
- Understand that general insurance companies hold a higher percentage of gilts than pension funds.
- Apprehend that UK pension funds hold about 6% of their assets in real estate.
- Recognise that some two thirds of real estate assets in the UK are held by institutional owners.
- Appreciate that foreign investors have become a major force with much of central London real estate now owned by foreign investors.

CASE STUDY Examples of Hedge Fund Activities

Privatisation of German Social Housing

In Germany, more than 500,000 social housing unit in the portfolios of housing associations were privatised between 1999 and 2006. Much of this housing was bought in many cases by United States based private equity/hedge firms that stepped in to exploit the low prices available from an asset new to the market. Hedge funds invested short term, often three to five years and with high gearing ratios that meant the funds only needed to find 10 per cent of the equity.

Entire housing associations were sold off to hedge funds. As the housing market recovered from the global financial crisis, the funds sold their real estate portfolios at higher prices or converted their German real estate subsidiaries into real estate companies that are listed on the stock exchange. Such a listing or sale enabled the funds to liquidate their capital tied up in the housing stock at a point in time when prices had risen from economic recovery. Returns were also enhanced by the acceptance of private investment in the social housing sector increasing the value of the assets. There was therefore a rise in company share prices with the establishment of a privatised market. Most private equity and hedge funds therefore withdrew from the social housing sector to be replaced by listed real estate companies with a longer-term investment perspective.

Purchase of European Real Estate Debt After the Global Financial Crisis

In the aftermath of the global financial crisis, many banks found themselves with many 'bad' real estate loans that arose from property company bankruptcies. They needed to find a way of disposing of these paper assets but were hampered by a lack of expertise and a depressed real estate market. One answer came in the form of hedge funds buying this distressed debt associated with portfolios of properties off the banks. These portfolios were sold at a discount reflecting the state of the market and banks desire to offload these unwanted assets. In some case, the banks even provided the finance to a hedge fund to purchase the debt and kept a share of the total debt as part of a partnership to resolve the distressed assets.

The control of distressed debt by the hedge funds enabled them to disentangle perhaps complex legal interests in individual properties that may have for example be subject to more than one debt. The aim would be to resolve these issues and ultimately sell these assets to realise cash as the market recovered from the crisis. These sales would ideally be at a much higher value than the book value of the assets in the bank's accounts. In some cases, there was a complex arrangement with the bank so that the hedge fund received a management fee for this asset stripping exercise and an agreed share of the uplift in value before residual profits were distributed.

The sales of these non-performing loans occurred across Western Europe at the beginning of the 2010s as part of medium term to long-term deleveraging plans by banks. The scale of the discounts to the value of the loans varied by the state of the national market. One major German loan portfolio had a discount of over 50%, while in the UK discounts were of the order 40–50% and in Ireland discounts were over 60%.

Reading

Investment Association (2020) *Investment Management in the UK 2019–2020*, Investment Association, London

Investment Property Forum (2020) *The Size and Structure of the UK Commercial Property Market*. Investment Property Forum, London

Investment Property Forum (2017). *Understanding UK Commercial Property Investments: A Guide for Financial Advisers*, Investment Property Forum, London

Jones, C. (2013) *Office Markets and Public Policy*, Wiley-Blackwell, Chichester

Jones, C., Cowe, S. and Trevillion, E. (2018) *Property Boom and Banking Bust: The Role of Commercial Lending in the Bankruptcy of Banks*. Wiley-Blackwell, Chichester. ISBN-13 978-1119219255

Powell, C. (1996) *The British Building Industry since 1800: An Economic History*. 2nd Edition, London

Scott, P. (1996) *The Property Masters*, Spon, London

Wijburg, G. and Aalbers, M. B. (2017) The alternative financialization of the German housing market, *Housing Studies*, 32, 7, 968–989

Market Efficiency and Asset Pricing

6

Introduction

The theory of pricing in property markets has been examined in detail in Chapter 2. This examined the concept of value and the use of discounted cash flow (DCF) models to distinguish between price, value and worth. The approach enables an investor to price an investment by examining its expected future stream of returns. However, the process of determining market prices cannot be analysed without investigating how efficient the market is at reflecting price and price movements.

Market efficiency is defined as the degree to which market prices reflect all available, relevant, information. It can have a significant bearing on how the prices of assets are established. In this context, we now examine market efficiency (perhaps more importantly market inefficiency!) and the implications that information inefficiency will have on the investment decision-making process.

If markets are efficient, then all information is already incorporated into prices, and there are no undervalued or overvalued securities available. The premise that asset prices are efficient is important and the assumption would certainly reduce the distinction between price, value and worth or at least make it easier to define. But are property markets efficient?

This chapter now explores these issues and starts by examining the efficient market hypothesis. In addition, this chapter describes ways to test the information efficiency of the property market and looks at irrational behaviour in the marketplace, an important marker of how well it is at handling information. In this context, this chapter undertakes a case study which analyses the UK property market during and after the global financial crisis (GFC) of 2007–2008 as an example of irrational behaviour in commercial property markets. It revisits the issue of mispricing of property assets and the part that valuations and their accuracy play in the mispricing of property assets. It is structured to cover the following main topic areas:

C. A. Jones and E. Trevillion, *Real Estate Investment*,
https://doi.org/10.1007/978-3-031-00968-6_6

- Efficient markets and their significance
- Tests for market efficiency
- Property market efficiency
- Pricing and mispricing in the market
- Valuation accuracy
- Market transparency
- Rational and irrational markets

This chapter finishes with a case study of the property boom in the UK market in the first decade of twenty-first century, an example of a boom in what was an irrational market. The case study not only complements material in this chapter on market efficiency but can be read in conjunction with the material in Chapters 3 and 4 on property cycles and real estate investment.

Efficient Markets and their Significance

The logical aim of any investor is to maximise return with a minimum of risk. An efficient market, where prices incorporate and reflect all relevant information, would minimise the risk to an investor allowing them to make rational decisions on up-to-date information and make accurate assumptions not only on value but also on investment returns. An efficient market ought also to bring some convergence to the distinction outlined in Chapter 2 of the value in use (worth), the value in exchange (open market value) and the outcomes of the interplay of the respective values in use of market makers (price). The ability to make rational decisions based on up-to-date information also reduces the possibility of irrational market bubbles.

The concept of efficient markets dates back many years and was first developed in the context of financial markets. Random-walk theory was used to define market efficiency in terms of the lack of dependence between successive price movements in a market (try reading *A Random Walk Down Wall Street* by Malkiel which popularised the random walk hypothesis in 1973). The basic idea is that a price series that demonstrates independence between current and previous price movements is said to follow a random walk. This occurs as a result of a market being efficient in informational terms. Stock price changes are considered to be independent of each other and so past trends or movements cannot be used to predict future movement. Accordingly, in the theory, it is not possible to outperform the market without assuming risk. These ideas and their subsequent development are now considered in detail.

Efficient Market Hypothesis

The Efficient Markets Hypothesis (EMH) refers to the information efficiency of the market. It requires that prices fully reflect all available information and that future price changes are unpredictable. The efficiency of price adjustments to new information refers to the speed and quality of the adjustment. Its importance is in its suggestion that it is impossible to 'beat the market' because stock market efficiency causes existing share prices to always incorporate and reflect all relevant information.

According to the EMH, stocks always trade at their fair value on stock exchanges, making it impossible for investors to either purchase undervalued stocks or sell stocks for inflated prices. As such, it should be impossible to outperform the overall market through expert stock selection or market timing, and that the only way an investor can possibly obtain higher returns is by purchasing riskier investments.

The theory that stock prices move randomly was suggested in the early 1950s and the random walk idea of market efficiency was supported in several studies throughout the 1950s and early 1960s. However, by the early 1960s this view of market efficiency was beginning to change when some studies concluded that stock prices do not follow a random walk.

Eugene Fama in 1965 proposed that in the real world there is no perfect or efficient market, but an efficient market is a benchmark, and ultimately recognised different degrees of efficiency. He divided market efficiency into three categories: *weak form* or how well do past returns predict future returns, *semi-strong form* or how quickly do security prices reflect public information announcements and *strong form* or how private information that is fully reflected in market prices. These degrees of efficiency are now considered in more detail.

Fama's Degrees of Efficiency

Weak Form Efficiency

This exists where:

- Past price information is available and current prices reflect this historical information. Current prices fully reflect the information implied by all prior price movements BUT movements in price are NOT dependent on past performance.
- New information behaves independently of history. Price movements are totally independent of previous movements. News inherent in any new piece of information concerning an asset, whether good or bad news, will be independent of the last piece of information. In addition, information will be absorbed quickly into the new equilibrium value in markets because there are many traders and lack of barriers to trading.
- Asset pricing reliant on past information is speculative and leads to mispricing and misinformation. It should not be possible to predict future movements from past price patterns.

Semi-Strong Efficiency
This exists when:

- All publicly available past information (company accounts, economic forecasts etc.) is compounded into prices. If new information is made available, then prices will respond instantaneously.
- Price responses are not biased towards new information.

Mispricing remains a possibility. Most markets are considered to be semi-strong, and forecasting improves with the increases in publicly available information.

Strong Form Efficiency
Strong form efficiency exists when all information (publicly available and information not available to the public) is reflected in prices. If the market were strongly efficient, then no one would be able to profit from privileged information as prices will reflect their intrinsic worth.

These three levels of efficiency are not independent of one another. For the market to have semi-strong efficiency then it must also be weakly efficient. This is because the tracking of price movements in a predictable path would imply that prices have reacted slowly or inaccurately to published information. For the market to be strongly efficient, then it must also be efficient in the weak and semi-strong forms for prices to capture all relevant information. The successful activities of analysts who assess market fundamentals and inside dealers imply that the market is inefficient. If the market was efficient, in the strong sense, then mispricing should not occur.

An efficient market does NOT imply that stock prices cannot deviate from true value. Deviation and mispricing can still occur, but in a random way. Under weak form efficiency no investor can earn excess returns from trading rules based on a past series of prices. Investors cannot 'beat' the market in any given time period. Investors will not beat the market in the long term as expected returns are consistent with the investment risk.

There is a market contradiction. While there is no possibility of beating the market in an efficient market there is a BUT, namely the market requires profit-maximising investors to consistently try to beat the market to make it efficient!

Tests for Market Efficiency

Various statistical tests have been used to empirically test markets for the existence of a random walk, and hence for efficiency. These tests on the stock market suggest that shares do follow a random walk and are weakly efficient. However, in a market where transaction costs are high enough to deter trading or where the dissemination of information to traders is slow (e.g. the property market) then the adjustment process is slow. There would be a trend in the asset price as it moved towards its new equilibrium. *This would give rise to price changes that are serially dependent rather than random, and excess return could be made by spotting the trends from charts or by trading on new information before prices fully adjust.*

Tests for semi-strong and strong form efficiency are a lot more difficult and technical. The most general of these models is the fair game model, which expresses efficiency in terms of the opportunities for speculators to earn excess returns. Empirical tests of stock returns suggest that equities may be semi-strong efficient.

Property Market Efficiency

Evidence

In the case of property markets, there is some limited evidence for weak form efficiency in the US residential sector and for hotels. However, evidence to the contrary appears to be stronger with other tests in US residential markets suggesting that real estate may be semi-strong.

Findings that 'price discovery' exists in the property investment market by Barkham and Geltner, in 1995 invalidate the assumption that the market is weak form efficient. Price discovery refers to the process by which asset prices are formed. It is a process of information aggregation through which market participant opinions about the value of an asset are combined into a single statistic, the market price of the asset. Barkham and Geltner found evidence that price discovery occurs by reference to the securitised or stock market and looking at price movements of REITs and property companies in both the United States and the UK. However, this price information was found to not fully transmit to the un-securitised or private markets for a year or more. The results suggest that the public securitised markets are more informationally efficient than the private un-securitised markets. Not only do the results raise questions about the application of weak form efficiency to these markets given that the private markets are not reacting instantaneously to new information, but they also suggest a potentially serious violation of semi-strong informational efficiency in the un-securitised markets.

There is very little evidence to support the hypothesis that the property market is semi-strong efficient. In fact, casual observation suggests that systematic mispricing is common in the property market. Notwithstanding that, it can be argued that real estate markets may be semi-strong based on the argument that if they were not, then investors would be encouraged by the consistent abnormal profits to switch their capital from other types of investments. Yet, it is acknowledged that market agents can earn abnormal profits from private information. For example, an individual may legitimately profit from buying land in the UK knowing that planning permission may be granted without that information being in the public arena. These occurrences dispel any suggestions that the property market exhibits strong form efficiency.

So, for the property market, the evidence one way or another is to some extent confused with the probable only conclusion being that the market does not exhibit weak form efficiency. There is mispricing in the market (see below) and in recent years, the notion of market efficiency has been refined. A market is considered to be efficient if investors are unable to consistently outperform the market once information, search and transaction costs are considered. No empirical study has been undertaken to consider this refined definition.

Price and Mispricing

In the property market, there can be problems with the determination of prices. Case studies of short leases and over-rented offices suggest that systematic mispricing over periods of time long enough for investors to react does occur. An over-rented property occurs when the passing rent is more than the market rent.

We have already noted in Chapter 2 and above that confusion exists in the property market between price, worth and values and have dealt with the distinction in some detail. But to reiterate, in an efficient market with homogenous goods, and perfect knowledge market price would equal market worth. Under such conditions, a valuation would be a good estimate of both. Worth to an individual investor may differ from market worth, but equilibrium would still prevail. In the property market with heterogeneous goods, and imperfect information, market price and market worth may diverge. In this situation, valuations might influence individual worth and subsequently market price.

Individual worth should vary from individual to individual according to the information and views they have, and their space requirements. These different views of worth among potential buyers will set the price of an individual property, which will influence the general price of properties in a market. The buyer's estimated worth of an individual property will at least be equal to the purchase price and may even be higher than the market worth. Systematic mispricing in a market will occur if the price does not equal market worth, the divergence driven by the systematic differences between individual and market worth.

Valuation Accuracy

If price equals market worth, then the valuation or appraisal of market price should equal market worth. If the market is mispriced, then valuations will reflect the mispricing rather than the true market worth. It can be argued that valuations may cause mispricing. The valuation may bias the market price because it may be used by a potential buyer or seller to establish a likely market price, although it could be argued that the bias may be deliberate reflecting that valuations can be influenced by customers. The heterogeneity of property, lack of a central market and information constraints make valuations difficult. However, traditional valuation methods may also contribute to the difficulty and imprecise nature of the valuation procedure. None of these techniques involve an assessment of worth so they fail to inform the investor on the individual or market worth of a property, and how that compares with the market price.

We have already outlined why the use of DCF is better at calculating worth compared with traditional approaches to valuation (Chapter 2). This requires an explicit cash flow analysis that includes forecasts of all expected incomes and expenditures, the exit value of the asset upon resale and the use of an appropriate discount rate. The discount rate needs to reflect the risk to the income flow and is discussed in detail in Chapter 2.

Traditional valuation methods rely on historical market transactions for comparable sales. They are backward looking and do not explicitly link values to the capital markets (e.g. investors' target return linked to gilt yields) or the wider economy (e.g. rental income forecasts). The use of traditional techniques, the limited range of comparable transactions used and the subjective adjustment of yields mean that a wide range of estimates of most likely selling price can be produced by valuers in the same sub-market. Two key valuation issues can be identified:

- *Bias*. This occurs when there exists any systematic difference between the true selling price and the average valuation. Also referred to as valuation inaccuracy.
- *Efficiency*. Inefficiency occurs when there is a spread of possible answers. Valuation inefficiency is also referred to as valuation variation.

Market Transparency

Market transparency is also covered in the international context in Chapter 9. Transparent real estate markets are considered as markets that are:

> *Open and clearly organised.... operating in a legal and regulatory framework that is characterised by the enforcement of rules and regulations ... and that respects private property rights'* (JLL, 2020)

These attributes are critical to the operation of efficient markets and are significant factors in helping to create healthy real estate markets. As the definition implies, it is not just about the provision of data. How the market is structured to allow transparent risk assessment and efficient and openly available flows of information is just as important.

Transparency is a major consideration for investors when investing at home and abroad (see Chapter 9) and Jones Lang LaSalle produces biennial transparency rankings on selected countries based on several attributes which are helpful in defining transparency (see JLL, 2020). They are closely associated with the operation of efficient markets and are as much about the barriers which affect information flows as the information itself.

The index of transparency that they produce includes the following attributes:

- ***Performance measurement*** Does the market have data that allows investors to make judgements on how well markets are performing? A transparent market would be expected to have access to direct property indices. In addition there would be indices that reflect the listed real estate securities market and private real estate fund indices such as those produced by real estate service providers or other organisations such as the Association of Real Estate Funds (see also below). Clearly valuation data either through such indices or publicly available is an important factor in informational efficiency.

The indices take information from banks and institutions and construct data sets that show trends in capital values, rental growth, yields and a range of other metrics on a monthly, quarterly and annual basis. In the UK, the main provider of performance data and data on market fundamentals is MSCI, formerly the Investment Property Databank (IPD). IPD began to generate a reliable UK specific commercial property index in 1985 but incorporated data back to 1981. The data sets, originally confined to the UK, now cover markets globally and have added enormously to market information, although the data is not publicly available and comes at a cost. This particular data set is considered in much more detail in Chapter 8 in the context of portfolio management.

In the United States, the NCRIEF property index has been the main standard for evaluating unlisted commercial property performance. It was launched in 1982 with data going back to 1977 and was the first attempt to build a comprehensive index that represented the performance of the commercial real estate.

In addition to these indices, there are AREF (Association of Real Estate Funds), Lipper and Morningstar indices. The AREF index covers the UK retail pooled property fund market. Lipper indices track the financial performance of different types of managed funds while the Morningstar indices track a range of asset performance on a global basis.

- ***Market fundamentals*** While performance measurement data is important in understanding the dynamics of market behaviour and directly impacts on market efficiency, a basic understanding of market fundamentals is also important. In this context, JLL has developed a transparency index of data to compare the market fundamentals in different countries. It recognises that, while performance data is important, investors and occupiers need to have access to data on metrics such as the size of markets both nationally and locally, the best locations, current rents, yields, typical lease lengths and conditions and so on—the bread and butter of transactions in the marketplace. The most transparent markets will have easy access to this kind of data though public and private sources, not only through the indices themselves but through real estate service providers and government and non-government information sources.
- **Regulatory**, **Governance** and **Professional Standards.** For this kind of information flow to happen transparent markets would also be expected to be open and well-regulated with regards to, governance and professional standards. These will include, for example, real estate tax and land use planning, building control, property registration and an openness with the transaction process. These issues are discussed in more detail in Chapter 9, and the reader is referred to the JLL Transparency Index (JLL, 2020) for a more detailed description of the index and its construction.

While all these transparency issues are important for informationally efficient markets, and there is a significant amount of information out there, it is questionable how accessible or publicly available it is. The index data especially comes at a cost and this is often supplemented by institutional data from their own transactions. In this regard, the data often represents the 'information not available to the public' element of the strong form efficiency reflected in prices.

Rational and Irrational Markets

A major factor affecting whether the EMH is sufficient to describe markets is the extent to which investor behaviour impacts on market behaviour overall. It seems logical to assume that for the EMH to apply we need something approaching a perfect (rational) market. What do we understand by that? According to neo-classical economic theory a perfect market is one where:

- All participants are rational and aim to maximise utility.
- There are many participants in the market, many buyers and sellers and monopolies are eliminated.
- Competition is 'perfect', there is no collusion or oligopolies.
- All transactions are mutually beneficial, and supply/demand adjusts instantaneously.
- There are no transaction costs.
- All participants have access to all relevant knowledge, 'perfect' information.

Equilibrium theory assumes that actors in the market behave in a rational way aided by perfect knowledge and in pursuit of clearly defined objectives and maximise utility. This view is not one that normal people would recognise as corresponding to reality. While financial markets are among those where expectations play an important part in the calculations of participants, it is precisely in these markets that rational behaviour is notable by its absence!

Irrational behaviour is where there is a divergence from pricing fundamentals in the market-place. Our discussions earlier have noted that in a rational property market capital value growth ought to be closely related to rental value growth through the DCF pricing model, and in the UK rental value growth has traditionally driven capital value growth. Any divergence from this close relationship is an indicator of irrational market.

Such behaviour is consistent with Shiller's 2005 view on the dynamics of bubbles based on 'irrational exuberance' a term first coined by Alan Greenspan, chairman of the US Federal Reserve Bank. Shiller notes that this term has become a useful name for the kind of social phenomenon that has happened again and again in history when markets have been bid up to unusually high and unsustainable levels under the influence of market psychology. He sees rational causes of this 'irrational exuberance' whereby initial external shocks instigate price increases that in turn encourage further investment demand through adaptive expectations that keep projecting forward capital growth.

The lack of rational behaviour chimes with behaviour exhibited in property markets on more than one occasion over many years. The best example of this is market behaviour in the lead up to the global financial crisis (GFC) of the mid/late 2000s and this is examined in more detail in the case study at the end of this chapter. The case study also has a brief assessment of the relationship between gilt yields and initial yields in the property market to illustrate the irrational disconnect between property fundamentals and capital growth in the UK market at this time (see also the analysis in Chapter 4 which undertakes an analysis using equivalent yields).

Summary

The concept of efficient markets in which prices fully reflect all available information and that future price changes are unpredictable is one that was developed through the 1950s and early 1960s. For the efficient market hypothesis to apply something approaching a perfect (rational) market was required, with actors in the market behaving in a rational way aided by perfect knowledge and in pursuit of clearly defined objectives and maximise utility. This view is not one that normal people would recognise as corresponding to reality where often rational behaviour is notable by its absence!

By the early 1960s this view of market efficiency was beginning to change and in 1965 Fama proposed that in the real world there is no perfect or efficient market, but an efficient market is a benchmark, and ultimately recognised three different degrees of efficiency: weak, semi-strong and strong.

For the property market the evidence one way or another for the degree of market efficiency remains confused with the probable only conclusion being that the market does not exhibit weak form efficiency. There are several problems with the determination of prices in the market. Case studies of short leases and over-rented offices suggest that systematic mispricing over periods of time long enough for investors to react does occur. Perhaps not surprising given the barriers to information flows that exist, the notion of market efficiency has evolved into one where a market is efficient if investors are unable to consistently outperform it once information, search and transaction costs are considered.

The notion of irrational markets (or a lack of rational behaviour) where there is a divergence from pricing fundamentals chimes with behaviour exhibited in property markets on more than one occasion over many years. The best example of this is market behaviour in the lead up to the GFC. In the UK, there was an optimism throughout the early 2000s that capital values would continue to increase and that there would continue to be strong rental growth. The consequence of this overoptimism throughout the early to mid-2000s was a departure from fundamentals. It was manifested in a growing disconnect between capital value growth and rental value growth.

In a rational market, long-term capital growth ought to be determined mainly by rental value growth and pricing by the income streams generated by the investment.

This has been generally true over the bulk of the last 40 or so years. However, the early years of the new millennium were heavily influenced by the exceptional high liquidity in the world financial markets and trends in property investment were shaped by conditions in other investment markets. Irrational behaviour contributed to a market that was detached from fundamental pricing, arguably a bubble (where the market appears to be driven by buyers operating on irrational exuberance, who take little notice of underlying value). This was ultimately unstable. ***It was a sobering reminder that considerations of efficient markets were not simply an academic exercise but came with potentially huge financial penalties if over relied upon.***

The financial crisis of 2007–08 led to renewed scrutiny and criticism of the EMH. Critics have blamed the belief in rational markets for much of the late-2000s financial crisis. However, Eugene Fama reacted by observing that the hypothesis held up well during the crisis and that the markets were a casualty of the recession, not the cause of it. However, he conceded that poorly informed investors could theoretically lead the market astray and that stock prices could become somewhat irrational as a result.

Critics have also suggested that financial institutions and corporations have been able to reduce the efficiency of financial markets by creating private information and reducing the accuracy of conventional disclosures. They also developed new and complex products, which were challenging for most market participants to evaluate and correctly price. Behavioural economists attribute the imperfections in financial markets to a combination of cognitive biases such as overconfidence, overreaction, representative bias, information bias and various other predictable human errors in reasoning and information processing.

As a result of these considerations and the irrational behaviour observed in the lead up to the GFC, the management of risk has moved up the agenda in UK fund management houses and with it much more interest in fair value models of the market. The recognition that behaviour is massively important in the operation of markets, however, was identified as long ago as 1841. The Scottish journalist Charles Mackay noted at that time: *"Men, it has been well said, think in herds .... they go mad in herds, while they only recover their senses slowly, and one by one".*

Learning Outcomes

Having completed this chapter, the reader should be able to:

- Explain the different levels of information efficiency.
- Comprehend the consequence of mispricing.
- Understand the important difference of worth and value.
- Discuss how valuations may cause mispricing.
- Understand the implications of irrational behaviour in the marketplace and its impact on property pricing.
- Make rational decisions in the acquisitions of investments.

- Understand the factors that determine the price of investments.
- Appreciate that property yields are determined by the redemption yields on long-dated gilts, and the investors' required yield premium and rental growth for new property.

Case Study A Property Boom in an Irrational Market—The UK Market in the First Decade of Twenty-First Century

A Property Boom

Initial yields and equivalent yields in the UK property market are strongly influenced by the redemption yields on gilts modified by the investor's perception of risk. Gilt yields and property yields are related through the risk premium equation discussed earlier in Chapter 2 and reprised below. Because the risk premium is not constant this relationship varies as Fig. 6.1 demonstrates for the UK. The chart shows historic trends in initial yield and the redemption yields on 10-year gilts and plots the yield gap between all property initial yield and the redemption yield.

The chart is important in as much as it clearly demonstrates the irrational nature of property markets over the period 2003 to 2009. From 2001 to 2007, gilt yields remained relatively steady while property yields fell as did the yield gap (a measure of the risk premium), which became negative in late 2006. This suggested a significant risk in the market, but despite this, money continued to be invested in

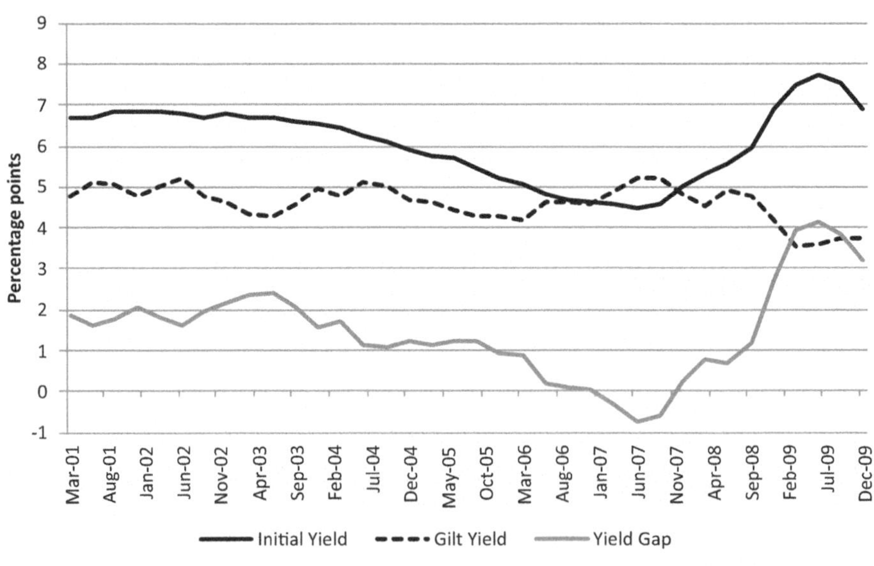

Fig. 6.1 The UK property-gilt yield gap, 2001–2009 (*Source* Jones et al. (2018))

property. The question is why and to answer this we must not forget the part that rental growth expectations play in determining risk premium.

In our discussion of risk premium in Chapter 2, we highlighted an important relationship (reproduced below in Eq. 6.1) between risk premium RP, initial yield k, the risk-free rate rf, as measured by the yield on UK 10 year gilts, rental value growth g_N, and depreciation, d.

$$RP = k - rf + g_N - d \tag{6.1}$$

It is worth bearing this in mind in any discussion of irrational or indeed rational behaviour in property markets. We can highlight this by considering the behaviour of the market during the period leading up to the GFC and the attitudes just before the GFC erupted.

Referring to Figure 6.1, the yield gap between initial yield and the risk-free rate in June 2007 was negative 0.73% points. However, at that time the rental growth assumption in consensus forecasts was for growth of around 2.7% over the next three years. If we assume a depreciation rate of 1% pa, then referring to Eq. 6.1 the implied risk premium at that time based on the yield gap was a little under 1%. Given that the long-term historic risk premium on property was assumed to be around 3%, there ought to have been some concern that the implied risk premium was low although it was still apparently positive. However, investment choices were based on a robust assumption on future rental growth. But these expectations were far too generous. Over the subsequent three years rents actually FELL by on average 1.5% pa. The reality in mid-2007 was that the risk premium was probably nearer -3.2% and much closer to the reality of what happened in the markets late 2007/2008!

The Consequences of Overoptimism

There was an optimism throughout the early 2000s that capital values would continue to increase and that there would continue to be strong rental growth. The consequence of this overoptimism throughout the early to mid-2000s was a departure from fundamentals. This was manifested in a growing disconnect between capital value growth and rental value growth (Fig. 6.2). Our discussions earlier have noted that capital value growth ought to be closely related to rental value growth through the DCF pricing model. What was happening over the period 2003 to 2007, however, was that capital values were yield driven i.e. they were being driven by the weight of money coming into property rather than by rental value growth. Discount rates in the pricing model were clearly not reflecting a rational required rate of return with the expectation that capital values would continue to rise to meet the shortfall.

This view is supported by two subsequent research papers by Burston and Burrell (2015) and Jones et al. (2014). Jones et al. (2014) looked at the relationship between property yields and government bond yields. Their work detected several

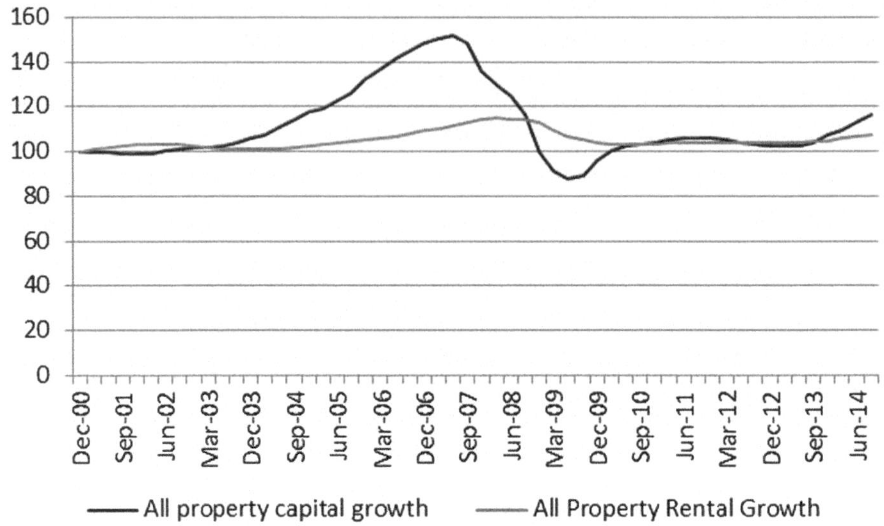

Fig. 6.2 The disconnect between capital and rental value growth (*Source* Jones et al. (2018))

structural breaks over the period 1985 to 2010. They suggested the one explanation of an apparent structural break that began in 2005 was probably, at least in part, the boom and subsequent bust in property lending and a re-evaluation of the risk premium or of expected rental growth or both. In other words, it could be investors responding particularly to property upturns and downturns differently, for example, being overly optimistic about rental growth expectations in a boom and overly pessimistic about forecasts in the bust. As the GFC began to unfold, investors were still projecting substantial rental growth, only for the lease expectations to be dramatically and swiftly downgraded.

Burston and Burrell (2015) took a statistical route that assessed the boom in the context of long run average returns from property. In particular, their study looked at the ratio of current rental income returns to capital value in each year and asked whether it was in line with historic experience. They concluded that there was a lengthy period of over valuation from the late 1990s, and most significantly so between 2005 and 2007. During the period 2004 and 2008, property was priced well above fair value.

To understand more about what was happening over this period it is useful to breakdown the components of capital growth and to look at this in the context of longer-term trends. Figure 6.3, repeated from Chapter 3, breaks down capital growth by yield impact and rental growth from 1981. Yield impact measures the effect of yield change on capital growth. The chart includes the residual term from the index. In the analysis of capital growth, the residual is that part of the change in value that is not attributable to either rental value growth or yield impact.

Approaching capital value changes in this way highlights starkly the relationship between rental value growth, which has traditionally driven capital value

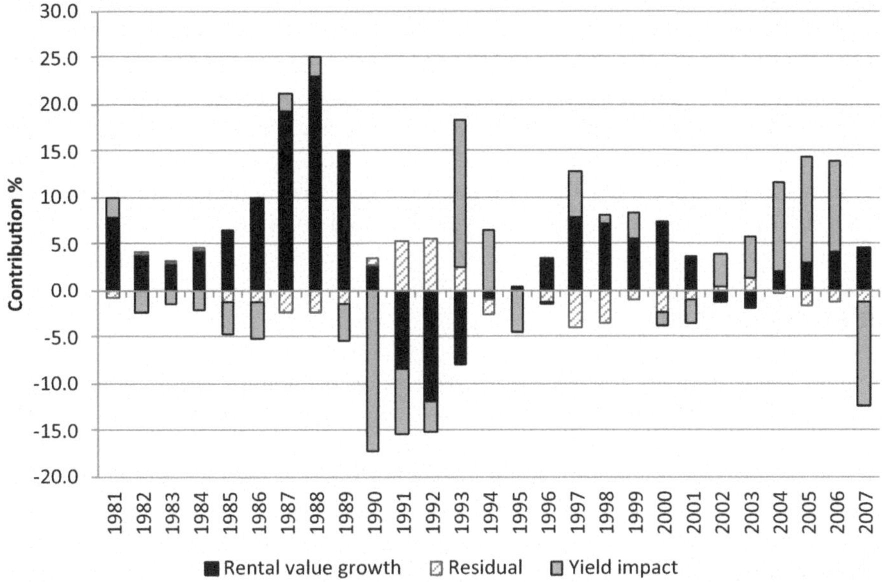

Fig. 6.3 Relative contributions of changes in UK rents and yields to capital value growth, 1981–2007 (*Source* Jones et al. (2018))

growth, and capital value growth overall and illustrates how post-2001 rental value growth was not the main driver of capital growth. From 2002 to 2007, capital growth was dominated by yield impact.

In general, the behaviour post-2001 was completely different from that in the years 1981 to 2001 where, apart from the year 1990 and the period 1992/1993, capital growth could be mainly attributed to rental growth, as one might expect in a rational market. It suggests some kind of structural shift in the market that can be explained by the increasing attractiveness of commercial property as an investment driving yields down and values up.

The evidence does support some kind of structural shift over this period. The five-year period preceding the global financial crisis of 2007/2008 was heavily influenced by exceptionally high liquidity in world financial markets. But from the early 2000s trends in property investment mirrored, and were shaped by, conditions in other investment markets. The investment landscape was changing. The 'dot com' share bubble that characterised the rise in stock market values for much of the previous decade was well and truly burst. Equity or share markets across the developed world tumbled over the period 2000/2003. Many company dividends were cut, hitting the incomes of retail investors, insurance funds and pension funds alike.

The challenges facing investors in maintaining a high level of equity income explain to some extent the way that retail investors turned to property. Returns from established asset classes fell as central banks cut interest rates to very low levels.

At the same time, high volumes of savings in the world economy attempted to secure the highest possible returns and a 'hunt for yield' developed which pushed down bond yields in the pursuit of higher returns. This global 'hunt for yield' by investors compressed yield spreads in a range of markets as money chased alternative investments capable of delivering a higher return including emerging market debt, corporate bonds and property. Investors, however, accepted lower risk premia with the expectation that low interest rates, low inflation and importantly higher returns and increases in capital values would continue.

An Irrational Bust?

In some ways, the period following 2007 was an economic mirror image of the period 2003 to 2007 but events took place over a shorter timescale. Figure 6.4 represents trends in capital value and rental value growth from December 2000 to 2014. It emphasises the world capital values fell through the GFC although rental growth continues to be positive. The figure highlights a number of the key events in the progress of the GFC as points of reference up to when Lehmans bank failed in September 2008.

There was a flip from investors projecting substantial rental growth and returns at the peak of the boom only for expectations to be dramatically and swiftly downgraded resulting in pessimistic forecasts in this past period that in May 2007 the

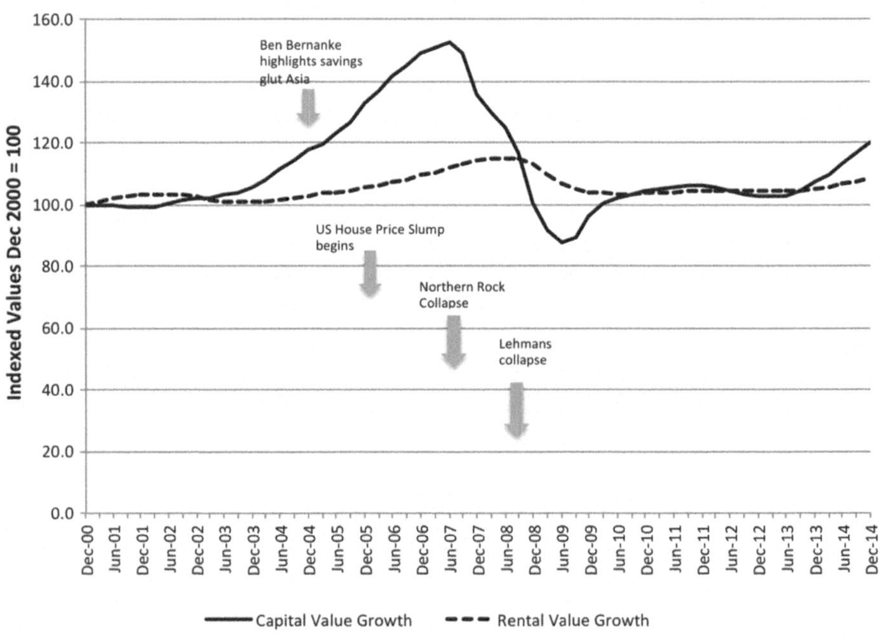

Fig. 6.4 Highlighted events during the market disconnect (*Source* Jones et al. (2018))

investment property forums consensus industry forecast was suggesting average rental growth over the following five years of 2.8% per annum. However, by June 2008, the rental growth forecast had fallen to 0.9% per annum (Investment Property Forum, 2009). Overall, the instability and irrational exuberance in the market in the period 2003 to 2007 was being replaced by perhaps an equally irrational pessimist about where the market could be driven.

From the end of June 2007 until the end of June 2009, when values began to stabilise, average capital values of properties held by financial institutions fell on average by 42.4%. What is interesting when events are superimposed on these trends, however, is that values were increasing even when there were early indications of potential issues in global market trends (as evidenced by warnings of a savings glut in Asia (and a potential impact on interest rates) and by the slump in house prices in the United States). Presumably, this was because of the perception that these problems were too far away to impact on UK commercial markets. Interestingly, though, the market had started to correct before the Northern Rock crisis and perhaps more interestingly still, there had already been a steep (23.3%) declining capital values (over half the eventual total decline) by the time of the collapse of Lehman Brothers' Bank in September 2008. That rate of decline was the most severe witnessed in the UK commercial property markets since meaningful records began in the early 1970s.

There is a suggestion that valuers were paying only cursory attention to property fundamentals and were tending to mark down all assets by almost identical amounts. The initial fall in capital values was virtually all the consequence of a rise in yields as rental growth remained positive. It was only in 2009 that negative rental growth became the main element of falling capital values. The market bust post-2007, like the boom years gently preceding the GFC, was yield driven as investment valuations markdown commercial property values (see Fig. 6.5). It suggests some kind of structural shift in the market post-2001 which persisted through both the boom and bust periods and into the recovery period post-2009.

Aftermath of the Global Financial Crisis

Overall, the falls in capital value through to at least the middle of 2009 represented a dramatic reappraisal of property investors perception of risk. Given the implied high-risk premiums and the deviations from long-term fair value following the GFC, it could be seen as an overreaction. It could be described as irrational pessimism, just as the boom could be seen as irrational exuberance. There then followed a period stretching into the mid-2010s that saw an unwinding process from this extreme.

This analysis has concentrated on behaviour in the UK property market, but the effects of the GFC on global property were just as severe (see also Chapter 9), and it must be remembered that the GFC was about more than just UK property. It was as much about the associated credit crunch and the requirement of banks to resolve the problems in their commercial property loan portfolios because of the falls in

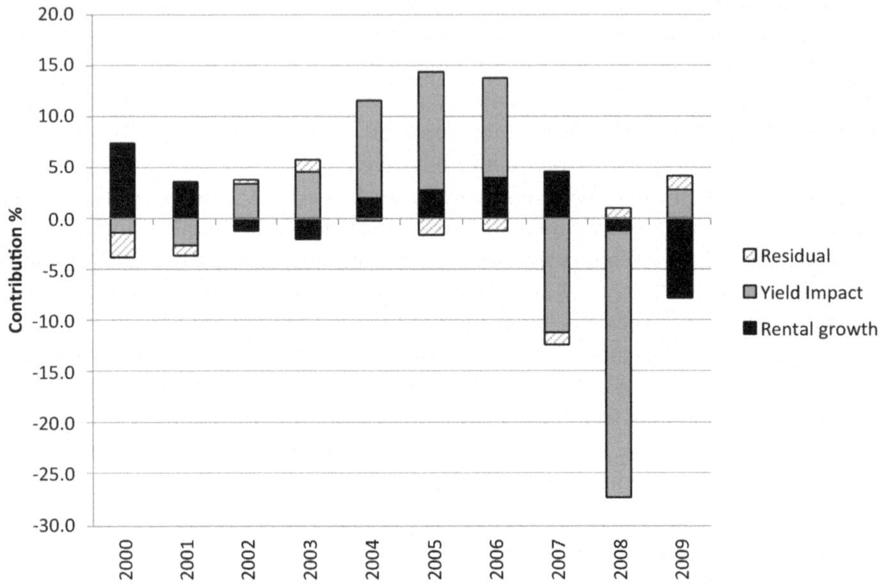

Fig. 6.5 Contributions to capital growth showing the bust period post-2007 (*Source* Jones et al. (2018))

capital values. The loans were originally negotiated against higher property values and many of the borrowers were in negative equity and unable pay the interest on their loan. As a result, the banks faced massive challenges to their fundamental viability which were mostly resolved with government intervention.

Like banks, large property investors also experienced a chastening time in the immediate aftermath of the global financial crisis. The property markets saw not just a rapid reduction in values but also a sudden lack of liquidity. Some institutional investors were forced to sell assets and overall the value of institutional investment dropped before eventually recovering in 2010. Up until the GFC banks typically lent up to 75% of development costs with low market markups over base rates and finance was readily available for speculative products. With the bust banks sought to rebuild their capital bases and adjust their impaired loans. There was limited lending for development or investment in commercial real estate. Annual bank lending to real estate fell by over £50 billion between 2009 and 2013.

Clearly, the consequences of irrational behaviour in the property market and the problems globally with the availability of credit resulted in a huge financial penalty. Consequently, the management of risk has moved up the agenda in UK fund management houses and with it much more interest in fair value models of the market, a much better appreciation of what constitutes fair value and risk premium, and an appreciation of the limited efficiency of property markets to accurately reflect market value (see Chapter 12).

Reading

Barkham, R. and Geltner, D. (1995) Price discovery in American and British property markets. *Real Estate Economics*, 23, 1, 21–44.

Burston, B. and Burrell, A. (2015) *What is fair value? Short paper 24*, Investment Property Forum, London.

Fama, E. F. (1970) Efficient capital markets: a review of theory and empirical work, *Journal of Finance*, 25, 383–417.

Investment Property Forum (2007) *Consensus Forecasts 2007,* Investment Property Forum, London.

Investment Property Forum (2009) *Consensus Forecasts 2009*, Investment Property Forum, London.

JLL (2020) *Global Real Estate Transparency Index*, JLL, https://www.jll.co.uk/en/trends-and-insights/research/global-real-estate-transparency-index

Jones, C., Dunse, N. and Cutsforth, C. (2014). *The Implications for Property Yields of rising Bond Yields, Short Paper 19*, Investment Property Forum, London.

Jones, C., Cowe, S. and Trevillion, E. (2018) *Property Boom and Banking Bust: The Role of Commercial Lending in the Bankruptcy of Banks*. Wiley-Blackwell, Chichester. ISBN-13 978–1,119,219,255.

Malkiel, B. (1973) *A Random Walk down Wall Street,* W. W. Norton and Company, New York. ISBN 0,393,062,457.

Mackay, C. ([1841] 2003) *Memoirs of extraordinary popular delusions*, reprinted as *Extraordinary Popular Delusions and the Madness of Crowds,* Harriman House Ltd, Petersfield.

Sewell, M. (2011) *History of the Efficient Market Hypothesis,* UCL Research Note RN/11/04. University College London, London.

Shiller, R.J. (2005) *Irrational Exuberance*, 2nd Edition, Broadway Books, New York.

Portfolio Theory and Property in a Multi-Asset Portfolio

7

Introduction

In Chapter 2, we discussed how to measure the risk and return characteristics of property investments. We defined risk as the potential variation in returns in the future but noted that it can be gauged by what has happened to a particular investment in the past. The risk can be quantified by calculating the standard deviation of past returns around the mean or average return. The greater the variation then the larger the standard deviation and the higher the risk.

We also examined how investors evaluate individual assets by comparing the expected returns from a range of probable outcomes with the risk attached to the investment. Since investors are assumed to be risk averse when they are choosing between different assets, they will select the one either with the highest return for a given level of risk or the lowest risk for a given level of return. This chapter, however, did not consider what happens to risk and return when we combine investments.

In this chapter, we now apply the concepts of risk and return to combinations of investments. Bundles of assets are called portfolios, and portfolio theory is the study of the risk associated with the combination of investments. Combining assets that react differently under certain economic and financial conditions can reduce a portfolio's risk and portfolio theory can help the investor to decide which combinations of investments give the best return for the risk involved. This chapter now examines:

- Risk reduction, diversification and a portfolio
- Property correlations with other asset classes
- Diversification
- Modern portfolio theory
- Post-modern portfolio theory
- The Capital Asset Pricing Model (CAPM)

C. A. Jones and E. Trevillion, *Real Estate Investment* ,
https://doi.org/10.1007/978-3-031-00968-6_7

- CAPM and property
- Property's target rate of return
- Property in a multi-asset portfolio
- Property as an asset class
- Overview of portfolio theory and practicalities

Risk Reduction, Diversification and the Portfolio

Don't Put All Your Eggs in One Basket!

Portfolio (diversification) theory is about relative risk. The variability of actual returns is being examined not between individual securities but relative to the market as a whole in which the investments are being traded.

Portfolios are a bundle of investments held or diversified to spread risk. Most rational people will spread their risk by holding a mixture of investments, usually with different income and capital performance qualities. A careful selection of a mix of investments can reduce the risk of incurring a loss in the portfolio's capital value and achieve the best possible returns from the bundle.

These portfolios might be bundles of the same asset class or bundles of a mixture of asset types, so-called multi-asset portfolios. We examine this issue later in this chapter and in Chapter 8, but it is important to recognise that the main theories of portfolios risk were developed for financial markets. This chapter, however, will consider how these theories relate to property in both mixed and stand-alone portfolios.

This mixing of investments with the intention of reducing the risk related to a portfolio is called ***diversification***. It is:

- A strategy of reducing risk by risk pooling across several assets whose individual returns behave differently from one another.
- The aim is to reduce risk on the whole portfolio without having to accept a lower average return on the portfolio.

Diversification can reduce the risk attached to a portfolio because different investments respond differently to different economic and financial conditions. Some investments may react one way to one set of conditions; other assets may react in another way. By carefully selecting assets that respond differently under various economic and financial conditions it is possible to eliminate some of the risk without reducing the expected return of the portfolio whether in multi-asset or real estate only portfolios. This risk reduction through diversification is the basis of modern portfolio theory.

We measure the relationship of one asset to another using correlation coefficients (ρ)—a statistic that measures the extent to which two investments' return move together (for the formal definition of correlation coefficient see Appendix to the chapter but EXCEL has a formula that will calculate this for any given series of data).

Correlation coefficients are in the range +1 to −1. By way of example, consider two assets, A and B. If the returns of asset A over a period of time move exactly the same as the returns on asset B, then the assets are said to be perfectly correlated. This results in a correlation coefficient of 1. Perfect correlation is not generally seen in practice as the two investments may react in the same way to an extraneous factor, such as the rate of interest, but not identically. In this case, the correlation coefficients will be in the range 0 to +1. They are still positively correlated, however, but to a lesser extent. The closer the returns move together then the higher the degree of positive correlation and the closer the correlation coefficient is to 1.

If the investor invests all their money in two positively correlated investments the benefits from diversification would be relatively low because changes in the returns from both assets are similar. If the assets are perfectly positively correlated, there would be no reduction in risk from diversification.

On the other hand, the returns of the assets may move differently. This is much more interesting from the diversification point of view. Negative correlation exists where two investments react in the opposite way to an extraneous factor. To take the rate of interest as a very simplified example, again banks will make high returns when interest rates are high but property companies' returns will be low because they have to pay the interest rates. When interest rates are low the reverse is true as banks make low returns while property companies benefit and make high returns. So, when one investment is doing well the other is likely to do less well and vice versa. The correlation coefficient for two negatively correlated assets will be in the range 0 and −1. The more negative the correlation then the more benefits the investor can achieve by diversifying between the two assets.

The extreme example of negative correlation is perfect negative correlation. This occurs when the returns of two assets move in exactly opposite ways so that the correlation is equal to −1. The diversification of a portfolio with investments that have perfect negative correlation would mean that the investor could remove a significant part of the risk attached to the portfolio (not all the risk since a part of the risk cannot be diversified away—see below). Yet, it is unlikely to find two assets that are perfectly negatively correlated because assets tend not to react to general economic forces in completely opposite ways.

Property Correlations with Other Asset Classes

Returns on UK property assets have been much less well-correlated with equities and gilts than equities and gilts have been with each other. By way of illustrating the benefits of keeping property in a multi-asset portfolio. Table 7.1 shows the correlation coefficients of property returns with equities, gilts, indirect property in the form of REITs/property companies and corporate bonds (another important

Table 7.1 Correlation of returns from direct UK property to other asset classes (to end 2017)

	Previous 30 years	Previous 20 years	Previous 10 years	Pre-2000	Post-2000
UK equities	0.41	0.50	0.58	0.21	0.48
UK gilts	−0.18	−0.20	−0.24	−0.12	−0.23
UK REITs	0.67	0.68	0.67	0.60	0.73
UK corporate (BBB) bonds			0.26		0.20

Note Data for REITs is from 2007. Property companies' data is used as a substitute before 2007. Corporate bond data is from 2003. Bonds with a BBB score are regarded as investment grade by rating agencies
Source Authors construct derived from Datastream and MSCI (2016)

investment class), over the thirty-year period to the end of 2017, a period that includes the turmoil of the GFC.

The table illustrates several important points. Correlation coefficients change with time. For equities (shares) and property, for example, these asset classes have become more positively correlated in recent years. Over the full 30-year period covered by the data, property has had a low positive correlation coefficient with equities (still allowing some diversification benefits). The reason why the two asset classes have become more correlated is as a result of the market turmoil of 2008. The returns on most asset classes came together with the GFC, although they began to re-establish their historical position post-2008.

Property has been negatively correlated with gilts, giving it strong diversification benefits when held in a multi-asset portfolio. However, direct property is strongly positively correlated with REITs and, as we noted in Chapter 6, there is evidence that returns from REITs anticipate those for direct property making them a good indicator of future property returns.

In terms of UK property, the table correlates *all property* total returns with the other asset classes. However, individual property sectors (retail, offices and industrial property etc.) will exhibit different behaviour within the umbrella of 'All-Property' (as illustrated later in our analysis of betas in the UK property market). This offers even more opportunities for diversification especially within an all-real estate portfolio.

With the knowledge that there are wide disparities in the way that assets react to market conditions the chapter now begins to analyse in more detail the potential risk reduction benefits from portfolios.

Diversification

We have noted that the risk associated with a portfolio can be reduced by selecting investments with returns that are not perfectly correlated. By combining these investments, the investor can expect to receive the weighted average of the securities' expected return but with less than the weighted average of their risk. But not all risk can be diversified away. There are two types of risk that are normally associated with portfolios of assets: systematic or market risk and unsystematic, specific or property risk.

The risk that can be removed through diversification relates to the individual characteristics of the investment. This is the so-called **specific or non-market risk**. It is the variability in return due to factors unique to the investment and for property include:

- Investment financing and gearing.
- Tenant selection.
- Property selection.
- Property characteristics.
- Location.

As the number of assets held increases so the overall variability of the portfolio return (risk), as measured by the standard deviation of portfolio returns, diminishes very rapidly (see Fig. 7.1). There are differing views as to the numbers of assets required for a sufficient diversification of specific risk but as a rule of thumb it ought to require at least 25–30 assets to diversify away about 70% of specific risk. Some researchers put the number in the range 16–88 depending on the assumption of whether returns follow a particular statistical pattern, namely a normal or non-normal distribution. Ultimately, whatever the precise pattern of returns, there are diminishing benefits to diversification with specific risk regressing to the market risk (see below) with increasing numbers of assets.

Market risk is the degree of risk that cannot be diversified away as shown in Fig. 7.1. This market (or systematic) risk is created by general economic conditions. It is the variability in return due to the dependence on factors that influence the return on all securities (assets) to varying degrees. Examples are:

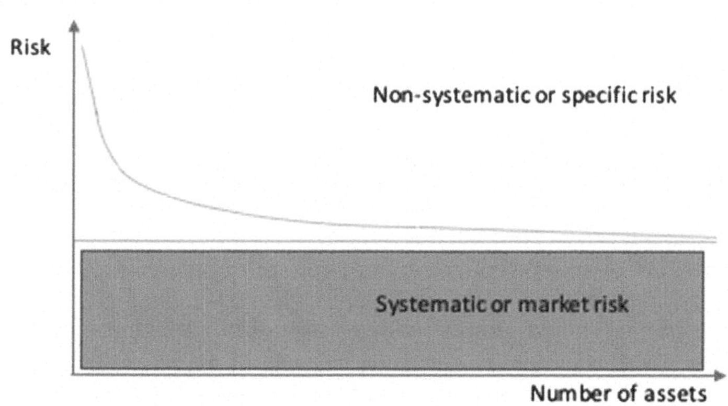

Fig. 7.1 Risk reduction by diversification

- Economic factors such as the prevailing interest rate and inflation.
- Social factors.
- Environmental factors.
- Political change such as changes in legislation and policy (e.g. planning).

Defining market risk, however, is problematic. It depends on the nature of the assets in the portfolio, and it is first necessary to define the market! An exact definition of a distinct market risk and the amount and origin of existing non-diversifiable market risk remains unclear, especially in a real estate setting. However, it will be related to the risk premium above the risk-free rate for the market in question and will be discussed later in the context of the Capital Asset Pricing Model (CAPM).

We will come back to diversification and its importance in portfolio management in Chapter 8 but now we will move on to models that have been developed to help quantify the impact of individual risk on portfolio risk and return.

Modern Portfolio Theory

Modern Portfolio Theory (MPT) was developed and first applied by Markowitz to the equities market in papers published in 1952 and 1959. The fundamental principle is that the risk and return attributes of individual investments are important not so much independently but in the way they contribute to the risk and return of a portfolio as a whole.

By combining securities/assets with correlations less than 1 in a portfolio an investor can expect to receive the weighted average of the securities' returns. At the same time, the risk from the portfolio will be less than the weighted average of their risk of individual assets. It can be a very complex process to calculate the risk/return behaviour of portfolios. There are an infinite number of risk/return combinations possible even with just a few securities. The 'opportunity set' of a potential portfolio shows the expected returns/risks of all possible investment combinations. Each asset's expected risk and return is calculated from all combinations of weightings.

As MPT is an analytical framework for calculating the balance of risk and return of a portfolio and for determining the optimal allocation to each asset, it relies on some simplified assumptions:

- That all investors behave rationally.
- All investors are risk adverse.

Investors are free to choose from countless assets from which they can construct their portfolio. We have already noted the dangers of assuming that investors are rational, and clearly not all investors are risk averse, so immediately there are some concerns with the approach, but it can be a powerful tool nonetheless.

The expected return from the portfolio is the sum of the weighted average of the expected returns of the constituent assets, expressed in the form of Eq. 7.1 below

$$E(Rp) = \sum_{i=1 \text{ to } n} w_i E(R_i) \tag{7.1}$$

where:

$E(Rp)$ = expected return of the portfolio
w_i = proportion of total funds invested in asset i
$E(R_i)$ = expected return of asset i
n = number of assets in the portfolio

The total risk of the portfolio is measured by the volatility of returns (as we have discussed previously) and is assessed using the weighted average of the risks associated with the individual assets in the portfolio (Eq. 7.2 expresses portfolio risk in terms of variance σ^2).

$$\sigma_p^2 = \sum_{i=1 \text{ to } n} \sum_{j=1 \text{ to } n} w_i w_j \sigma_i \sigma_j \rho_{ij} \tag{7.2}$$

where:

σ_p^2 = Total portfolio risk (as variance).
$w_i w_j$ = Individual asset weights
$\sigma_i \sigma_j$ = Standard deviations of the individual assets
ρ_{ij} = Correlation coefficient between returns to assets i and j

If asset returns are not perfectly correlated, portfolio risk is less than the weighted average of risks.

The Efficient Frontier

The risk-return profiles for all possible combinations of n assets of potential interest to an investor is called the opportunity set available, as noted earlier. Within the opportunity set the expected risk and return can be calculated for all combinations of weightings of each asset. The *efficient frontier* represents the best risk/return trade-off for the given securities. Any portfolio represented by the efficient frontier has a higher return for the same risk or a lower risk for the same return than any other possible portfolio under the curve. Note standard deviation (σ) rather than variance (σ^2) is generally used as the risk measure.

In reality, plotting the efficient frontier is very complex as it requires a forecast of future expected returns, the likely standard deviation of those returns as well

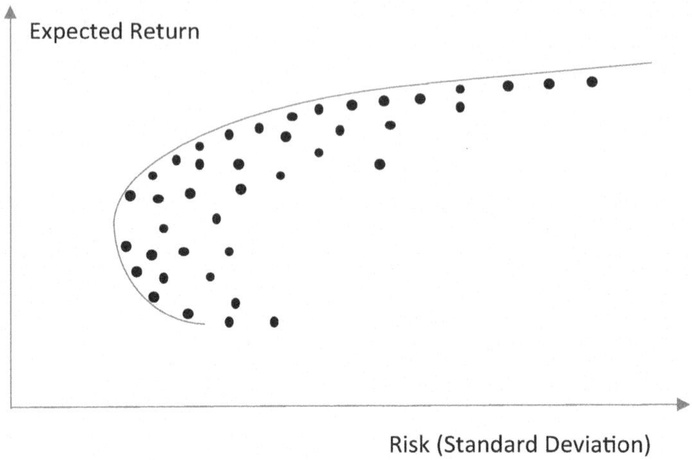

Fig. 7.2 The efficient frontier

as the calculation of the correlation between investments. It remains a difficult process even with modern computer software.

Figure 7.2 shows an efficient frontier for a hypothetical portfolio. Contained within the boundary are many sub-optimal combinations of risk return. The points along the frontier indicate the best possible risk/return combination for the portfolio. A numerical example is given in the Appendix to the chapter.

Investor's Preferences and Indifference Curves

How do investors choose a portfolio? Do they want to minimise risk or take on higher risk in return for higher returns? Each investor will have a preference, and this can be represented by a so-called curve of indifference. In standard economics, this is a line that shows all the possible combinations of two goods between which a consumer is indifferent—i.e. a line that shows the consumption of two goods that will give the same utility (or satisfaction) to the person. In the present context, it is a line which shows combinations of the level of risk and return to which an investor is indifferent. Investors with different attitudes to risk will have different shaped indifference curves.

Each indifference curve represents different combinations of assets (with different expected return and risk attributes) which the investor perceives with the same benefits (utility). There are a family of these curves for each investor, each one representing a different level of satisfaction. An investor will wish to be on the highest possible indifference curve as that represents greatest satisfaction. The highest possible indifference curve that can be achieved is the one that is tangential to the efficient frontier.

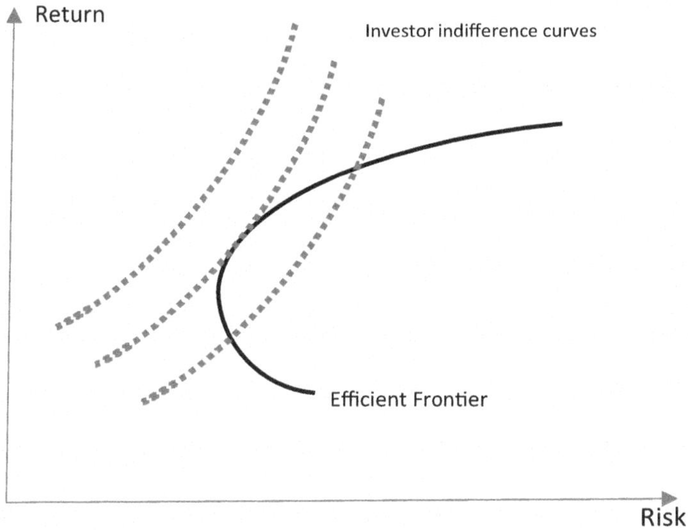

Fig. 7.3 Indifference curves and the efficient frontier (*Note* Indifference curves depend on the subjectivity of the investor while the efficient frontier depends on statistical calculations carried out)

So, the tangent between an investor's indifference curve and the efficiency frontier represents the optimal combination of return and risk, and portfolio weights as shown in Fig. 7.3. In this paradigm, more risk averse investors will have steeper curves while risk takers will have flatter ones. Nevertheless, in practice, finding this optimal point may be difficult, if not impossible.

An investor will probably not know their utility function or be able to plot his/her family of indifference curves. Investors are more likely to structure their portfolios based on their pre-defined maximum risk tolerance or minimum expected return requirement, rather than use MPT to find the optimal portfolio. The portfolio yielding the highest utility that each investor can achieve is identified at the point where the efficient frontier is tangential to the highest indifference curve Table 7.2 provides the advantages and disadvantages of MPT.

Post-Modern Portfolio Theory

From the early 1990s, some assumptions of MPT have been reviewed mainly around the assumptions around the nature of risk and how it should be treated in portfolios. These considerations have been developed into what is now known as post-modern portfolio theory (PMPT). It is a portfolio optimization methodology that uses the downside risk of returns instead of the mean variance of investment returns used by MPT.

Table 7.2 Summary of pros and cons of MPT

For	Against
• Increased technological know-how has led to increased use of MPT • Helps to understand the relationship between assets and the importance of choosing asset classes for the investor • Useful in the stock market for rebalancing portfolios, creating a more optimum structure (less market/info restrictions and more liquid)	• MPT rarely used in practice as the data requirements are substantial • Historical data problematic for future forecasting. Based on expected returns • Ignores subjectivity of investor • Limited application in the property market (data restrictions, future forecasting and illiquidity)

Both theories describe how risky assets should be valued, and how rational investors should utilise diversification to achieve portfolio optimization. The difference lies in each theory's definition of risk, and how that risk influences expected returns. The differences in risk, as defined by the standard deviation of returns, between the PMPT and the MPT is the key factor in portfolio construction. The MPT assumes symmetrical risk whereas the PMPT assumes asymmetrical risk (see also below—there is evidence of asymmetric risk in UK property markets).

While MPT remains the main method for constructing portfolios (and is the basis of passive investing see Chapter 8) PMPT offers a way for portfolio managers to understand and incorporate negative returns in their portfolio calculations. It potentially increases returns beyond what passive investing can bring or reduces risk in a more significant way.

The Capital Asset Pricing Model (CAPM)

MPT relates to risk in the portfolio and how that might be managed as collectively. It highlights the types of risk when several assets are combined but it is not helpful in establishing a target rate of return for an investor. Because specific risk can be reduced through diversification it can be argued that it is the market risk of a portfolio that matters most in this regard. This section looks at the CAPM as a way of assessing returns in relation to market risk. Again, the model was developed with financial markets in mind but has been adapted for use with property markets with some reservations.

All assets are influenced by market trends to some extent, but some are more sensitive to such movements that others. It is this sensitivity which is the nature of market risk and is measured by what is called the beta (β) ratio, the measure of market risk. The market as a whole has a β of 1. A share/asset with a β of 1.5 is expected to vary by 15% for every 10% movement up or down in the market. Assets with a β of 0.5 would vary by only 5% given a 10% change in the market.

It can be argued that because of the relative ease with which specific risk can be eliminated by diversification the type of risk that an investor is principally concerned with is market risk and specific risk goes largely unrewarded. This is the basis of the CAPM. According to the CAPM, an investors target return is a combination of the return available from a riskless investment plus an extra return (the risk premium as discussed in Chapter 2) *which is proportional to the investment's market risk* (β).

The model was developed during the 1960s by a series of authors beginning with Sharpe in 1964 to overcome the problems of calculation involved in MPT and to develop and extend the analysis. It again examines the relationship between risk and return in a portfolio, considering this trade-off to establish if the asset is correctly priced. It purportedly calculates an assets 'correct' risk premium.

CAPM observes that most shares are positively correlated because of a common market response in their returns. It postulates therefore that the expected return of any share is a function of the expected return of the market. If we bought until we held all shares on the market we would end up bearing the risk of the market which cannot be diversified away—the market risk. It effectively assumes that investors have diversified away specific risk. This kind of assumption led to a 'market model' whereby the expected return of a security can be expressed as a linear function of the expected return on the market.

Simplifying Assumptions

Again, as with MPT, there are some wide-ranging simplifying assumptions:

- The approach assumes that the only common factor affecting returns is the return from the market and that there are no economic factors which effect only some sectors or industries.
- It simplifies the calculations by relating the returns on any asset to a common index (the market as a whole) rather than to each other. All assets are seen as marketable.
- Investors are risk averse and maximise their returns over a single period.
- The market is assumed to be efficient and a notional market portfolio is used (generally via indices for property, for example, the MSCI/IPD index).
- Investors make their decisions solely on the expected return and standard deviation of these portfolios and have identical risk expectations.
- Standard deviation and return can be consistently calculated.
- Investors are price takers (no individual can affect the market by buying and selling), there are no taxes or transaction costs.
- There is free and available information for all investors.
- Assets are divisible.
- All investors agree on the time period considered (it affects the annual/quarterly/monthly etc. returns on the market).

Main Relationships

There are three main relationships:

- The Capital Market Line, which derives an optimum portfolio of risky and risk-free assets.
- The Characteristics Line, which expresses the relationship between the expected return on a security for given values of the return expected on the portfolio (market).
- Securities Market Line, which relates the expected return of any asset to its risk.

These are now considered in turn.

The Capital Market Line (CML)

The CML given in Fig. 7.4 is the tangent to the envelope of the efficient portfolio of risky assets drawn from the expected return of the risk-free asset (Rf) shown on vertical axis. The return on a risk-free asset could be that from long-dated government bonds. The tangent point itself, M, has an expected return, ER(m) and risk, σ(m).

Immediately, it introduces the concept of a risk-free rate and the relationship of this to the efficient frontier. It indicates that the optimum portfolio is a linear combination of a risk-free asset and the market portfolio combination at M. Any combination along the CML (except the M itself) is superior to any combination of risky assets alone i.e. investors can obtain more desirable risk-return combinations

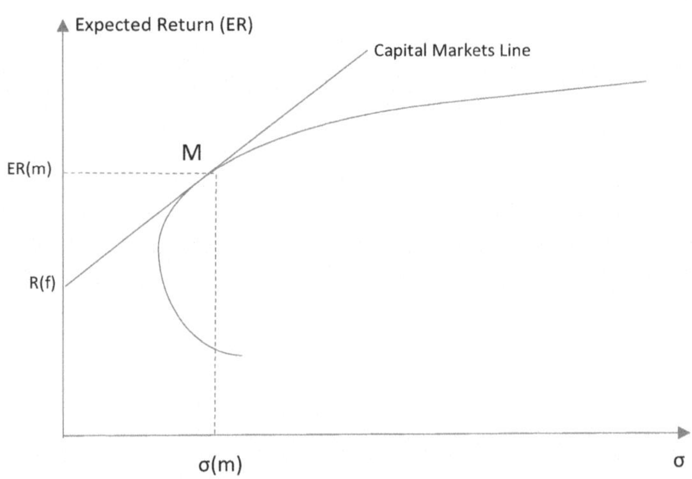

Fig. 7.4 The Capital Market Line

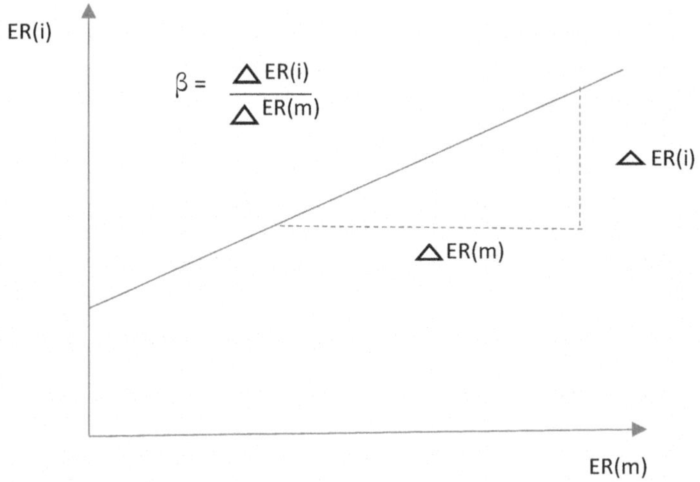

Fig. 7.5 The characteristics line

by mixing the risk-free asset and the market portfolio to suit their preferences. The slope of the CML defines the best available terms for exchanging risk and return.

The CML may be represented by Eq. 7.3 which expresses the expected return on the *portfolio* as a function of the risk-free rate (Rf) and the expected return on the market.

$$ER_p = Rf + [ER(M) - Rf]\sigma_p/\sigma_m \tag{7.3}$$

where σ_p/σ_m is the ratio of the risk associated with the portfolio as defined by the standard deviation to that of the market as a whole.

The Characteristics Line

This now expresses the general relationship between the expected return on a security ER_i (rather than the portfolio) for given values of the return expected on the portfolio (market) ER_m. The slope of the line is β. Beta indicates the degree of systematic risk of the security. Although not a direct measure of systematic risk, it is an important indicator of relevant risk. The characteristics line shown in Fig. 7.5.

Securities Market Line (SML)

The equilibrium relationship between risk and return which holds when all securities are 'correctly' priced is indicated by Eq. 7.4. It has the same form as the CML but is now linked to individual assets not the portfolio as a whole. It indicates the appropriate required return on individual assets in an *efficient* portfolio.

The equation of the SML is:

$$E(R_i) = RF + [(E(R_m) - RF)]\beta_i \tag{7.4}$$

where:

β_i = Slope of the line
$E(R_i)$ = Expected return on asset i
$E(R_m)$ = Expected return on the market
RF = Risk-free rate

In the equation, the expected return on the asset i is related to the risk-free return and the expected return on the market. For most purposes this is the most important equation arising from the CAPM. It measures the expected return of any asset to its (market) risk.

Using betas helps us to assess the effect of including the asset within a portfolio. If beta is one then the asset has the same risk and expected return as the market. If beta is >1, then the returns on the asset will outperform the market in a 'bull' phase (prices rising upward market trends) but underperform in a 'bear' phase (prices falling, downward market trends). If beta is <1, then the return is less volatile than the market. If beta is 0, then the asset has no risk and the return is equal to the risk-free asset, the optimal return.

As we have noted, the assumptions here are that we are dealing with an efficient market. In the real world, the question is can we get excess returns in practical terms. Alpha (α) is a term used in investing to describe an investment strategy's ability to beat the market. Alpha is thus also often referred to as 'excess return' or 'abnormal rate of return'. If we assume that markets are efficient in theory at least there is no way to systematically earn returns that exceed the broad market as a whole.

Practical Limitations to CAPM

The CAPM analyses the sources of risk and offers key insights into what rewards investors should expect for bearing these risks. However, like all economic models it should not be applied blindly, notwithstanding its apparent simplicity. In particular:

- There are reservations that the model does not reflect investor behaviour regarding risk. This was clearly demonstrated in the property market over recent years, particularly during the global financial crisis of 2008–2010 (see also our discussion of efficient markets in Chapter 6). It does give a broad indication of fair value, however, and a guide as to what investors ought to expect from the market.
- It assumes an efficient market in equilibrium which exhibits a linear risk-return relationship.
- A key assumption is that investors adopt a one period time horizon for holding securities. Whatever the length of the period the rates of return incorporated in investor expectations are rates of return over the whole holding period, assumed

to be common for all investors (see also below and note the way that property betas change over time).

Despite these limitations, the CAPM does provide a way of assessing the rate of return required from investments albeit based (partly) on past returns. If the beta is known, and a view is taken on the future return from the market then the expected rate of return for a given asset follows. It becomes the cut off rate for new investment projects, at least for those with similar systematic risk to existing activities.

CAPM and Property

The assumptions used to create the CAPM model mean that its application within the property market is relatively difficult.

- It makes the strict assumption that markets are efficient and that all information is available to all investors. The difficulties with this assumption are already set out in Chapter 6.
- It assumes that each investor is looking at a specific time period and has the same risk characteristics.
- Calculation of beta is difficult as beta is calculated with historical data (past performance may not indicate future performance).
- Beta will depend on the time period being analysed.
- Calculating market return is subjective as it is derived from published property indices that are primarily based on professional valuations. Valuations also suffer from potential smoothing over a property cycle that underplays variations in returns as noted in Chapter 4. In addition, it is important to recognise that real estate universes or data sets change over time, with ramifications for the calculation of property betas. It is also questionable whether a published property index is free of specific risk as it cannot practically be based on the whole market. Indices are based on subsets of the market and so the assumed market return may be actually contaminated by an element of specific risk.
- What risk-free rate do we use? In the case of property, the redemption yield on 10-year government bonds (gilts) is normally taken as the risk-free rate as explained in Chapter 2. However, although gilts are not riskless, they provide a better comparison than short term Treasury Bills (see glossary), for example, because they are a closer substitute for property for a long-term investor, and there is a close relationship between their yields and property yields over time (see Chapter 2).

The issue of timing is illustrated by UK commercial property investment given in Fig. 7.6. This presents the long run risk and equivalent beta figures for properties held in MSCI/IPD portfolios over different periods. Beta has been measured for the main property sectors against the UK All-Property MSCI/IPD Universe over

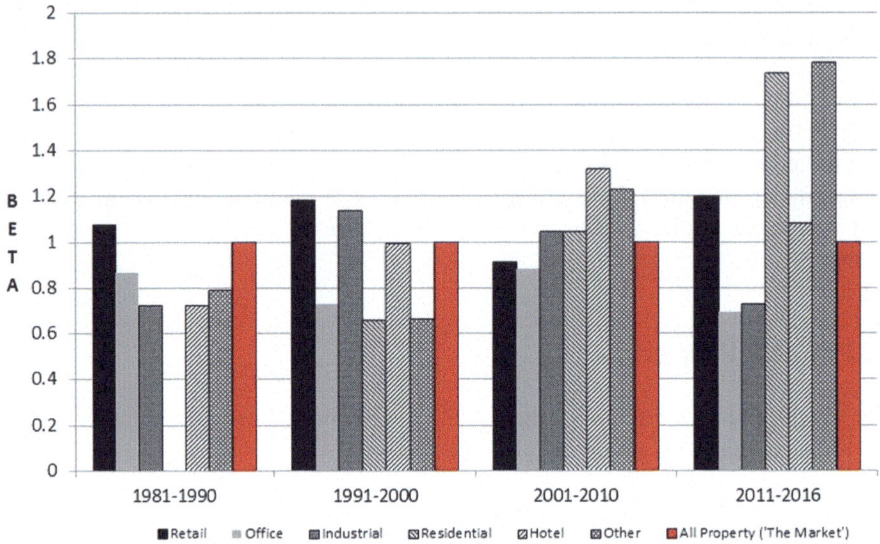

Fig. 7.6 Selected UK property market betas, 1981–2016 (*Source* Jones et al. [2018])

periods from 1981 to 2016. The chart highlights the difference in performance of these sectors over time as indicated by their respective betas, but perhaps more importantly that these betas vary over time. For example, retail has the highest beta in three of the periods compared to offices and industrial units but the industrial has the highest one in the decade following the millennium. This finding emphasises the need to clearly define the time period when comparing performance in these terms.

Property's Target Rate of Return

The analysis so far has highlighted the benefits of holding properties (or any asset for that matter) in a portfolio that diversifies risk. In addition, the CAPM allows an investor to relate an expected return on an asset to the risk in the wider market. We have also noted that an investor will aim to match their indifference curves with the efficient frontier of a portfolio to give an indication of the most efficient portfolio composition. This in theory puts us in a position to reach some conclusions about what an investor's target rate of return should be.

It would be expected that the target rate of return would be at least the risk-free rate plus a risk premium (see Chapter 2), largely determined in relative terms by the market within which the individual asset sits. Historically, the industry has assumed that the target rate of return on good quality property investment is 2% (risk premium) above the redemption yield on **10-year government bonds**. However, as Chapter 4 demonstrates this gap is variable with the state of the economy and with inflation in particular. The risk premium has also been negative on some occasions (see Chapter 6 and the GFC).

The elements that make up this risk premium for real estate and their relative contributions are therefore more complex than the CAPM implies. It is clear that while there are risk factors common to real estate as a whole the premium varies over time, and it is not possible to assign consistent contributions in any specific sector.

Property in a Multi-Asset Portfolio

Property can be held either in stand-alone property portfolios or funds or held in larger multi-asset funds such as pension and insurance funds which include equities, fixed interest bonds and other investment vehicles. Quite often the property element of multi-asset funds will be operated as if it were a stand-alone fund.

Asset allocators in investment houses are making day to day decisions on the weighting they should give to the different asset classes in multi-asset portfolios. As part of this process, they will consider the risk-return characteristics of the asset classes and the benefits that might accrue because of diversification.

While commercial property is a significant investment medium in the UK, it is still small compared to other asset classes. To recap on Chapter 5 by the end of 2018, the total stock of commercial property in the UK was valued at £951 bn of which £512 bn was so-called investable stock (stock held for investment purposes). The equities market in the UK at the end of 2018 was valued at around £3,881 bn and the fixed income market (total debt, securities) at £5,174 bn in Q3 2020, of which £2,531 bn was government debt.

Ordinary shares, bonds and property assets offer investors a wide range of benefits. We have discussed some of the benefits and limitations of these investments earlier in Chapter 4. Direct property has quasi-equity characteristics. Between rent reviews, the income from property is fixed like a conventional bond, however rent reviews, including 'upward only' clauses where applicable, and lease renewals offer investors the opportunity for real rental growth. This results in the income and capital value of direct property (just like ordinary share assets) being variable in real terms.

Table 7.3 The returns from the UK investment spectrum 1971–2016

Asset class	Annualised total returns (% pa)	Standard deviation	Return/risk
UK equities	12.0	27.8	0.43
Gilts	9.7	13	0.74
UK direct property	10.8	10.8	1.0

Source Authors construct derived from MSCI (2016) and Barclays Annual Equity Gilt Study (2017)

Property as an Asset Class

So far this chapter has considered the role of real estate investment primarily in the context of portfolio theory, and its risk relative to other investments. However, the traditional case for property has been wider, namely that:

- Real estate remains a good diversifier for portfolios dominated by equities and bonds
- It performs well relative to other investment categories (risk/return).
- It provides a secure and stable cash flow
- It has low volatility of returns

This section assesses the verity of these arguments based on historical data from the UK.

In the context of the UK, property has hybrid features. These are covered in detail in Chapters 4 and 5 but it is worth recapping some of these here. In times of economic growth, upward-only rent reviews allow an equity type return linked to the real economy. In times of negative growth, fixed nominal income between reviews and upward-only rent reviews give it conventional bond features. Generally speaking, real income is variable like conventional bonds and equities as opposed to the fixed real income exhibited by indexed linked gilts. Likewise real capital values are variable compared to the fixed nature of indexed linked gilts, as are nominal expected returns and real expected returns. As we have noted in Chapter 4, property is an illiquid asset unlike equities and bonds.

The investment properties can be effectively used as a hedge, a safeguard of value, as noted in Chapter 4 (see also below). Over the long term, in the UK, property has exhibited annualised total returns that were lower than equities and marginally higher than government 10-year gilts over the period 1971–2016 (Table 7.3). At the same time, the volatility of property returns was less than both of these other asset classes. Superficially at least the statistics show a higher return to risk ratio for real estate over the period. However, as discussed previously the MSCI/IPD property index is based on valuations that smooth market values and may have artificially lowered the volatility of the property returns.

These characteristics, however, have changed with time. Of note here is that over the 30-year period to the end of 2017 the return/risk characteristics of UK direct property changed in absolute and relative terms (compared with the other asset classes) as shown in Table 7.4. Over the whole of this 30-year period it was 0.87, compared to 0.59 for equities and 0.94 for gilts. However, in the 10 years to the end of December 2017, a period which includes the GFC, it had fallen to 0.54. During this 10-year period, the ratio was about the same as equities but now well below gilts and corporate bonds. This was largely due to the GFC when total returns of all asset classes came together over the period 2007–2009. Over the long term, however, property has delivered good returns on a risk adjusted basis (but bear in mind the smoothing issue).

Table 7.4 Changing UK risk adjusted returns, 1987–2017

	Total return (% pa)	Standard deviation	Return/risk
30 yrs to December 2017			
Direct property	8.65	9.92	0.87
UK equities	9.32	15.82	0.59
UK gilts	7.93	8.45	0.94
UK REIT's	7.59	27.17	0.28
20 yrs to December 2017			
Direct property	8.58	9.20	0.93
UK equities	6.26	15.95	0.39
UK gilts	6.35	7.44	0.85
UK REIT's	7.39	24.67	0.30
10 yrs to December 2017			
Direct property	5.85	10.87	0.54
UK equities	6.32	15.77	0.40
UK gilts	6.61	7.82	0.85
UK REIT's	5.48	25.95	0.21
UK BBB bonds	6.59	7.92	0.83

Source Authors construct derived from MSCI and Datastream. REITs from 2007. Property Companies before 2007. Corporate bonds data from 2003

Thus far in this chapter, the focus has been on direct property. Table 7.4 now highlights the performance of indirect property (discussed in detail in Chapter 4.) in the form of REITs and property companies. Because UK REITs have been a relatively recent addition to property portfolios in the UK, the data relating to them in Table 7.4 only runs from 2007 and property company data has been used pre-2007. Of particular note is the much lower risk adjusted return achieved from this asset class compared to direct property.

Table 7.5 UK property returns and inflation, 1970–2013

	Total returns % pa	Inflation % pa
1970–2013	10.4	6.0
1970–1980	16.3	13.8
1980–1990	11.6	6.4
1990–2000	9.2	2.9
2000–2013	7.3	3.0

Source Authors construct derived from MSCI +

Both direct and indirect real estate offer diversification benefits in multi-asset portfolios. For direct property, the type of property is also important for diversification although there is a view that location has a greater impact. Locational diversification benefits are especially relevant to an international context (see Chapter 9). Indirect real estate investment also offers diversification benefits in both multi-asset and property only portfolios and may take the form of a range of vehicles.

Evidence of Asymmetric Returns

The assumption in the theories so far is that risk can be assessed using the standard deviation of returns around a mean as per modern portfolio theory. But, consistent with our discussion of PMPT earlier, there is evidence that might challenge this assumption. It means that portfolios derived from mean–variance analysis are sub-optimal (Lizieri et al. 2013).

In weak economic conditions, such as those experienced in the GFC, real estate returns appear to be skewed and to have 'fat tails'. Put another way there is a higher probability of extreme downside returns than would be expected for a normal distribution. There is also evidence that valuation smoothing effects are more pronounced in extreme markets so that appraisal-based performance indices may particularly understate property risk in these circumstances.

Property as an Inflation Hedge

The impact of inflation on the value and income of a financial asset is an important concern for investors. They wish to safeguard the value and purchasing power of their investments. To do so, they aim to select assets with inflation-hedging characteristics. An asset is regarded as an inflation hedge when its nominal value increases broadly at, or above, the rate of inflation over the long term. It is deemed a real asset as its real value is maintained over time. Property was traditionally regarded as a good hedge against inflation as identified in Chapter 4.

In fact, rental growth from commercial property tends to lag economic activity and importantly inflation. In one sense, this is not helpful since the effect of lengthy rent review periods is to cause a delay before rental growth is converted to higher investment income. Property can suffer in the short to medium term in periods of high inflation but importantly gain in periods of low inflation when properties can become over rented and property can produce higher than expected income yields.

While property may not be the complete hedge against inflation that was traditionally thought it can provide some protection against expected inflation. Table 7.5 compares the annualised UK returns from property to average inflation for different periods up to the immediate post-GFC period. Overall direct property outperformed inflation over the 43-year period from 1970 to 2013 by 10.4% to 6%. But it should be noted that equities and gilts have also generally beaten inflation as well—there is nothing special about property in this regard with the annualised total returns for equities and gilts over this period 12.6% and 9.7%, respectively.

As an asset class real estate cannot cope with high un-expected inflation. It is a hedge but perhaps a poor one. Despite this, historically property continued to be viewed as a hedge because of its long-term returns, and as such suitable for matching the long-term inflation linked liabilities of life and pension funds. As far as financial institutions and pension funds are concerned this is not now perhaps the main reason for investing in property. The case for investing in property as a hedge against inflation has declined as inflation has declined and this has been further undermined by the introduction of indexed linked gilts (see Chapter 4).

Overview of Portfolio Theory and Practicalities

This chapter has set out the case for property investment in a multi-asset portfolio by reference to portfolio theory. Even a few decades ago property portfolios were viewed as simple aggregations of individual buildings with little reference to portfolio theory. The arguments for property investment as considered above have traditionally been wider than benefits of diversification and return. In addition, property also benefits from rent as a contractual obligation like interest on debt, while dividends are not. Often in times of economic downturn, tenants will stop paying dividends before they stop paying rents providing property with a relatively secure income yield.

Despite the positive arguments for real estate investment, the proportion of property held in institutional portfolios is limited. Figure 7.7 shows how the over-

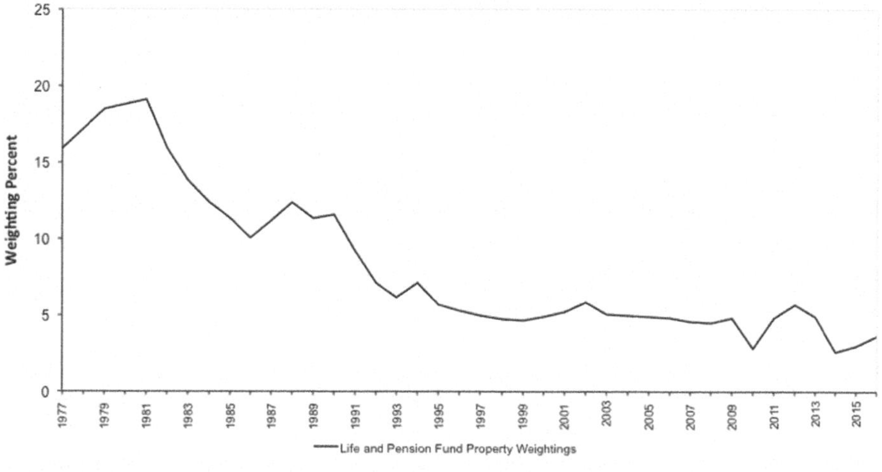

Fig. 7.7 UK institutional property holdings as a proportion of funds under management, 1977–2016 (*Source* Authors construct derived from MSCI data and Investment Association Annual Survey 2020)

all proportion of property held under the management of UK institutional funds has generally fallen since the mid-1970s. It peaked in 1981 at just over 19% but has fallen progressively ever since. At the end of 2016, the proportion held by life and pension funds was around 3.6%.

There are several reasons why the proportion has fallen:

- The use of indexed linked bonds in portfolios has been an attractive option for asset allocators.
- The realisation that property is only a partial hedge against inflation (expected inflation).
- A better understanding of the real value of total returns from property, partly, because of the greater market transparency resulting from the publication of MSCI/IPD indices.
- The removal of exchange rate controls in 1979 allowing institutions to achieve greater diversification overseas and reducing the importance of property as a diversifier.
- Dividend controls were also removed on UK companies at about the same time allowing dividends on equities to be increased making them a more attractive investment medium.

Summary

This chapter has focused on how the concepts of risk and return can be applied to combinations of investments. It has examined modern portfolio theory and although it has limitations its basic ideas are widely applied in the property industry. The usefulness of portfolio theory has been in establishing and reinforcing the ideas of market and specific risk and underpinning naïve ideas on diversification.

Portfolio (diversification) theory is about relative risk. The variability of actual returns is being examined not between individual securities but relative to the market in which the investments are being traded.

Portfolios are a bundle of investments held to diversify or spread risk. Most rational people will spread their risk by holding a mixture of investments, usually with different income and capital performance qualities. A careful selection of mixed investments can reduce the risk of incurring a loss in the portfolio's capital value and achieve the best possible returns from the bundle.

Not all risk can be diversified away. There are two types of risk that are normally associated with portfolios of assets: systematic or market risk and unsystematic and specific or property risk. The risk that can be removed through diversification is referred to as **specific or non-market risk**.

Market risk is the degree of risk that cannot be diversified away. Market (or systematic) risk is created by general economic conditions. It is the variability in return due to the dependence on factors that influence the return on all securities (assets) to varying degrees.

MPT holds that the risk/return attributes of individual investments are important not so much independently but in the way they contribute to the risk and return of the portfolio. By combining securities with correlations less than 1 the investor can expect to get the weighted average of the securities expected return but with less than the weighted average of their risk.

MPT relates risk and return in a portfolio of risky assets and how that they might be balanced as a collective. It is not helpful in establishing a target rate of return for an investor.

The CAPM extended and to some extent simplified these ideas relating the expected return from portfolios and individual assets to market risk. It postulates that the expected return of any share is a function of the expected return of the market. It effectively assumes that investors have diversified away specific risk. This assumption led to a 'market model' whereby the expected return of a security can be expressed as a linear function of the expected return of the market.

The CAPM analyses the sources of risk and offers key insights into what rewards investors should expect for bearing these risks. However, like all economic models we should not apply it blindly. There are reservations that the model does not reflect investor's behaviour regarding risk. Despite these limitations, the CAPM does provide a way of assessing the rate of return required from investments albeit based (partly) on past returns.

The strict assumptions within the CAPM limit its practical application to real estate investment. In particular, it makes the strict assumption that markets are efficient while the property market is not. The calculations of betas for different property sectors are variable over time and suffer from being based on data sets derived from valuations. The risk premium for real estate is variable over time and so the relative contributions to the required rate of return for property is more complex than the CAPM implies.

The traditional case for property has been wider than that set within MPT and includes that it provides a secure and stable cash flow and has low volatility of returns compared to other asset classes. In addition, it has been seen as a hedge against inflation. The evidence for these views is not straight forward and have varied over time.

PMPT suggests that only the downside nature of risk is important to investment decisions. This is an issue for property investment as appraisal based performance indices may particularly understate property risk in downturns, for example following the GFC.

Despite the positive arguments for real estate investment, the proportion of property held in institutional portfolios is limited. The proportion of property held in UK institutional portfolios peaked in 1981 at just over 19% of all assets but has fallen progressively ever since. At the end of 2016, the proportion held by UK life and pension funds was around 3.6%.

This chapter has reinforced the traditional case for property as an investment medium and for a place for it in multi-asset portfolios. It should be remembered that one of the powerful arguments for property as an investment medium is that property investments are rights over land and buildings. Consequently, they are tangible and durable assets. Rent is a contractual obligation like interest on debt, dividends are not. Often in times of economic downturn tenants will stop paying dividends before they stop paying rents providing property with a relatively secure income yield.

Learning Outcomes

After completion of this chapter, the reader should be able to:

- Understand the concept of diversification and how total portfolio risk can be reduced.
- Have a grasp of modern portfolio theory and the efficient frontier.
- Understand that total portfolio risk consists of market risk and specific risk, and that the specific risk constituent can be diversified away.
- Know how to determine the investor's optimal combination of assets.
- Measure a portfolio's expected return and risk.
- Understand the Capital Asset Pricing Model and appreciate how this technique is simpler to apply than Modern Portfolio Theory.
- Understand some of the practical limitations of applying CAPM. In particular, the strict assumption of an efficient market does not hold for the property market.
- Calculate the beta for an asset.
- Note that the betas for different property sectors are variable over time and suffer from being based on data sets derived from valuations.
- Understand the place of commercial property in multi-asset portfolios.
- Appreciate that the traditional case for property is that it provides a secure and stable cash flow and has low volatility of returns compared to other asset classes, as well as a hedge against inflation. The evidence for these views is not straight forward and have varied over time.
- Note that PMPT suggests that only the downside nature of risk for investment decisions and that property indices may particularly understate this risk in downturns.
- Be able to discuss the similarities and differences in the risk and return characteristics of the main asset classes.
- Appreciate that property offers investors diversification benefits.

Appendix

Correlation Coefficient Formula

Correlation coefficient can be expressed as follows:

$$\rho_{ij} = \frac{\mathrm{COV}_{ij}}{\sigma_i \sigma_j}$$

where COV_{ij} represents the covariance between each pair of investment returns of assets i and j, $\sigma_i\ \sigma_j$ are the standard deviations of the individual assets and the covariance is as follows:

$$\mathrm{COV}_{ij} = \sum \left[E(R_i) - E(\overline{R}_i)\right]\left[E(R_j) - E(\overline{R}_j)\right] P_{E(R)ij}$$

where:

$E(R_i)$ = expected return of asset i
$E(\overline{R}_i)$ = average expected return of asset i
$E(R_j)$ = expected return of asset j
$E(\overline{R}_j)$ = average expected return of asset j
$P_{E(R)ij}$ = probability of each return being achieved

Calculating the Efficient Frontier

Let us assume that there are two assets A and B in a particular portfolio and that they have the following expected returns and standard deviations associated with those returns:

	Asset A (%)	Asset B (%)
Expected return	10	20
Standard deviation	15	30

The returns have a correlation coefficient of −0.5%

Now consider a number of possible combinations of these two assets in a portfolio:

Portfolio	Weight (%)	
	A	B

1	100	0
2	75	25
3	50	50
4	25	75
5	0	100

To calculate the efficient frontier, we need to relate the expected portfolio return to the associated risk. We use the following equations for Expected Return and Portfolio Risk:

$$\text{Expected portfolio return} = w_A * R_A + w_B * R_B$$

$$\text{Portfolio risk} = \text{sqrt}\left[w_a^2\sigma_a^2 + w_b^2\sigma_b^2 + 2w_a w_b \rho_{ab}\sigma_a\sigma_b\right]$$

where

w_a = weight of asset A
w_b = weight of asset B
R_a = return on asset A
R_b = return on asset B
σ_a, σ_b = standard deviations of the individual assets
ρ_{ab} = correlation coefficient for assets A and B

For example, for portfolio 2, the expected portfolio return is $(0.75*10+0.25*20)$ or 12.5 and the associated portfolio risk would be:

$$\text{Sqrt}\left[\left(0.75^2 * 15^2\right) + \left(0.25^2 * 30^2\right) + (2 * (-0.5) * 0.75 * 0.25 * 15 * 30)\right] \text{ or } 9.9$$

We can calculate the portfolio risks for each of the portfolios considered above as follows:

Portfolio	Risk	Return
1	15	10
2	9.9	12.5
3	13	15
4	20.9	17.5
5	30	20

The efficient frontier is obtained by charting risk (on the X-axis) against portfolio return (on the Y-axis) as shown in Fig. 7.8.

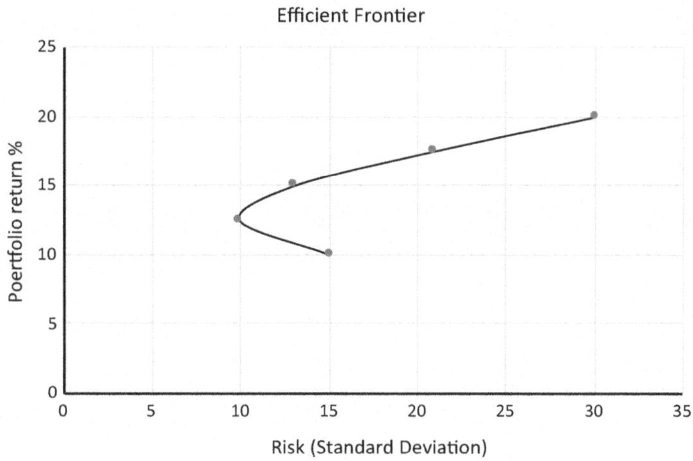

Fig. 7.8 Efficient frontier for the portfolio of assets A and B

Reading

Barclays Bank (2017) *Annual Equity Gilt Study*. Barclays Bank, London.

Hoesli, M. and MacGregor, B. D. (2000) *Property Investment: Principles and Practice of Portfolio Management*. Pearson Education, London.

Investment Association (2020) *Asset Management in the UK 2019–2020: Annual Survey*, Investment Association, London.

Investment Property Forum (2020) *The Size and Structure of the UK Commercial Property Market*. Investment Property Forum, London.

Jones, C., Cowe, S. and Trevillion E. (2018) *Property Boom and Banking Bust: The Role of Commercial Lending in the Bankruptcy of Banks*. Wiley-Blackwell, Chichester. ISBN-13 978-1119219255.

Lizieri, C., Alcock, J., Steiner, E., Satchell, S. and Wongwachara, W. (2013) *Real Estate's Role in the Mixed Asset Portfolio: A Re-examination*. Investment Property Forum/University of Cambridge Department of Land Economy, Cambridge, March.

Markowitz, H. M. (1952) *Portfolio selection*. Journal of Finance, 7, 77–91.

Markowitz, H. M. (1959) *Portfolio Selection: Efficient Diversification of Investment*, Cowles Foundation Monograph No. 16. Yale University Press, New Haven.

MSCI (2016) *Annual Digest*. MSCI, London.

Sharpe, W (1964) Capital asset prices: A theory of market equilibrium under conditions of risk. *Journal of Finance*, 19, 3, 425–442.

Property Portfolio Management 8

Introduction

In this chapter, we adopt a broader perspective and examine the overall investment strategies used by investors when constructing and managing a portfolio. These strategies can be linked back to the nature of investors described in Chapter 5. The chapter examines the investment process including the choice of portfolio (fund) assets, how these choices match the preferences of potential investors, the ongoing monitoring of performance and how that is judged against certain reference behaviours (benchmarking). The chapter also looks at important elements of monitoring and managing performance including the use of indices.

An investment strategy should be shaped by the objectives of the portfolio. An investor or fund manager can only set these objectives after determining certain characteristics about the investment preferences of the investor(s). For instance, the investment objectives need to reflect the required risk and return of the investor(s), details of their existing wealth, their tax position, liquidity requirements and future liabilities. Only, after these objectives are established can an investment strategy and relevant policies be devised, and a suitable monitoring programme constituted.

The chapter is structured to cover the following main topic areas:

- The property portfolio investment process
- Property portfolio investment approaches
- Benchmarking
- Portfolio strategy and property selection
- Analysis of a portfolio's performance and reviews of strategy
- Problems with the construction of property indices
- Portfolio forecasting
- Additional management issues

C. A. Jones and E. Trevillion, *Real Estate Investment* ,
https://doi.org/10.1007/978-3-031-00968-6_8

It includes an outline of how performance measures such as capital and income returns are calculated and briefly examines issues around property forecasting. It finishes with a case study of the benchmarks in a balanced multi-asset fund.

Before we start, it is useful to spell out some relevant fund management terms. Summarised below are important terms commonly used in the fund management industry. They set the tone for the chapter, and they apply to multi-asset portfolios as well as property only portfolios:

Fund management: The administration of a pool of capital with the intention of investing the majority of the capital in a group of assets. This is distinct from *portfolio management* which is the administration of assets within the fund and *asset management* which is the administration of individual assets.

Fund mandate: The mandate of a collective investment vehicle is a statement of its aims, the limits within which it is supposed to invest, and the investment policy it should follow.

Pooled fund: A fund in which at least two investors pool their capital in an investment account. Groups such as investment clubs, partnerships and trusts use pooled funds to gather resources to invest. It can be a specialist fund as well. Investors can include financial institutions and retail funds (such as unit-linked or Property Unit Trusts).

Segregated fund: This term is used interchangeably with the term separate account. It is a portfolio managed for a single investor. This could encompass public or private pension funds, insurance companies, charities, sovereign wealth funds, etc.

Balanced fund: A fund investing across the investment spectrum, latterly taken to imply in proportions reflecting the market.

Specialist fund: A fund dedicated to one country, currency, asset type or class.

Retail funds: Such funds are sold directly to third-party investors, typically on a daily trading basis. In some cases, they are open to institutional investment as well.

Institutional funds: These are generally pension and life funds that are often not distinguished separately and can be typically put into the pooled or segregated fund category. They could also represent money managed by financial intermediaries, such as German open-ended funds.

Active management: A fund where investments are purchased and sold on a regular basis according to perceived investment opportunities.

Indexed fund: Refers to the generation of market returns from a portfolio that has been constructed to copy the structure of a market or an index.

Benchmarking: Benchmarks provide the basis on which performance is monitored and judged. They can also be used to determine strategic asset allocations and form the basis of, and characterise, investment mandates.

The Property Portfolio Investment Process

The construction and management of a property portfolio starts with the development of an investment strategy and a clear view of performance measures. These should be inter-related and there are a number of fundamental stages in this investment process which are now considered in detail.

The Asset Decision

Decisions within property portfolios are straightforward in the sense that a decision has already been made in terms of the asset of choice. Investment decisions revolve around sector and property choices and the balance of these within the portfolio.

In large multi-asset portfolios, there is a 'pre-step' which involves the decision of how to weight the different assets of choice. In such large institutional portfolios, there will be an 'asset allocator' who will be making such decisions as:

- Should the portfolio (fund) acquire tangible or intangible assets?
- How much should be invested?
- In what projects/assets?
- How much capital is available, and should additional capital be raised?
- What is the best mix of financing? Shares/Debt? Geared funds? Equity directly from investors?

Allocations to property will be managed in such circumstances as a sub-unit of the main institutional fund—with a fund manager answerable to the asset allocator and the trustees of the multi-asset fund. It is important to recognise this process in the big institutional funds, but the rest of this chapter will concentrate on the management of stand-alone property funds whether retail, segregated or specialist funds.

First Steps in Portfolio Construction

The basic first steps in portfolio construction should include the following:

- *A clear understanding of who the client is*: The aim here is to provide an initial key to understanding the client, their motivation, risk attitude, the currency of operation, etc. Is the client a private client, institutional client or is the fund a retail fund managed by the investment house for itself? This process of understanding should include an assessment of the client's financial situation including total net worth (private client), how and where assets are spread, liability matching requirements and cash flows.

- *A clear statement of its objectives*: Different investors have different objectives, for example, pension funds need to consider long-term liability matching, retail funds are probably concerned with more short-term higher risk. The development of a viable strategy involves the clear identification of the fund's investment objectives in consultation with the client. The exercise should define what the fund is trying to achieve. This should include an examination of the fund's taxation status and liability objectives (although these issues tend to be considered at the broad multi-asset level rather than the individual property level), the nature of the returns (income? capital gain? high, average or low growth?) and liquidity? The objectives have a massive and critical effect on asset allocation.
- *What are the investors' return objectives?* Are they expecting the fund to pursue a high, average or low growth strategy? However, the growth prospects tend to be linked to risk. The higher the growth target then the more risk the fund should be expected to accept.
- *Risk appetite*: How risk averse are the investors in the funds? The answer to this will clearly define the fund's risk objectives. Is the fund in pursuit of the efficient frontier (see Chapter 7) and are they market tracking (pursuit of beta?), are they pursuing abnormal returns (alpha)? Alpha (see Chapter 7) is the term used in investing to describe an investment strategy's ability to beat the market. It is often referred to as *excess return* or an *abnormal rate of return*. Alternatively, is the investment strategy aimed at achieving a required rate of return?
- *What is the time horizon for the portfolio?* The timescale over which the objectives are achieved and performance is measured is important. In modern portfolio management, three-to-five-year averages have become common. Shorter timescales for measuring the fund's achievements are regarded as unrealistic because investors cannot expect good returns every year. In addition, new managers need time to implement a new strategy and for the fund to reap the benefit of the changes.
- *Investment spectrum*: For property portfolios, the management needs to consider what the sector weighting will be and should the portfolio/fund include derivatives or other indirect investments such as REITs or fund of funds. A 'fund of funds' is an investment vehicle that holds a portfolio of other investment funds.
- *Fund mandates* normally specify restrictions. These may be severe on life and pension funds, e.g. liquidity requirements because of the need to liability match. They will include maximum investment limits, but will also consider whether it should be limited to ethical investments.
- *Investment authority*: Can the fund managers invest on their own authority (discretionary management) or what approval procedure is required? Is the mandate sufficient to allow the fund manager freedom to invest within limits?

Property Portfolio Investment Approaches

The management process for a fund (portfolio) is intimately wrapped up with the fund investment objectives and the nature of the client. The investment objective sets the tone for both the structure and management of the fund and in turn the benchmark.

In the wider investment market, the terms active, passive and tracker are used to describe a fund/vehicle's approach to management/risk. Active management is designed to beat the market's average returns and take full advantage of short-term price fluctuations. However direct property is a heterogeneous asset and unlike equities and bonds, it is not possible to have a fund/vehicle that invests in direct assets which is not active. It is possible to obtain passive and tracker-style exposure to UK property through a fund/vehicle that invests in listed property securities and/or property derivatives.

Investors will have return objectives in terms of a nominal or real total return over a given time period. A common approach that has emerged over the last 30 years is the generation of market returns from a portfolio that has been constructed to copy the structure of a market or an index. A fund that exactly replicates an index is called an index fund (or more recently still *a balanced fund*). They are developed from the view that it is not possible to beat the market or benchmark index consistently without taking higher risks, and higher management costs. In the UK, it is common to use the MSCI/IPD indices to construct a property index fund.

In competitive markets, fund managers may also choose a strategy where they benchmark the structure and performance of their fund with their competitors. This approach is like an index fund but in these circumstances, the expected return of the fund is measured relative to a competitor rather than a market index.

The risk associated with deviations away from the benchmark is called '*Tracking Error Risk*'. The closer the composition of a fund is to the structure of the benchmark then the lower the tracking error risk. The reverse is also true: other things being equal, the further away from the benchmark, the greater the tracking error risk.

A fundamental problem with creating an index or benchmark fund is that the heterogeneity of property makes it difficult to construct identical portfolios. This inevitably generates tracking error risk as the performance of the fund may differ from the market/benchmark because the specific risk of its properties may differ. The smaller the fund then the more significant is the impact of the specific risk of the properties in the portfolio because smaller funds are less able to diversify these risks away.

It can be costly to set up a diversified fund that reflects the market. In Chapter 7, it was noted that at least 25–30 assets are required to diversify away about 70% of specific risk. Theory has suggested that approaching 200 properties are required to ensure that the market explains 95% of a fund's performance and over 1000 properties are required to reflect 99% of the market. This approach is not very practical for small funds and even larger institutional funds are questioning the validity of this approach. Instead, they are adopting a more stock picking active management approach in recent years. The use of benchmarking in this way can produce a 'beta tracking' attitude in the fund manager, i.e. it doesn't matter what the total return of the fund is as long as it is better than the benchmark. This issue was amply demonstrated during the GFC when values and returns were falling significantly, but if the fund was producing returns even slightly better than the benchmark, the trustees were happy!

To address this problem, investors may simply adopt an absolute return approach where the fund is managed against an agreed target rate of return benchmark which is absolute and not index-based. These different approaches to benchmarks are now considered.

Benchmarking

Benchmarking is at the centre of this investment process and provides the basis on which performance is monitored and judged. It is also used to determine strategic asset allocation and forms the basis of investment mandates.

A benchmark may be narrowly defined as a point of reference that is used to compare investment performance. It forms an objective test of the effective implementation of an investment strategy for all asset classes. Benchmarks allow returns and variations in investment returns to be measured and attributed, thereby making it possible to determine how effectively managers have performed against them.

Benchmarks can also be used to compare the structure and the weighting of property portfolios to the constituents of a particular index. A benchmark may therefore not just be simply about financial performance in terms of returns but also about perceived risk relative to an industry investment norm in terms of the location and property sectors. In this context, the benchmark may reflect the market as a whole and hence beta. It may, however, relate to the level of risk that reflects permitted deviations from market returns.

Assessing performance against market-based benchmarks is common in the real estate investment business. These benchmarks are useful to evaluate the performance of active investment strategies or to summarise the performance of any given segment of the market. In the UK MSCI/IPD produce indices for segments of the market. Such segmentation may be geographical, by land use sector/segment, etc. Investment managers/funds that specialise in a particular sector or segment are often referred to as pursuing an 'investment style'. It is logical to have a suitable benchmark that reflects a specific market sector or investment style/specialism.

It should be made clear that benchmarks and indices are not the same thing. They are related but should not be confused. Conceptually, an index is a historical record of the performance of a market or defined market segment. Indices therefore reflect the investment performance of standing assets. On the other hand, a benchmark is a yardstick defined for the purpose of assessing the performance of investors (or managers) participating in those markets.

An index becomes a benchmark when it is used as a reference point to quantify the relative performance of an asset or a portfolio of assets. It can be argued, however, that the primary role of a benchmark is to characterise an investment mandate. The assessment of performance relative to that mandate remains important, but secondary.

A benchmark should also be distinguished from a target. A target is not used as a formal comparator of performance. Nevertheless, benchmarks can be used as targets to decide remuneration of investment managers. Investment managers may also operate within guidelines that set limits on permitted deviations in portfolio construction. They can determine the impact of benchmark composition on the standard, 'day-to-day' investment process.

In some asset classes, investment performance can be compared against an agreed index of returns from an investment universe or an appropriate index of investment opportunities. This is not straightforward in commercial property markets. The problems are that not only do index construction methodologies vary from index to index but so also does the breadth of market coverage and their representativeness. This is a global issue and an array of academic papers have detailed the differences and issues for both listed and unlisted real estate.

The choice of benchmark will be different, depending on the objectives of an investment fund, and may differ in the short- and long-term. Income-orientated funds may prefer income-related benchmarks rather than total return-based benchmarks. 'Style' or 'property type' based funds that are logically measured against a defined property type also need to address how their specific sector/segment performance relates to the broader property market. Approaches therefore differ across the industry, even within investment houses, reflecting both the nature (structure) of the fund and the specific requirements of fund mandates. The different fund characteristics mean that market-based indices may not necessarily be appropriate.

Peer Comparison

In the case of peer comparison, a specific universe is selected to reflect the performance of 'competitor funds' or those that invest and manage real estate in the same style or specialist area. These funds have similar investment strategies as that under consideration, e.g. large/small life and pension funds or similar sized and managed retail funds. The definition of size may be explicit, e.g. £50–500m or relative to the size of the benchmarked fund, e.g. half to double the size.

In the UK, this peer group comparison has been accepted by many investors. The peer group may be defined as a component or segment of a transparent index, e.g. one defined by MSCI or by a group of funds defined by the Lipper or Morning Star indices. The principal benefit of this approach is that it is a transparent method for the comparison of the constituent funds and proves relatively easy for advisors to understand and advocate.

Relative Return

Relative return benchmarks are closely related in as much as the fund performance can be measured relative to the 'peer universe' but it may simply be the return that an asset class achieves over a period of time compared to the market or sector of the market as a whole. The relative return being the comparison (difference or ratio) between the absolute return achieved by the asset/fund and the return achieved by its comparative benchmark. A relative return allows the evaluation of a manager over and above what an investor could achieve by investing directly into an index or the respective benchmark.

Absolute Return

An absolute return benchmark assesses the return of a fund/portfolio/asset over a period of time relative to an investor's target rate of return. The latter will require some assessment of the risk premium attached to property over and above some 'risk-free rate' rate of return, e.g. 10-year government bonds. The methodology has the advantage compared to other benchmarking methods in that it is simple and allows the direct comparison of performance, not only against the investors target rate of return but also against market returns globally. This approach also reduces the scenario whereby managers are rewarded when delivering negative total returns to investors simply because their returns have proved 'less negative' than the benchmark as a whole. It avoids managers being rewarded for beating the benchmark although they have delivered relatively poor returns at a property level.

Portfolio Strategy and Property Selection

The practicalities of the relationship between benchmarks, fund mandates and the choice and retention of individual assets is now considered. Buy/sell decisions translated at the individual property level will vary from organisation to organisation and clearly will be determined by the overall strategic approach. Indexed/balanced funds will buy and sell according to the property sector weightings in the index to which the fund is being compared. In this top-down approach, the focus is more strategic with property considered in the same context as other capital markets and the wider economy. The structure is integrated with stock selection to add value to the portfolio. Fund managers using this top-down strategic approach first allocate their assets to main asset groupings and sub-groupings, and then select individual securities to satisfy that allocation. Property selection factors include considerations of geography, quality, risk profile, return profile, lot size, pricing valuation and stock availability.

There is more flexibility regarding sector allocation where absolute return strategies are concerned, but regardless of the overall strategy, managers will continue to actively manage the property in their portfolios (see also earlier). In this context:

- Fund managers are constantly seeking ways to improve the performance of the portfolio both at the individual property and portfolio level.
- Each specific investment is selected for its 'attractiveness' and individual merits.
- The general aim is to add value through careful risk management.

Decisions about the ratios of cash, indirect and direct property held in the fund/portfolio may be determined by a fund asset allocation committee but the upper limits for each of these will ultimately be determined by the fund mandate. The direct property holdings are set in the fund business plan using a model portfolio for the benchmark based on top-down property forecasts. The target portfolio would consider the realities of trying to move to this position in terms of the cost/benefit and the cash available for investment.

IRR is often used in individual asset decisions since it offers a convenient method for choosing from mutually exclusive projects when capital rationing prevails. Comparison between alternatives is simplified by ranking projects according to their rate of return. However, the popularity of IRR is in part psychological—managers simply prefer a measure of investment worth which is expressed in percentage terms. However, it is not uncommon to find that the margin between a project's success and failure hinges on the enthusiasm and commitment of the person sponsoring and implementing it.

A decision also needs to be made as to whether the IRR should be compared to a defined hurdle (target) rate of return. One clear danger of simply using hurdle rates in the decision-making process is that there are potentially large errors on the forecasting of returns. Basing decisions simply on hurdle rates could result in missed good opportunities for added value later in the life of the asset. Using market forecasts and IRRs simply as a guideline allows scope for later improvement.

Analysis of a Portfolio's Performance and Reviews of Strategy

Any ongoing management of a portfolio (fund) should involve a cycle of:

- Analysis of portfolio performance
- Periodic review of current investment strategy
- Response to the review of strategy which may involve devising a new forward strategy

Performance Measurement

Performance measurement should try to answer:

- What returns have been achieved?
- How do these returns compare with other portfolios and assets?
- Has the timing of purchases been good?
- Has the ability to select good performers been good?
- Can good performance be maintained at a consistent level from period to period?
- How well-diversified is the portfolio (if appropriate)?
- What is the risk of the portfolio?
- Where are the returns coming from? Skill or luck?

Performance is measured at regular intervals to evaluate how well a fund has achieved its investment objectives. This should involve an explanation of the fund's current structure, and analysis and an explanation of the fund's recent performance. Typically, the returns would be aggregated from the performance of individual property assets based on the approaches set out in Appendix 1 of this chapter.

The overall aim is to determine if the fund has met its objectives, and to assess its performance. Specifically, the fund manager would measure the total and market risks of the portfolio to decide on the level of diversification achieved by the fund. It should also find out if the fund has under- or outperformed the market and identify the properties that performed well and those that under-performed.

Reviews of Current and Future Investment Strategy

A process of review would be undertaken on how the fund and its constituent parts (structure and stock) performed and are expected to perform in the future. It would also examine the fund's risk strategy and objectives of the portfolio to see if they are still appropriate under future market conditions. This stage involves the use of economic and property market forecasts. The property forecasts should predict expected rental values, yields, rental value growth and risk premiums. If the conclusions of the review stage are to continue with the existing portfolio structure with no changes to the assets held, then the fund manager needs to forecast the future performance of the fund to see if it will attain its investment objectives.

However, if the review recommends a revamp of the portfolio's holdings, then the fund manager needs to consider the constraints and other practicalities that may arise from restructuring the fund's stock characteristics. The fund manager may propose a new strategy for the portfolio which identifies which buildings to sell, specifies which type and location of building to buy and identifies which buildings to maintain for asset management. These changes (and resulting return/risk characteristics that are forecast) would keep the fund in line with the agreed strategy and objectives.

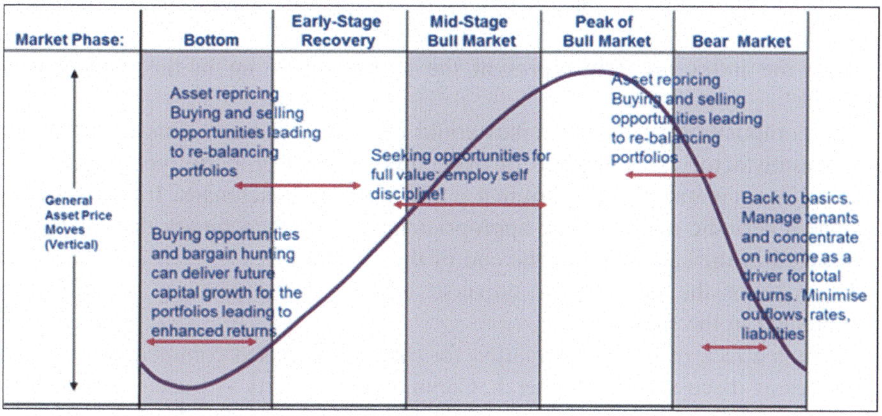

Fig. 8.1 Decision and market cycles

Inevitably the fund strategy will change and evolve over an economic cycle. An illustration of the kinds of decisions that might have to be considered over a market cycle is given in Fig. 8.1. The figure shows how at the bottom of the market cycle fund managers would be looking for buying opportunities in a market where prices have fallen with a view to capital growth as the cycle progresses. At the peak of the market consideration ought to be given to rebalancing portfolios before market prices once again fall (assuming that forecasting models are in place to anticipate these changes). At the bottom of the market, it is important to manage tenants and concentrate on current income flows as a driver for total returns where capital growth is low or negative.

Problems with the Construction of Property Indices

Property portfolio monitoring depends on real estate indices but it is important to recognise their limitations. It is easy in the share and stock market to construct an index by aggregating the market value of assets. The assets being monitored are homogeneous and the prices are precise and openly disclosed. For example, the FT index is measured hourly. The FT-SE100 index mimics a basic market portfolio that is frequently measured as a weighted index of the top 100 shares quoted on the London Stock Exchange. Investors who wish to hold a market portfolio can easily copy the structure of this portfolio because the shares held in the benchmark are identical to the other shares available in the market. It is not so easy for direct property. There are several important questions around the use of property market indices.

- To what extent does the index fully represent the total market under consideration?
- Does the index properly represent the sector weighting in the market as a whole?
- The composition of the universes could change over time. This could create an unsatisfactory bias in terms of the composition of property types, sectors or areas in comparison to the original purpose of the benchmark. It could necessitate a periodic review of the appropriateness of the benchmark that is applied as noted in the case study at the end of the chapter.
- The size of the data set or universe influences the property specific risk contained in the sample.
- There is a lack of price information for transaction-based commercial property indices as discussed in Chapter 1. Commercial property is traded infrequently with very little information made available on the finer details of the transactions. This does not make it impossible to construct indices based on transaction prices, but it does make it difficult. Commercial property indices are generally appraisal-based. This issue is considered further in Chapter 12.
- Depreciation of property occurs over time. Do we include depreciation on individual assets when the market as a whole will not be depreciating?
- Smoothing. Most commercial property market indices are based on valuations. As noted previously, this can result in smoothing with the volatility of the valuation-based indices being lower than actual market values. It tends to be worse for monthly and quarterly series than annual series.

There are issues with information accessibility and transparency of data, although this is improving, but there remains the potential for misinformation and data manipulation.

Portfolio Forecasting

All investment decisions (regardless of the strategy taken) are concerned with the future performance of a portfolio. The practical application of the investment process requires the calculation of the expected return and risk to the portfolio structure assuming a fund remains the same. This forecast can be for any appropriate period although annual forecasts are most widely used.

Expected return is based on forecasts of rental income which are applied to the appropriate pricing model. It is not just a question of adding the individual return that an additional property provides but what are the implications for the risk and return of the whole portfolio? The selection of properties for a portfolio cannot be undertaken in isolation but must also consider the covariance of returns between them.

A further issue is the size of the property portfolio required to minimise specific risk. As we have noted above, the expected risk can be measured by the variance of the expected returns, although expected risk can also be calculated as tracking error risk associated with tracker funds. An investment with a high variance of returns but a low correlation of returns with other investments in the portfolio may be less risky, from a portfolio perspective, than an investment which has a lower variance but a higher correlation with the other investments in the portfolio.

The practical application of monitoring and property stock selection requires a range of market forecasts. Over the years, property researchers have produced models which attempt to describe how the commercial property market works and to forecast future behaviour. Many of these models are econometric-based and although they may partially capture how the market works at the aggregate level, it is questionable whether they offer any real insight into the underlying processes at work. The practicalities of these models are considered further in Appendix 2 of this chapter.

Additional Management Issues

After reviewing the historic and predicted future performance, fund managers will attempt to identify the under-performing properties held in a portfolio. They will also involve monitoring the property market to find mispriced properties and identify sectors of the market expected to perform above average. The consequence of this review is that they may decide to sell existing stock but purchase new assets. However, there are several other practicalities that a fund manager must consider when restructuring a property portfolio. These are:

- **Lot size**: The average lot size varies across property type and location. The small size of a fund may constrain property selection by limiting investment to smaller properties, which in turn will influence its strategy. However, larger funds may be able to buy larger, more expensive properties and still achieve a well-diversified portfolio.
- **New money expected in fund**: New cash inflows may be available for the restructuring of a portfolio. This would allow the fund manager to acquire new assets without disposing of existing holdings. However, if sales are required, this may influence the scale and timing of the implementation of a strategic change in a portfolio's structure.
- **Market conditions**: In poor market conditions, difficulty may arise in selling properties because it is essentially a buyers' market. On the other hand, prices in weak markets are depressed so this is the ideal time to acquire new assets.
- **Market size**: The sale or purchase of a property may influence the market. This depends on the scale of the market, the size of the property and possibly the nature of the property fund itself. The smaller the market and the larger the size of the property then the greater the impact a disposal or acquisition will have on market prices.
- **Costs**: Transaction and implementation costs also need to be built into the calculations. For example, can the restructuring be achieved in the desired period

with existing staff and money resources? Such constraints will impede the restructuring of a portfolio.

All funds have a mandate and in the end a fund manager is answerable to the investors. The trustees of a fund/investors expect several things from a fund/fund manager:

- *Good performance*: As noted, the investment objectives are generally set over 3–5 years but performance is monitored regularly (with quarterly reports typical).
- *Performance explanation*: How and why the fund performed in a language the trustee understands! These should include explanations of poor performance periods.
- *Continuity of management*: Fund managers preferably with the fund for a number of years offering a chance to build up a relationship with the trustees.
- *Regular and clear reports.*
- *Good and efficient administration.*

Summary

The chapter has examined the overall investment strategies used by investors when constructing and managing a portfolio and has looked at the investment process including the choice of assets in a portfolio and the ongoing monitoring of performance and how that is judged against certain reference behaviours (benchmarking).

An investment strategy should be shaped by the objectives of the portfolio. An investor or fund manager can only set these objectives after determining certain characteristics about the investment preferences of the investor(s). For instance, the investment objectives need to reflect the required risk and return of the investor(s), details of their existing wealth, their tax position, liquidity requirements and future liabilities. A clear understanding is also required of who the client is, the time horizon of the portfolio and the manager's investment authority. Only, after these details are established can an investment strategy and relevant policies be devised, and a suitable monitoring programme be constituted.

Whereas in the wider investment market, a fund/vehicle's approach to management/risk encompasses active, passive and tracker type management, the choices for property funds are restricted by the very nature of property assets. Direct property is a heterogeneous asset and unlike equities and bonds it is not possible to have a fund/vehicle that invests in direct assets which is not active. Fund managers are constantly seeking ways to improve the performance of the portfolio both at the individual property and portfolio level. The general aim is to add value through careful risk management.

The ongoing management of a portfolio (fund) should involve a cycle of performance measurement, the periodic review of current investment strategy and, inevitably, a response to the review of strategy, which may involve devising a new forward strategy.

Benchmarking is at the centre of this investment process and provides the basis on which performance is monitored and judged. It is also used to determine strategic asset allocation and forms the basis of investment mandates. The choice of benchmark will be different depending on the objectives of investment funds and may differ in the short and long term.

In the property market, indices are derived as estimates of market activity and to benchmark the performance of property against the performance of other investment media. The chapter notes the problems associated with the use of indices to benchmark funds, particularly with regard to the nature of the index universe and how that changes over time. It potentially requires a periodic review of the appropriateness of benchmarks.

Notwithstanding the potential problems associated with indices, they are a fundamental aid that enables investors and fund managers to make informed decisions when they are constructing and measuring the performance of multi-asset and property only portfolios.

In all of this, it is important to recognise that inevitably the fund strategy will change and evolve over an economic cycle. At the bottom of a cycle, the managers' objectives ought to be quite different to their approach at the top of the cycle. On the one hand, they ought to be looking for buying opportunities, at the same time managing their existing tenants while on the other, they should be looking to rebalance their fund where opportunity allows.

Learning Outcomes

Having completed this chapter, the reader should be able to:

- Appreciate the different approaches to property portfolio management.
- Understand the objectives behind the development of a portfolio investment strategy.
- Appreciate the constraints a fund manager may face.
- Understand how fund managers and financial institutions monitor the performance of property portfolios.
- Be aware of the data available to measure and monitor the performance of property assets.
- Understand how different indices are constructed and what they measure.
- Appreciate the difficulty in constructing property indices.
- Understand how total returns and its components are calculated.

Case Study: The Benchmarks of a UK Balanced Multi-Asset Fund

This case study is taken from Trevillion et al. (2021). It is of a balanced institutional portfolio within a substantial multi-asset investment house that has invested in commercial real estate over a long time period. It is included to demonstrate how benchmarks do change over time to represent both the changing face of the fund and of the benchmark data itself.

This real estate portfolio has been in operation for decades and is a segregated mandate that accepts no external investment. It retains substantial holdings across the three traditional United Kingdom property sectors of retail, office and industrial. The portfolio also invests directly in some of the more recently established alternative sectors. The portfolio now sits within an expanded real estate offer that includes retail investment products, and specialist and international investment vehicles.

During the research study, the authors spoke directly with members of staff who had responsibility for the development and implementation of benchmarking policy, leading towards its formal establishment with the adoption of IPD in 1985. Prior to that date monitoring was very rudimentary, comprising crude cash flows of the portfolio. The fund has participated in IPD benchmarking since its foundation. Since that time, the portfolio has had only five managers, which has contributed to the stability of the fund with consistent preference for relative benchmarking.

Benchmark A

From the outset until 2003, the benchmark applied was the returns of non-unitised life funds in IPD.

Benchmark B

By the late 1990s and early 2000s, the mis-selling of endowment policies produced serious challenges for life assurance companies, particularly in relation to their with-profits business. These policies proved not to be value for money and fell out of favour with the public. There was also increased competition driven by the establishment and success of lower-cost unit-linked vehicles. This led to a major reduction in the number of non-unitised life funds, so the benchmark was redefined in 2004 as Life funds greater than £1bn in the IPD database.

Benchmark C

In a similar vein, the benchmark had to be adjusted again to reflect changes and consolidation in the market after the global financial crisis. As a result, the benchmark was changed to extend it to encompass pension funds while reducing the threshold size required. In addition, one IPD market segment was deleted from the benchmark because the view was taken that the sample contained in that data was not representative of that particular subsector. The benchmark was then defined from 2011 as Life & Pension Funds >£500m, with specific benchmarking data removed from the IPD database.

Benchmark D
In 2015, a decision was taken to remove the exclusion of benchmarking data on the subsector agreed upon when implementing the previous change in 2011. The benchmark therefore was simplified to Life & Pension Funds >£500m.

Benchmark E
In the middle of 2018, the benchmark was changed to the IPD Quarterly Universe. The principal driver behind the change was again the declining sample of the database.

Appendix 1: Performance Measurement

Typically, the return from a property asset is used as the measure of performance. This can take the form of capital or income returns or a combination (total returns). Rental growth and yield are also important measures of performance.

In a *single month period*, **total return** is the sum of capital appreciation (net of capital expenditure) and receipts plus net income expressed as a percentage of capital employed (Eq. 8.1)

$$TR_i = \frac{(CV_t - CV_{(t-1)} - CExp_t + CRpt_t + NI_t)}{CV_{(t-1)} + CExp_t} \tag{8.1}$$

where:

TR_i = total return in month t
CV_t = capital value at the end of month t
$CExp_t$ = total capital expenditure in month t
$CRpt_t$ = total capital receipts (including sales) in month t
NI_t = day-dated rent receivable during month t net of property management costs, ground rent and other irrecoverable expenditure

Income return is the net income receivable for the month expressed as a percentage of the capital employed (value at the beginning of the period), as noted in Eq. 8.2.

$$INCR_t = NI_t/(CV_{t-1} + CExp_t) \tag{8.2}$$

where:

$INCR_t$ = income return for period t
NI_t = net income received during period t (net of outgoings/expenses)

The income from investment property is the rental income minus any outgoings paid by the investors (e.g. internal and external repairs, management costs, insurance premiums and general services). The rental income is usually measured as the current contractual rent paid by the tenant for the occupation of the subject property. For unoccupied properties or properties subject to a rent review, the expected rental income is calculated (otherwise stated in the unexpired lease) as the open market rental value. This is estimated using recent comparable market transactions.

Capital growth is the increase in the value of properties net of capital expenditure expressed as a percentage of the capital employed over the month as set out in Eq. 8.3.

$$CVG_t = \frac{(CV_t - CV_{(t-1)} - CExp_t + CRpt_i)}{CV_{(t-1)} + CExp_t} \tag{8.3}$$

Rates of Return

There are two main approaches to calculating the rate of return, the money-weighted rate of return and time-weighted total return.

Money-weighted rates of return (MWRR) are the same as the IRR of a discounted cash flow and are calculated by finding the discount rate which equates the initial outlay with the present value of all future income and expenditure flows over the period. Generally, MWRR is used as a measure of return over a single time period and is appropriate for funds where the manager has control over cash flows. It takes account of the amount invested in each period.

The time-weighted total return is more complex and allows a fund manager to take account of inflows and outflows occurring at different points. It breaks up the return on a portfolio into separate intervals based on whether income was added or withdrawn from the fund.

Appendix 2: Practicalities of Forecasting

A fund will forecast a string of variables for a range of property sectors. In the UK, these typically use indices such as the MSCI index as the basis for the forecasts with the main outputs being rental growth, equivalent yields, capital growth , income return and total return. These will be attempted for a range of property sectors and, where data exists, at the national and regional/sub-regional level.

The nature of UK and regional economic output, employment, retail sales and government bond yield forecasts stamp their mark on the shape of property forecasts. Macro-economic factors such as interest (swap) rates and inflation in particular impact on yield forecasts but investor preferences and the weight of money coming into property are clearly also important. In general, real estate forecasts are built on a foundation of macroeconomic forecasts for growth, retail sales, manufacturing and services employment and output, inflation, interest rates and gilt yields.

The forecasting of yields is particularly difficult as it brings together assessments of several components and drivers of yield. These include swap rates, long run rental trends, gilt yields, estimates of the current and future risk premium, inflation and depreciation. These are combined with a reversion parameter which dictates the extent to which yield forecasts are brought back to their long-term fundamental value.

In order to calculate returns and capital growth, it is necessary to make assumptions about a variety of other factors. This is generally done in some form of simulation model, effectively a cash flow model applied to forecast rents and yields for the various sectors. The models take into account market void rates, lease lengths/renewals, degree of over-renting, etc., to produce estimates of: income returns, total returns and capital growth.

Limitations

The limitations of these models to reality are well-understood, in particular, their inability to understand the process of change and to forecast turning points in the market, because their behavioural properties are weak. Matysiak et al. (2012) and Watkins et al. (2012) provide broader explanations of the problems.

For models of the market to be truly representative, it is necessary to understand and model the process of change, as well as modelling the system's longer-term behaviour. Econometric models have some difficulty in doing this. They are relatively successful in a stable market with slow changes, but they have not been able to cope with rapid change in the cycle as was experienced, for example, during the GFC. There was a total failure to forecast the severe drop in values and returns experienced over the period 2007–2009, or for that matter the recovery. To some extent, this is the fault of the economic forecasts used as inputs to property forecasts but also partly as a result on the linear nature of the econometric forecasts used for property markets. These models do not account for investor behaviour but really just extrapolate existing trends.

Notwithstanding their limitations, econometric type models will represent the mainstay of forecasting approaches for some time to come. However, a more inductive type of approach is now being explored to incorporate behavioural aspects into forecasts (see Trevillion 2021) but whatever type of approach is adopted, the forecasting of yields will remain problematic because of the behavioural components of this variable.

Reading

Baum, A. (2015) *Real Estate Investment: A Strategic Approach.* Routledge, London.

Brown, G. and Matysiak, G. (1995) Using commercial property indices for measuring portfolio performance. *Journal of Property Finance*, 6, 27–38.

Brown, G. R. and Matysiak, G. A. (2000) *Real Estate Investment: A Capital Market Approach.* Financial Times, Prentice Hall, Harlow.

Investment Property Forum (2017) *Understanding UK Commercial Property Investments: A Guide for Financial Advisers.* Investment Property Forum, London.

Matysiak, G., Papastamos, D. and Stevenson, S. (2012) *Reassessing the Accuracy of UK Commercial Property Forecasts, Research Report*. Investment Property Forum, London.
MSCI (2014) *IPD Indexes and Benchmark Methodology Guide*. MSCI, London.
Trevillion, E, Gardner, A., Cowe, S. and Jones, C. (2021) Current practices in benchmarking real estate investment performance. *Journal of Real Estate Portfolio Management*, 26, 2, 118–131.
Trevillion, E. (2021) Using system dynamics modelling to understand behaviour in UK commercial property markets. *Journal of European Real Estate Research*, forthcoming.
Watkins, C., White, M. and Keskin, B. (2012) *The Future of Property Forecasting, Investment Property Forum Research Report*. Investment Property Forum, London.

The Internationalisation of Property Investment

9

Introduction

The organisation of economic activity, and with it commercial property markets, has become increasingly global and integrated over the last three decades. Despite trends in some regions towards nationalism and fragmentation, markets are much more integrated compared to the early 1990s. The single European market is largely still intact rivalling the economic strength of North America, and the rise of the economies in the Far East and Asian Pacific Rim has led to the formation of a third large integrated trading bloc.

China has emerged as the world's fastest growing large economy, and more recently, India has also begun to open up to, and benefit from global economic forces. This integration has created a wide choice of investment opportunities but with sufficient segmentation to allow for diversification at home and abroad, and the opportunity for a variety of investment strategies. How BREXIT will impact on UK markets, both financial and property, is yet to be fully realised at the time of writing, but the UK remains a strong player globally, at least, in the short to medium term.

This chapter aims to provide an analysis of this internationalisation process. It undertakes an in-depth analysis of investment issues relating to the ownership, management, valuation, development and acquisition of property in international property markets. Specifically, it includes:

- Globalisation
- Real estate market segmentation and integration
- The case for international real estate investment
- Formal and informal barriers to overseas investment
- Global real estate investment
- Internationalisation of real estate cycles
- Market maturity

C. A. Jones and E. Trevillion, *Real Estate Investment*,
https://doi.org/10.1007/978-3-031-00968-6_9

- Internationalisation and property related practices.

As part of the discussion of market maturity, case studies analyse some emerging markets in Eastern Europe and Asia and separately examine the characteristics of global cities. The chapter also looks at the impact of political risk and nationalism on segmentation in the context of BREXIT and Scottish independence.

Globalisation

For much of the twentieth century international property markets were fragmented with mature (established) markets limited, generally speaking, to Europe, North America and British Commonwealth countries on the Pacific Rim. Even in these countries there was no real harmonisation of market practices apart from countries where legal systems mirrored those of the UK.

The globalisation of financial and property markets really only developed towards the end of the twentieth century and was driven by socio, economic and political changes worldwide. Although it has been argued that the globe has become more democratic, and there is no doubt that this has led to greater harmonisation in general, the real game-changer has been the move to economic neo-liberalism and global capitalisation. Irrespective of whether governments are considered democratic or not, it is recognised and accepted that this economic approach had the potential for providing greater market efficiency compared to strict command economies.

With this change came, in many cases, the removal of barriers to international interaction, for example, because of the fall of command economies in Central and Eastern Europe, the collapse of apartheid in South Africa and the adoption of more liberal economic policies within the communist regimes of China and Vietnam.

A very early step towards the integration of global financial services came with the Bretton Woods Agreement in July 1944. It had the principal goals of creating an efficient foreign exchange system, preventing competitive devaluations of currencies and promoting international economic growth. The Bretton Woods Agreement also created two important organisations—the International Monetary Fund (IMF) and the World Bank. The broad aim of the IMF was to establish an exchange rate regime and facilitate the balanced growth of free international trade, and to encourage the provision of private investment. The World Bank started business in 1947, and the intention was to link it to the IMF.

While the Bretton Woods System was dissolved in the 1970s, both the IMF and World Bank have remained strong pillars for the exchange of international currencies. The current aims of the IMF and World Bank are to control balance of payment deficits and provide the funds and technical advice on finance to less developed countries.

Other important changes in the way financial markets were structured occurred during the 1970s and 1980s and these also helped to promote free markets and trade. They encouraged the international movement of capital by de-regulating and liberalising financial institutions. The period saw the deregulation of stock markets in the United States in 1975, in Japan through the mid-1980s and in the UK in 1986. These large-scale changes were referred to as 'the Big Bang'. There were also changes in regulatory banking legislation from the 1970s including for example in the United States during the early mid-1980s. In parallel, the rapid development of international information networks that linked the major financial centres of the world enabled a 24-hour trading day, although a downside was that this promoted the potential for a much higher volatility in financial markets because of the interlinking of these markets.

The globalisation of business activity was also a continuing process driven by the desire to command global presence through organic growth and/or acquisition. It led to the conversion of ownership of successful companies from domestic to multinational concerns and the increasing opportunities offered to corporations, institutional investors and banks to own overseas assets through globally traded stock markets.

Collectively these changes fundamentally altered the flow of capital and foreign direct investment (FDI) from existing mature economies. It ultimately resulted in notable increases in the levels of global trade and with it flows of international capital seeking the highest risk adjusted return. In this context, *The World Trade Organisation* recognises two types of capital flows:

- Portfolio investment where an investor resident in one country invests in stocks, bonds and other financial instruments in another country.
- FDI where an investor based in one country acquires physical assets in the other country with the intention of managing them.

However, FDI involves the transfer of much more than capital alone. Technological expertise, marketing and management skills and other firm specific resources are transferred to the host country as well. Portfolio investors exercise very little, if any, control of the asset and thus are typically passive investors. As a result, FDI is much more likely to influence local property markets since both goods and services may be (are) supplied locally.

The type of property in use markets is determined by the nature of FDI. The increasing importance of FDI is reflected in the global growth of inflows from \$51.4bn in 1980 to \$1631bn in 2019 (The World Bank 2021).

This increase in international trade has seen trade relationships increasingly formalised. Thus the period since World War II has seen the creation in Europe of the European Union (1993), with its origins in the European Coal and Steel Community founded in 1951. Other continents have seen the North America Free Trade Association (NAFTA), founded in 1994, and the Association of South East Asian Nations (ASEAN). The latter was initially a political grouping founded in 1967 but progressively became a trade organisation which expanded over the period 1984–1999. In 2020 the Regional Comprehensive Economic Partnership was set up, a trade arrangement between China and 14 countries in the ASIA–Pacific region.

These new alliances reinforced the apparent benefits of free trade and the acceptance that this economic approach had the potential for providing greater market efficiency compared to strict command economies. The removal of trade and market barriers has led to greater international economic integration and has given rise to an increase in cross-border mobility of raw materials and goods; business activity and services; technology, information and expertise; as well as knowledge and education. They have altered the location and mix of industries throughout the globe. These phenomena have also given rise to major alterations in occupation and investment demand that have reshaped the built environment.

However, despite this major change in attitude over the last 60 or so years, the benefits of economic openness have been under increasing scrutiny in Western countries, giving rise to nationalism and populist politics. Communities in the United States, the UK and other countries in the EU have felt a threat to their livelihoods from global competition, both offshore and at home. There have also been concerns about immigration. It has been argued that the rise of populism can be attributed to many people's perception that the economic system is rigged for the benefit of 'insiders', enabling huge gains for an elite set of gatekeepers without benefitting ordinary citizens.

Real Estate Market Segmentation and Integration

Although there is now much greater interaction between markets, there are still barriers to the harmonisation of asset values (whether financial or property based) allowing plenty of opportunity for diversification. Constraints may exist in many countries that prevent investors from investing in overseas markets or inhibit the speed by which investment flows can switch between markets. The constraints may be financial, or legal or due to differences in working practices. If these constraints give rise to significant additional costs and risks to the foreign investor, then they may cause market segmentation through affecting asset prices. If segmentation occurs, then the simple pricing relations between different markets will break down so that assets with the same risk characteristics will have different values.

Property markets are no different. International market imperfections and constraints will prevent the integration of a 'global' property market and the full synchronisation of property values. A few examples of the factors that may segment property markets include:

- Differences in the quality and amount of market information available.
- Language barriers.
- Psychological barriers to foreign investments and investors' perceptions of risk.
- Different valuation practices and legal frameworks.
- Taxes, penalties and restrictions to cross-border transactions.

The process of removing these barriers is called harmonisation. However, this a-synchronicity is a major motive for international real estate investment which is now covered in the next section.

The Case for International Real Estate Investment

Diversification is the principle motivational factor for institutions holding international property investments. The principles of overseas diversification are no different to those discussed around portfolio theory in Chapter 7. International investment can provide access to higher potential returns than are available domestically. It allows access to a larger universe of properties as well as faster growing economies and access to different sectors of the market at different stages of maturity as well as an opportunity to obtain higher returns. However, the appetite for investing overseas (and the type of international asset to hold) varies according to the institution/individual/organisation involved and their investment preferences.

Diversification by institutional investors is a powerful driver of international activity. If domestic returns are perceived to be disappointing, then domestic money will seek returns overseas. The sheer pressure and weight of money arising from a variety of sovereign wealth funds (see Chapter 5) has also driven overseas investment and it is now very unusual for a large investor not to have a global property strategy.

Whether overseas or domestically, one of the main reasons given for diversification is the reduction of specific risk (risk diversification). We will not dwell too long on this aspect here since it is covered in detail under portfolio theory earlier in Chapter 7, but it is worth reprising elements of the theory. The risk of a portfolio is a function of the standard deviation of individual asset's returns (volatility) and the correlation of returns between assets. The removal of non-market (specific or non-systematic) risk may be achieved by constructing diversified portfolios of assets whose correlations are less than unity. Specific risk is that risk which relates to the individual characteristics of an investment and it is this element of risk that can be diversified.

The other element of risk in a portfolio, which it is not possible to diversify away, is market risk, also referred to as systematic or non-specific risk. This risk relates to the economic and financial factors that affect the performance of all assets and asset classes. The systematic risk of a portfolio within a single country is linked to country specific factors. These include national monetary policies that affect interest rates, inflation, the cost of capital, the political situation, the business cycle and institutional, social and demographic factors.

A country's economic policy has a big impact on diversification so that market risk is just as important as specific risk in investment decision-making. On this basis the rationale behind international diversification is that a global portfolio strategy enables investors to select markets which have different economic drivers or are at different stages of their economic cycle. This is less manageable where portfolios are structured across a number of borders. It is still difficult in trade groupings where, in theory, there is more uniformity in economic practices, for example, in the EU where economies are converging, and market risk are coming together. Even here though there is sufficient segregation to make market risk an issue, so cross-border investment in the same portfolio may still be problematic in this regard.

The question arises as to whether buying into large foreign markets with different market risk means that the cost of reducing *specific* risk is higher because to gain benefits the investor needs to invest significantly in each market rather than a single market.

Corporate investors will also invest overseas for operational or strategic business reasons, such as matching liabilities in a particular country. As these organisations expand their core businesses, they will acquire land and buildings in these markets, partly to meet liabilities. In a properly functioning international capital market, it is unlikely that a rational firm would invest in foreign property unless they possess some advantage over local firms or there are clear diversification benefits. Typical advantages may be that foreign investors have lower costs of capital or domestic firms may be restricted from investing in property.

City level effects are important even where countries in different world regional economies have come together but institutions and institutional behaviour and their attitude (prejudice?) is still an important factor regarding where to invest overseas.

Diversification opportunities still exist worldwide and mature property markets appear to have been effective diversifiers against all domestic assets, especially gilts and equities. In addition, diversification possibilities amongst mature European markets remain despite economic harmonisation in those markets.

Formal and Informal Barriers to Overseas Investment

There are a series of barriers which still need to be addressed regardless of the reasons behind an investor choosing to invest in foreign property. These may be both formal and informal. Formal barriers include problems around national professional accreditation, restrictions on foreign ownership and restrictions on foreign residents. Informal barriers include traditions concerning market practice, the status of professions, business culture and language and cultural factors.

Higher costs and market restrictions are the most cited reasons for being unable to compete on an even playing field. Some examples of these disadvantages could be higher information costs, cultural barriers to understanding the market, unfamiliar real estate practices, the high costs of acquisition and monitoring and the riskiness of adverse currency movements. An example of legal restrictions that disadvantage institutional investors in foreign markets are the laws imposed on German pension funds that control the location of their investments and the proportion of funds held in 'risky' assets like property. The legal requirements for real estate funds in Germany are quite narrow and some extend only applicable to domestic investment vehicles.

Solnik (1996) identifies five major difficulties associated with investing in all international capital and financial markets:

- *Familiarity*: The investor may not know or fully understand the practices or operations involved in an overseas market. They may also have difficulty obtaining and assessing information on market opportunities and performance.
- *Regulations*: These may restrict or prohibit foreign ownership, have a restrictive regulatory framework and constrain the repatriation of capital and profits.
- *Market efficiency*: In some markets, particularly smaller markets, liquidity problems, pricing inefficiency and manipulation/obstacles to capital flows may affect the efficient operation of the pricing mechanism.
- *Risk perception*: Concerns over political and currency stability may discourage investors.
- *Cost structures*: International assets may generate higher costs in terms of information gathering and monitoring, management fees and currency transmission costs. These costs may not be fully reflected in performance measures.

These five difficulties are largely related to information costs and are compounded in the real estate market by property's characteristics together with the institutional structure of markets and a range of management costs.

These issues are not as significant as they were. Although they continue to represent barriers to cross-border investment they have been mitigated in recent years by the increasing involvement of international real estate consultancy service providers as overseas markets have matured, the gradual development of international indices by the likes of MSCI/IPD and the use of joint ventures with local partners. Some specific problems are now considered in more detail.

Currency Risk

Currency risk to international investment is a general issue. A devaluation of a currency could have disastrous implications for the returns from a real estate investment in a particular country, wiping out any rental returns and leading to a real fall in capital value. It has been mitigated in Europe with the almost universal use of the Euro across countries of the EU. But with this exception it is a barrier to international investment across countries of the world.

There are three main types of currency risk:

- *Transaction risk*: Currency movements can result in a price differential arising between the sale price agreed in an overseas property transaction and the price paid upon legal transfer. This can be mitigated in the short term with currency hedges.
- *Translation risk*: Currency movements may affect the value of notional repatriated income streams and capital values in a company's accounts from one year to the next.

- *Economic risk*: The value of an asset when sold depends on the economic and political policies of the country the property resides in. Changes in exchange rates expose assets held within the country to economic risk. It is difficult to totally hedge against economic risk.

Exchange rates can therefore have a large impact on the returns to investors since currency fluctuations can be significant and, if left of unhedged, currency exposure can significantly increase the overall riskiness of the investment. Hedging is the process of reducing the uncertainty associated with exchange rate movements. It is used to protect against changes in the value of an investment due to currency fluctuations. Possible hedging instruments include forward contracts, future contracts, various currency options and currency swaps.

Forward contracts are negotiated contractual agreements to purchase (sell) a sum of foreign currency at a specified price (in domestic currency) on a specified date. No money is exchanged when contracts are signed. They are typically for one year or less.

Future contracts are like forward contracts, but they are standardised contracts traded and regulated on exchanges. They are more liquid than forward contracts. There are daily cash flow adjustments as the exchange rate and settlement price changes (marked to market).

Currency options are the right, but not the obligation, to buy or sell an amount of foreign currency at a particular price on a particular day. An up-front premium payable to acquire the option makes it an expensive vehicle. They also suffer from the absence of long-term contracts that can be bought or sold in a secondary market. This makes the hedging of income cash flows complex.

With currency swaps the investor agrees with a financial intermediary to swap a set capital sum and fixed cash flows from the domestic currency into the required foreign currency. The currency swaps are designed to have the same value (in the domestic currency) as the capital required for the purchase (sale) of property investment at the time of the acquisition (disposal).

A more straightforward way of hedging currency risk is by using local currency in transactions (leveraging or using debt provision in the local currency for transactions). Borrowings in foreign currency perfectly hedge the currency risk of the debt component of the investment made.

An investor is also able to hedge the rental income where it is known with some certainty. However, while hedging products can help reduce exchange rate risk for income returns, they are perhaps less helpful for the capital gain element, which is only realised on final sale, and this component will be more exposed to currency volatility.

Taxation Issues

Returns achieved by investors are reduced by taxes and fees. Pension funds, which are tax exempt in their own domicile, may suffer some taxation when investing internationally. For an investor, taxes may be applied in the domicile of the fund or in its own domicile (e.g. capital gains, income taxes).

Taxes may also be applied to the holding entity (e.g. a special purpose vehicle) in the domicile of the property (local taxes) or the domicile of the fund. Taxes may be applied to the entity in the domicile of the entity and taxes can be applied to the property in the domicile of the property. This can be a complex and expensive business and potentially a major barrier to overseas investment.

Political and Title Risk

This problem often express itself in the form of inflation, high taxation, lower GDP growth and other impacts which are not conducive to successful property investment. Political risk can encompass a range of hazards, from unexpected punitive taxation for investors and exchange controls, new limits on nondomestic ownership of real state, and even land and property nationalisation. Political risk can also be extended to cover the risk of defective legal title, a potential problem in the former communist countries of Central and Eastern Europe. At its most extreme, however, founded or unfounded perceptions of political risk can make the country un-investable.

The advantages and disadvantages of investing overseas are summarised in Table 9.1.

Global Real Estate Investment

As noted above globalisation has brought a significant expansion in international real estate investment but it is notoriously difficult to estimate the size of the global property market. MSCI (2020) estimates the total global professionally managed investable stock at £9.6 trillion of which \$3.16 trillion was in Europe, \$3.78 trillion in North America and \$2.57 trillion in Asia Pacific. These estimates only cover 32 markets and exclude Russia, so do not give a complete view of global markets, but the estimates do cover most of the professionally managed invested stock worldwide. Other estimates place the global stock of property that is of sufficient quality to become institutional much higher at \$32 trillion at the end of 2014 (Baum 2015).

Table 9.1 Some of the pros and cons of investing in overseas property

Pros	Cons
• Access to a larger universe of properties • Potential access to faster growing economies • Access to different sectors of the property market and at different stages of maturity	• Currency risk • Lack of transparency and liquidity in some markets • Concerns over title/legal issues • More limited data

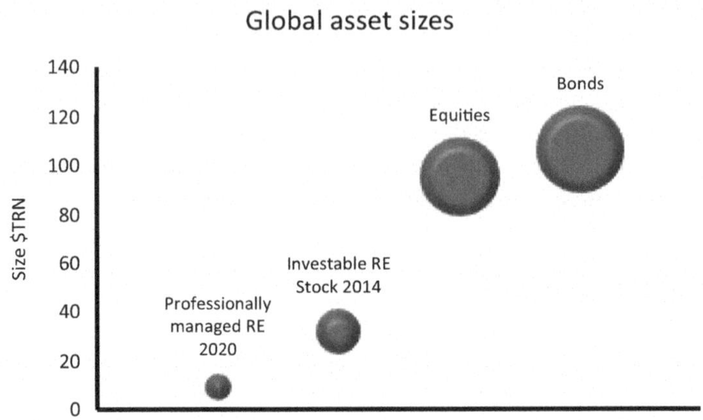

Fig. 9.1 Global asset sizes (*Source* Authors construct derived from SIFMA [2021] and MSCI [2020])

Although commercial property is a significant asset class, it is small compared to equities ($95 trillion global equities capitalisation) and fixed income ($105.9 trillion global bond markets outstanding value) in 2020. These relative sizes of these asset classes are shown graphically in Fig. 9.1.

Foreign investors, notably the Asians and Americans, and more recently Europeans have become increasingly active in overseas markets. Figure 9.2 illustrates the main cross-border capital flows for property in 2020 and demonstrates the significance of American investors.

The UK real estate market has been a particular focus of the expansion in foreign investment. Prior to the mid-1980s, British institutions dominated in the UK property market. However, this position radically altered in the late 1980s when foreign institutional funding into UK property equalled the level of UK institutional investment. The most important investors then were the Japanese and Swedish. The reasons for this increasing trend can be attributed to the good and stable long-term prospects that investors expected in this established market, especially the London office market. The trend was supported by the freeing up of the financial markets through 'big bang' in 1986. In the mid- and late 1990s, German investors were the dominant players undertaking over one-third of total European activity. By the late 1990s many landmark buildings in London were owned by overseas investors.

By 2017 nearly 50% of all-property purchases in the UK were undertaken by overseas investors (£32.3bn of £65.7bn). The proportion in the UK office market was even higher at 65% (£15.8bn of £24.22bn). By 2020 the UK was the top destination for cross-border capital flows (Fig. 9.3).

Although historically financial institutions have been big players in international property markets, sovereign wealth funds have been increasingly active. A sovereign wealth fund (SWF) is a state-owned investment fund comprised

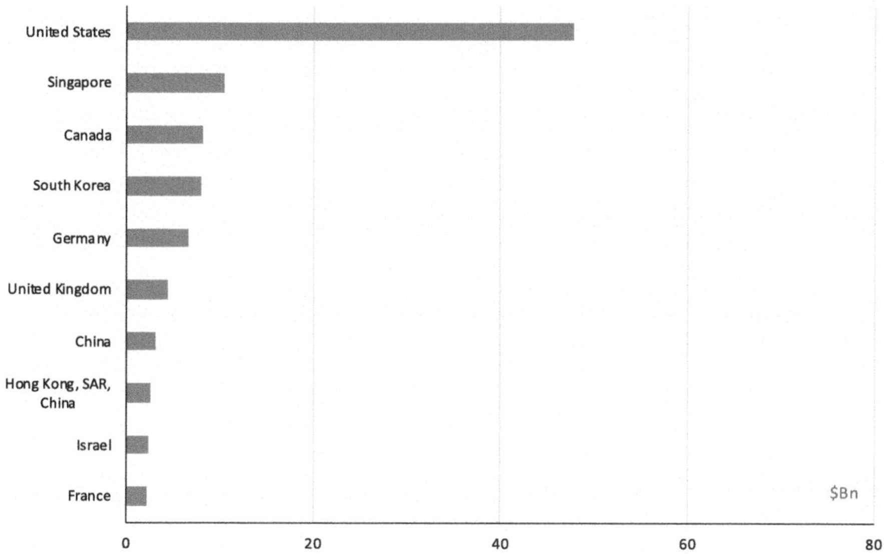

Fig. 9.2 Top 10 sources of cross-border capital into property globally in 2020 ($Bn) (*Source* Derived from MSCI Real Capital Analytics [2020] with permission)

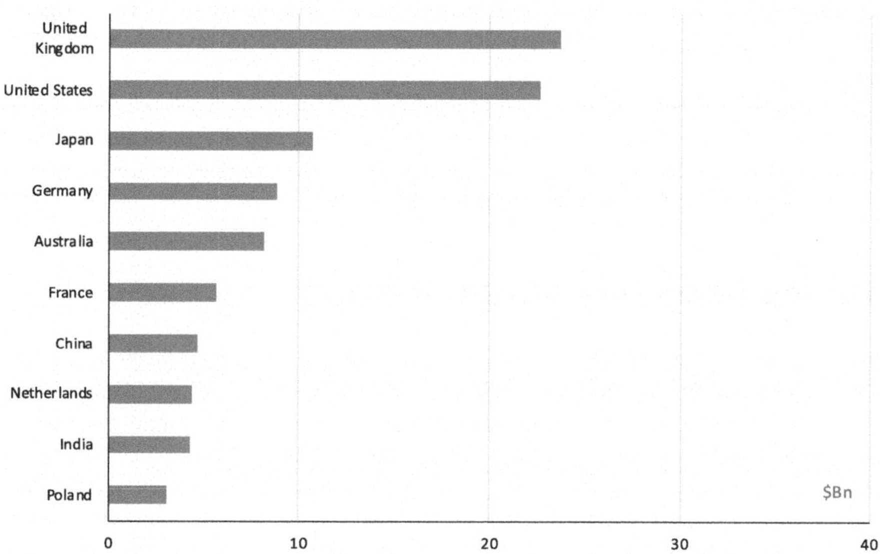

Fig. 9.3 Top 10 destinations of capital for commercial property in 2020 (*Source* Derived from MSCI Real Capital Analytics [2020] with permission)

Table 9.2 Sovereign Wealth Funds in 2021

Rank	Profile	Total assets ($bn)	Type	Region
1	Norway Government Pension Fund Global	1323.3	Oil	Europe
2	China Investment Corporation	1045.7	Non-commodity	Asia
3	Hong Kong Monetary Authority Investment Portfolio	580.5	Non-commodity	Asia
4	Abu Dhabi Investment Authority	579.6	Oil	Middle East
5	Kuwait Investment Authority	533.6	Oil	Middle East
6	GIC Private Limited	453.2	Non-commodity	Asia
7	Temasek Holdings	417.4	Non-commodity	Asia
8	Public Investment Fund	399.4	Oil	Middle East
9	National Council for Social Security Fund	372.1	Non-commodity	Asia
10	Investment Corporation of Dubai	301.5	Non-commodity	Middle East

Source Authors construct derived from SWFI (2021)

of money generated by the government, often derived from a country's surplus reserves. They represent a huge source of global investment funds (Table 9.2). It is only in the last decade or so that they have participated in global property markets and allocations to property are now comparable to investments by UK institutions.

The Norwegian SWF, the largest of the global SWFs can now invest up to 7% of its holdings in real estate. Real estate investments were initially in well-developed European markets. However, from 1 January 2013, the mandate to invest in real estate was broadened to include countries outside of Europe.

Internationalisation of Real Estate Cycles

Chapter 3 noted both the close relationship between commercial property performance and a nation's economy as well as common international real estate cycles. The reason for the added international dimension is that real estate markets in major cities are increasingly linked by global economic factors. A fundamental driver of international real estate market activity is economic growth and development. As real incomes have grown over the long term and economies have developed there has been an increasing demand for real estate assets across all-property sectors, retail, office, industrial and residential.

This link makes investment values in the property market vulnerable to global shocks and liquidity crises. The instability is further enhanced by the direct influence that the global economic cycle has on occupation demand. Global booms and recessions now drive national rents and with it yields and capital values. Recent decades have seen the convergence of national property cycles in major economies.

The main mechanisms are changes in demand and supply but as trade and financial markets become increasingly integrated, national property cycles increasingly co-move.

Interest rates, exchange rates, and actual and anticipated inflation are increasingly influencing international capital flows, which in turn are influencing the value of property in key global centres. The outcome is the synchronised fluctuations of national property cycles within the global economy. However, the extent of the volatility of property values in individual countries will depend on fiscal and tax policies, and supply factors within each individual country (see later).

Economic integration has meant that property cycles can almost simultaneously occur in distant cities in different parts of the world. In particular, cities with similar economic structures in different parts of the world have more synchronised property cycles than other locations. The implication, though, is that countries integrated into the international capital markets are destined to suffer from common 'boom and bust' scenarios, but they will inevitably be mediated by local factors. Importantly, user demand is correlated with investor demand for property as an income-producing asset, and so both user and investment markets can be affected by global events.

The integration of financial, capital and business creates instability and makes the entire global economy vulnerable to shocks. In recent years, there have been several instances where shocks experienced in one country have been transmitted around the global system and created crises in other countries. Perhaps the clearest indication of this link was the GFC of 2007, which started in the US residential market and brought about the longest and deepest global recession since the 1920s.

This close relationship between the behaviour of commercial property markets and economic behaviour is clearly illustrated by market trends from 2000. The global economic expansion experienced over this period fed through to increased commercial property demand, and so rental and capital values rose with yields falling. As noted in Chapter 3 many countries experienced a common commercial property boom, especially those that were more intimately linked in with the global capital cycle. This phenomenon was linked to long-term changes in the nature of cities and the growth of financial and business services that resulted in similar property market trends. However, the commercial property boom began generally later in the first years of the millennium. This aspect of markets has been discussed in Chapters 3, and in the case study in Chapter 6, but it is worth re-examining this aspect of international markets in more detail.

Inevitably there were differences in the scale of the upturn in commercial property values as despite economic globalisation international markets are *not* homogeneous and not all countries were starting from the same base at the beginning of the economic upswing. Different countries have distinct institutions and varied legal systems which, with different informational property market efficiencies (information quality and interpretation) and transparency, mediate behaviour. In this context, while yields fell, and capital values increased across many countries in the boom years, they did so to different extents and over varied timescales inevitably mediated by local market conditions and institutions.

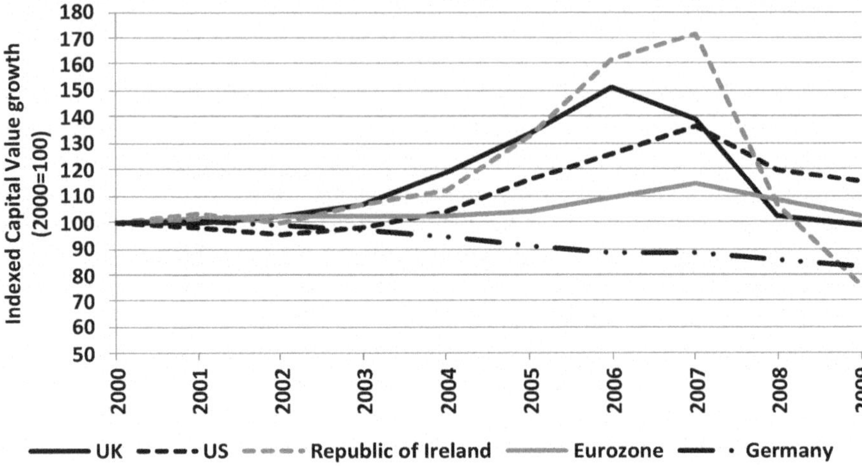

Fig. 9.4 Commercial property capital growth in selected countries 2000–2009 (*Source* Jones et al. [2018])

These distinctions can be seen in the international real estate boom of the early 2000s. Capital values had begun to rise in many countries worldwide from 2003 but the UK had shown growth from 1996 with strong growth from 2002. In the United States there was no growth in commercial property values in 2001 or 2002 but capital growth was seen from 2003 and had reached 11.4% per annum by 2005. Ireland had experienced a sustained growth in capital values from the early 1990s, and this resumed in 2003 after a year of contraction. Growth reached double figures by 2005 and a staggering annual 21.9% by 2006.

Geographical differences in both the onset of the rises of capital values and the extent of growth during the boom years are illustrated in Fig. 9.4 (repeated from Chapter 3). Taken as a whole the Eurozone average values did not show any real growth until 2005, but there are considerable differences beneath this average.

The capital values of commercial properties rose by 70% from the millennium to the peak of the boom in Ireland. The equivalent figures for the UK and United States were lower, just over 50% and almost 40%, respectively. The aggregate statistic for the Eurozone is much less, just 15%, but this is substantially influenced by falling valuations in Germany.

Figure 9.4 clearly illustrates the completely different growth (contraction) pattern in Germany compared with other mature property markets. In Germany values fell during the whole period in which values boomed in other countries, but this may be down to valuation practices in that country.

Valuation approaches more generally vary from country to country (see later), so a precise international comparison of the increase in capital values is difficult. With these caveats it is interesting to note that the climax of the boom varied across countries. Capital growth in Ireland and the United States peaked a year later than in the UK.

This phenomenon of markets moving in similar directions but at different rates could be viewed as undermining the case for international diversification because of the existence of common circles. On the other hand, there are individualities in these cycles in terms of precise timing and amplitudes. It is also important to remember that not all economies and markets are linked into globalisation, and these may offer better opportunities for diversification. These latter markets are arguably immature and the next section considers the concept of market maturity.

Market Maturity

The concept of market maturity is a useful one when assessing the relative development of markets worldwide and with it their investment potential and associated risk. It is closely linked to the concept of transparency discussed in Chapter 6 (see later). The terms mature and emergent markets have been used loosely for many decades in financial markets but have been ill defined for property markets until relatively recently. However, the classification of where property markets sit in a maturity spectrum remains subjective despite attempts to inject rigour into the definition of maturity (see below). In this context, the concept of a mature market seemed to be straightforward and based largely on how well established they were, but the definition of markets that did not totally meet these criteria less so.

A property market may take a traditional and simple form in which the real estate sector is poorly developed and lacks an identifiable separate market for users' and investors' interests. Alternatively, it may be highly mature with a sophisticated and well-established real estate profession providing the essential requisites for use and investment real estate markets.

Keogh and D'Arcy (1994) identified six factors that are indicators of real estate market maturity and influential on market performance, and proposed that:

- A mature market should provide investors and users with a diverse selection of property products so individuals can tailor their property rights to their specific needs.
- A mature market has mechanisms to enable demand and supply to respond rapidly and be flexible in both the short and long run, so that market participants can react effectively to new information and opportunities.
- Mature markets have extensive information flows so that participants are informed of changing market conditions. The market will also be well researched.
- The most open markets in spatial, functional and sectoral terms are generally more mature. The greater the level of openness then the wider the information available to outsiders. This facilitates information flows throughout the market and allows market participants to operate across boundaries.
- A mature real estate market contains a sophisticated property profession with the quality of service regulated by codes of practice and/or laws.

- The more mature the market then the more market practices and property rights are standardised.

These six broad criteria still represent the starting point for more recent assessments of market maturity which generally assess maturity in terms of how well markets meet these criteria. Mature/established markets meet the criteria most closely.

Emerging markets are perceived as being markets where the criteria defined above are less well developed. The term 'emerging market' derives from a macroeconomic policy debate of the 1970s and 1980s. These markets were generally associated with nations having low to middle per capita income. This worked well for macroeconomic analysis but has been less well defined for property markets. Burrell (2015) suggested that an economic-based definition was still appropriate for the purposes of real estate markets and defined emerging markets as follows:

> Emerging market is a term that investors use to describe a developing country, in which investment would be expected to achieve higher returns but be accompanied by greater risk. Global index providers sometimes include in this category relatively wealthy countries whose economies are still considered under-developed from a regulatory point of view. (p. 2)

In addition to mature and emerging markets, the terms transitional and frontier have been used for markets which are relatively newcomers to international commercial property investment and which are placed at the bottom end of the maturity spectrum. The term transitional markets were found to be particularly useful when it came to defining markets moving from a command to neo-liberal economies and related initially to Central and Eastern European countries emerging from Soviet style economies.

Frontier markets can be characterised by low levels of per capita income, property investment and market transparency, which again defines markets in relative rather than absolute terms. The so-called transitional markets have evolved over the three decades to 2020 into what might now be better classified as emerging markets and this trend is analysed later in the case studies at the end of the chapter.

However, the maturity characteristics of markets are fluid and vary across and within markets over time. Consequentially the elements of the maturity spectrum will change through time. Furthermore, it is important to recognise that markets do not progress through the same stages of maturity to reach a common end state. They may develop criteria at different rates and at any point in time may be stronger in one category or another. Maturity should not be seen as an end state as markets need to continuously evolve as the requirements and perceptions of users and investors change. It is issues such as these that make absolute judgements of 'maturity' complex.

It is also a very institutional view of markets, being related essentially to investability and arguably a partial picture of property market characteristics, combining selective institutional inputs that shape property markets and outputs.

Examples of this include sustainability and governance issues, not featuring at all in Keogh and D'Arcy's original criteria.

It is fair to say that the starting point for both the market maturity concept and transparency is developed countries and neither approach sits easily as measures of the relative state of property markets in developing countries. In this context, it is important to recognise the distinction between formal and informal mechanisms in the operation of land and property markets, including residential markets.

All of this still begs the question that although market maturity may be a good conceptual framework for decision-making what data do you use to establish a hierarchy of markets? The next section outlines some of the data that can be used in this context.

Indicators of Maturity

The maturity characteristics we have discussed in this chapter are not unrelated to the market transparency framework developed by Jones Lang Lasalle in the late 1990s and first published in 1999 (JLL 2020). Their definition of transparency shares many of the elements of what we would consider characterise as a mature property market and transparent markets can be defined as:

> Open and clearly organised real estate markets operating in a legal and regulatory framework that is characterised by the enforcement of rules and regulations and that respects private property rights.

JLL produce biennial transparency rankings on selected countries based on several attributes. The 2020 assessment (JLL 2020) survey covered 99 countries and territories, and 163 city regions. A composite score is made up from the 6 (sub)-indices (see Chapter 6 for more detail). These include whether market performance can be adequately monitored through the use of published indices, and the extent to which market data is accessible. Such data would need to be provided through government or other sources such as by real estate service providers. The indices also assess the transparency of the governance of listed vehicles in terms of whether financial aspects are disclosed and managed. In addition, an index assesses whether there is a regulatory infrastructure in place that allows a range of property market processes to be clearly followed with protection for the actors involved in these processes. Importantly the survey covers sustainability, an area not included in Keogh and D'Arcy's original concept.

Transparency is critical to the operation of efficient markets and is a significant factor in helping to create healthy real estate markets. Countries with immature real estate markets can be seen as less transparent where there is a lack of market information and historical data, no standardisation rules or processes, no investment by benchmarks, problems with the deeds and perhaps arbitrary expropriation of private property. It can be shown that real estate market transparency is broadly

Table 9.3 Selected transparencies from the JLL transparency index

2020 transparency level	Market (in order of transparency)
High	UK, United States, Australia, France, Canada, New Zealand, The Netherlands, Ireland, Sweden, Germany
Transparent	Switzerland, Finland, Belgium, Singapore, Hong Kong, Japan, Italy, Denmark, Spain, Poland, Austria, Norway, Czech Republic, Portugal, Hungary, Slovakia
Semi-transparent	India, Romania, UAE Dubai, Israel, Russia, Greece, Bulgaria, Turkey, Slovenia
Low	Egypt, Morocco, Colombia, Costa Rica, Ukraine, Iran
Opaque	Oman, Belarus, Tunisia, Tanzania, Iraq, Libya

Source JLL (2020)

positively related to GDP per head, low levels of corruption and an attractive business environment.

Data also suggests that countries that have more mature or transparent real estate markets receive more international real estate investment than less mature or transparent markets. For example, the UK, which has a high level of transparency, receives a disproportionately large amount of foreign investment into direct real estate. In general, market maturity and transparency characteristics tend to be highly correlated with economies that have a relatively high level of inward investment in relation to their national GDP. However, this view can be slightly circular in as much as higher satisfaction of the criteria used to define market maturity and transparency act as a magnet for inward investment because market and specific risk are lowered.

Scores on the transparency characteristics for each country provide the basis for a hierarchical grouping or categorisation by JLL. Selected markets are outlined in Table 9.3 according to the JLL categories—highly transparent, transparent, semi-transparent, low and opaque.

An alternative way of ranking countries according to their level of maturity has been developed by Burrell (2015). The approach recognises national GDP as a driver of market development and change, but not the sole differentiator of market maturity. This makes categorisation harder. Past property and equity classification surveys are the starting points in this assessment. This approach divides global markets into developed, emerging and frontier groups based on an assessment of investment flows, market transparency and GDP per head. Burrell's assessment of market maturity is summarised in Table 9.4.

For comparison, JLL transparency ratings have been added to the various countries included in the table using bold and italics text. Not surprisingly the categorisation of markets as emergent is related to their transparency and the markets defined as emergent fall generally into the *transparent* or *semi-transparent* categories of the JLL Transparency Index. However, the complex (and to some extent dangerous) nature of this categorisation is illustrated by countries like Thailand and South Africa. These are deemed to be transparent and yet are designated as frontier when other factors are considered.

Another useful non-property market specific market categorisation is the Global Index of Economic Openness (Legatum 2019). This index measures the extent to which the economic systems of 157 countries enable trade, competition and productivity. It measures policy choices on market access and infrastructure, investment environment, enterprise conditions and governance (all contributors to market maturity). While this index has not been specifically incorporated into the considerations of property market maturity above, it is useful to use this index to illustrate the, sometimes, different picture that can emerge from different indices.

The top ten most open economies according to this index at the end of 2019, in order, were Hong Kong, Singapore, The Netherlands, Switzerland, Denmark, Norway, UK, Sweden, United States and Germany. All of these are considered to be developed/mature in the categorisation given in Table 9.4, but Hong Kong, Singapore, Switzerland and Denmark are lower in the transparency index in relative terms. Other measures of competitiveness at the city level are considered in the case studies later.

Internationalisation and Property Related Practices

Part of the challenge of international real estate investment is the variations in the operations of markets between countries, even those that have mature markets. This section reviews the, sometimes, wide disparities that exist in property related practices worldwide. These differences segregate property markets and inhibit the ease by which market players can operate in different national markets. A range of topics that are specific to market transparency in overseas property markets are examined. These include variations in lease structures and differences in valuation methods.

Lease Terms

The investment returns on property assets are determined by changes in their capital value and net income flows. Arguably, the most significant variable in determining an asset's value is the lease terms governing the conditions under which it is let. They are important factors because they dictate the conditions for rent reviews and rental growth, the length of the lease (term), repair obligations and local real estate taxation liabilities. These in turn influence the relative liquidity of the asset, the size and timings of income return the volatility and security of income and capital and the responsiveness of income return and capital values to changes in economic conditions.

Table 9.5 summarises the lease terms typical in foreign office and industrial markets. Little has changed since this table was assembled in 2011. The figures

Table 9.4 An alternative view of markets and their maturity

Market categorisation	Countries
Developed (mature, advanced)	**United States, Australia, The Netherlands, UK, Singapore, Sweden, Hong Kong, Canada, Germany, France, Norway, Switzerland, Finland, Ireland, Denmark, Japan, Belgium, Italy, Spain, Austria, New Zealand**
Emerging (growth, transitional)	**Taiwan**, **South Korea**, **Poland**, **Czech Republic**, ***Russia***, **Malaysia**, **Portugal**, ***Brazil***, ***Greece***, **Hungary**, **China**, ***UAE***, **Slovakia**, ***Mexico***
Frontier	***Saudi Arabia***, ***Israel***, **Thailand**, **South Africa**, ***Croatia***, ***Turkey***, ***Romania***, ***India***, ***Chile***, ***Bulgaria***, ***Indonesia***, ***Vietnam***, ***Philippines***

Source Adapted from Burrell, Investment Property Forum (2015)
Notes **Countries designated highly transparent or transparent in JLL Transparency index**
Countries designated semi-transparent in JLL Transparency index
Countries designated low or opaque in JLL Transparency index

Table 9.5 Selected typical lease terms for global office space in 2011

Country	Lease terms	Break options
Australia	3–10	Negotiable
Belgium	9 years	3 years
Canada	5–10 years	Usually none
China	2–3 years	NA
Czech Republic	3–5 years	Negotiable
Denmark	3 and 5 years	Negotiable
Finland	3–5 years	Not typical
France	3/6/9 years	Every 3 years
Germany	5–10 years	Option at year 5
Greece	12 years	None
Hong Kong	3 years	Only for large areas
Ireland	10–25 years	10–15 years
Italy	6 + 6 years	6 years
Luxembourg	9 years but negotiable	3 years
Norway	4–6 years	Only when stated
Poland	3–7 years	Standard fixed term common
Russia	3–5 years	3 years
The Netherlands	5–10 but negotiable	5, 10 years
UK	5–15	3–5 years
United States	5–10	Not standard

Source Selected data adapted from CBRE (2011)

in the table illustrate that standard institutional leases in the UK are on average longer than for other countries. Even so they are on average shorter than they were 20 years ago when standard institutional office lease was around 25 years. Average lease lengths in the UK continue to fall, however, and currently stand at around 9 years. Lease terms in the United States and Germany are for five years while three years is the norm in Finland and Denmark. These differences in lease structures have arisen due to differences in historical and cultural factors, government legislation on landlord and tenant relationships (see Chapter 10), market forces and investor preferences.

Tenancy and Landlord Obligations

Tenancy and landlord obligations range across responsibilities for repairs, break clauses and security of tenure also differ between countries. The variation in allowances for break clauses and security of tenure is also illustrated in Table 9.5.

The UK is unique as types of leases can vary. Some leases are based on rents net of removing management, insurance and repairing obligations. There are also FRI (Full Repair and Insurance) lease terms that place the onus on tenants to cover these costs. There are also IRI leases whereby tenants are responsible for internal repairs. In other countries, it is unusual to make tenants responsible for all repair liabilities because civil codes exist that prevent it. However, greater responsibility for repairs on tenants is being sought in other European countries.

Rent Reviews

The lease contract will specify when and how rents may be reset after the start of the lease. Three dominant types of provision for rental change in European leases can be identified.

- *Periodic rent review to open market value*: The rental income is fixed with the rent set at initial letting and will change to the open market level at pre-agreed intervals. The main feature of this type of lease is that rental income is stable between rent reviews. This type of lease is very common in the UK, Italy and the Republic of Ireland.
- *Rent linked to inflation*: The rent rises at pre-agreed intervals (in some cases annually) in line with an inflation-related index, usually a retail or consumer price index. This means that the rental income is inflation proof with the nominal rent rising in line with inflation. Any changes in the contract rent to the open market value would only be possible either at renewal of the lease or a new letting. In France, for example, rents can be revised every three years at the request of either party, even if a formal rent review is not provided for in the lease. However, the parties may agree on an automatic indexation of the rent—often stipulated on a yearly basis. The most frequently used indexes are the Tertiary Activities Rent Index (indice des loyers des activités tertiaries—ILAT), the Construction Costs Index (indice du coût de la construction—ICC) and the Commercial Rents Index (indice des loyers commerciaux—ILC). They are all published by the National Institute of Statistics and Economic Studies (INSEE). The index chosen by the parties must have some connection with the activity carried on by one of the parties or with the purpose of the lease.
- *Rent linked to turnover*: Turnover (or percentage) leased property is let on the basis that all or part of the rental income is directly related to the turnover the occupier achieves (see Chapter 12). It is a type of lease that is associated primarily with the retail sector, and is very common in the United States. Turnover rents are rare in Europe, except for France and Germany.

International Valuation Methods and Practices

Valuation methods across the globe can be quite different. They depend on the standard techniques and definitions adopted by these countries set by government legislation and recommendations, and by institutions or professional bodies/associations within the country. An understanding of these differing techniques is important because they impact on the apparent volatility of markets and make a comparison of property markets often quite difficult. It affected analyses of the impact of the GFC on property markets when, for example, the apparent volatility of some Western European markets during the GFC appeared to be much less than for the UK.

An additional problem, certainly in the UK, is that many quoted market valuations relate to those monitoring the portfolios of financial institutions. These valuations do not necessarily relate to market transactions and are undertaken according to professional rules and practices which vary between countries.

A technique used in Germany and not yet widely applicable, certainly not in the UK at the time of writing, is the use of a long-term sustainable valuation, an approach that underpins Germany's Pfandbrief bond market and might help mitigate risk when assessing loan-to-value (LTV) ratios when advancing debt. The rationale is that the increased risk arising as the market overheats can be mitigated significantly through the use, in addition to current appraised LTV, of a measure that compares the amount of the loan to the long-term sustainable value of the property. The latter is the average value of the property through the market cycle. In this approach, the most important element of pro-cyclicality would be removed. Although this is based on a significantly more cautious valuation, it allows a better insight into the risks involved. The use of this approach probably explains the different volatility seen in German markets, as discussed earlier (see Fig. 9.4 and a wider discussion in Chapter 12).

Summary

The chapter has provided an analysis of how the globalisation of financial markets has internationalised property investment worldwide. It has done this against a background of economic growth, which has concomitantly encouraged the growth of commercial property markets worldwide.

The globalisation of financial and property markets developed towards the end of the twentieth century and was driven by socio, economic and political changes worldwide. With this change came, in many cases the removal of barriers to international interaction, including those in command economies in Central and Eastern Europe, China and Vietnam.

Collectively these changes fundamentally altered the flow of capital and FDI from existing mature economies and ultimately resulted in notable increases in the levels of global trade. They also brought flows of international capital seeking the highest risk adjusted return, influencing local property markets.

Despite this major change in attitude over the last 60 or so years, the benefits of economic openness have been under increasing scrutiny in Western countries, giving rise to nationalism and populist politics.

Although there is now much greater interaction between markets, there are still barriers to the harmonisation of asset values allowing plenty of opportunities for diversification. Property markets are no different from FDI generally. International market imperfections and constraints will prevent the integration of property markets and the full synchronisation of property values.

The principles of overseas diversification are equivalent to those discussed around portfolio theory in Chapter 7. International investment can provide access to higher potential returns than are available domestically. It allows access to a larger universe of properties as well as faster growing economies and access to different sectors of the market at different stages of maturity.

Formal barriers to overseas investment include problems around national professional accreditation, restrictions on foreign ownership and constraints on foreign residents. Informal barriers include the traditions of market practices, the status of the local profession, business culture and language and cultural factors.

Currency risk generally remains an issue for investors, although it has been mitigated in Europe with the almost universal use of the Euro across countries of the EU. It clearly remains an issue for most countries of the world. There are three main types of currency risk: transaction risk, translation risk and economic risk.

The uncertainty associated with exchange rate movements can be reduced by hedging. It is used to protect against changes in the value of an investment. Possible hedging instruments include forward contracts, future contracts, various currency options and currency swaps.

Foreign investors, notably the Chinese and Americans, but more recently Europeans (especially the Germans in London office markets) have become increasingly active in overseas markets. The UK has been a particular focus for the expansion in foreign investment. By 2017 nearly 50% of all-property purchases in the UK were undertaken by overseas investors.

Economic integration has meant that property cycles can almost simultaneously occur in distant cities in different parts of the world. Countries integrated into international capital will be destined to suffer from common 'boom and bust' scenarios, but they will inevitably be mediated by local factors.

The concept of market maturity is a useful one when assessing the relative development of markets worldwide, and with it their investment potential and associated risk. A property market may take a traditional and simple form in which the real estate sector is poorly developed and lacks an identifiable separate market for users' and investors' interests. Alternatively, it may be highly mature with a sophisticated and well-established real estate profession providing the essential requisites for use and investment real estate markets.

In addition to mature and emerging markets, the terms transitional and frontier are identified for markets which are relatively newcomers to international commercial property, and which are placed at the bottom end of the maturity spectrum. The term transitional markets are used to define markets moving from a command economy to economic neo-liberalism and related initially to Central and Eastern European countries emerging from Soviet style economies. Frontier markets can be characterised by low levels of per capita income, property investment and market transparency.

The concept of transparency shares many of the elements of what we would consider characterise the definition of maturity. Transparent markets can be defined as markets which are open and clearly organised real estate markets: operating in a legal and regulatory framework that is characterised by the enforcement of rules and regulations and that respects private property rights.

The UK, United States, Australia, France and Canada are among the group of countries with the most transparent property markets in the world.

There are wide disparities in property related practices worldwide. These differences segregate property markets and inhibit the ease by which market players can operate in different national markets. The chapter examines a range of topics that are specific to market transparency in overseas property markets. These include variations in lease structures and differences in valuation methods.

Learning Outcomes

Having completed this chapter, the reader should be able to:

- Explain that international diversification is possible when national capital and financial markets respond differently to economic conditions.
- Understand the pros and cons of investing overseas. Investors can reduce the risk attached to a global portfolio by selecting markets that have different economic drivers or are at different stages in their economic cycles. However, the more markets become integrated then the more diversification opportunities will be eroded.
- Understand that portfolio analysis must be undertaken at the international level, however, the lack of directly comparable performance measures makes this difficult.
- Understand how currency risk can be hedged.
- Critically assess the case for foreign investment.
- Understand the drivers of change and restructuring of world cites over the last three decades and the consequences for their property markets.
- Understand and define the characteristics of global and world cities.
- Identify ways in which world cities have been ranked and the limitations of these methods.

Case Studies

To help understand the global changes in property markets over recent decades, four specific case studies are considered in this supplement. These aim at complementing and expanding on the underlying principles discussed in this chapter.

Rather than a country-by-country analysis, the studies take a broader regional view and, in keeping with the theme of the book, have focussed on investment trends. The studies start with a look at global cities and then examine trends in Asia–Pacific and emerging markets in Central and Eastern Europe. The latter are particularly interesting as they document a fundamental change in the way their local markets changed from a command economy to one based on neo-liberal economics.

A fourth case study reviews the potential impact of the UK vote to leave the EU (BREXIT) on UK property markets.

Case Study 1: Global Cities

Over the same period that changes were occurring in financial, capital and business systems, many world cities underwent a process of restructuring. As economic activities became global, and financial and business systems expanded, the nature of cities changed, and the global economic expansion fed through to increased commercial property demand.

Many countries experienced a common commercial property boom, especially those that were more intimately linked in with the global capital cycle. In addition, the growth of financial and business services resulted in similar property market trends and cities with similar economic structures in different parts of the world were more likely to have more synchronised property cycles than other locations. Developing countries increasingly became industrialised but at the same time these structural changes were often associated with an increased demand for office space in the major city centres.

A global city is now considered to be an important node in the global economic system. The cities play important roles in the global network of finance and control and have increasingly concentrated on international business and financial services functions. They are major business centres showing significant growth in GDP, infrastructure and population and which are attracting investment capital or have the potential to attract significant investment.

This has been influenced by the greater agglomeration of economies and attractive cultural facilities that they have to offer. Pashley identified a range of common characteristics of these world cities:

- They have a variety of international services, especially financial and marketing.
- They have HQs of several multinational corporations.

- They are typified by the existence of financial HQs, a stock exchange and major financial institutions.
- They dominate the trade and economy of a large surrounding area.
- They can be centres of major manufacturing industry, although increasingly financial and business services dominate.
- They have considerable decision-making power on a daily basis and at a global level.
- They are centres of new ideas and innovation in business, economics, culture and politics.
- They are also centres of media and communications for global networks.
- They show a dominance of the national region with great international significance.
- A high percentage of residents in the cities are employed in the service and information sector.
- They possess high-quality educational institutions including world recognised universities with international student attendance and research facilities.
- They have a multi-functional infrastructure offering some of the best legal, medical and entertainment facilities.

More recently, the term 'gateway' cities has been coined. These are effectively the best of the best of the 'global cities'—the world's most prominent cities, and at the time of writing include London, Paris, New York, Singapore and Hong Kong. Investors are attracted to these cities, which are experiencing significant employment growth and increasing influence. They are attracting both capital and highly skilled employees on an increasingly international basis.

The activities of the gateway cities have been complemented by a concentration of service activities in other world/global cities such as Frankfurt, Shanghai, Mumbai, Tokyo and Sydney. These global cities tend to be major cities that make-up the upper level of the international 'urban hierarchy' and are attractive locations for the headquarters of firms with national and international markets. They are expanding the service base, experiencing employment and infrastructure growth and are attracting people and capital.

The world's largest and fastest growing cities offer many opportunities to property investors. However, they exhibit very different characteristics. Some are particularly successful at attracting international labour and capital and experiencing strong growth and rapidly rising affluence. Such cities usually have: an excellent infrastructure, quality of life, investability and transparency. From an investors point of view, the very best also have an element of property supply constraint, whether physically or due to planning controls, and can deliver particularly strong performance.

Like market maturity there is no universally accepted way of ranking these cities, although there are indices which rank them according to various criteria. If cities are grouped according to the extent to which they meet the criteria already discussed in this chapter, then in addition to grouping New York, Singapore, London, Hong Kong and Paris as gateway cities global cities would include Mumbai, New Delhi, Shanghai, Beijing, San Francisco and Frankfurt.

Unsurprisingly, many of the gateway/global cities are in the top tier countries of the JLL transparency index. The changing international hierarchy of cities per se though is demonstrated in two indices which specifically address the health of cites overall rather than just their property markets. These are the Global Financial Centres Index and the A. T. Kearny index both useful as indicators of future city performance.

The Global Financial Centres Index, first published in 2007, provides profiles, ratings and rankings for financial centres specifically, drawing on a number of factors and looks at competitiveness. It produces a score (rather like the JLL transparency index) drawn from a range of sources/other indices including The World Bank, OECD and the Economic Intelligence Unit and on-line surveys based on five main areas:

- Business environment
- Financial sector development
- Infrastructure
- Human capital
- Reputational and general factors.

These are combined with a financial centre assessment based on an ongoing questionnaire completed by international financial services professionals. The 2021 report (GFCI 29) covers 120 centres and again produces a hierarchy of cities in relative terms. Although the index has a short history, it does demonstrate how cities move up the spectrum of maturity in a relatively short period of time. The first index produced in 2007 showed the top ten in order as London, New York, Hong Kong, Singapore, Zurich, Frankfurt, Sydney, Chicago, Tokyo and Geneva with Shanghai at 23 and Beijing at 36. By March 2020 (GFCI 29) the top ten cities were in order New York, London, Shanghai, Hong Kong, Singapore, Beijing, Tokyo, Shenzhen, Frankfurt and Zurich reflecting the fundamental changes that have occurred in global financial and business service centres in recent years.

The A T Kearney index has been collecting data on global cities since 2008 and now includes both a global cities index (GCI), which examines cities performance, and a global cities outlook (GCO) which evaluates their potential. The GCI assesses how globally engaged cities are across five dimensions: business activity, human capital, information exchange, cultural experience and political engagement. The index and outlook are based on composite scores that include a wide range of metrics. In 2020 it analysed 151 cities in six world regions (A T Kearney 2020). Like the GFCI it examines maturity at the city/regional level rather than the country level, although the cities examined often drive a country view of maturity especially for property markets. Like the GFCI, the index is not property specific but can be used to give an indication of commercial property sectors of importance.

New York, London, Paris and Tokyo have led the index consistently for a number of years. This consistency of performance highlights the wide range of positive attributes a city must have to reach the top of the index and to stay there. It also demonstrates the difficulty of building such a broad platform of strengths for cities further down the chain. It also shows that for those cities able to do so, global status has so far been reinforcing.

What the index also demonstrates is a degree of fluidity in these maturity rankings with Beijing unseating Hong Kong from its long-held top five positions in the A T Kearney index. It could prove to be a sign of further changes to come with weakening governance issues in the latter. While Beijing's strong economic growth and human capital investments paid off, the political chaos in Hong Kong undoubtedly dampened its performance across all dimensions, with significant drops in business activity, information exchange and cultural experience.

The longer-term usefulness of these reports is that they identify cities on the rise—those creating the right conditions for future global status, and with it the changing maturity of markets. In this case, while London maintained its top ranking (interestingly despite risks around BREXIT), cities with a strong commitment to innovation and strong governance, where long-term investments were beginning to show results, scored strongly in terms of outlook. Cities considered to have a strong outlook because of these factors included Toronto, Singapore, Tokyo, Paris, Munich, Abu Dhabi, Stockholm, Amsterdam and Dublin.

Case Study 2: Property Markets in Asia–Pacific

This case study relates to the so-called Asia–Pacific countries bordering on the South China Sea and the Western Pacific Ocean. It groups countries which have had broadly similar experiences in terms of the way they have responded to the forces of globalisation but whose property markets have moved at different paces along the maturity spectrum because of their individual histories. Rather than undertaking a detailed country-by-country case study, the section looks at selected countries in the context of a regional response to these global economic forces. The group includes China, Hong Kong, Singapore, Thailand, Vietnam, Japan, Malaysia and Taiwan.

In order to understand the significant changes that have occurred in the property markets of this group of countries, it is useful to understand how globalisation has impacted on their economies, since this has determined the characteristics of their property markets.

A common feature is that they have responded to the forces of globalisation by reducing barriers to trade and investment and have witnessed significant changes in economic and institutional structures over the last six decades. The region has also witnessed major political and economic reforms.

Although it can be argued that the region has become more democratic in some areas (it is questionable whether this is true in absolute terms), the real game-changer has been the move to economic neo-liberalism and global capitalisation.

Fig. 9.5 GDP growth in selected Asia Pacific countries, 1961–2019 (*Source* Authors construct from selected data World Bank Open Data [2021])

This has happened irrespective of whether their governments are considered democratic or not. Coupled with this has been the recognition or acceptance that this economic approach has the potential for providing greater market efficiency compared to strict command economies. This is especially true of China and Vietnam. These transformations have had a significant impact on investment interest in the respective property markets.

The Asia–Pacific region has, in general, grown at a much faster rate than the rest of the world over the past three decades despite economic downturns during the 1980s, 1997 and 2008 (Fig. 9.5).

The downturns in GDP in 1997 and during the GFC in 2008 were experienced across the group to different extents. In addition, all have experienced fluctuating growth since the early 1960s, with China consistently showing the strongest growth over the period. On average, the region has experienced higher growth rates compared with other global regions and has witnessed a remarkable degree of macroeconomic stability.

Economies were not affected to the same extent as Europe and North America during the GFC and consequently experienced a much less severe impact on property markets than other global markets. Data for Vietnam is less comprehensive but what there is suggests that GDP growth in that country has remained in the range 2.7–9.5% pa since 1985.

Economic growth in these countries followed a pattern which started with high growth in Japan during the post-World War II period. The newly industrialised economies (NIEs) of Hong Kong, South Korea, Singapore and Taiwan followed Japan with Indonesia, Thailand, Malaysia, Philippines and Vietnam following later

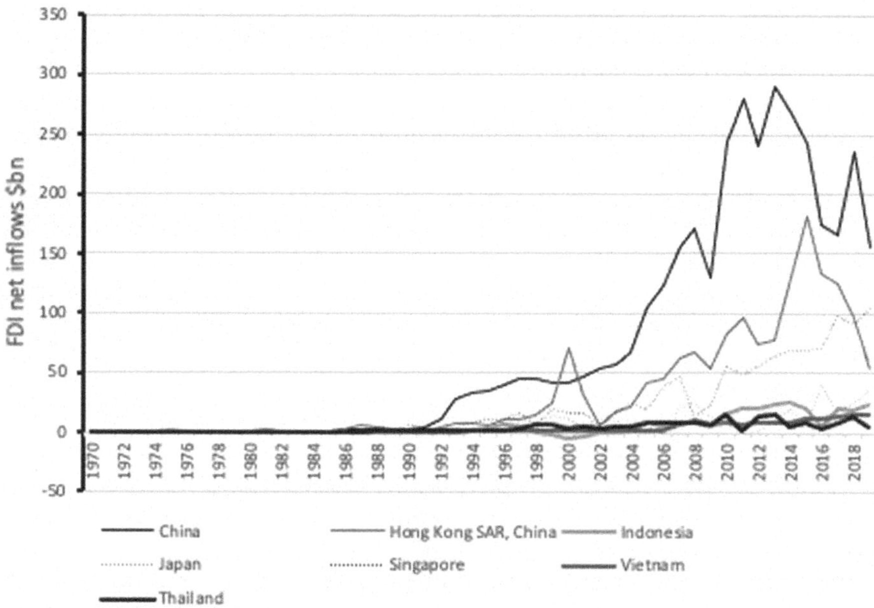

Fig. 9.6 Foreign direct investment in Asia Pacific countries (*Source* Authors construct from selected data World Bank Open Data [2021])

at various stages. A common feature across the group, shown in Fig. 9.6, has been the growth of FDI but its role has differed widely across the region at various stages of their development and to different extents. NIEs have generally been less dependent on foreign investment than others in the group.

China experienced significant FDI much later than others in the group that was encouraged by a new more neo-liberal approach to economic matters. In 1978, the country embarked on an open-door policy and began for reaching economic reforms. From 1980 it began to develop special economic zones (SEZs) and other initiatives as part of the drive to open up the country. These special SEZs are areas in which foreign and domestic companies can trade and invest without the same control and regulation from central government as other parts of China. The areas were designed to encourage overseas investment in China and boost the country's economic growth. Shenzhen, in southern China near the border with Hong Kong, was among the first of four locations to be given SEZ status. It is now one of China's largest cities and one of the country's main import–export hubs as well as a leading manufacturing base.

The SEZs have been complemented by Economic and Technological Development Zones (ETDZs). These are generally smaller than the SEZ's and place a larger emphasis on specific industries, particularly on developing high-tech research and development. Latterly several Free Trade Zones have also been established which have more relaxed regulations on currency exchange and less stringent rules on the types of companies that can be set up. However, the state continues to control activities in these zones through restrictions on the type of activities allowed within them.

This massive growth in economic activity throughout the group of countries has triggered significant urban development across a range of property sectors. In particular, the maturing of Asia Pacific's logistics sector has been one of the region's most impressive growth narratives over the 2010s. Before 2016, the sector was heavily dominated by Japan and Australia, which together accounted for three quarters of all logistics property trading activity. However, in recent years newer markets emerged in South Kores and then in China. In addition there was an increase institutionalisation of logistics ownership. As early as the post-GFC recovery years, institutional involvement was already on the rise at the opportunistic end of the spectrum.

However, the level and diversity of property market activity depend not only on economic fundamentals but also on market maturity, and Asia–Pacific markets are at different stages of maturity. In economic terms, Japan is the second largest economy in the world, but on the JLL market transparency scale as of 2020 it ranks 16 putting it in the second transparency tier.

Singapore (14) and Hong Kong (15) are perceived as the most mature markets in the Asia–Pacific region, with a full range of use and investment opportunities, well-developed property professional services, market flexibility, availability and standardisation of information, good quality product property products and stability of development activity. Thailand (33), the Philippines (44), Indonesia (40) and Vietnam (56) have all improved their transparency dramatically in recent years and are now among the JLL Index's top improvers due to regulatory reforms, enhanced market data and sustainability initiatives (JLL 2020).

Mainland China has progressively improved in terms of the availability of market data and has a more coordinated approach to land use planning. These improvements have helped mainland China's leading cities Shanghai and Beijing into the 'transparent tier' of the JLL Index.

The changes in regional economies and the relative improvements in their transparencies have resulted in a marked improvement in the sizes of their professionally managed real estate markets in recent years (Fig. 9.7).

In global terms, while these trends are not surprising given the established nature of the Japanese, Hong Kong and Singapore markets, it is a major indicator of the changes that have occurred in the Chinese economy over the period covered by the case study. Another indicator of the changes happening in the region are changes in the sources of capital funding in property markets shown in Fig. 9.8. While transborder capital flows remain important and are a feature of the early investment in the region, they are now much less important and domestic sources of capital now represent the major source of capital in the region.

There is to an extent a common narrative in these trends reflecting the fundamental changes in the region over the last 50 years. Rapid economic growth supported by foreign investment was accompanied by a maturing of real

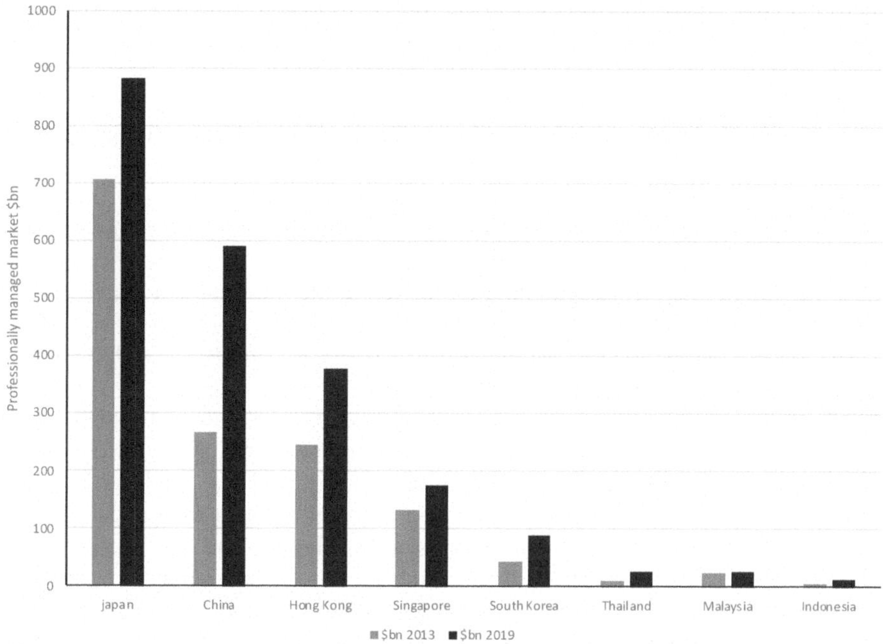

Fig. 9.7 Size of the professionally managed property market in Asia–Pacific area (*Source* Author construct from selected data MSCI [2020])

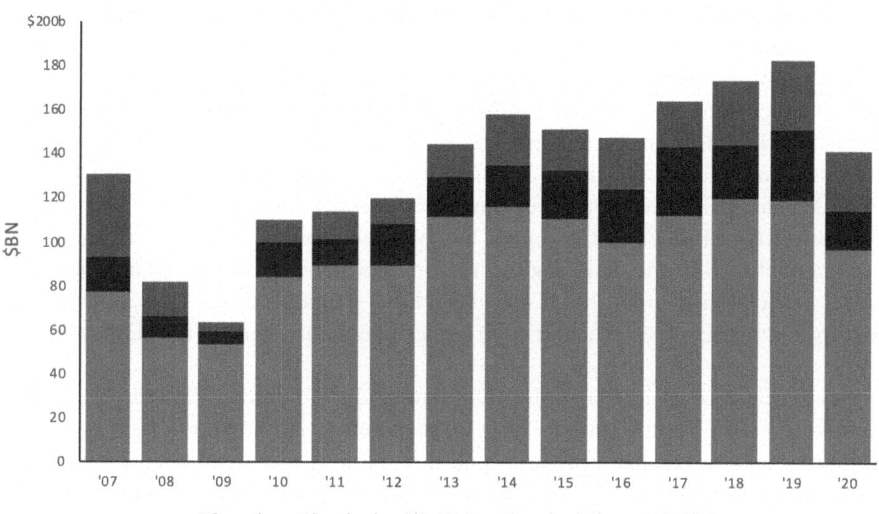

Fig. 9.8 Asia–Pacific investment 2020 by source of capital (*Source* Derived data from MSCI Real Capital Analytics [2020] with permission)

estate markets. These real estate markets are now widely accepted localities for international investment.

Case Study 3: Emergent Markets in Central and Eastern Europe (CEE)

The emergence of countries in Central and Eastern Europe as neo-liberal economies, with open semi-transparent/transparent property markets, represents one of the most interesting economic narratives in the latter part of the twentieth century.

The post-World War II economic history of CEE countries has led to certain common trends and responses in terms of the local interplay of economic globalisation processes. There is a commonality across the region of globalisation interacting with societal transformation and the transfer from a central command economy to a private market economy. In this context, the case study again takes a more regional view of investment trends in this region rather than undertaking a country-by-country analysis. It concentrates on Czechia, Poland and Hungary with a briefer look at Russia and Slovakia, mainly because these letter two countries remain hampered by a lack of in-depth data. Up until 1 January 1993 Czechia (The Czech Republic) was joined to the Slovak Republic (Slovakia) to form Czechoslovakia. At that point, they became independent countries, and the case study treats them as separate countries throughout.

All the CEE countries considered in this case study are classed as emerging markets, although until recently they were termed transitional markets, a useful term to describe relative newcomers to international commercial property markets who were transforming from command economies. Like countries in the Asia Pacific region, a common feature has been that they have responded to the forces of globalisation by reducing barriers to trade and investment. They have witnessed significant reforms in political and institutional structures over the last three decades that have brought economic changes.

Irrespective of whether the region has become more democratic in some areas (questionable), like the Asia Pacific region the real game-changer has been the move to economic neo-liberalism and global capitalisation. This change has occurred irrespective of whether their governments are considered democratic or not.

An indicator of their transition from command economies is that they have progressively improved in terms of market transparency. All are now classed as being among those countries in Europe which now have strong regulatory frameworks, governance structures and transaction processes. However, market fundamentals in terms of data and performance measurement are still areas for improvement.

Russia is among countries classed as semi-transparent by JLL, but it has made steady improvements in recent years. However, concerns remain around corporate governance and regulatory enforcement. Despite the poor performance of Russia in both *economic openness* and transparency scores, Moscow remains of some

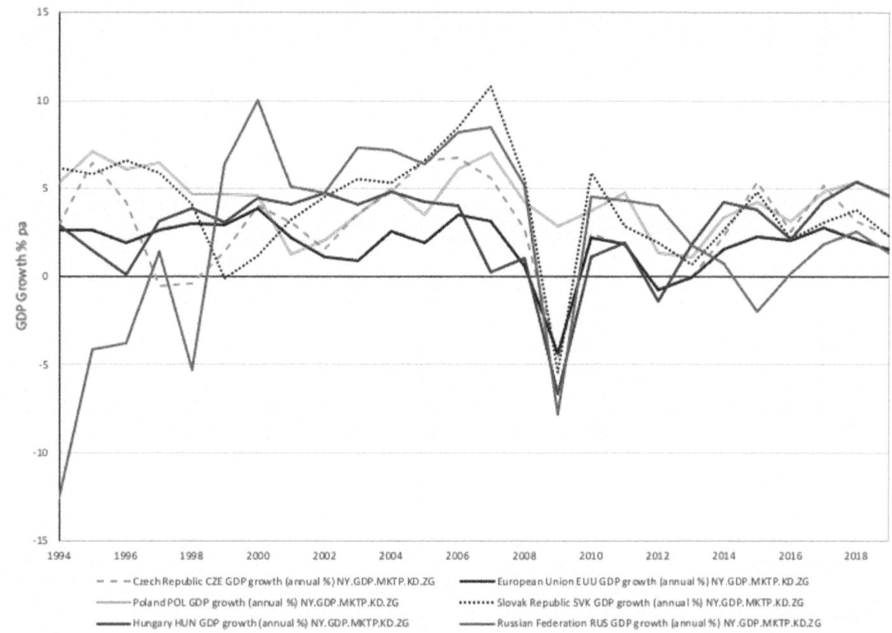

Fig. 9.9 Economic growth in selected CEE countries, 1994–2019 (*Source* Authors construct from selected data World Bank Open Data [2021])

importance as a 'global financial centre'. The city is classed as a global specialist despite being ranked 57 of 126 centres in the GFCI 29 index. In a similar vein, Budapest is considered an 'established financial centre' although ranked 85 in the GFCI 29 index. Prague, Warsaw and Bratislava are still considered local centres although ranked 76, 61 and 66 respectively.

As Fig. 9.9 indicates all the CEE countries have experienced good growth in their economies since the early 1990s. The Russian economy took longer than other CEE countries to exhibit stable growth post the reconstruction of their economies. However, on average, all countries showed growth above the EU average. Apart from Poland, all countries showed synchronised negative GDP growth during the GFC from 2007 to 2009.

This above-average growth reflects the progressive expansion in their economies stimulated by the new socio-economic conditions and investment began to progressively improve. This is reflected in the growth of inward investment in the decades following the dissolution of the Soviet Union as shown in Fig. 9.10, albeit in some cases the experience has been mixed.

Russia in particular saw significant inward investment in the early to mid-2000s before experiencing a fall towards the end of the decade. Inward investment in Hungary, while being significant, has been volatile. Both countries have possibly suffered from falling perceptions of openness and transparency (see above and

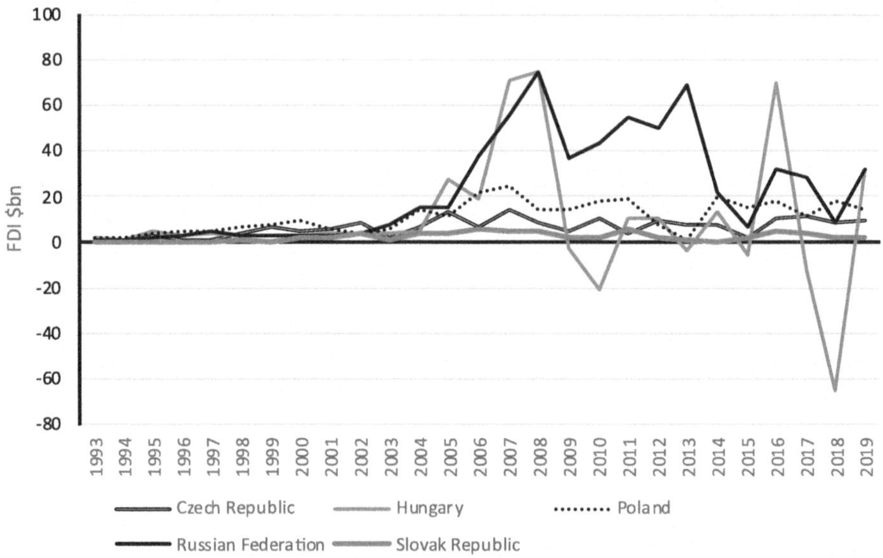

Fig. 9.10 Foreign direct investment in selected CCE countries (inflows US$), 1993–2019 (*Source* Authors construct from selected data World Bank Open Data [2021])

later). Czechia, Slovakia and Poland, on the other hand, have experienced steady flows of investment as their markets matured.

The establishment of real estate markets, however, required radical changes and successful economic and legal reforms. Various transformational adjustments were required as part of this process as set out in Table 9.6, drawing on perspective provided by Sykora and Simonickova. A sustainable economic environment was essential since real estate markets do not function in isolation (increasingly satisfied during the 1990s). Open and liberal economies were necessary to foster economic growth which would allow domestic users to expand and attract international users into the market. In addition, a stable political climate and a clear regulatory framework that embraced the different interests in landed property were prerequisites to the operation of real estate markets.

Only after these conditions were in place could a sustainable real estate market be created with investment, user and development sectors, and an appropriate professional infrastructure.

Table 9.6 Transformation processes in CEE countries

Object of transformation	Transformation process
Management of resource allocation	Public to market
Ownership structure	State to private
Exchange measures	Regulated to liberalised

The experience in central Europe showed that the evolution of markets in transition underwent broadly three distinct phases:

- The initial transformation period took place between 1988 and 1992 whereby state prices were liberalised and real estate assets were privatised. This led to the establishment of market rents and a sharp rise in real estate prices.
- In the second stage (1992–1994), there was the entry of foreign users into the markets who saw opportunities to tap into these untouched markets.
- The expansion in demand and the shortage of property acceptable to international companies/investors led to huge growth in capital and rental values. The increase in values attracted overseas investors and developers and triggered a wave of major developments.

However, the exact pace and nature of change between different countries were different and largely reflected the various institutional frameworks in place. There were a range of common barriers to investment in the early stages of the transition process. These included problems with regard to limited financial resources, different taxation regimes (particularly relating to property transfer taxes), a paucity of information sources and issues around land ownership, some of which still exist.

An important element of the transition was the restitution of private property rights. For real estate in particular there was a need to legally define private property rights that could form the basis of exchange. Under the communist regimes, land and buildings were primarily state owned. To establish an investment market these resources needed to be transferred to private individuals and organisations. However, the previous owners claiming the right to restitution (the process whereby properties taken from their owners under the communist regime are given back to their owners or heirs) made the process difficult in some countries.

Different approaches were adopted to restitution. In Russia, there was no restitution policy. Rather property was transferred from the state by transaction. In Hungary, re-privatisation of land was permitted where there was a five-year commitment to farm the land. The Polish government chose to return property to previous owners or their successors. Applicants had to prove administrative violations of the pre-1949 laws that allowed the state to take private property. State-owned land/real estate was transferred to municipal authorities who were required to clarify ownership claims.

The Czech Republic, and with it, Slovakia (as part of the original Czechoslovakia) was unusual in that they had retained a culture of entrepreneurship and it was easy to reconnect the institutions that existed in the 1930s and 1940s. The government in Czechia opted for the principle of restitution. Legal reforms ensured the clarification of property rights by introducing guarantees of private ownership. These legal changes were encompassed within the new constitution that became effective in 1993.

It was also essential for emerging markets to put other effective property market structures in place, such as standardised valuation practices, market research and the provision of market data. Increasingly the larger and more experienced multinational real estate agents from elsewhere in Europe and the United States became involved with these countries and standards have improved. With the growth of domestic and international firms, there has been a drastic improvement in the market data available and the research undertaken.

In addition, from an institutional framework, international real estate services providers such as JLL and CBRE can be seen to reduce transaction costs for property users and investors who operate in different institutional and cultural environments globally. They play a key role in the delivery of property services to a demand that is international.

All of these issues have progressively addressed and improved market maturity ratings and with it the transparency ratings of the CEE countries, although issues of data transparency remain to be addressed satisfactorily in Russia and to some extent in Slovakia. This improvement has been reflected in the growth of the professionally managed property markets in Poland and Czechia as shown in Fig. 9.11 between 2013 and 2019. Growth in Hungary remains sluggish. These numbers reflect the attractiveness of the countries to investors, whether domestic or overseas, an important distinction, and hence growth in managed portfolios in the respective countries.

In the absence of market size data for Slovakia and Russia, transaction volumes are compared for all countries in Figs. 9.12 and 9.13 to give a relative indication of investor interest in these markets. Figure 9.12 charts volumes for the period Q3 2018 to Q4 2019 (PWC 2019) showing Poland is the most active of the markets considered in this case study.

A slightly different picture emerges when real estate transaction volumes are considered in relative terms. Figure 9.13 expresses transaction volumes relative to population size and GDP per capita. On this basis, given the GDP per capita and population size (both reflecting potential economic activity), Czechia is the most

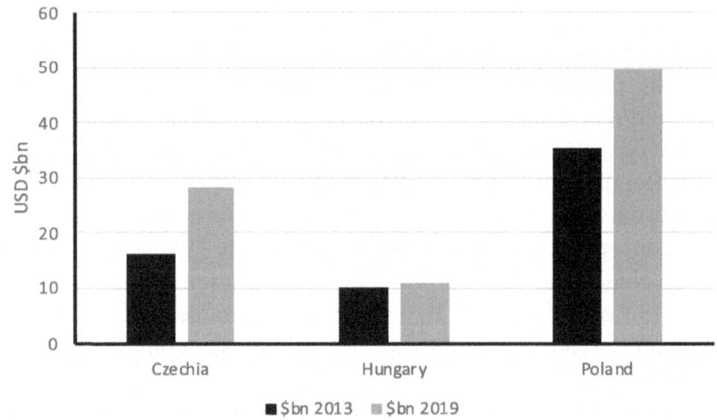

Fig. 9.11 Size of the professionally managed property markets in Czechia, Hungary and Poland ($bn) between 2013 and 2019 (*Source* Author construct from selected data MSCI [2020])

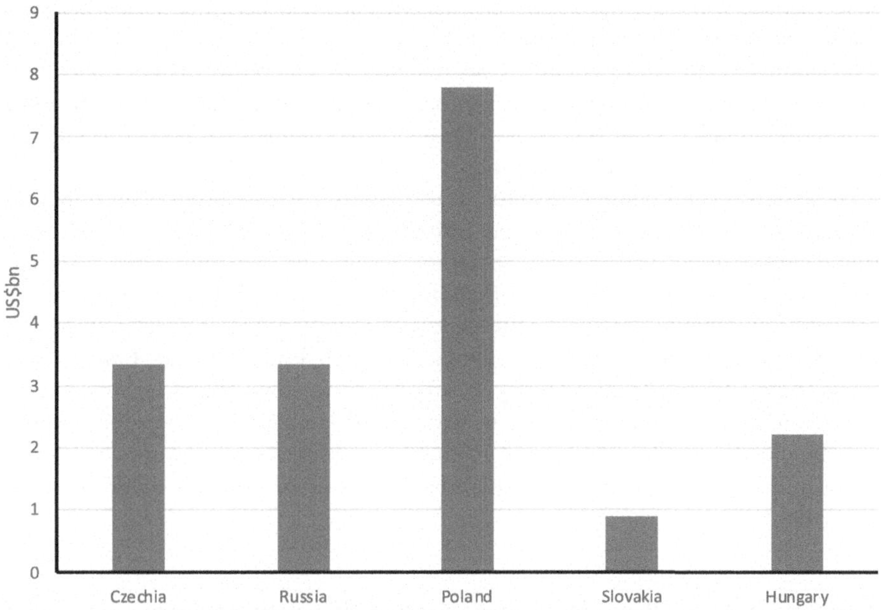

Fig. 9.12 Real estate transaction volumes ($bn) for selected CEE countries, Q4 2018 to Q3 2019 (*Source* Author construct derived from MSCI Real Capital Analytics [2020] with permission)

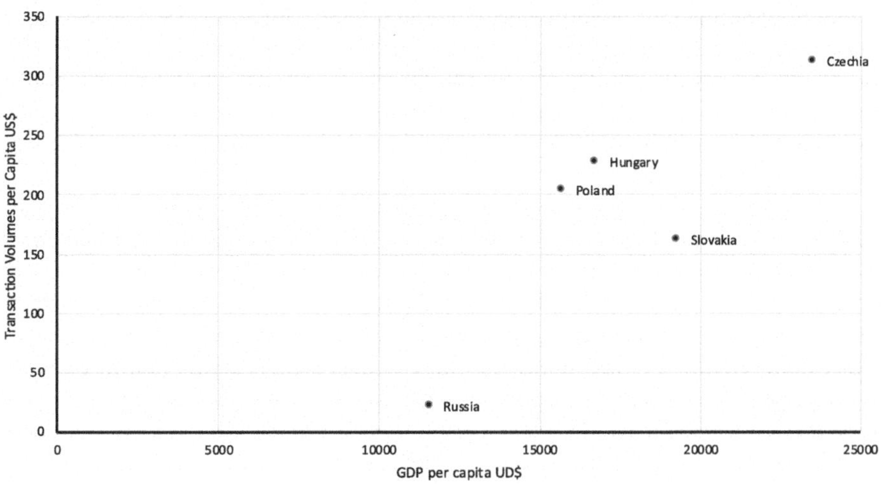

Fig. 9.13 Real estate transaction volumes ($) of selected CCE countries in relative population and GDP per head terms (*Source* Author construct from selected data MSCI [2020] and World Bank Open Data [2021])

active market, while Russia is the least active. Slovakia performs much better in relative terms and Poland much less.

In summary, all these countries are classed as emerging markets and have outgrown earlier descriptions as transitional markets, a useful term at the time to describe relative newcomers to international commercial property markets transforming from command economies.

There have been common features in this transformation process and the way they have reacted to globalisation, but ultimately property markets have moved in different ways along the maturity spectrum because of their individual histories. The establishment of real estate markets required radical changes and successful economic and legal reforms. Since the late 1980s/early 1990s they have improved transparency and market maturity ratings, although issues of data transparency remain to be addressed satisfactorily in Russia and to some extent in Slovakia.

There remain governance issues in Russia and Hungary but, overall, property markets and the institutions related to them have developed. Inward investment generally has grown along with professionally managed property markets across the region.

Case Study 4: Political Risk and Recent UK Referendums

International investment needs to be aware of potential political risk when choosing countries to invest in. Political risk relates to the potential negative implications on real estate values of government policy and leadership, and political and economic instability. It may encompass policy conflicts, ethnic and social tensions and even the prospects of war. There could be concerns about the stability of national governments, regimes and prospects and falling currency values. To a degree the issues can be seen as part of foreign investment risk generally and do not apply only to developing countries.

The nature of political risk is quite nebulous in the sense it is difficult to quantify. The scale of political risk can also change with events that are in some cases unexpected or because policies have evolved over time. The source of political uncertainty could be the immediacy and consequences of a referendum such as with that for Scottish independence from the UK or on Britain leaving the European Union (BREXIT). The impact of these events are discussed below, drawing on and updating a paper by Jones entitled, *The impact of political risk on real estate investment: evidence from the Scottish 'neverendum'*, and published in Property Management in 2019. However, while a referendum is a binary decision, the ramifications can be complex. Political uncertainty can also arise from long-term ongoing and intractable internal divides in a country.

Political risk creates uncertainty and hence can dampen investment. Political risk is also not stationary and so investment sentiment and associated risk premiums vary according to the state of instability or lack of clarity. The political risk impacts are to a degree a matter of perception and can be viewed differently by (types of) investors. In fact, falls in investment values can be seen as an opportunity by some investors.

Scottish Independence Referendum

The Scottish independence referendum on whether to leave the UK took place in September 2014. It was envisaged as a once in a generation event, but a series of subsequent political events conspired to create a 'neverendum'. Seven years on at the time of writing another referendum is anticipated but no one is sure when. The political risk created by the neverendum increased uncertainty and had a negative effect on sentiment, with reduced real estate investment by UK investors and increasing property yields/lowering capital values. Increasing real estate yields in turn reduced development viability and led to lower new supply. Even though the underlying basics of the Scottish real estate market were sound political risk had a profound effect on investment attitudes.

The degree of uncertainty/risk had varied with political events even before the referendum, rising in the lead up to it and then recovering quickly in the last quarter of 2014 with the remain majority vote. However, uncertainty then rose again as the spectre of a second referendum became more likely so that there was a cumulative negative impact on real estate investment sentiment.

Political risk was interpreted differently by overseas investors compared with domestic UK funds because they had different investment mandates. Many UK investment funds were required to invest in the country and began divesting their Scottish portfolio. Overseas funds saw opportunities to purchase (in European terms) prime real estate at low historic investment prices supported by a decline in the value of sterling.

The political risk of investment in Scotland ebbs and flows with the changing probability of constitutional change but without a date for a second referendum it has been a negative influence. The COVID pandemic has prolonged the process to what many regard as an inevitable second referendum. An element of the political risk can be deemed to be specific risk linked to UK institutional fund mandates that stems from concerns about possible forced sales with independence. In addition, political risk is in the eye of the beholder with overseas investors in Scotland unfazed by the prospects of independence.

BREXIT Referendum

The BREXIT vote to leave the European Union (EU) took place in June 2016 and the polls were on a knife edge in the lead up creating uncertainty. Given the economic and political uncertainty Land Securities, the largest REIT in the UK sold £1.1bn of its assets in the six months up to the end of March of that year. The decision to leave in June was determined but the terms of the divorce from the EU were still to be negotiated. Even after a deal was agreed in December 2019 there were continued disputes notably about the trade arrangements between the borders of the UK, Northern Ireland and the Republic of Ireland (EU). These disagreements cast doubt about the long-term sustainability of the 2019 deal.

In addition, some transitional arrangements have some years to complete and the 2016 deal excluded an agreement on a framework for financial services that in 2021 had yet to be resolved. The result is that uncertainties will continue as political events including future elections to the UK Parliament and the Northern Ireland Assembly on the horizon could impinge on eventual BREXIT outcomes. The outcomes could also influence the probability of Scottish independence and even ultimately the reunification of Ireland.

In the immediate aftermath of the vote investment into UK commercial real estate fell to a four-year low in the third quarter of 2016, with investment in the second half of the year over a quarter lower than in the first six months. The picture was starker in London where British real estate investment in 2016 fell by more than half compared with 2015, and there was an 8% fall in central office values in the first nine months of the year.

The uncertainty derived from the referendum was exacerbated by the UK political context that saw, first, one prime minister resign in the immediate aftermath. His successor called a general election ostensibly to empower her to negotiate with the EU only to achieve a reduced majority. This minority Conservative government elected in 2017 was in a weak position in Parliament, with the ruling party also split on the nature of the trade deal it wanted. There were continuing negotiations with the EU on trade arrangements, but the government did not have the power in Parliament to ensure any proposed deal could be ratified. The result was gridlock with a series of twists and turns on likely outcomes as political factions vied to get the upper hand. The prime minister resigned in 2019 and a subsequent general election finally gave the government a large majority in Parliament to enable a deal to be completed in December 2019.

The real estate market waited for the political hiatus to be resolved. The initial response identified central London offices as the area of the real estate market most negatively exposed by BREXIT. It reflected fears of a mass exodus of financial services to cities in the EU. However, there has not been as severe an impact on the demand for office space in the central London as first expected even though as yet there is no formal agreement on the trade of financial services to the EU. Some business has moved to Europe but five years on there is a market view is that the current status quo is likely to continue suggesting stability for the London office market. Nevertheless, it is still uncertain how much new business can be generated from the rest of the world to replace that lost to the EU.

In the first four years that passed after the BREXIT vote arguably the central London office investment market stood still with office yields at a relatively high representing an uncertainty risk premium despite falls in long-term UK bond yields. For these four years office yields in central London were higher than in other major mainland European cities and overseas investors stayed away. 2021 saw the eventual return of overseas investors as political uncertainty began to lift with the trade deal. The impact of the pandemic also has slowed market activity.

Overview

The examples of Scottish independence and BREXIT referendums show how political risk can impact on real estate investment over a number of years pushing up yields. One decision was for the status quo and the other for change, but both led to long-term investment inertia as the results still left much uncertainty about the future. The uncertainty began in the lead up to the votes and the complex political angst that followed simply created a continuing unstable investment environment. Nevertheless, the impact on international investment was very different. In Scotland European investors in particular grasped the real estate opportunities as UK funds divested but in London hesitant overseas investors stayed their hand. A further difference is that the neverendum is not yet over whereas BREXIT is, or at least real estate investment sentiment in 2021 takes this view. However, as discussed above, there is considerable scope for political events to unravel this market consensus and for BREXIT uncertainty to go on for some time to come.

Reading

A T Kearney (2020) *Global Cities Index 2020; New Priorities for a New World.* https://www.kearney.com/global-cities/2020.

Baum, A. (2015) *Real Estate Investment: A Strategic Approach*, 3rd Edition. Routledge, London.

Burrell, A. and Investment Property Forum (2015) *Emerging International Real Estate Markets, Investment Property Forum*, Short Paper 28. Investment Property Forum, London.

CBRE (2011) *Global Office Occupier Guide.* CBRE, London.

The Global Financial Centres Index 29 (March 2021) https://www.longfinance.net/programmes/financial-centre-futures/global-financial-centres-index/.

JLL (2020) *Global Real Estate Transparency Index.* JLL, London.

JLL (2021) *Office Property Clock Jan 2021.* JLL, London.

Jones, C. (2019) The impact of political risk on real estate investment: evidence from the Scottish "neverendum". *Property Management*, 37, 5, 610–626.

Jones, C., Cowe, S. and Trevillion, E. (2018) *Property Boom and Banking Bust: The Role of Commercial Lending in the Bankruptcy of Banks.* Wiley-Blackwell, Chichester.

Keogh, G. and D'Arcy, E. (1994) Market maturity and property market behaviour: A European comparison of mature and emergent markets. *Journal of Property Research*, 11, 3, 215–235.

Legatum Institute (2019) *Global Index of Economic Openness.*

McGreal, S. Parsa, A. and Keivani, R. (2002) Evolution of property investment markets in Central Europe: Opportunities and constraints. *Journal of Property Research*, 19, 3, 213–230.

MSCI (2020) *Real Estate Market Size 2019/2020.* MSCI, London.

MSCI Real Capital Analytics (2020) *Global Capital Trends Report for 2019.* Real Capital Analytics, New York.

Pashley, R. (2000) *Excel HSC Geography.* Pascal Press.

SWFI, Sovereign Wealth Fund Institute (2021) https://www.swfinstitute.org/fund-rankings/sovereign-wealth-fund. Accessed Feb 2021.

SIFMA (2021) *Securities Industry and Financial Markets Association (2020).* US Fact Book.

Solnik, B. (1996) *International Investments*, 3rd Edition. Addison-Wesley.

Sykora, L. and Simonickova, I. (1994) From totalitarian urban managerialism to a liberalised real estate market: Prague's transformation in the early 1990s, in M. Barlow, M. Dostal, P. and Hampl. M. (eds) *Development and Administration of Prague.* Institute voor sociale Geografie, Amsterdam.

Tiwari, P. and White, M. (2010) *International Real Estate Economics*. Palgrave Macmillan, London.

The World Bank (2021) *World Bank Open Data*. World Bank, Washington, DC. http://data.worldbank.org/.

Part III

Developing Real Estate Paradigms

10 State Intervention and Implications for Investment

Introduction

Governments set the framework for the operation of the real estate market and hence the returns to investors. They act at a number of different levels from the local level through to international treaties. Local governments in general have responsibility for land use planning although they usually operate within a set of rules determined by national governments. Planning systems vary from country to country in how and to what degree they intervene in real estate markets.

Increasingly governments are looking to real estate development and the use of the stock as a means to address the issues raised by climate change and in particular energy use. In some cases, there is direct regulation of the green standards of new buildings. In other cases, governments try to 'guide' the real estate market by providing information to shape decisions.

There is also a long history of government regulation in the housing market around the world through residential rent controls and security of tenure for tenants. The terms of commercial leases can also be subject to legal constraints. There are also instances where governments have sought to control commercial rent levels.

When regulation is reversed or reduced, there is inevitably a market response as controls unwind. However, in some cases, this process can take some time to come to fruition, as it may involve other supporting factors also responding to the new policy environment. In the most recent past, the deregulation of banks has had the most severe impact on the commercial real estate market and investment values during the global boom of the 2000s. Not surprisingly there has been a reaction through tightening of international banking regulations notably through new Basel Accords.

This chapter examines the intricacies of the role of governments in these different areas and the interface with real estate markets, and is structured to cover the following main issues:

C. A. Jones and E. Trevillion, *Real Estate Investment* ,
https://doi.org/10.1007/978-3-031-00968-6_10

- Planning and urban management policies.
- Government green agendas.
- Environmental, Social and Governance.
- Market Regulation.
- Deregulation.
- International banking regulations.

Planning and Urban Management Policies

Land use planning is almost ubiquitous in countries around the world. While much of the motivations for planning are seen in social terms, it is essentially an intervention into real estate markets with consequences for values, development constraints and investment activity.

One overarching argument for planning centres on addressing 'market failure' especially in real estate markets that are imperfect and inefficient. Market failures encompass negative externalities where the actions of an individual firm say are imposed on others without payment, the failure to supply public facilities and 'unacceptable' market outcomes.

Examples of negative externalities that planning could address are stopping the building of high office blocks that obstruct a neighbouring building's light or view, and new developments generating increased traffic and bringing excessive noise or congestion. Similarly, planning controls development to ensure that it meets society's needs. With this in mind, planning may constrain the supply of shops or offices at a given location say because it is not accessible for public transport. Alternatively, planning may positively intervene to stimulate development if the market left to its own devices produces insufficient supply.

Planning tools are typically passive by a combination of zoning for specific uses, applying density constraints and requiring planning permission. Proactive policies can involve grants to developers or tax incentives to locate in an area. A broader view of planning encompasses acceptable building standards and the provision of public infrastructure including water, sewerage, etc. It also incorporates a strategic perspective on the spatial structure of urban areas to enable them to operate efficiently. The latter goal can be described as urban management and includes shaping and redirecting traffic flows.

There is a broad consensus of the need for planning and urban management as a way of setting a framework for development and hence real estate markets and investment. Even in Houston in the United States where there is no land use zoning there are still some restrictions on development, and some developers employ private covenants and deed restrictions on adjacent 'incompatible' developments. In fact, it is in the interest of real estate investors that planning restricts detrimental uses close by to their properties. The extension of this argument is that in many cities where planning is weak or ineffective, as in some developing countries, there are often even more market constraints on commercial real estate investment and development. When there is controversy it is not about planning itself but about precise policies and the degree of constraint applied.

Planners have a range of social, economic and environmental goals but in meeting these goals they are in effect agents that manipulate the real estate market. By intervening in real estate markets, planning inevitably distorts prices applicable in a free unfettered market. Planners can be viewed as shaping, regulating and stimulating real estate markets. Two examples illustrate how planning can distort values by constraining or promoting development.

First, say in order to promote economic development in a town suffering from deindustrialisation local planning policies zone an amount of land for industrial use say sufficient to meet the demands for decades to come. With 'too much' land zoned for industry, this will lead to depressed industrial land values. It could also create a shortage of land for other sectors of the local economy and push up land values for these uses in the town.

Second, an historic city centre is often subject to development constraints on new office developments. These constraints are brought about by strict rules on the conservation of existing buildings or the permitted floor area to plot size or building heights. There are consequences for the local real estate market. As a result of these planning policies, demand is greater than supply and values of the existing offices increase. The policy requirement for low density development could lead to an expansion of the area covered by the city or firms simply moving to an alternative city.

More generally, the impact of planning, where it limits supply's response to rising demand, is the generation of higher land and real estate values that otherwise would have been the case. One study by Cheshire and Hilber noted that the office occupation costs of a provincial city in the UK in the early part of this century were 44% higher than in Manhattan, New York. They contend that this fact can be partly attributed to the planning regulations in the form of height restriction, conservation requirements and limitations to land allocated to offices (although there is no formal zoning). More broadly they argue that the British real estate market is more highly regulated than other European countries by an order of magnitude, and that Europe in turn is more regulated than the United States. While these precise conclusions are crucially dependent on the research technique applied, they do illustrate the potential for differential planning regulations to influence the market.

The study also draws attention to the differences between the severity of planning regimes between regions. In general, less prosperous areas tend to have less restrictive planning policies. Localities with depressed economies cannot afford to be overly prescriptive about new development and the prospects of new employment to the area. On the other hand, in prosperous areas severe planning constraints are often in place to restrict development with the consequent crowding out of economic activity and increased real estate values. This may be because the costs are not recognised or because prosperous areas can bear the additional cost. The differential perspective on planning contributes to a spectrum of real estate values between rich and poor areas.

Where planning is a strong restraining force then land prices are much higher than otherwise would be the case. In the housing market, it can be evident at the margins of growing urban areas with a gulf between land valued and zoned for housing compared to agricultural land. Planning constraints inevitably generate a market response with developers seeking ways to respond to higher values by adjusting the intensity of the use of urban land in the long term. In the short term, the increased value of land breeds where possible new development densities that are higher than they would be without planning. In addition, a highly constrained real estate market creates higher values that benefit existing real estate investors in these urban areas who make substantial capital gains over time.

It is important also to recognise that planning policies in their broadest sense also aim to manage and change urban form. Urban regeneration can stimulate new land use patterns with consequences for real estate values in different parts of cities. Through either tax incentives or grants to developers new real estate forms can be supported and established in parts of a city suffering from dereliction caused by say deindustrialisation. The most prominent and most extreme example in the UK is the concentration of offices centring on Canary Wharf in the former docklands of east London. In the process, land/real estate values in the area rose from zero to become some of the most valuable in the country. More generally urban generation projects have the possibility of high returns but there are also high risks.

Perhaps of wider importance for investors is that transport policies, including new infrastructure, road pricing or parking constraints, can benefit some locations while others lose out. The rest of this section considers potential implications through examples for the retail and office real estate sectors. In a city centre pedestrianisation or new route restrictions can change the pattern of pedestrian shopping flows. Over time the prime locations of retailing and real estate values evolve leaving some retail locations gaining while others lose out.

Travel constraints to reduce congestion too can have negative consequences for the retail centres affected and consumer spending directed to the benefit of those without constraints. A congestion charge or a car parking fee can add considerably to the cost of a shopping trip shifting demand to decentralised shopping centres. Policies aimed at reducing congestion are aimed at improving travel times to city centres and seek to make the city centre more attractive to office workers and businesses. These policies work directly on congestion by inducing workers to switch from their cars to public transport However, for some offices, the long-term impact is to reduce the attractiveness of a central location and encourage a switch to a business park. Overall travel constraining policies potentially moderate city centre real estate values.

Government Green Agendas

There are increasing global concerns about the warming of the planet. The Paris Agreement in 2015, developed from the United Nations Framework Convention on Climate Change in 1994, was the first legally binding, global agreement against to address climate change. Along with the UN Sustainable Development goals, it provided a target which individual countries needed to aim for to ensure global warming remains under 2 degrees by reducing greenhouse gas emissions. The COP conference in Glasgow in 2021 subsequently sought a common way forward to a 'net zero' future. The sustainable policy agenda has become almost universally accepted by governments. In the UK, the Climate Change Act 2008 committed the country to an 80% reduction in carbon emissions by 2050 relative to the levels in 1990. In June 2019, the target was increased to at least 100%.

The carbon footprint of buildings and the energy consumption of offices as principal workplaces represent a central element of this problem. Changes to the real estate sector have the ability to make a significant impact on climate change. It is therefore not surprising that governments have focused on the sector to reduce climate change on a global scale. In the commercial real estate sector, government policies have been promoting greener buildings. These policies have been seen in energy usage certification for buildings and higher green standards for new buildings in some countries.

There are many governments around the world that have building codes in place to support energy efficient designs for new development. These are mainly in European and Australasia countries. There are notable gaps in regulation in Latin America, Africa and the Middle East. In general, governments are not insisting to date on green accreditation for new commercial buildings (see Chapter 11). However, there are local variations. At least one city in the UK requires through its planning guidance that new offices have green accreditation. Large office blocks of more than 1000 sq m are now required to have green accreditation.

There is also a focus on improving the energy use of existing buildings. In Europe in 2008, the EU Energy Performance of Buildings Directive instigated Energy Performance Certificates (EPCs) for offices. An EPC shows the current energy efficiency capability of an office and is required on completion, on sale or on letting (or every ten years). EPCs are actually an estimate based on a building's characteristics. Buildings are graded from A the top score down to G. Large public offices are also required to display 'Display Energy Certificates' (DECs) that show the actual energy consumption of the building.

Since 2018 in the UK there has been a Minimum Energy Efficiency Standard of E for new lettings. In other words, grades F and G ratings are no longer legally acceptable for new leases. From 2023, the rule is to apply to all tenancies. Furthermore, the government has announced it intends to make it unlawful to continue to let commercial property with an EPC rating of below B by 2030. *If this happens it could bring 85% of buildings into the failing energy category with dramatic implications for the real estate market.*

Governments have also been nudging (not just real estate) investment towards a greener future. The European Union, for example, has issued a Sustainable Finance Disclosure Regulation that came into force in 2021 that requires financial institutions to disclose all the sustainability risks in their investment process that could have a potential negative return. As a result, institutions and financial advisors in the EU, offering portfolio management or financial advice, must publish information on their websites about their policies. This information should explain the integration of sustainability risks into their investment decision-making processes. In addition, the European Banking Authority has set out the nature of the required disclosures covering transitional and physical climate change risks, mitigating actions and governance arrangements. For real estate investment assets, these disclosures relate to energy consumption and flooding.

Another example is building energy disclosure policies in a small number of states in the United States. These regulations require residential and commercial properties above a certain size to disclose the energy consumption to prospective purchasers, tenants and lenders. These disclosures are aimed at improving energy efficiency by increasing consumer awareness. They may also impact on the investment value of individual properties and stimulate energy conservation. These energy disclosures have the same goals as EPCs (see above) in Europe although the latter is based on an estimate of consumption.

All these initiatives demonstrate that the direction of travel of government policy around the world is on promoting greener buildings. The speed of policy adoption varies by country but there is no doubt about the destination. The policies have been clear for some time and, certainly in Western economies, in the relatively near future more strict environmental standards for buildings are to be anticipated. For real estate investors, it is evident that new green developments reduce the potential of not meeting future regulations and the risk of obsolescence (see Chapter 11). New technologies are also driving down the cost of green buildings.

For these reasons, green has become the norm for new office buildings since 2010 in many Western economies. In the UK, the previous decade was a period of transition with a dramatic upward step change in the number green of office completions in the latter part as government policy clearly shifted in a green direction. A similar trend occurred in the United States. In addition, financial institutions are increasingly adopting environmental and social governance (ESG) real estate benchmarks for real estate investment that explicitly address climate resilience, climate change risk, zero-carbon targets, wellness and governance issues. The application of ESG is discussed in detail in the case study at the end of the chapter.

Market Regulation

An important factor for investment in different real estate sectors is the significance of regulation on returns. Regulation goes hand in hand with tax incentives and subsidies but also extends to security of tenure for tenants. Without security of tenure rent controls are ineffective. The tax treatment of investors is particularly important and has shaped commercial real estate investment vehicles: pension funds have benefitted from tax advantages and the establishment of real estate investment trusts (REITs) has enabled indirect investors to not pay double taxation on their income.

Historically regulation is especially important in the housing market and rent controls have been applied in many parts of the world. Often they were introduced at times of excess demand when rents were rising as a means of helping tenants. Rent controls are usually operated together with security of tenure for tenants to make it more effective. If these rent controls hold rents below the 'market level' for some time, there are inevitable negative consequences for investment. There is likely to be limited or no new investment and hence no new development. Furthermore, rent control acts as a revenue constraint on landlords who can seek to maintain profits by reducing maintenance expenditure. The result is a decline in the quality of the stock.

In addition, the owner-occupied sector offers an opportunity for landlords to sell their properties rather than let as they become vacant. The owner-occupied sector also often benefits from tax advantages that also make it more attractive to be an owner rather than a tenant if it is affordable. The sale price to a homeowner is much higher than the discounted value of the accommodation as a tenanted property. The result is that the size of the private-rented sector declines while the home ownership rate rises.

This type of rent control is often described as first generation as opposed to second generation controls. The latter do not set rent levels but regulates rent increases. In this latter approach, annual rent increases are typically limited to increases in inflation, wages or a specific benchmark. Such regulation has been applicable for example in Germany and New York. This type of regulation still favours the tenant, especially when there is excess demand pushing rents up. On the other hand, many landlords prefer tenants they expect to stay only for short periods, such as young professionals or students, as they can raise the rent for new tenants. Second generation rent controls reduce returns to investors but have fewer negative effects on supply than first generation ones.

In second generation rent controlled markets, the initial rent is agreed between the tenant and the landlord and only subsequent increases are regulated. In practice, there have been a wide range of variations in these basic two versions of rent control, linked for example to different rules on security of tenure or to particular segments of the rental market. In Germany, for example, legislation introduced in 2016 has meant that rents applicable in new contracts within overheated or overstretched markets have to be linked to a local reference rent. Rents for these new tenancies may not exceed the local reference rent by more than 10%.

Overall while residential rent controls are introduced to help tenants, there is an argument that the negative impacts on investment and supply do not help renters in aggregate. In some forms of rent regulation, landlords also choose mobile professional households over low-income families. An alternative is income related subsidies to spend on housing, but this strategy too has its limitations.

Commercial real estate leases can also be subject to regulation although as with residential tenancies there is considerable variation between countries. Leases vary by country mainly according to custom as noted in Chapter 9. In some countries, there are legally definitive lease lengths as these two examples illustrate. In Poland, the maximum commercial real estate lease term is ten years, otherwise it is indefinite subject to appropriate notice. In France, commercial leases have a minimum duration of nine years although leases may be terminated after three and six years. The tenant then has a renewable right after nine years. In most countries, there are rent reviews as part of lease arrangements that periodically upgrade rents. In some countries, rents are subject to statutory indexation in line with a measure of inflation.

Leases and their associated rent reviews act to provide a (often statutory) framework for the commercial real estate market. In doing so, rents are normally set at market value and then can remain constant until raised at the subsequent reviews to take account of inflation. This process shapes the investor's flow of income and commercial real estate is ultimately a form of an equity investment. It is fundamentally different from residential rent controls with frozen rents that can deter investment as they are analogous to a fixed income investment but with rising maintenance and management responsibilities/costs.

Statutory regulations on commercial leases that limit rent rise to inflation are designed to protect tenants against potential excessive increases (as in the residential sector). There are some limited examples of explicit commercial rent 'freezes' driven by supply shortages and rising rents (much like in the residential sector). Increases in commercial rents were limited by statute in New York under the Police Acts for eighteen years from 1945 to reduce the pressures caused by market shortages. The UK operated a full commercial (and residential) rent freeze from 1972 to 1975 as part of a general suite of restraint policies to curb inflation. One highly publicised impact of the policy at the time was that some newly completed office developments were left empty as the owners waited for the freeze to end at which point rental values were anticipated to be much higher.

Deregulation

Just as regulation constrains real estate markets not surprisingly deregulation has the converse effect and is the catalyst for change. Over the last thirty years or so there has been a trend towards the deregulation of the private residential rented sector (PRS). The most extreme deregulation during this period has occurred in Spain, Finland and the UK. A detailed impact of the removal of residential rent controls and security of tenure in the UK is now considered.

Rent controls were introduced in 1916 in the UK as a temporary measure during World War I but were applied in different guises until 1989. Over this period, comprising most of the twentieth century, the privately rented sector was in decline, and by the end of the 1980s it was almost moribund. Investment in the PRS was also significantly impaired by subsidies to other tenures and a relatively poor tax treatment compared to other investments.

This platform for fundamental change was new legislation that led to virtually all new private tenancies from January 1989 not being subject to rent regulation, and with security of tenure very limited. This relaxed regulatory environment provided the basis for the revival of the PRS although not immediately as there was inevitably a (unfounded) suspicion that a change in government would reverse the policy. It took time for investment in the sector to respond. It was supported by the phasing out and ultimate abolition of subsidies via tax relief on mortgages to owner occupiers. Meanwhile private landlords continued to receive this tax relief. Investors were also encouraged to invest in the PRS because of the general fall in share values at the turn of the millennium.

Nevertheless, an essential underpinning to the growth in investment in the PRS was the availability of mortgage finance with the arrival of the buy to let (BTL) mortgage scheme in 1996. BTL mortgages enabled private individuals to invest in property to let without being penalised by high (previous) mortgage surcharges. The result was a major surge in small private investors stimulated by favourable housing market conditions that saw a sustained rise in house prices and dramatic investment returns.

By the top of the housing market boom in 2007, the PRS in England represented 12.7% of all households, a growth of 39% from the mid-1990s, and it has continued to increase to over 19% by 2019. In doing so, it transformed the business and characteristics of private landlords.

This experience of the deregulation of the PRS in the UK demonstrates that deregulation in itself may not be sufficient to stimulate substantial change even if it is an essential prerequisite. The long period of regulation resulted in key pillars of support for private landlords being missing. In particular, investment in the sector did not begin to take off until loan finance was freely available at reasonable interest rates.

Deregulation of Banks

This example demonstrates the importance of the availability of finance to real estate markets and the role of banks. Variation in the availability of finance from banks has been critical to property cycles as outlined in Chapter 3. Increased availability of funds in turn is often associated with the deregulation of banks. There are numerous examples through history. Deregulation of the UK banking system at the beginning of the 1970s was the precursor of a real estate boom as property companies went on a spending spree supported by the ready availability of loan finance.

The influence of financial deregulation took on an international dimension during the 1980s as monetarist governments came to power, notably in the UK and the United States. It was supported by the abolition of exchange controls and globalisation that brought increased cross-border capital flows and wider international perspectives for banks. Banks not only became more internationalised but also entrepreneurial, competing across continents offering, amongst other services, real estate loans and development finance. Banks shed their traditional conservative approach to lending and took more risks in their lending practices in the pursuit of growth.

In the 2000s, it also brought wholesale borrowing, as noted in Chapter 3, whereby existing bank loans are bundled together and the income from them used as the basis for the issue of bonds. The revenue generated by these mortgage-backed securities could then be recycled to issue more loans. This practice, known as wholesale funding, occurred globally and enabled banks to grow rapidly by raising capital on a worldwide basis without much scrutiny by regulators or company auditors.

There was a spirit of deregulation during this period that related to the long upswing in economic growth around the world and the associated growth in real estate capital values. The long boom contributed to a delusion of certainty and the underestimation of risk. There was little or no recognition that globalisation and wholesale funding had changed the standard banking model and brought with it new risks and increased fragility. Ultimately the mortgage-backed bonds funding stream or banks came unstuck when it was discovered that some of the loans supporting bonds in the United States had been mis-sold and were worthless. As a corollary, the bonds were also worthless and more generally the funding mechanism was fundamentally undermined, and with it the banks themselves. The details of how this occurred are in the book, *Property Boom and Banking Bust*, by Jones et al. published in 2018.

The linkage between deregulation and globalisation is seen in a world capital market that has intertwined banking systems and macroeconomies inextricably connected by trade in goods and services. The resultant interlinkages of economies have also created a synchronisation of real estate market behaviour giving rise to global cycles as indicated in Chapter 3. The more countries are integrated into international deregulated capital flows the more likely they experience common 'boom and bust' scenarios. This phenomenon is moderated by the distinct institutions and legal systems of countries that generate different informational efficiencies and transparencies in real estate markets.

International Banking Regulations

Financial deregulation was a major contributor to the global financial crisis (GFC) and led to insolvency of many banks around the world. It is important to realise that when a bank issues a loan to a real estate investor it is also participating in that investment. In retrospect bankers unburdened by regulation took risks on a quite unjustified scale in lending to real estate investors during the boom of the 2000s believing the good times would roll on and on. The banks had no apparent memory of the banking losses in past downturns of commercial real estate cycles, experiences that had been repeated around the world.

The lack of financial prudence by the banking system in the 2000s was made possible by the weakness of self-regulation. Regulation had been deliberately watered down by governments to give banks greater freedom to generate innovation and profits. There was also a belief that self-regulating financial markets tended towards stability. What regulations there were, were not fit for purpose. They could not cope with the new entrepreneurial banks, developing new products, expanding dramatically their commercial real estate lending portfolios and raising vast sums of money via international bond markets.

The failure of many banks can be traced directly back to their excessive lending to commercial real estate investors. Not surprisingly given the financial support and nationalisation of banks following the GFC were demands for greater regulation. In the United States, the Dodd-Frank Act was enacted in 2010 that established a new system of oversight of financial services including credit rating agencies, etc. The increased regulation went beyond just banks themselves because the crisis had been caused not just by banks. For example, the credit rating agencies had failed to properly accredit the risks involved in mortgage-backed securities. Their overly favourable ratings supported the excessive bank lending of the 2000's boom.

By regulating bank lending for real estate developments and investment purchases, the real estate market is also regulated. One specific goal is to moderate real estate cycles. The introduction of greater regulatory structures of financial services through state appointed agencies occurred in all major economies within an international framework. The G20 countries set up the Financial Stability Board to coordinate the regulation of financial services around the world. The original countries have been augmented by Hong Kong, Singapore, Spain and Switzerland. The European Banking Authority was also established in 2011 with a goal to develop a single set of prudential rules across the European Union to enable better monitoring and regulation of banks. In general, there has been a move towards a greater consistency of banking definitions with regard to risks.

A further outcome of the greater monitoring is periodic stress testing of individual banks around the world to assess their resilience to adverse market developments such as a recession or an international banking failure. With regard to real estate, the key question is does a bank have sufficient capital to survive if investment values fall on the properties that they have loans outstanding (see Basel III below). These tests assess, in particular, the capital adequacies of individual banks to meet the strains, and if they do not a bank has to put in place plans to address the issue.

A further element of the increased international regulation was the introduction of 'Basel III' in 2011, or the Third Basel Accord. The Basel Accords were originally developed in the late 1980s. The accords are so named because the Basel Committee on Banking Supervision (BCBS) is headquartered in Basel, Switzerland. The extensive list of member countries includes Australia, Argentina, Belgium, Canada, Brazil, China, France, Hong Kong, Italy, Germany, Indonesia, India, Korea, the United States, the UK, Luxembourg, Japan, Mexico, Russia, Saudi Arabia, Switzerland, Sweden, the Netherlands, Singapore, South Africa, Turkey and Spain. It is useful to review how they have been developed.

Basel I

The Basel I accord was originally organised by central bankers from the G10 Countries. It was issued in 1988 and focused on monitoring the capital adequacy of financial institutions to deal with the risk of an unexpected loss in their loan portfolios. A ratio was calculated that compared the capital of a bank with its assets weighted by their degree of risk. The assets of a bank include loans such as mortgages and loans to real estate. Loan assets were weighted by their degree of risk in terms of supporting collateral with, for example, residential mortgages twice as safe as commercial real estate loans. A bank's capital was also differentiated by the degree of liquidity to assess a bank's financial strength to cope with a crisis. Only certain types of capital were deemed eligible to be considered as a liquidity base for lending. International banks were recommended to broadly hold eligible capital equal to at least 8% of their loan assets (adjusted for their degree of risk) to reduce the risk of insolvency.

Basel II

The second Basel Accord in 2005 augmented the original accord. It extended the minimum capital requirements by adding another layer of more risky capital to be included in the capital adequacy formula. It introduced a requirement for an operational supervisory review of an institution's capital adequacy, and the effective use of disclosure as a lever to strengthen market discipline and encourage sound banking practices.

Basel III

In the wake of the GFC of 2008 and the collapse of many banks, including Lehman Brothers, around the world, the BCBS decided to update and strengthen the Accords. It was considered that poor governance and risk management, inappropriate incentive structures and an overleveraged banking industry were reasons for the crisis. These issues have been discussed at length in this book with regard to commercial property holdings and loans.

The banking industry faced a legacy of the GFC in which many outstanding loans had been negotiated against higher property values that now applied. The falls in capital values following the crisis meant that many outstanding loans to investors and developers were greater than the values of the properties. The banks became effective owners of properties where the loan was in default, and sought ways of reclaiming some of their capital, often with the help of hedge funds (see Chapter 5). Basel III was a response to these problems in both financial and real estate markets.

In November 2010, the Basel III agreement was reached on a capital and liquidity reform package. It strengthened bank capital requirements by increasing minimum capital requirements, encouraging holdings of high-quality liquid assets and decreasing the gearing of banks. Amongst a range of changes to achieve this goal the relative risk associated with commercial real estate loans was upgraded in the capital adequacy formula from Basel I. Mortgage backed securities were also taken into account as off balance sheet risky commitments.

Basel III also introduced micro-prudential management of banks. Banks need to be subject to external credit assessments that are independent and based on publicly available criteria. The results have to be made available to interested parties. There are also requirements to have internal risk compliance procedures that are robust and fully documented, and that are subject to periodic external review. Banks are also required to develop operational risk measurement systems where operational risk is defined as the risk of loss resulting from inadequate or failed internal processes, people and systems or from external events.

Basel IV

The Basel IV standards that are due to take effect in 2023 and can arguably be seen as an extension of Basel III. It increases the capital requirements of banks and primarily fine-tunes and simplifies the calculations of credit risk, market risk and operational risk for financial institution set out in Basel III. It also reduces national discretion to interpret the regulations.

It should be noted that a Basel Accord is not legally binding in any jurisdiction but rather is intended to form the general basis for national (or regional) rule making. Member countries of the Basel Committee have taken different approaches to implementing accords. These international regulations are therefore to be policed by national bank supervisory authorities. In the UK, for example, banks and financial institutions continue to be supervised by the Prudential Regulation Authority, part of the Bank of England, and the Financial Conduct Authority.

Notwithstanding the increased state regulation following the GFC, the real estate industry itself is now more focussed on the risks of severe real estate downturns. In the UK, all of this precipitated an industry wide assessment of the threat the real estate cycle can pose to the stability of financial systems in the UK. In 2014, the Investment Property Forum published A *Vision for Real Estate Finance* in the UK. It made recommendations that could protect systemically financial institutions and the financial system more generally from the commercial real estate cycle. To achieve this goal, it proposed that financial institutions hold sufficient capital to withstand a market crash reflecting the recommendations of Basel III. The vision also saw the moderating of the flow of credit to the commercial real estate sector and the establishment of systems to ensure that financial institutions are positioned to support commercial real estate lending after a market crash.

The increased regulatory environment since the GFC is still to be tested. It is designed to moderate bank lending in general. Regulations have been introduced to make banks hold s higher amount of (liquid) capital to support lending activities. However, at the time of writing, there has not been a significant upturn or downturn in real estate markets to generate the stresses that the new regulations are designed to address. On the other hand, the banks were able to cope with the negative consequences of the pandemic in terms of debt holidays.

Summary

Across the globe land use planning regulations intervene in real estate markets with implications for values, development constraints and investment activity. It takes various forms, including refusing developments that could have negative consequences for neighbouring sites or because they are in locations deemed not appropriate. Planning is normally in the form of rules including a combination of zoning for specific uses, applying density constraints or requiring planning permission.

In some circumstances, planning can take a proactive approach by offering grants to developers or tax incentives to locate in an area. It can also encompass a strategic perspective on planning urban areas to ensure the operation of an efficient urban form, including the management of traffic flows.

Planning is generally beneficial for the real estate market and in countries where it is ineffective it can unnecessarily constrain investment and development by generating uncertainty. While planning can have negative impacts on land values of a certain use if it zones too much land for that use in the main it supports land values. Where planning limits development despite rising demand, for example, then there are higher land and real estate values that otherwise would have been the case. The more severe the planning constraint the greater are land and real estate values. The higher values benefit existing real estate investors and push up densities as land is used more intensively.

There is evidence to suggest that the British real estate market is more heavily regulated by planning than other European countries and that Europe in turn is more regulated than the United States. But there are differences within countries: less prosperous areas tend to have less restrictive planning policies because of the need for new employment to the area.

Planning policies also proactively manage and change cities through for example urban regeneration that can involve grants or tax incentives to developers and investors to develop in specific areas. Transport policies too are designed to improve the management of traffic flows in a city but can alter the spatial pattern of land uses. In the city centre, it could lead to the reconfiguration of the shopping centre. There could be significant impacts on investment values with some locations benefitting while others lose out. More generally constraints on travel into city centres are likely to favour alternative locations and relatively deflate city centre real estate values.

Countries around the world are committed to a green agenda to address climate change and it is recognised that the real estate sector needs to adapt by in particular reducing energy consumption.

There can be policy requirements for new buildings to be energy efficient but there are also strategies to reduce the energy use of existing buildings as exemplified by EPCs in Europe. In the UK, there are now minimum efficiency standards for buildings that are set to become more stringent in the near future.

On a wider front, the EU has been placing requirements on financial institutions and advisors to disclose all the sustainability risks in their investment process that could have a potential negative return. These disclosures relate to energy consumption and flooding for real estate investments. In a similar vein, some states in the United States require large buildings to disclose energy consumption to prospective purchasers, tenants and lenders. All these disclosures are aimed at increasing awareness of the need for investors and tenants to address the green agenda. Given this imperative, it has led to nearly all new office buildings being built to green specifications in Western economies. It has also been seen in the introduction of ESG real estate benchmarks by many financial institutions in Western economies.

Regulation of real estate markets has taken different forms and its impact needs to be taken together with the tax treatment of investors. Residential rent controls are the most widespread form of regulation around the world and designed to protect tenants from excessive rises in rents. When residential rents are kept below market levels, it leads to potentially no new investment in the sector and a decline in the quality of the stock. Indeed, the sector will decline if it is possible to sell vacant property for owner occupation, especially if the latter sector has tax advantages.

In some countries, there are 'second generation' rent controls that just moderate rent increases. This type of control means that many landlords favour tenants who landlords expect to stay only for a short period. This type of rent control lowers returns to investors and dampens rather than stifles investment. In practice, wide variations on these two models of rent control have been applied across the globe. An alternative to the introduction of rent control to support low-income tenants is income related subsidies to spend on housing.

In the commercial real estate leases may also be regulated. The nature of leases differs by country mainly according to custom but can be controlled within a legal framework. In some countries, rents are subject to legal constraint that index them in line with a measure of inflation even though lease lengths are not. There are only a few international instances of commercial rent 'freezes' that have lasted a number of years.

Deregulation of real estate markets has the potential to unleash fundamental change. There has been a trend towards the deregulation of the PRS in many countries. An extreme example is the UK where decontrol happened in 1989 after almost a century of regulation in different forms. It was the beginning of a transformation of the PRS which appeared up to that point as in terminal decline.

Re-investment in this sector took time to respond and the timing of the revival was also dependent on other factors linked to changes in the taxation of owner occupation and the fall in returns from stock market investments. A crucial impetus was provided by the emergence of readily availability of mortgage finance and a house price boom. This UK experience of the deregulation of the PRS demonstrates that deregulation in itself may not be sufficient to stimulate substantial change and other supporting pillars are needed.

Deregulation of banks normally leads to the expansion of the availability of credit and often provides a platform for real estate booms. From the 1980s, deregulation combined with globalisation led to banks becoming more internationalised and entrepreneurial in their approach to real estate lending. In the 2000s, banks were able to grow and expand their lending using wholesale borrowing with very little oversight from regulators or company auditors. It was a major contributor to the real estate boom of that decade. When the wholesale funding stream collapsed following the sub-prime lending crisis in the United States the GFC that followed brought a sudden end to the bank lending spree and the real estate boom. The linkage between deregulation and globalisation led to the synchronisation of a real estate boom and bust across many Western countries.

The follies of the deregulation or self-regulation of the banks were exposed by the GFC. In particular, there had been excessive lending to commercial real estate investors. The policy response around the world was greater regulation. The 2010 Dodd-Frank Act in the United States, for example, brought a new system of supervision of financial services. In fact, tighter regulation via public agencies occurred in all major economies within an internationally coordinated framework. In addition, there was also an international effort towards a greater consistency of the identification of banking risks.

Periodic stress testing of individual banks was introduced around the world to assess their resilience to adverse market developments such as the fall of real estate investment values in a recession. The essential idea was that if banks were found to lack sufficient capital resources to meet the strains they would be required to make plans to resolve the problem.

The increased international regulation of the banks also occurred through the establishment of '*Basel III*' in 2011. Basel Accords are traced back to the late 1980s. They began with *Basel I* in 1988 when the central bankers of the G10 countries decided to monitor the capital adequacy of financial institutions. A recommended minimum prudent ratio was developed for a bank that was based on the capital held by each bank (partly in liquid form) with its assets (including loans to real estate) by their degree of risk.

Basel II in 2005 introduced greater requirements for public disclosure but after the GFC it was realised that the accords needed to be strengthened. In November 2010, the *Basel III* agreement increased bank capital requirements, encouraged holdings of high-quality liquid assets and lowered the gearing of banks. The risk status of commercial real estate loans was increased, and mortgage-backed securities were also taken into account as off balance sheet risky commitments.

Basel III also brought in micro-prudential management of banks with external credit assessments, internal risk compliance procedures and operational risk measurement systems. *Basel IV* standards are to be applicable from 2023 and again extend the capital requirements of banks. These Basel Accords are policed by national bank supervisory authorities and the revisions have not been tested by a significant downturn in real estate markets since the GFC. However, banks coped with the negative consequences of the pandemic.

Learning Outcomes

After completing this chapter the reader should be able to:

- Understand that land use planning regulations intervene in real estate markets with implications for values, development constraints and investment activity.
- Recognise that planning is normally in the form of rules including a combination of zoning for specific uses, applying density constraints or requiring planning permission.
- Note that planning can take a proactive approach by offering grants to developers or tax incentives to locate in an area.
- Appreciate the strategic perspective on planning urban areas to ensure the operation of an efficient urban form including the management of traffic flows.
- Planning is generally seen as beneficial for the real estate market by reducing uncertainty and increasing land values.
- Recognise that the influence of planning regulations varies between and within countries.
- Be aware that planning policies can lead to the reconfiguration of land use patterns.
- Appreciate that the global green agenda to address climate change has requirements for reducing the energy consumption of buildings.
- Note that many governments have required buildings to be graded by their energy consumption and have set minimum standards.
- Recognise that the EU requires financial institutions to disclose sustainability risks in their investment process that could have a potential negative return.
- Understand how the regulation of real estate markets takes different forms and its impact needs to be taken together with the tax treatment of investors.
- Recognise that residential rent controls below market levels stifle new investment in the sector and a decline in the quality of the stock.
- Note the differences between first and second generation rent controls.
- Appreciate that commercial real estate leases may be regulated.
- Recognise that there has been a trend towards the deregulation of the PRS in many countries.
- Understand that deregulation of the PRS in the UK suggests that decontrol is in itself not sufficient to stimulate substantial change and other supporting pillars are needed.
- Note that the deregulation of banks normally leads to the expansion of the availability of credit and often provides a platform for real estate booms.
- Appreciate how deregulation and wholesale funding together with globalisation in the 2000s led to banks being a major contributor to the real estate boom and bust of that decade.

- Understand how international banking regulations have been tightened up after the GFC to require banks to hold more capital to support lending together with a recalibration of the risks involved in commercial real estate lending and mortgage-backed securities.
- Note also that banks have become subject to more monitoring and external risk assessment. These measures include periodic stress testing of an individual bank to assess their resilience to adverse market developments as well as internal risk compliance procedures and operational risk measurement systems.

Case Study: Application of Environmental and Social Governance (ESG)

With the increasing acceptance of the urgency of climate change, ESG criteria are becoming embedded in investment decision-making. Climate change is directly impinging on the real estate market and investment. The fear of rising sea levels could engulf much prime real estate in major world cities. In some parts of the world, long-term drought threatens the viability of cities. Extreme weather events across much of the world have included extensive flooding and largescale wild fires with consequent property damage. As a result, insurance premiums have increased and there is a need for investors to quantify risks and recognise the importance of resilience to climate change.

But there is a wider imperative about the need to reduce greenhouse gases and energy consumption. Although green buildings are becoming the norm for new buildings, there is now a realisation that net zero carbon emission buildings are required to meet the aims to address global warming. As a result, governments are raising required environmental standards for properties as detailed in this chapter. In addition, the social and economic impacts of building design on workers through wellness and productivity are now widely recognised by employers with implications for the demand for offices and ultimately real estate values.

These concerns are expressed in ESG real estate benchmarks addressing climate resilience, climate change risk, zero-carbon targets, wellness and governance issues. ESG benchmarks can be used not only to give a broad strategic assessment of investment performance but also permit improvement goals. Despite the ESG title, many social aspects of sustainability such as diversity receive little attention. These benchmarks are clear risk management tools but also act to serve the wider community.

There are a number of companies that prepare consistent scores based on ESG benchmarks for real estate investors. GRESB, the market leader, was set up in 2009 and is used by more than 1500 real estate investors including financial institutions, developers and REITs to assess their sustainability performance relative to their peers. Participants provide data for GRSB to be scored and benchmarked on an annual basis. For investors, there are two dimensions to the benchmarks.

A management component assesses the investor's governance procedures including strategy and leadership, risk management and stakeholder engagement. The second dimension reviews the performance of the portfolio of assets in terms of energy consumption, GHG emissions, water consumption and waste. At the individual asset level besides green accreditation of design there are agencies in some countries that score energy consumption and wellness. Some companies have also developed internal bespoke benchmarks but this a resource intensive process.

A study of ESG by Newall et al. for the Investment Property Forum published in 2020 and based on a survey of investors within the real estate industry found:

- ESG benchmarking was still a work in progress and needs supporting data and metrics.
- Benchmarking was viewed as the starting point not the end point of an ESG strategy.
- ESG was seen as an effective risk management procedure and more important than just for profile or PR purposes as part of say 'corporate social responsibility'.
- ESG benchmarking in real estate was viewed as fundamentally important as part of overall best practice in real estate investment.
- There was a considerable variation in ESG benchmarking and implementation across the world. Australia and Europe were the leading regions in adopting best practices, with North America catching up. Asia and the Middle East were some way further behind in embracing ESG. These differences partly reflected the distinction between developed and emerging markets.

Reading

Cheshire, P. and Hilber, C. (2008) Office space supply restrictions in Britain: The political economy of Revenge. *Economic Journal*, 118 (June), 529, F185–F221.

Deschermeier, P., Haas, H., Hude, M., and Michael Voigtlander, M. (2016) A first analysis of the new German rent regulation. *International Journal of Housing Policy*, 16, 3, 293–315.

Investment Property Forum. (2014) A *Vision for Real Estate Finance in the UK*. Investment Property Forum, London.

Jones, C. (2021) *Urban Economy: Real Estate Economics and Public Policy*. Taylor & Francis, Abingdon.

Jones, C., Cowe, S. and Trevillion, E. (2018) *Property Boom and Banking Bust: The Role of Commercial Lending in the Bankruptcy of Banks*. Wiley-Blackwell, Chichester.

Newall, G., Moss, A., and Nanda, A. (2020) *Benchmarking Real Estate Investment Performance: The Role of ESG Factors*. Investment Property Forum, London.

Oyedokun, T., Jones, C., and Dunse, N. (2015) The growth of the green office market in the UK. *Journal of European Real Estate Research*, 8, 3, 267–284.

Investment Consequences of Changing Occupier Needs and Obsolescence

11

Introduction

In Chapter 5, the changing composition of real estate investment portfolios by financial institutions was noted. It reported how UK institutional investors shifted from preferring retail property to offices and then back again over several decades. This chapter examines the reasons for these swings in more detail and looks at the changing nature of the main real estate sectors.

It focuses on how changing occupier needs are framed by the state of technology and demonstrates how technological advances lead to new built forms in the different sectors. In particular, the emergence of these new forms is shown to replace traditional buildings causing obsolescence in the existing stock. The chapter reveals how no real estate sector is immune from obsolescence and that in turn there are consequences for investment decisions and the composition of portfolios.

The chapter begins by considering an overview of the reasons for depreciation and obsolescence in real estate markets before assessing changes in individual sectors. The chapter is structured to cover the following main topic areas:

- Defining and measuring obsolescence
- Green labelled buildings
- Retail change including online sales
- Information and communications technology (ICT) and warehousing
- Hot desking and demand for offices
- Serviced Offices including a short case study of *WeWork.*

C. A. Jones and E. Trevillion, *Real Estate Investment* ,
https://doi.org/10.1007/978-3-031-00968-6_11

Defining and Measuring Obsolescence

The causes of the depreciation in values of real estate can be distinguished between physical deterioration and obsolescence with the latter derived in turn from changes linked to market forces. In fact, there are a variety of forms of obsolescence defined by reference to their cause. These causes are:

- *Economic obsolescence* that occurs when underlying market conditions, independent of the state of the structure, leads to falling values, and perhaps eventually redevelopment or abandonment.
- *Functional obsolescence* is created specifically by technological change leading to changed occupier demand requirements for individual properties. An example would be the replacement of analogue telephone exchanges by digital technology.
- *Aesthetic/visual obsolescence* as society's norms reject certain building forms or designs
- *Environmental obsolescence* is caused by a rise in acceptable standards for the quality of work and changing environmental standards.
- *Legislative obsolescence* is generated by new laws that raise the standard of building regulations, for example, with regard to fire safety and external cladding.

An important distinction between physical deterioration and obsolescence is that the latter is outside the control of property owners. Very often, commercial and industrial buildings reach the end of their functional or economic lives well before they reach the end of their physical lives. Physically sound buildings suffering from functional obsolescence can be converted to alternative uses such as redundant banks to restaurants.

While physical deterioration and obsolescence can be differentiated by their causes, both can be measured by falls in rental and capital values. More precisely depreciation can be defined as a loss in the real existing use value of a property. Declines in value do not normally follow a linear trend. Depreciation in property values is linked to age and is most likely to take the shape of a convex accelerating curve rather than linear deterioration. Studies have found that building quality is an additional factor beyond age in explaining depreciation. Similarly, there are arguments that ownership retention and lease structures affect depreciation. Longer lease structures with tenants responsible for full repairs could generate greater depreciation whereas short leases and frequent sales of an individual property are likely to stimulate active management and physical improvement. This argument points to variations between countries with different lease structures.

Economic and functional obsolescence are both linked to market forces, with the latter dependent on the pace of change of the adoption of technological innovation. Obsolescence therefore varies over time. The relative comparative rental and capital values of offices and industrial units that are new, 10 years or 25 years old would be very different in the 1980s than in the 2020s. Part of the reason why the impact of obsolescence varies over time is that functional obsolescence is linked to technological change that tends to come in waves.

Depreciation not only varies over time periods but also between locations, even within cities. First, depreciation is likely to be highest where land values are lowest and vice versa lowest where land values are highest. This is because the depreciation/obsolescence may apply simply to the building and its use. Put another way, the land component of the rental or capital value is not depreciating just the property on it. Indeed, as the value of physical buildings fall, the rate of rent/price depreciation is tempered by the land value component that may even be rising if there is an increase in demand for that locality. In these circumstances, the different components of the property's investment value could balance out.

To take an example the initial value of a new office skyscraper on a prime city centre site may comprise a high component that can be attributed to the building itself. Over time the rental value of the office block may suffer as newer offices are built offering better quality accommodation to users. The building will suffer economic obsolescence so the rents achieved may fall in real terms. However, the land could keep its market value because of its prime central location. The result is that the contribution to the overall investment value of the land rises and that of the building falls. Eventually, the underlying finances could lead to the redevelopment of the site with a new office with up to the minute specifications.

In a similar vein, it is likely that the main contribution to the investment value of a city centre shop is the price of the land on which it is located. A city centre is the most accessible point of the urban area and the apex of retail rents and land values. Traditionally there is excess demand ensuring that rents do not fall (but see later). The result is that the investment value of shops in the city centre will be shielded from economic obsolescence by both high land values and continuing demand.

In contrast, there are many substitute locations for industrial property and they are more susceptible to competition from new property. It is relatively quick to build a new industrial unit. Construction costs are low as is the land used by industrial property. For these reasons, falls in rental values of industrial property from competition are not balanced by land price rises. The investment value of industrial property is therefore prone to economic obsolescence.

Local market conditions also influence the rate of economic obsolescence as the following examples illustrate. Strong demand pressures in a local market could mean an old building may find a taker at a rent close to that attainable for a new building. In contrast, the reverse would be true in a local market with over supply. In general, the higher levels of real estate development in an area the greater the rate of property depreciation.

In addition, land value as well as the physical structure can be subject to economic obsolescence, for example, if the optimum location for specific land uses change. There are several ways this can occur, and the following examples are not exhaustive. To recap on Chapter 10, it was noted that a local authority planning policies can influence the relative attractions of shopping locations within a city centre. If certain localities become more popular then retail rental and land values increase while areas losing demand experience a fall in land values. Similarly, the building of a new motorway that changes accessibility relationships brings with it modifications to associated land values.

Functional obsolescence as noted earlier is related to technological change. An important example is the emergence of the office obsolescence problems of the 1980s with the beginnings of the ICT revolution. Many offices built as late as the 1960s were unable to cope with the heavy cabling demands of ICT and hence were obsolete at that time. It led to the depreciation of office rental and capital values and the attraction of investing in offices floundered. And as a result, it contributed to the office development boom during the 1980s as many existing buildings were replaced.

Empirical studies in the UK on depreciation from the early 1980s to the early 2010s have generally not differentiated between falls in property values caused by physical deterioration and obsolescence. They have centred on the impact of age on property values without separating land value. These studies find annual depreciation rates that are quite low, of the order of 1 to 3%, and confirm how land prices can cushion the fall in the value of physical property. However, there is considerable variation in these rates between different locations (and properties) and research also only relates to properties owned largely by financial institutions.

Depreciation rates could be very different in other segments of the market, but this evidence suggests offices are most prone to depreciation followed by industrial properties with standard shops least. These findings are very period specific, and since these studies for example online sales have revolutionised retailing and seen the value of shopping centres fall.

Further sections in this chapter examine recent experiences of functional obsolescence on investment in different real estate sectors. The next section considers the influence of the arrival of new technologies that have brought new green labelled buildings with higher environmental standards. The following section charts the arrival of online sales and the consequences for existing retail units. The online revolution and new applications of ICT to the distribution of goods are then assessed for investors in warehousing.

Green Labelled Buildings

As noted in Chapter 10, governments around the world are now following a green agenda that is seeking a zero-carbon future. Part of this strategy is the greening of buildings, but this will have consequences for real estate markets and investment. The promotion of greener buildings requires a market identifier in other words a green label for buildings that meet the requisite environmental standards. However, there is no one definition of a green building.

There are a range of voluntary accreditation green label systems around the world with different measuring schemes. These green label schemes began with BREEAM, the first scheme originated in the UK that has been adapted in other parts of Europe, China and South America. LEED is the primary North American version and it too is exporting its accreditation system overseas. France has its own scheme entitled HQE while GBTool is used in many countries such as South Africa.[1] Green Star accreditation is applied in Australia.

There are inevitably differences between schemes reflecting local circumstances. Climate is important because of the impact on work conditions and hence the need for air conditioning in some localities. All these schemes are based essentially on receiving credits for a wide range of different green building features that range over energy, health and wellbeing, water, waste, materials, transport, land use and ecology, and management.

The criteria have changed over time reflecting developments in the state of the art of green technology. The schemes have also been extended to rate existing buildings and refurbishment. The green scores do not relate to actual benefits but to individual design characteristics. Sustainable transport scores, for example, are calculated not by travel usage but by such features as the nearness to public transport, car parking spaces, bicycle friendliness and so on.

For investors, there is also an issue of equivalence between the scores in different schemes. Different countries use different criteria and different classifications. These differences are an issue for consistency in the increasingly globalised real estate portfolios of large investors. In some countries, there are parallel schemes that measure actual energy use including Energy Star in the United States and NABERS in Australia/UK.

A key reason for green labelling is so that the real estate market can recognise the environmental standards of buildings and price them accordingly. Tenants can then appreciate that the environmental standards of these buildings would mean for example lower heating bills and improvements in the productivity of the workforce. Tenants might then pay a higher rent, a green premium, for the benefits of these buildings. The existence of a green premium could potentially drive investment and development of new green labelled buildings as well as green refurbishment of the existing uncertified buildings.

Through this price mechanism increased rents and capital values could make green developments more viable. If the premium is sufficiently high enough, it could stimulate the viable development of say new green offices and refurbishment of the existing stock of office buildings. However, in practice, not all tenants are prepared to pay a green premium. The choice of an office involves normally considering a range of substitute properties in which the choice balances a range of attributes such as rent, location and size with green features. A tenant's choice is likely to involve the trade-off between the 'positive' and the 'negative' characteristics of the different offices.

Historically, the greenness of offices was a secondary demand characteristic for tenants, subservient to location and the suitability/functionality of space. In

[1] BREEAM Building Research Establishment Environment Assessment Method
LEED Leadership in Energy and Environment Design
HQE Haute Qualite Environmentale.

many localities, non-labelled offices constitute the larger proportion of the market and green labelled offices are a small submarket. A growing acknowledgement of the attractions of green buildings could ultimately lead to the labelled submarket expand to become the dominant component of the market. If and when the advantages of green offices to tenants become widely accepted, and such offices become standard, then there could be negative consequences for the values of non-green stock.

The greening of the office stock is more than simply the building of green offices. The logic of this process is that eventually rather than a green premium existing there is a non-green discount rent. In other words, the rents/capital values of non-green offices depreciate in relative terms. These market changes can be viewed as 'green obsolescence' that is a combination of functional, aesthetic, legal, social, physical and environmental obsolescence. Ultimately, these offices would need to be replaced or refurbished.

This process of change could take a long time even if supported by government policies. Real estate markets can be slow to adapt because of their imperfections. The development of new buildings and green refurbishment takes time with the latter subject to many physical barriers derived from the original building form.

The pace of change can also be slowed by national economic downturns. As noted in the previous section, there is also a local dimension to the obsolescence process shaped by the nature of demand and supply restrictions caused by the urban physical characteristics and planning/conservation (see Chapter 10). Local demand may have concentrations of large multi-national companies who seek green buildings as part of their corporate social responsibility agenda.

In many countries, this progression towards green labelled buildings has been limited to the construction of new accredited buildings. Green refurbishment is often prohibitively expensive. It means that a green premium for older stock is elusive. To date green investment decisions are bound up with the development of new offices and their characteristics. The influences on investment are not directly from a green premium but part of a wider requirement to attract quality tenants by offering better-specified offices.

Certainly, in the UK at the time of writing, there is a general belief by real estate agents that there is not a green rent premium but a 'green letting premium', namely that a green office is easier to let. It is more subtle than a green rent premium but ultimately means a greater revenue stream. A green label is therefore important to investors therefore as it acts a guarantee of future income streams and ultimately higher capital values.

Investment Consequences

There is an inevitability about the greening of office and the obsolescence of the non-green stock. However, the timeline to achieve this could be very protracted. Nevertheless, owners and prospective owners of existing non-green office blocks will need to factor in a future that eventually sees falling values and green refurbishment/redevelopment.

Retail Change including Online Sales

The impact of online sales on retailing is only the latest of a long line of changes that have impacted on the retail sector with consequences for investment. Many of these changes were brought about by the growth of car usage and led to new retail forms and locations. This section first examines this process of change, and then considers the response of large investors.

For centuries, the primary focus of shopping was at the centre of urban areas, latterly in the form of high/main streets in the 1800s. Until relatively recently the core retail area was the essential location for shops selling comparison goods such as clothing and footwear. There were also a series of suburban high streets (often along arterial roads) selling primarily convenience goods with neighbourhood centres offering a more limited range of goods and choice.

The advent of the family car restructured patterns of shopping, and the flexibility enabled larger catchment areas. People no longer had to walk to a local shopping centre or take a bus to shop in the urban core. Access to a car meant that a person did not have to shop at the nearest centre but could travel on to a more attractive one. The use of cars also contributed to the decentralisation of cities, and as households moved out to suburbs the spatial pattern of retail catchment areas was also inevitably altered, including their hierarchical structure. The combined influence of population suburbanisation and car bound shopping freedom led to the decentralisation of shopping centres. The United States led the way where the first suburban covered shopping mall opened in 1956.

Retail decentralisation has followed distinctive paths in different countries, both in terms of timing and retail formats. The chapter now spotlights how this decentralisation occurred in the UK. Schiller identifies three waves of decentralisation from the 1970s on in the UK. In the first wave, supermarkets open up outside town centres. Standalone retail warehouses (big box shops) begin to be built in the early 1980s representing the second wave with out-of-town shopping malls following in the third.

The initial retail warehouses were sometimes converted units on industrial estates. However, by the end of the 1980s, warehouses were now new box units grouped together to form 'retail parks' around common car parking. These developments in the United States are called 'power centers'. Over time the units on retail parks increasingly looked like shops and the park was often co-located with a grocery superstore.

Initially, retail warehouses sold mainly bulky products including DIY, furniture, carpets and electrical appliances. The bulk of these goods made decentralised locations very appropriate as there was the advantage of space and lower rents than the traditional high/main street. The extensive adjacent parking made it easy for consumers to load their cars. Given the type of products on sale, these developments were at the beginning viewed as helpful to central urban locations. The shift of these stores from the centre relaxed space constraints on high/main streets, enabling a wider range of retail opportunities.

This position has been transformed over time as the bulky goods stores were replaced by mainstream national 'high street' retailers. In this guise, retail parks now represent significant threats to town centres. Similarly, urban retail cores are suffering from the displacement of consumers to out-of-town shopping malls.

The characteristics of urban retail core shopping centres have also changed in response to customer demands for more convenience. Department stores, once the historical anchors of town centres, have been superseded by new in town shopping malls. Nevertheless, small-town centres have been undermined by car parking constraints in comparison with out-of-town centres. The move to out-of-town has also been supported by retailers' demands for larger specification retail units, in part the result of the rise of brands. Many small shops have become functionally obsolete.

Retail change has not been confined to change within cities, but also to between urban areas. Improved inter-urban road networks have led to shoppers abandoning local towns for comparison goods, such as clothing, and travelling to larger regional centres with more choice. At the same time, as noted, small-town centres have also suffered from the competition from retail parks at their urban edge. As a consequence, most shopping centres of small towns have high levels of vacancies.

These changes can also be seen in a wider context. The rise of retail parks and out-of-town centres can be seen in the long-term rise of real incomes bringing increased spending and a demand for more shops. Traditional high/main street shopping centres were too physically constrained to expand and hence the out-of-town revolution. But eventually new supply outstripped demand, and there were beginning to be too many shops. The problem became clearly evident with the recession following the GFC which saw vacancies balloon in small-town centres rising to unprecedented levels, in some cases over 20% by 2009.

At this point, the emergence of online sales is added to the changing fortunes of retailing. Online sales in the UK at the beginning of 2009 were just over 5% of sales but a decade later they were over 20%, the highest share in Europe. The most severe initial impact on shopping centres was through the many closures of bank branches, travel agents, and book and music shops. Such closures reduced the reasons for visiting high/main streets and dampened passing trade of the remaining shops.

Online purchases have now had a much wider impact on shopping centres, although physical stores are still important to shopping. Many British retailers now operate a popular arrangement of customers ordering online and collecting in a store known as 'click and collect'. The popularity of click and collect has worked to the benefit of out-of-town shopping centres for collection by car. Nevertheless, the continuing ascent of online sales inevitably siphons off revenue from physical stores, and in the process worsens the surplus of shops.

By the beginning of 2020, with real incomes falling or stagnant for over a decade after the global financial crisis, many national fashion retailers had begun closing branches. The subsequent disruption caused by the COVID pandemic of 2020/2021 led to an extension of previous plans to reduce store networks. While in the recession following the global financial crisis, it was small towns that primarily suffered this time round additional redundant excess space was concentrated in shopping malls and retail parks (power centres).

The recent account of retail change related above is the British experience that demonstrates the interaction between decentralisation and shopping. The history in other countries will be different. There will be shared elements including the long-term expansion of real incomes in Western economies in the decades after the Second World War. Recent stagnant or falling real incomes in many countries is also a common strand. Likewise, the suburbanisation of the population/urban decentralisation is a ubiquitous phenomenon that has inevitably led to pressure for the development/expansion of retail centres away from traditional central locations.

There are other commonalities across countries as new technologies and products linked to food preparation/storage reduced the frequency of local shopping trips. The rise of family car ownership has also extended distances households are prepared to travel. Together these innovations have brought increased flexibility in shopping patterns.

The overall result has been fundamental changes in the way people shop, a rearrangement of the retail hierarchy with new out-of-town retail formats. This is reflected in a changing mix of shops over time both in long-standing shopping centres and newer decentralised localities. There is also a growing surplus of shops. The scale of the surplus depends on the nature of national planning policies with the more liberal the approach to suburban shopping malls the greater the clear excess (see Chapter 10).

Investment Consequences

The long-standing attractiveness of shops as an investment was based on two key pillars. First, rental income (growth) was supported by the long-term rise in real incomes/consumer expenditure. Second, shops were located in high/main streets particularly in urban cores. As such the supply of shops was constrained by the urban fabric limiting development opportunities to the advantage of the existing retail units.

In addition, the prime shopping pitch was at the central location within the high/main street representing the apex of the retail hierarchy in a town/city. As the most accessible point of the urban area, it meant that there should always be excess demand for this location. These prime shopping locations represented the least risky of investments. If one tenant left, there would be another queuing to replace it. If one type of shop was no longer viable, there would be other shops selling different goods waiting in the wings to occupy the premises. In other words, the specific risk of the investment was low and risk was very limited.

A further positive factor of high street shops relative to other real estate sectors was the absence of obsolescence fears (but see below). While industrial properties

Table 11.1 The changing retail real estate institutional portfolio in the UK 1981–2010

Retail Segment	1981 %	1985 %	1990 %	1995 %	2000 %	2005 %	2010 %
Standard Shop	54.1	53.7	47.6	35.8	28.4	20.9	19.3
Shopping Centre	33.5	34.8	36.0	36.9	37.9	37.6	33.5
Retail Warehouse	2.1	2.6	8.2	16.6	25.5	34.7	36.3
Department/Variety Store	6.8	5.2	5.4	4.7	3.7	2.9	2.4
Supermarket	2.5	2.6	1.4	4.5	3.1	2.7	7.1
Other Retail	1.1	1.1	1.4	1.5	1.4	1.2	1.5
Total (%) Retail in 'Institutional' Portfolio	28.1	34.8	35.3	46.9	48.6	52.1	53.5

Source Derived from MSCI/IPD (2010)

have always been recognised as having a relatively short life and offices as noted above became subject to functional obsolescence from the 1980s shops were relatively immune. This position of the high street was also supported by the planning system (in many countries) that sought to protect the hegemony of core shopping centres. The exception was the impact of changing pedestrian flows where shopping centres were subject to reconfiguration as discussed in Chapter 10. This issue was primarily a risk for secondary rather than prime locations. Furthermore, in the UK at least, leases ensured that the periodic refitting of high street shops and the revamping of shop fronts were the responsibility of the tenant.

This picture began to unravel from the 1970s in the UK as outlined above. Table 11.1 records the subsequent changes to retail investment by financial institutions in the UK as decentralised retailing took hold. The table maps the changing share of types of real estate retail assets owned by financial institutions over the period, 1981–2010 using the MSCI/IPD database (see also Chapter 12). These three decades represent a period of substantial upheaval in retail forms.

Over this period retail assets as a percentage of the total value of all real estate investment by financial institutions grow consistently. Indeed, its share of real estate investment in 2010 is almost double that in 1981. But beneath this macro-trend, there are significant upheavals taking place. Standard shops suffer a dramatic slide from over half the value of retail assets to less than a fifth. At the other extreme retail warehouses rise from insignificance to become the largest type of retail asset and account for 36% of the value of retail assets. While shopping centres maintain a consistent share of retail assets, the aggregate increase in retail investment hides the fact that they rise from 9% of real estate assets held by financial institutions to 18% by 2010.

These statistics demonstrate the scale of the economic obsolescence of standard shops on high/main streets. The number of standard shops owned by financial institutions in 2006 was less than half that a decade earlier. They also show how financial institutions have had to adapt to urban and retail change. In 2010, retail warehouses represented almost one fifth of the value of real estate assets owned by financial institutions in the UK. They hardly existed as a retail form thirty years earlier.

The process by which new real estate forms are accepted by financial institutions as suitable investments can be slow and more complicated than perusal of Table 11.1 suggests. It is useful to examine the process by which retail warehouses rose to have the largest share of institutional investment. Initially in the 1980s, these new real estate forms were built by specialist development companies. To begin with profits from these new innovative retail forms were weak because rent levels were low to attract demand. The concept of a retail warehouses was also evolving so capital values were very low to reflect the risk of obsolescence. Eventually, the product was reshaped into clusters and became retail parks.

Financial institutions only began to invest once the market for retail warehouses had 'matured' and started buying out developers. Nevertheless, there was continuing perceived risks of obsolescence as the product developed and with it uncertainty about the long-term acceptability to occupiers. These concerns ensured that investors required a return that factored in a high-risk premium, namely a higher yield, in comparison to traditional standard shops. Eventually after a period of sustained letting activity and an active resale market yields fell and capital values increased.

At the beginning of this process in the 1980s, there was an investment 'risk premium' differential of approximately 2% between retail warehouses and standard shops. Only in 2000 does the risk premium on retail warehouses fall below that of standard shops. By then, all retail parks were predominantly owned by financial institutions. This suggests that the process of market establishment for retail warehouses took almost twenty years. The length of time reflects that they were a new real retail form in non-traditional locations, and that initial designs were subject to functional obsolescence. There were also uncertainties created by UK retail planning policy discouraging retail warehouses.

It is not just the pains of change that are important for retail investment because of the transformation of shopping centres. Retail real estate investment is no longer the passive activity it was when city centres were the primary shopping locus. Decentralised shopping centres mean that there is no supply constraint. An owner of a shopping mall or retail park can easily find itself subject to competition from a new shopping centre say ten minutes away by car, although there may be some protection from the planning system in some countries. Investment returns are no longer dependent on location but the quality of the centre. With the prevalence of shopping malls responsibility for refurbishment no longer lies just with tenants. To maintain the attractiveness of a shopping centre to customers and tenants, and hence protect rental values it may be periodically necessary for an owner to upgrade facilities and finishes.

Shopping centres are now prone to economic obsolescence, an issue that has been heightened by the growing excess shops compounded by the rise of online sales. For example, in the UK, there was a tsunami of major retail brand closures and others in financial difficulties at the end of the 2010s. It was brought about not only by online sales but also partly by a decade of austerity policies that stifled consumer spending in shops. The result is vacancies in shopping malls and retail parks. There is the probability that some of these centres will not survive as fickle customers simply drive past those with vacancies. It creates a potential downward spiral and falling capital values. Such is the scale of economic obsolescence that many centres will have to 'repurpose' to alternative uses.

The pace of change has also brought demands for more flexibility by tenants to respond to market forces that have been translated into shorter leases. Historically financial institutions in the UK required a 25-year lease with five year upward only rent reviews. These began to be less prevalent at the turn of the millennium and terms have consistently fallen since then to an average of less than ten years. In addition, the greater choice of properties in the retail sector has led to the power in negotiation switching to tenants from landlords.

This section has chronicled the changing nature of retailing in terms of decentralising locations and formats over the last half century. The focus has been on the UK, but the same processes and associated phenomena are occurring around the world. There are investment challenges in coping and adapting to the emergence of new retail forms and the demise of others. Online sales are the most recent important element in the cumulative shift to excess shops. The ultimate investment consequences are seen in increasing obsolescence and a need to take a more positive or proactive approach to asset management. The result is a fundamental reappraisal of investing in retail real estate.

ICT and Warehousing

Warehouses have a long history and were originally constructed to store local agricultural produce. Over the centuries, warehouses have been subsequently needed to store goods at ports and at rail heads or canal terminuses. The arrival of efficient inter-urban motorway/freeway networks led to warehouses decentralising to be adjacent to road junctions.

It is not just the location of warehousing that has changed over time but also their structures. Warehouses have increased significantly in size and technological advances have periodically changed their design. Warehouses abandoned the historic multi-storey model to become a single story 'shed' from the 1960s onwards supported by the invention of the forklift truck together with standardised pallets. Containerisation followed in the 1970s stimulating trade and increasing the demand for warehousing.

Warehouses have therefore been subject to evolution. As motorway networks have improved, large distribution centres have been able to service national/regional markets with the closure of small depots. One central location can now distribute to a number of countries in mainland Europe.

New technologies, such as barcodes, too have shifted warehousing from a passive storage function to one of inventory management. Warehousing is now an integral part of the distribution of goods, and warehouses are now better described as distribution centres within a wider 'Just in Time' supply chain management.

Where goods were once stored either in factories or in the backrooms of shops, from the 1980s retailers set up central distribution centres to which suppliers then delivered to. The retail chains then delivered goods directly to their shops.

These distribution changes led to larger and larger warehouses, as well as an increase in number. 'Mega-sheds' mushroomed around the world, comprising over 10,000 sq. metres in size. It was made possible by automation and improved management systems that encompass internal racking systems getting taller. Warehousing is also set up for sorting and picking goods rather than storage and as a result there is a speedy turnover of inventories necessitating parking spaces for a heavy throughput of lorries.

The growth of online sales has expanded the demand for distribution warehousing and reconstituted distribution processes to provide for home delivery and returns. To address the home delivery challenges hub and spoke networks have been established whereby regional/national warehouses link with local urban depots. These local depots are parcel sorting stations, that enable goods to be transferred for local delivery to homes, workplaces and stores (as part of click and collect). This local delivery task is known as 'the last mile'. These smaller warehouses can be newly built but also many factories and light industrial units have been converted for this use.

Investment Consequences

There has almost been a revolution in the warehousing process facilitated by technological change. Large national or regional distribution centres have become a real estate asset class in their own right. Initially, some large factories were converted but since the mid-1990s, there has been a rapid expansion of large purpose-built new distribution centres (DCs) with floor space in excess of 100,000 sq. ft (9300 sq. m).

In the UK, in the first two decades of this century 50 DCs were being built every year during the property boom, and even after the downturn following the global financial crisis annual construction rates dropped only marginally. New warehouse space is also clustering in dedicated distribution parks.

The precise sources of demand for this space are varied. Over 20% of the large DC space in the UK is directly occupied by high street or grocery retailers who undertake their own distribution. Many of their DCs are owner occupied. Third party logistics companies occupy a similar amount of space but provide services to a wide range of customers so the links to other sectors of the economy are complex and varied. An analysis of lease lengths on new properties, over the period 2010–2018, found that 90% of leases on logistics units were over 10 years, and a quarter more than 20 years. Some occupiers prefer to operate on a freehold basis often designing and building their own facility.

The logistics warehousing sector therefore has a high proportion of new stock with a high occupancy rate secured on particularly long leases (relative to say the retail sector) with national tenants representing strong covenants. These characteristics suggest that properties in the sector represent an attractive real estate investment.

Nevertheless, it appears that the proportion of warehousing owned as investments by financial institutions is low. In 1981, only 1% of the UK MSCI/IPD database was accounted for by distribution warehouses, rising to 3% in 2004 and 4.4% in 2014. While the warehousing numbers in this database rose from 46 in 1981 to 531 in 2014, this rate of growth is much lower than for the sector as a whole. Indeed, the numbers owned by financial institutions have not risen during the expansion of ecommerce since 2008. A much higher proportion of DCs are owned by specialist operators or owner occupied compared to the retail sector even though the two sectors have many common occupiers.

The reasons for this relate to the changing nature of DCs in parallels with the development of retail warehousing in the 1980s. Earlier it was noted that the emergence of the retail warehouses concept evolved through a product life cycle, just as DCs, to meet occupier demands. As part of the product development retail warehouses moved from individual units locating separately to spatial concentrations or parks. However, the experience of DCs highlight that there is a distinction between the evolution of a product to meet customer demand and its acceptance as an investment class by financial institutions.

A comparative analysis for the evolution of distribution relative to retail warehousing reveals some initial similarities to this process. Initially speculative and specialist developers primarily build these warehouses but there is a continuing trend towards bespoke building (often with a pre-let to a retailer) and owner occupation. As noted, institutional investors have not positively responded to this new investment class.

This lack of interest is despite evidence of a rising demand for distribution warehouses since the GFC at a time of stagnant national economic growth, high specification modern buildings and respectable tenants on relatively long leases. The explanation lies in the impact of technological change. DCs as an investment class has been subject to perpetual obsolescence over recent decades.

There is a continual march of technological advances in the sector, such as enabling automated packing systems and mechanised storage, and the rethinking of optimum distribution processes, including locations. It has meant that often businesses choose new facilities over vacant warehousing. At best it leads to long letting periods for vacant property and lower rents for second-hand properties. With a relatively short development timescale, logistical innovations accelerating there is investment uncertainty that suggests a high-risk premium for this investment class. In recent years, the risks have further increased by the woes of physical retailing with a contraction of the numbers in store networks with ramifications for distribution networks.

Overall financial institutions' reluctance to invest in DCs is based on their assessment of the risk. It is the obsolescence risk, primarily associated with technological change, that has been the main barrier to investment by financial institutions in this asset class.

Hot Desking and Demand for Offices

The demand for offices is at its simplest relates to the number of workers employed in services. However, the relationship between employment and the demand for office space has always been more complex than it at first seems. Inevitably space requirements are linked to the technology available. (New) offices are designed to meet the specific requirements of work based around the current technology.

Over the last fifty years, information technologies have been transformed spectacularly with consequences for the demand for and the design of offices. In the late 1970s, individual offices rarely contained a computer and usage involved a main frame centralised installation for the organisation. The 1980s brought new computer technology and many offices that proved unable to adapt became functionally obsolete. Decades on the contrast with then and today is night and day and in today's information age standardised software together with the ubiquitous laptop enables 'office' work to be conducted anywhere.

Work practices have been rethought and then rethought again. And so has the way business itself has been organised with the arrival of e-business and call centres. Company web sites are now used for promotion, with customers of many businesses ordering and paying online. Increasingly firms are focusing on their core business by outsourcing to subcontractors. Business decision-making structures have become less hierarchical with more team working and greater fluidity and flexibility in the use of labour.

There is an inevitable change in the demand for the type of office premises. Open plan offices became the norm. For many offices, it was possible to reconfigure existing space, and so the changes were evolutionary rather than revolutionary, but unavoidably some offices became obsolete. During this process, the office space per worker required fell marginally over time but the increasing demand for services saw a continuing rise in the number of offices.

Despite this trend, it was becoming increasingly evident that a high proportion of total office space was unused on any one day due to either absences, flexible working or team meetings. With the high cost of real estate, there is clear pathway to potential saving by introducing hot desking and hence downsize the required office space. Arguably it is not just the amount of space that is changing but also the nature of office environment as space is allocated to meeting rooms and collaborative and activity-based work.

Recent technological advances, through for example smart phones and cloud computing, have created a spur to flexible working trends and working from home. Home working and telecommuting have become common at least for part of the working week. In 2010, just over 10% of the UK workforce were primarily based at home and half of these were freelancers who had set themselves up as a company. The move towards a flexible hybrid working model is very much on an upward trajectory and the numbers increased over the decade aided by changing work practices due to the COVID pandemic.

Flexible working has also spawned a new form of coworking office format. Across the world, there are suppliers who now offer multi-tenanted offices incorporating supporting services with flexible space. The goals of these new coworking spaces are not only designed to offer flexibility in terms of short-term contracts but also an ambience that is a combination of working from home and the traditional office. These offices have seen exponential growth since the millennium albeit from a very low base. Coworking spaces still represent only a few percentage points share of the prime office stock.

When the COVID pandemic struck, working from home became essential. Many firms found it improved productivity and employees also saw the advantages. Businesses had to invest in the necessary technology, and it is likely that there has been a sea change towards greater remote and hybrid working. The corollary is that firms will reappraise their office needs in terms of both location and the physical accommodation. It seems likely that at least some firms will downsize to reduce costs while coworking office space is likely to become more popular.

Investment Consequences

The nature of office work has changed over the last half century driven by waves of technological advances. Each wave brought with it revised demands for office space and with it functional or economic obsolescence. The latest technological innovations have enabled hybrid and remote working. As a result, hot desking and serviced/coworking space have grown in popularity since the millennium.

The COVID pandemic has accelerated these trends. It has generated a positive step change towards hybrid working and remote working. The scale of the likely consequences at the time of writing is unknown but any market adjustments will be ameliorated by existing leases. Hybrid working brings more efficient space utilisation, and there seems to be an inevitable ultimate reduction in the demand for offices. It leads to question marks over current rental and capital values of some offices.

The demand for offices is not going to vanish rather those meeting the new requirements of tenants are likely to benefit. It could be characterised crudely as a flight to quality, and the role of green offices (as discussed earlier) could be part of the adjustment to a new normal. There is expected to be demands for a configuration of existing offices towards more meeting and even wellness space with capital expenditure by landlords. Serviced offices are likely to continue to grow in prominence but as the case study below shows there are risks to investors who take this route. The office market is about to go through one of its periodic metamorphisms and investors will need to adjust their offering.

Summary

The chapter has focused on how changing occupier needs are framed by the state of technology and has demonstrated how technological advances lead to new built forms in the different sectors. In particular, the emergence of these new forms is shown to replace traditional buildings causing obsolescence in the existing stock.

Depreciation in real estate values is linked to both physical deterioration and obsolescence. The latter can be classified as economic, functional, aesthetic, environmental or legislative. The first two are the main forces considered in this chapter and are linked to market forces. Obsolescence usually occurs before the end of a building's physical life, and in some cases a property can be adapted to alternative uses.

Depreciation in property values is linked to age but it is also affected by building quality, ownership and lease structures. Short leases and the frequent sales of individual properties are likely to lead to active management and physical improvement. Waves of technological innovation bring functional obsolescence and falls in the rental and capital values of the real estate affected.

Depreciation/obsolescence is ameliorated by the value of the land component of a property. While the value of a physical property may be in decline the value of the land on which it is situated may be rising. The result is that value of land can dampen any depreciation.

Rates of economic obsolescence are influenced by local market forces and dependent on the strength of local demand for real estate. Economic obsolescence can also be affected by external factors to the market that change the business attractions of a given location in favour of another.

A prominent example of functional obsolescence was the impact of ICT on offices in the 1980s. However, studies in the UK on depreciation suggest that land value inflation has mitigated its impact on properties in prime locations.

Green labelling of buildings provides an identifier for the market so that tenants can recognise the enhanced environmental standards and price them accordingly. Logically tenants would then pay a higher rent, a green premium, for these benefits. This premium would provide the financial base for the greening of the stock through investment, development and refurbishment.

The market processes by which the office stock is eventually greened are not straightforward. The greening process is more subtle than investment stimulated by a rent premium. In the UK, it seems there is no green rent premium, but a green office is viewed by investors as easier to let, thereby guaranteeing a future income stream and higher capital value.

The nature of retailing and retail forms have seen substantial change from broadly the middle of the last century culminating in the impact of online sales. The wide access to a family car has enabled the suburbanisation of homes and decentralisation of retail outlets. The United States was in the vanguard of these changes with the first suburban covered shopping mall opening in 1956.

Three waves of decentralisation from the 1970s can be identified in the UK. It began with supermarkets opening up outside town centres, followed by retail warehouses and then out-of-town shopping centres. Over time retail warehouses were grouped into retail parks. Retail warehouses are now mainly occupied by mainstream national 'high street' retailers.

The changes in retailing have led to a comprehensive overhaul in shopping patterns and retail real estate. There has been a reorganisation of the urban retail hierarchy incorporating new forms of decentralised shopping centres. There is also a growing surplus of shops although this depends on the constraints on retail development by national planning policies.

The traditional attractiveness of shops as an investment class was supported by rising real incomes and the constraints on supply created by the limited development opportunities in urban cores. It meant that prime shopping locations were subject to excess demand. Retail investment in prime locations was therefore protected from functional obsolescence.

Decentralisation from the 1970s in the UK changed the fundamentals of retail investment. While investment in retail assets by financial institutions continued to grow, there were dramatic revisions to its composition. While standard shops fell from grace, investment in retail warehouses rose from non-existence to become the largest type of retail asset with over a third of the portfolio of financial institutions by 2010. Shopping centres also increase from 9% of real estate assets held by financial institutions to 18% over this period.

These changes introduced the economic obsolescence of standard shops on high/main streets and showed how the portfolios of financial institutions adapt to urban and retail change. The process of this change was not straight forward with retail warehouses first seen as risky investments. They were also initially prone to obsolescence as the concept evolved to being clustered in a retail park. Initially, the capital values of retail warehouses factored in a risk premium of 2% over standard shops and it took twenty years to disappear.

The metamorphosis of shopping centres has not only changed the physical nature of the asset class but also the nature of retail real estate investment. Investment returns are no longer simply a function of retail location but the quality of the centre. Excess space has resulted in all shopping centres now being susceptible to economic obsolescence and some have to repurpose to encompass alternative uses.

As a result of these changes power now lies with tenants in negotiations with landlords and demands for more flexibility by tenants to respond to market forces has resulted in shorter leases. The wider investment corollary is the increasing significance of obsolescence and hence a potential rethink of the basis of retail real estate as an investment class.

Warehousing is a long-established building form that originated in agricultural economies. With technological change, the role of warehousing has now changed from simple storage to being part of the distribution process within wider 'Just in Time' supply chain management. Goods are no longer stored in factories or in the backrooms of shops. In the process, warehouses have become 'mega-sheds' because of automation and improved management systems that encompass internal racking systems getting taller.

The retail chains now collect goods then deliver goods directly to their shops. The recent growth of online sales has further reconstituted distribution processes to provide for home delivery and returns. The home delivery challenges have produced hub and spoke networks so regional/national warehouses feed to local parcel depots for local delivery.

Technological change has contributed to this rapid expansion of large purpose-built new DCs, with this new warehouse space clustering in dedicated distribution parks. Many of these DCs are owner operated by national retailers and third-party large logistics companies. Most of the tenanted DCs are let on leases of a least ten years. These modern units with a high occupancy rate and strong covenants appear to be attractive investments. However, in the UK, the percentage of warehousing owned as investments by financial institutions is low.

Over the last fifty years, information technologies have fundamentally altered the nature of office work and currently much 'office' work can be conducted from a laptop located anywhere. Technological advances have also impacted on the way business is conducted through the umbrella term e-business. This has also encouraged outsourcing and subcontracting. Along the way, offices have adapted or become obsolete. Nevertheless, a high proportion of total office space is no longer utilised at a particular point in time, motivating firms to downsize their offices using hot desking.

Continuing technological advances have encouraged flexible working and working from home, at least for part of the working week. As part of this trend, a new form of serviced office with a coworking format offering flexible space has been established and is growing fast (from a small base). The COVID pandemic has provided a major stimulus to these trends and there is likely to be an acceleration towards hybrid working with at least some office occupiers downsizing. It leads to question marks over current rental and capital values but some offices that can meet the demands for more meeting and even wellness space (possibly after capital expenditure) will thrive.

Learning Outcomes

Having completed this chapter, the reader should be able to:

- Understand that depreciation in real estate values is linked to both physical deterioration and obsolescence.
- Appreciate that the different causes of obsolescence that can be classified as economic, functional, aesthetic, environmental and legislative.
- Note that while depreciation in property values is linked to age it is also affected by building quality, ownership and lease structures.
- Understand why the value of land can reduce depreciation.
- Grasp that green labelling of buildings provides a market identifier of high environmental standards that enables them to be priced accordingly.

- Realise that the eventual greening of the office stock will lead to the depreciation in values of non-green buildings.
- Appreciate that while in the UK at present there is no green rent premium, a green office is seen as easier to let generating a higher capital value.
- Understand how retail centres have decentralised over time and why.
- Be able to analyse why small-town retail centres have struggled to compete with other centres and as a result have high levels of vacancies.
- Understand the impact of online sales on different types of shopping centres within the long-term context of retail change.
- Be able to explain why there is a growing surplus of shops in many countries.
- Grasp the historic attractiveness of shops as an investment class.
- Appreciate the changing pattern of real estate investment from 2010 in the UK.
- Understand why the incorporation of retail warehouses into the portfolios of British financial institutions took twenty years.
- Be able to discuss how the nature of retail real estate investment decisions has changed with retail decentralisation.
- Recognise how the history of warehousing has evolved together with the distribution process.
- Explain how online sales have reformulated the distribution process and the real estate implications.
- Appreciate why British financial institutions own few DCs as investments.
- Be able to provide a commentary on the impact of information technologies have had on transforming the nature of office work and the implications for offices.
- Have a view on what the future of office investment is in the light of the new hybrid approach to work and companies offering serviced workspaces.

Case Study Serviced Offices—We Work

We Work is one of several companies that offer flexible office space on a short-term basis. In the serviced office sector operators typically supply accommodation, property services and business support services including catering to their clients. Space can be let on a daily basis, even hourly. The business model is based on tenants being prepared to pay a premium to locate in premises on short flexible leases with access to business services including secretarial, ICT and meeting facilities.

Flexibility is the core of the business. WeWork was started in 2010 in New York and now offers business space in many cities across North and Central America. It further operates in thirteen countries around Europe and ten in Asia. The company also has a presence in Australia, South Africa and South America. WeWork was able to expand quickly through the use of leased offices. These leased premises are then subdivided into coworking suites and a premium rent charged. The rapid expansion contributed to high losses and an attempt to launch itself as a public company as a result failed in 2019 because it exposed the financial difficulties.

It continues to make losses at the time of writing with its future profitability dependent on the continued growth of hybrid office working, but more importantly cutting its cost base.

While WeWork is a high profile pioneer of providing serviced offices that have suffered significant losses, other international firms have produced more successful business models. The success of serviced offices operations depends on the management and design of the flexible space as well as maximising usage. The expected services by tenants are increasing to encompass wellness/health facilities, organisation of community events and the 'hotelisation' of the shared office suites.

Serviced office operators like WeWork typically lease rather than own their premises but can occupy it based on operational real estate arrangements that are considered in more detail in Chapter 12. Instead of leasing the serviced office operator can enter into a management agreement and pay a fee to the landlord. Even in a lease arrangement there can also be an equity sharing arrangement with the landlord. In such an arrangement, the operator typically pays a proportion of the open market rental value (say 50–80%) together with a fee linked to the profitability of the business. This arrangement is similar to a base plus turnover rent arrangement that can occur in retailing. Landlords can also enter into a franchise arrangement with an established operator.

The short-term nature of the business means that there is a high turnover of clients but there are unlikely to be high vacancies at any one time. However, in recessions the short leases (rather than the long leases of normal offices) enable firms to downsize rapidly so that the values of serviced offices are very susceptible to market downturns.

Reading

Crosby N. and Devaney, S. (2011). *Depreciation of Commercial Investment Property in the UK*, Investment Property Forum, London.

Dunse, N. and Jones, C. (2005). Rental depreciation, obsolescence and location: The case of industrial properties. *Journal of Property Research*, 22, 2/3, 205–223.

Jones, C. (2010). The rise and fall of the high street shop as an investment class. *Journal of Property Investment and Finance*, 28, 4, 275–284.

Jones, C. (2013). *Office Markets and Public Policy*. Wiley, Chichester.

Jones, C. (2021). *Urban Economy: Real Estate Economics and Public Policy.* Taylor & Francis, Abingdon.

Jones, C. and Livingstone, N. (2018) The 'online high street' or the high street online? The implications for the urban retail hierarchy. *The International Review of Retail, Distribution and Consumer Research*, 28, 1, 47–63.

MSCI, IPD, Investment Property Databank. (2010). *IPD Digest*. IPD, London.

Oyedokun, T., Dunse, N. and Jones, C. (2018). The impact of green premium on the development of green-labelled offices in the UK. *Journal of Sustainable Real Estate*, 10, 81–108.

Real Estate Opportunities and Challenges

12

Introduction

Real estate markets are constantly subject to change as the previous chapters exemplify. Change inevitably offers opportunities and challenges to investors. The years since the millennium have been dominated by the economic boom in the first half of the subsequent decade, the global financial crisis and then its continuing aftermath. This is the essential backdrop to the developments discussed in this chapter although their origins in some cases began earlier.

The motivations for changing the way real estate investment are undertaken and the market operates have often been shaped and stimulated by external macroeconomic forces, what is happening in the stock market, and facilitated by technological advances. This period is no different.

Speculative market expansions, such as those seen in global property markets in the first decade of the new millennium, have often been associated with popular perceptions that the future is brighter or less uncertain than it was in the past. The term *new era* has periodically been used to describe these times. Shiller in his 2005 book, *Irrational Exuberance,* notes that by many measures the world has indeed been growing into a new and better era. Shiller also notes that the most salient characteristic of popular new era thinking is that it is not continuously in evidence but occurs in pulses. This is the context to this chapter and its review of the decades of change in the commercial real estate market around the turn of the millennium.

Some of the challenges and opportunities examined have spun out of the global final crisis (GFC) and the need to re-examine risk assessment and valuations, but those relating to pension reform had been developing before the GFC. The chapter also examines some of the structural consequences of the GFC, the usefulness of transaction-based indices to monitor performance and the potential for using sustainable valuations, and their possible mitigating effects on bubbles when assessing new loans for property investment.

C. A. Jones and E. Trevillion, *Real Estate Investment* ,
https://doi.org/10.1007/978-3-031-00968-6_12

We also look at the opportunities arising from the use of AI and other new technology as well as examining the need to include behaviour in our models of the market. Finally, the chapter examines the emergence of alternative real estate assets to the traditional sectors and considers different ways of generating return from property. The chapter is structured to cover the following main topic areas:

- The impact of pension reform on real estate investment
- The consequences of the global financial crisis
- Sustainable valuations
- The impact of behaviour in property markets
- The practicalities of transactions-based versus market price indices
- Alternative investments and operational real estate
- PropTech, artificial intelligence and the commercial real estate industry

The Impact of Pension Reform on Real Estate Investment

As Chapter 5 notes, pension plans have been in existence since the nineteenth century and expanded significantly in the immediate post-World War II period across developed economies. To recap, regular payments are invested to provide for a pension on retirement. In a company scheme, both individual employees and the employer contribute into a pension fund to offer pensions on retirement. Until recently these pensions have been linked to an employee's final salary and their years of membership.

Across the world, there has been fundamental change to this approach to pension provision partly driven by the difficulties in achieving the traditional defined benefits (DB) set out in the schemes without significantly raising the level of contributions. There is an increasing awareness that current funding levels are insufficient to meet future pension obligations. As a result, private pension schemes have moved towards an alternative defined contributions (DC) approach whereby members receive a pension based on the sums that have been paid in, and how these contributions are invested.

There are also several other reasons for the shift from DB to DC pension plans. From a long-term perspective, factors such as increased workforce mobility associated with demographic and industrial change appear to have been important drivers of the shift away from DB pension plans. All else being equal, mobile workers have less of a preference for DB pensions because they favour long-tenured employees, and because DB benefits are not easily portable from one employer to another. In addition, the recent acceleration of the trend towards DC plans appears to be linked to moves to more market-based accounting and increasing regulatory burden identifying the long-term financial black holes in the schemes. It has also been influenced by plan sponsors to improve their management of the financial risks.

In addition, in many countries, there has been a move towards universal coverage of pension plans by governments requiring companies to offer a scheme. In the UK, for example, the government decided in 2012 to force companies to 'auto-enrol' workers in a pension scheme if they did not otherwise have one. These new schemes were based on DC as many of the companies and their employees affected could not afford to contribute to DB plans. Even in existing pension schemes, DB arrangements have been replaced by a DC approach, for example by requiring new staff to enter a DC arrangement. Pure DB pension schemes for all a company's staff, certainly in the UK, are increasingly rare, and there is often a hybrid arrangement.

This step change has impacted on the way real estate assets are managed in pension funds and the part they play in the fund's investment spectrum of assets. The following analysis now examines the challenges resulting from these changes, specifically regarding commercial property assets, but first outlines the detailed nature of DB and DC occupational pension schemes.

What Are Defined Benefit and Defined Contribution Pension Schemes?

A DB scheme is one where the amount a person is paid as a pension when they retire is based on how many years they have worked for their employer and the salary earned. The schemes pay out a secure income for life which increases each year, normally in line with a measure of inflation. They are usually backed by a sponsoring employer, although the benefits may be secured by transferring to a financial institution such as an insurance or pension company. Both employers and employees may contribute to the scheme, the ratio of that contribution varying depending on the employer.

Typically, DB schemes are run by a Board of Trustees on behalf of the employer. Trustees are responsible for all aspects of the scheme including paying out benefits to retired members. Daily management of the scheme is typically done by the scheme administrator, who reports to the Board of Trustees.

A DC pension works more like a tax-friendly savings account. They normally use independent pension providers and the amount of money a DC pension is worth on retirement depends on how much has been paid in and how well the pension provider has invested its cash flows and their performance. A person pays money into their 'pension pot' and an employer can contribute too. The pension provider claims tax relief on an investor's behalf and adds it to the pension pot. Like other investment funds, including those associated with a DB scheme (see Chapter 5), the pension provider usually invests the money in several asset categories including shares, property, bonds and cash.

In the UK, the DC market consists of workplace and personal savings schemes. Spence and Libre in 2018 identified three types of workplace scheme:

- **trust-based schemes** like DB schemes that require trustee boards and other governance structures.
- **contract-based schemes** are technically individual contracts between the member and the pension provider, but in reality are managed by the company sponsoring the scheme.
- **master trusts** are multi-employer DC schemes. Trust-based schemes operate under a deed of covenant and are managed by a board of trustees. Often, in larger companies, it will be the same board that manages both a company's DB and DC scheme. Trust-based scheme investments are sometimes managed internally, but usually rely on external advice.

There are risks with both types of pensions—but the nature of this risk varies. For DB schemes, the risk lies mostly with the scheme sponsor—usually the member's company. This is because they have promised their members a defined pay out level at retirement. The company is responsible for addressing deficits on the pension scheme. The risk attribution has changed with the growth of DC schemes which leave employers with no obligation beyond the contributions they agreed to pay into the scheme. Instead, scheme members bear the investment risk that could, potentially, leave them with a smaller than expected pension pot on retirement.

Investment in DC and DB Schemes

As Chapter 5 shows the assets held in pension schemes are significant. Despite the fall in the number of DB schemes, the study by Spence and Libre in 2018 for the UK finds that the assets held by them are still much larger than those of DC schemes, £1.3trn compared to £300bn respectively in 2015. But of course the assets held in DC schemes are rising and had reached £338bn by 2018.

The Investment Property Form reports that commercial real estate holding in these funds is 8% or £42bn of the investment stock in the UK at the end of 2017, with £6.2bn held in DC pension schemes. The implications of the shift to DC schemes for real estate investment need to be seen in the wider context of changing institutional attitudes towards the asset class. The proportion of real estate investment in pension fund portfolios in the UK had suffered a long-term decline for almost twenty years from their allocation popularity heyday in the early 1980s. After the turn of the millennium, there was a modest increase in real estate weighting, partly reflecting the fall in stock market values but also a reappraisal of the scale of property investment.

Almost all large pension funds have an exposure to property but amongst small funds, real estate investment was and remains not common place. Spence and Libre suggest that 1.8% of the assets of workplace DC pension schemes are invested in property, and that virtually no real estate investment by DC schemes is undertaken through directly held property. In other words, real estate investment is placed indirectly through for example REITs. This is significant and relates to the perceived need of these schemes to maintain a good degree of liquidity. However, property is still a popular investment medium offering diversification opportunities and perceived higher longer-term returns, and 30% of all DC schemes currently invest in property, either through property funds or via multi-asset funds.

While the assets held in DC schemes are forecast to grow in coming years, the value of assets in DB plans is expected to flatten. In the UK membership of private sector occupational DB schemes fell from 2.8 m people in 2008 to 1.1 m people in 2019, as these schemes close and mature. Meanwhile, DC pension scheme membership has increased, from 1 m people in 2013 to over 10 m people in 2018. This significant increase is driven primarily by the government's decision noted above, to force companies to 'auto-enrol' workers on a pension scheme if they did not otherwise have one.

Impacts and Challenges for Real Estate Investment in Pension Schemes

The move towards DC from DB changes the nature of decisions. As DB schemes mature, they become more risk averse, reflecting the need to reliably pay out pensions month after month, rather than investing contributions for the long term and not worrying too much about short-term cash flow. This risk aversion tends to involve selling (riskier) equity type assets and buying (safer) bond type investments including secure income producing commercial real estate.

New DC funds may have a strong inflow of capital while mature DB funds may have net outflows. Consequently, the matching of assets to liabilities is no longer the same and pension funds, as noted, may approach risk differently. There is a greater demand for transparency, guaranteed levels of pay out, and portability/liquidity for DC schemes, hence the trend in DC schemes to diversify into real estate through more liquid indirect property. The demand for liquidity in DC schemes is very strong, so property vehicles with daily pricing, such as REITs, are favoured. Lack of liquidity remains the key barrier to holding property in DC schemes while this demand is much less strong in DB schemes. For real estate investment, the need for liquidity in DC schemes remains a challenge.

Consequences of the Global Financial Crisis

Real estate capital values around the world fell dramatically in the short term following the GFC driven by forced sales, as Fig. 3.2 demonstrates. The property markets saw not just a rapid reduction in values but also a sudden lack of liquidity. The importance of the GFC lies not only in the short to medium term impacts it had on property market values worldwide but also in the way it highlighted longer-term structural issues in property markets and associated financial systems, including behaviour. The former has been discussed at length in earlier chapters, but we now highlight the consequences and challenges of the latter.

It must be remembered that the GFC was about more than just UK property. It was as much about the associated credit crunch and the requirement of banks to resolve the impairments in their commercial real estate loan bank. Outstanding loans had been negotiated against higher property values that applied in the aftermath of the GFC. The falls in capital values following the GFC meant that many outstanding loans to investors and developers were greater than the values of the properties.

In their book, *Property Boom and Banking Bust*, Jones et al. report on the massive challenges to banks and their fundamental viability which were initially resolved around the world by government financial support. The banks became effective owners of properties where the loan was in default, and sought ways of reclaiming some of their capital, often with the help of hedge funds (see Chapter 5).

Up until the GFC, banks typically lent up to 75% of development costs with low market markups over base rates and finance was readily available for speculative products. With the bust banks sought to rebuild their capital bases and adjust their impaired loans. There was limited lending for development or investment in commercial real estate, with consequences for values.

Some large property investors also experienced a chastening time in the immediate aftermath of the global financial crisis. But not all investors were affected badly from the fall in value of assets if they did not have to sell. Many pension funds suffered from early retirements of members and unemployment in the short term affecting their income and outgoings. For some the need to sell properties could have been shielded by the low percentage, 5–6%, of assets held in real estate. Overall, the value of institutional real investment dropped before eventually recovering in 2010.

Specialist real estate unit linked and unit trust funds were very susceptible in the recession that followed as detailed in Chapter 5. These funds were in the vanguard of property sales and arguably drove the market down. As a result, many of these funds changed their investment mandate with unit holder approval. The maximum amount permitted to be invested in direct property assets was reduced while the amount permitted in more liquid assets was increased. In some cases, the maximum amount allowed to be invested in direct real estate was cut to 60%.

The constrained availability of debt from the traditional banking sources spawned new providers of debt. Some opportunistic funds obtained shareholder funds with which to lend to suitable projects, so-called debt funds. Other new sources of debt are coming from the life funds of financial institutions with more and more life companies offering loans to property investors or developers. Technically, these loans form part of a fund's fixed interest (bonds) portfolio and not the direct property portfolio, but these areas of a life company's operation will work together on assessing and managing the loan. For the life companies, it is very much back to the roots. Loans issued by the life funds now account for over 10% of all loans granted in the UK.

There were other ramifications. What became clear was that forecasting models were inadequate in anticipating the scale of the falls in values that resulted from the GFC, not just property forecasts but economic forecasts as well (a fundamental flaw since the latter are used as major inputs to property market models). Part of the problem is that published forecasts by real estate researchers are not pure statistical forecasts but also reflect sentiment and professional judgement. In addition, these models take no account of the behaviour that drove yield shift during the GFC. In terms of the UK, and elsewhere, a challenge for the industry is how to address this aspect of modelling and the irrational behaviour (and related aspects) of the market (see also later).

A further general problem exposed by the GFC for investors was the consequences of gearing and the associated risk. Many investment funds were shown in the downturn to have over-extended levels of borrowing. The cocktail of falling capital values and stationary rents while interest payments continued was explosive. Investors needed to repair their balance sheet, if they could, to avoid forced sales, and so for example in the immediate aftermath REITs turned to raising additional funds from their shareholders to rebuild their capital base.

Following the GFC, property investors' perception of risk increased massively. The management of risk moved up the agenda in UK fund management houses and with it a much better appreciation of what constituted fair value and with it a recognition of the consequences of irrational exuberance (see Chapter 6). With this came the building of larger liquidity buffers in retail funds and property unit trusts (see above). Due diligence that in the boom years only received cursory attention from both the banking and real estate industry has also moved up the risk agenda.

All of this precipitated an industry wide assessment of the threat the real estate cycle can pose to the stability of financial systems in the UK. In 2014, the Investment Property Forum published *A Vision for Real Estate Finance in the UK*. It brought recommendations that could protect systemically financial institutions and the financial system more generally from the commercial real estate cycle. To achieve this goal, it proposed that financial institutions hold sufficient capital to withstand a market crash.

The vision also saw the moderating of the flow of credit to the commercial real estate sector and the establishment of systems to ensure that financial institutions are positioned to support commercial property lending after a market crash as being important. In this context, as part of post-GFC considerations, the potential application of long-term sustainable valuations when assessing commercial property loans has been proposed as a way of mitigating risk when advancing debt. These are considered in the next section.

These changes show that the overall impact of the long boom up to the GFC, the dramatic bust and slow recovery shook investors attitudes towards commercial real estate. The events challenged the underlying pricing of commercial property by investors. In particular, the impact was a reappraisal of the risks associated with the property as the recession exposed its frailties. The challenge is whether the revisions to investment behaviour generate a resilience to the next significant economic downturn.

Sustainable Valuations

The increase in property investors' perceptions of risk following the GFC stimulated a debate in the UK and beyond about the role of valuations in bank funding of investment purchases. It raised questions about what constituted fair value and the potential need to consider the use of sustainable valuations by banks when deciding on whether to agree a loan. This could be applied when assessing the loan-to-value (LTV) ratio for commercial property. There has been a recognition in the UK that long-term sustainable valuations might help mitigate risk when advancing loans.

Sustainable valuations are not widely used in UK markets, but the approach underpins values applied in Germany's Pfandbrief commercial bond market. In determining this value only, the durable characteristics of the property and the revenue that the property can guarantee for each proprietor through correct use are considered. German legislation interprets market value as the price which would 'probably' be achieved under normal conditions, namely when the vendor is willing to and competent to sell, etc. This definition means that it is the most probable value which lies at around the average level of potential values. In the UK and elsewhere value follows RICS guidelines and is interpreted as the estimated amount for which a property should exchange on the date of valuation between a willing buyer and a willing seller in an arm's length transaction after proper marketing.

The rationale for using sustainable valuations is that the increased risk arising as the market overheats can be mitigated significantly through their use. It represents a measure that compares the amount of the loan to the long-term sustainable value of the property, in other words, the long-term sustainable LTV. It can be seen as being the average value of the property through the market cycle. Under this approach, the most important risk element of using valuations at the peak of a boom would be removed.

Application of Sustainable Valuations in the UK

Discussions continue in the real estate profession as to how and whether sustainable valuations might be applied in the UK as there are challenges associated with their use. The Bank of England has also commenced publication of a series of commercial property market valuation-based indicators of over and under-pricing within their Financial Stability Report.

Three approaches have been examined by researchers (Mansley et al., 2020):

- **adjusted market value (AMV)** AMV is derived by comparing current market value, as reflected in an appropriate capital value index, to a long-term trend line. It is extremely simple and inexpensive to use, although this simplicity may also limit its versatility as a tool.
- **investment value (IV)** This is based on a traditional discounted cash flow (DCF) model valuation approach. The inputs comprise current rental values (derived

from MSCI indices), rental growth forecasts, a long run exit yield (a 15-year backward-looking rolling average of the relevant MSCI equivalent yields series) and a target rate of return (comprising a risk-free rate and a static undifferentiated risk premium). IV differs from a standard DCF model because of its use of a 15-year backward-looking rolling average of the relevant equivalent yields series, rather than current yields or forecasts of future yields. IV can be used relatively flexibly at individual property or index levels.
- **Mortgage lending value (MLV)** MLV is based on Beleihungswert, the mortgage lending value approach that forms a key element of the German bond market, the Pfandbrief. The German rules (see also above) aim at a 'prudent valuation'. It represents the value at which experience suggests a property may be sold at any point throughout the life of a loan, irrespective of speculative or cyclical commercial real estate market fluctuations. The result is almost always below market value, and it is achieved by following a statutory valuation methodology that prescribes, among other things, specified minimum capitalisation rates and rental and operating expenditure inputs.

The research concluded that long-term value could improve cycle awareness and lender risk management, and that AMV was the most reliable of the three methodologies although IV has potential.

Challenges

These valuation approaches are based on a significantly more cautious approach than traditionally used and they allow a better insight into the risks involved. However, criticism of changes in the UK centres around the view that the German valuation system is incapable of reflecting a prolonged downswing in the property market. The use of this approach probably explains the different volatility seen in German markets, shown in Chapter 3, and the apparently more stable behaviour.

Challenges remain with applying German MLV to the UK market, especially regarding rental inputs (as for IV). In addition, there are issues around adapting other prescribed German MLV parameters, so they can fit for generalised use in the UK market. The whole process of establishing long-term sustainable value is complex and not simple.

Although there is not a full commitment to the MLV approach used in Germany, there is support for the use of sustainable rents to monitor any over-heating in UK occupier markets. In addition, the use of sustainable or equilibrium capital value estimates to monitor if investment markets appear to be over-heating has been recommended by an Investment Property Forum report. These values would be based on both econometric modelling of capitalisation rates and the ex-ante estimation of these rates (potentially with some scenario analysis).

Notwithstanding the use of these estimates of 'sustainable values' in the UK, a wider view of market behaviour is recommended including the monitoring of leverage/gearing in the market. Such a review would enable checks as to whether there is excessive growth in gearing within commercial real estate lending (i.e. higher LTV lending). We consider these in the next section.

The Impact of Behaviour in Real Estate Markets

In Chapter 6, we examined the consequences of overoptimism in UK and global real estate markets and the way that irrational behaviour drove yield change in the years before the onset of the GFC. There was a misplaced confidence throughout the early 2000s that capital values would continue to increase and that there would continue to be strong rental growth. The consequence of this overoptimism was a departure from fundamentals manifested in a growing disconnect between capital value growth and rental value growth.

The implication of this irrational behaviour for the real estate market, and the problems globally with the availability of credit, was a huge financial penalty. In turn, the management of risk moved was priortised in UK fund management houses. There was subsequently much more interest in fair value models of the market, but the risk associated with irrational behaviour still represents a challenge to the industry.

Part of the challenge has resulted from the continuing belief in the application of the efficient market hypothesis (EMH) to property markets. We noted in Chapter 6 that a major factor affecting whether the EMH is sufficient to describe markets is the extent to which investor behaviour impacts on market behaviour overall. It seems logical to assume that for the EMH to apply there needs to be conditions approaching a perfect (rational) market. What do we understand by that? According to neo-classical economic theory, a perfect market is one where:

- All participants are rational and aim to maximise utility.
- There are many participants in the market, many buyers and sellers and monopolies are eliminated.
- Competition is 'perfect', there is no collusion or oligopolies.
- All transactions are mutually beneficial, and supply/demand adjusts instantaneously.
- There are no transaction costs.
- All participants have access to all relevant knowledge, 'perfect' information.

In this paradigm, equilibrium arises because actors in the market behave in a rational way aided by perfect knowledge and in pursuit of clearly defined objectives and maximise utility. This view is not one that normal people would recognise as corresponding to reality. If we assume that the market is informationally efficient then there is an assumption that investors correctly process available information on prospective cash flows, discounted at a rate appropriate to available information on risk. So, prices change only with new information on cash flows.

But Is It True That Individuals Do a Good Job at Evaluating Probabilities and Making 'Rational' Choices?

Behavioural theory (as manifest in behavioural finance) suggests that this is not all true. 'Anomalies' can be both important and widespread, leading to substantial and systematic effects that are not transient but persist. Departures from rationality can be measured by laboratory simulation of investor choices or, as in Chapter 6 by the observation of actual investor choices. Behavioural explanations of market 'anomalies' can be seen as bubbles, momentum and systematic mispricing.

Price differences from fundamental value persist because there are limits to arbitrage and behavioural finance would expect that irrational investment behaviour determines prices at least some of the time. The challenge is whether we are good at judging the probabilities of outcomes in the market.

Market actors arguably often do not properly assess the probabilities of outcomes, instead they use mental shortcuts (heuristics) in their reasoning and so arrive at biased conclusions. This manifests itself in three main ways: representative thinking, availability and anchoring:

- In *representative thinking,* the probability of an event is judged by its similarity to a pattern or template—often the true pattern is misjudged, sometimes because of the lack of data. For example, a good large company, with a record of profit growth, well covered by analysts etc. must represent a good investment.
- *Availability* is where the probability of an event is assessed by the ease with which we recall similar events. The likelihood of extreme events is badly misjudged.
- *Anchoring* is where judgements are made by anchoring on what first enters the mind. This anchor is then used as a reference when new information is reviewed—but the adjustment is very frequently an under-adjustment. Anchoring may (in part at least) cause overconfidence: people think they know the 'answer' and won't move much towards accepting other possibilities. They are, or can be, overconfident in their predictive abilities and skills and put very narrow confidence ranges on their estimates. As result, the element of skill in what happens is exaggerated and the role of chance is denied (illusion of control). Confidence' in judgement grows when it is confirmed by outcomes—but not weakened when it is contradicted (biased self-attribution). Overconfidence can result in excess trading, with lower returns.

Some examples of the consequences of these behavioural issues are that investors will be reluctant to shift from previous decisions, there might be home bias in global portfolios, over-weighting of home countries, valuers may produce 'sticky' valuations and are swayed by other irrelevant anchors, and the risk-management models banks use may underestimate the savage effects of big shocks.

Challenges

Recognising that behaviour is an important element in real estate market systems suggests that behavioural economics ought to be applied more widely to understand market dynamics. Behavioural economists attribute the imperfections in financial markets to a combination of cognitive biases such as overconfidence, overreaction, representative bias, information bias and various other predictable human errors in reasoning and information processing.

Economic systems such as the real estate market are imbued by cultural values and underpinned by social and psychological customs that influence the way in which people understand their options and make their choices. Trevillion argues that treating property markets as a complex system can address and integrate this diversity and offer a multi-dimensional framework for analysis. The approach applies not only to the system structure but also to behavioural aspects within the system itself.

Systems theory is a well-established conceptual framework for understanding complex systems. Such systems typically exhibit non-linear behaviour. These notions of complex systems and non-linear behaviour have been known about for a long time, and evolutionary theories of economic growth have applied themselves to the process of change. They are as much concerned with the forces that displace systems from equilibrium as those that move systems towards equilibrium, and use the same models of human motivation and behaviour as the rest of the social sciences.

Despite the wide application of the systems theory to business and other related areas, particularly evolutionary economics and policy, its use in commercial real estate research has been limited and has not gained much traction as a research tool. There have been only a few behavioural studies including analyses of corporate real estate and relocation decision-making.

This lack of application is despite the clear advantages and opportunities that the approach offers in terms of understanding the dynamics of market cycles and behaviour within the real estate market system. It offers an alternative to the econometric based models used for forecasting returns and other important property investment metrics.

Chapter 8 notes the limitations of these econometric based forecasting in particular their inability to understand the process of change and to forecast turning points in the market, because their behavioural properties are weak. The more inductive approach offered by systems theory offers a way of incorporating behavioural aspects into forecasts. More generally the challenge is to incorporate the impact of behaviour into the understanding of the market.

Practicalities of Transaction-Based Versus Market Price Indices

In Chapter 8, it was noted that property indices can be differentiated by the techniques used to collect data and compile the series, either appraisal-based (market price) or transaction-based approaches. There are challenges in constructing and using both types of indices and these are now examined, along with the opportunities presented by applying transaction-based indices, commonly used in residential markets, to commercial real estate markets.

Appraisal-Based Indices

The choice of a real estate index is not straightforward; indices vary both in the construction methodologies used and the breadth and representativeness of their market coverage. As previously described the commonly used benchmarks for market comparison and benchmarking in the unlisted sector of the UK are based on data provided by MSCI/IPD. It was established by a range of surveying practices and institutional investors to pool data.

To recap IPD began to generate a reliable UK commercial property index in 1985 but incorporated data back to 1981. The database is drawn from records of property funds and the valuation agencies sponsoring the database. The index is appraisal or valuation based rather than derived from transactional data of actual prices. The list of countries where now MSCI operates the same database model encompasses countries in Europe, Asia, North and South America, Australia and New Zealand.

Appraisal base indices are the most common type in the commercial property market as information on transaction prices is scarce. Large real estate databases such as those used by the MSCI/IPD indices are based on valuations because few of the properties in the sample universe are sold during each period. Indices are constructed by valuing the estimated market prices for a sample of individual properties on a regular basis. These valuations are aggregated into one measure.

In the UK, the frequency of the valuations determines the size of the sample. Usually, the larger the sample then the less frequent the index observation. For example, the UK MSCI/IPD Annual index is based on a sample larger than the sample it uses to construct the monthly and quarterly series. The monthly index is based on a sample of only unitised funds that require monthly valuations. It represents a market movement index while the annual index is a performance measurement index.

As explained earlier in the United States, the NCREIF Property Index (NPI) has been the main standard for evaluating unlisted commercial property performance. The NCREIF Property Index is also an appraisal-based index. The NPI was launched in 1982 (with data going back to 1977) and was the first attempt to build a comprehensive index that represented the performance of a commercial real estate market.

Transaction-Based Indices

These are common in the residential market where more information on property transaction prices is available, although Real Capital Analytics (RCA) are now producing transaction-based indices for commercial property in the UK and the United States. These can be constructed by averaging transaction prices in a given time period, using statistical modelling which assumes that property values depend on the sum of the property's individual attributes. The price of a standard property at any one point in time can be estimated by summing the price of its individual characteristics. The analysis is repeated for different points in time to produce a time series index.

An alternative approach is the repeat sales method where the construction of this type of index is based on calculating the price change that occurs when properties in a database are sold more than once in a specific period. Based on these individual price changes the statistical analysis estimates market price trends.

These types of indices are in their relative infancy. In 2006, Real Capital Analytics and Massachusetts Institute of Technology Centre for Real Estate (MIT/CRE) launched a commercial real estate index that adopted this repeat sales approach. The index is fundamentally comparable to typical securities indices, such as stock market indices, which are based on same-stock price changes from one period to the next.

A second generation of the index was launched in 2011 by Moody Investor's Service and RCA, based on price changes in the United States and the United Kingdom. It is now simply known as the RCA Commercial Property Price Index (RCA CPPI) and provides a broad measure of commercial property price trends. RCA is the first and only producer of an international transaction-based price index. The RCA CPPI covers traditional commercial property types (office, industrial, retail) as well as apartments and hotels encompassing North America, Europe and Asia–Pacific. CoStar also produces a transactions-based index for the United States using repeat sales.

Challenges and Opportunities

The principal concerns with appraisal-based indices such as that produced by MSCI/IPD are around valuation smoothing as well as with temporal and spatial aggregation within the appraisal process. Valuations tend to smooth out market movements in a real estate cycle by for example underestimating price falls in a downturn. Aggregate indices also hide spatial variations say between cities.

As a result, these indices produce statistics that do not provide investors with an accurate quantification of market risk. It is also questionable whether appraisal-based indices accurately reflect the scale of market movements, particularly when placed under extreme conditions. The degree of auto correlation, namely the correlation between different time periods, and predictability in appraisal-based returns is a major challenge to the degree of market efficiency in commercial property markets (see also Chapter 8).

Even in stable market conditions, the degree of representativeness of the indices depends on its coverage of the market which is not always complete. In many countries, the valuation data is based only a small number of investment funds. In the UK, the MSCI/IPD index has suffered from overseas investors buying a significant amount of real estate, especially in central London since the millennium. The properties owned by these investors are not in the database. In addition, the process of draft valuations and structure of client relationships result in a conflict-of-interest that can impugn the degree of independence that even the most effective evaluation professionals can exercise. The basic methods of conducting valuations can introduce a degree of subjectivity that restricts the production of open and transparent market pricing.

While a key question for appraisal-based indices is what the significance or bias of these indices are as benchmarks in terms of smoothing market trends, the steepness of the distribution of returns, and not capturing turning points, transaction-based indices measure market movements and returns on investment based on the actual prices of properties sold.

A study by Trevillion et al. for the Investment Property Forum published in 2020 that reviewed current practices in benchmarking real estate investment performance recognised these challenges. However, notwithstanding these issues, it was clear that MSCI/IPD remains the index of choice when constructing market benchmarks in the UK. Users recognised that, to some extent, the issues reflect the 'nature of the beast' in establishing a pooling of the data required to produce the benchmark measures, particularly when based on asset level metrics.

There are drawbacks to transactions-based measures with regard to opacity in how they are calculated. Data requirements are very demanding. In particular, the use of the repeat sales technique invariably removes a substantial proportion of the actual transactions conducted from the sample. As a result, market coverage may be biased by where there is a high turnover of properties. The reliance on the existing repeat sales techniques therefore brings about some basic practical issues. The complex mathematics used within the process by its very nature also restricts its use as a practical tool.

Many operators within the industry from a traditional professional surveying background are unlikely to have in-depth experience of the mathematics involved in the creation of repeat sales measures. The process compares unfavourably with the aggregated appraisal approach undertaken by MSCI. Within a real estate context, at least this latter process is far more transparent and easier to understand.

Generally speaking, there is no enthusiasm in the United Kingdom for using transaction-based indices as benchmarks although they are seen as useful analytical tools. There seems to be little trust in using them for performance measurement, but there is interest in using transaction-based indices as an early warning system, for example at very specific points in the market cycle, when asset prices change rapidly.

Although there are concerns around the lack of comparability and reliability that exist in appraisal-based indices, transaction approaches are primarily seen only as augmenting them. The latter are only seen as having a role when there are enough transactions and challenges remain in convincing real estate investment professionals to apply them more widely. These practical issues, however, should not mask the opportunities that they may offer especially during periods when asset prices are changing rapidly.

Alternative and Operational Real Estate

Real estate investment in its traditional model involves a property owned by a landlord who receives a rental income from the tenant. This arrangement is governed by a lease with periodic rent reviews that usually upgrade the rent with inflation or to market value. However, as noted in Chapter 11, technological change is creating substantial upheaval in the ownership and use of the industrial, office and retail real estate sectors. It is driving innovation in the way property is used and paid for, including developments such as the rise of flexible office working and the renting of individual desk spaces. In the retail sector, the normal rental model in some instances has been replaced by use of turnover leases in which the rent paid by the tenant is based on sales revenue.

Besides the three traditional real estate sectors, investment by financial institutions in recent times has seen a move into 'alternative assets' as set out in Chapter 4. There are a range of reasons and include the desire for higher returns than that are available in the long-established sectors. Motivations also embrace the desire for more diversification supported by the growth of leisure properties and the opportunities created by the privatisation of public amenities. In particular, the returns from alternative assets may have a different relationship over time with the economic cycle creating the potential for diversification. The popularity of investing in alternative assets can be seen by the growth of specialist REITs in these sectors.

Alternative assets are an eclectic collection of asset types including those listed in Table 12.1. They can be divided into two types:

- Operational entities or trade related properties
- Social infrastructure.

Both types involve the operation and management of a specialist real estate form. Both types tend to have generally low transaction volumes, poor liquidity and information on performance is limited compared with traditional sectors.

This section considers the characteristics of these alternative assets and the use of an operational approach to real estate investment. It draws on a report, *Operational Real Estate Risk and Reward*, published in 2021 by the Investment Property Forum.

Table 12.1 Categorisation of real estate

Traditional	Alternative	Alternative
	Operational entities/Trade related properties	Infrastructure
Industrial	*Hotels and leisure* *Student accommodation*	*Medical facilities* *(Hospitals/Medical Practices)*
Offices	*Self-storage facilities* *Data centres*	*Education facilities* *(Schools/Colleges/Universities)*
Retail	*Care homes*	*Energy*
	Pubs and bars	*Public facilities* *(Libraries/Courts/Museums)*
Residential	*Cinemas and bowling alleys* *Serviced/Coworking offices*	
Agriculture	*Airports* *Car parks*	
Forestry		

Investment Perspectives on Selected Alternative Trade Related Real Estate Types

Greater understanding of the nature of alternative assets can be discerned from the investment attributes of three selected trade related case studies considered below. They illustrate the nature of investment decisions and the role of the operators of real estate.

The success of a facility broadly depends on location, but it is based upon the income from tenants renting units on a short-term basis with a high turnover of tenants. There is no guaranteed income so while location is a key to success good management is essential to maximising revenue.

These three examples illustrate the greater complexity of investing in trade related assets but also some commonalities with traditional asset classes in terms of the fundamentals of real estate investment. A good location is a prerequisite to success but so is the predictability and security of the underlying revenue stream. There is a further key component of success, namely the importance of the operator.

Example 1 Hotels

Hotel cash flows are determined from income from a potential range of sources—rooms, food and drink, gym/spa/swimming pool, conference facilities and other related activities. The larger the hotel the larger the range of these facilities. These cash flows depend on location, brand and quality of the building, but crucially also the operator's management efficiency. The role of the operator is likely to have a key influence on cash flows. The periodic upgrading of the physical internal and external environment is essential and is also an important operational decision.

Example 2 Petrol Stations

Petrol stations are income-generating businesses that are highly dependent on passing trade and competition. There is little requirement to refurbish. Profits per litre are very low so the scope for increasing profits lies primarily in the associated convenience goods sold on the site or in some cases a cafe. There may also be an opportunity to offer collection lockers for goods purchased on the internet. As an investment, the attractiveness of a petrol station is dependent on the expertise of the management to develop non-petrol retail activities.

Example 3 Self-Storage

Self-storage is the term applied to facilities offering rental on a month-to-month basis where the tenant has sole access to his unit. A self-storage facility usually constitutes a large former industrial building with a range of unit sizes, security cameras, removable steel partition walls, lifts and moving equipment. There is an onsite manager.

Self-storage has relatively low barriers to entry compared to other forms of real estate investment. There is a low-initial capital outlay to convert an existing industrial unit. When tenants leave, there is no need to provide a refurbishment of the interior unlike an office building. The building is also low maintenance. This makes it very attractive to investors as there is seldom a need to provide a large capital outlay for refurbishments and repairs.

A Comparison of Traditional and Alternative Real Estate Investments

These three examples provide just a flavour of the attractions and constraints of what alternative investments offer. Their relative merits are now seen in a wider more generalised review of the spectrum of real estate assets but with a focus on the role of their management and contractual arrangements between occupier and owner.

Traditional Sectors

Traditional real estate assets are fundamentally dependent on future income streams linked to the performance of a property sector and location. There is normally a degree of contractual certainty given by leases and rent reviews. There is some specific risk associated with business failure and temporary voids that can be attributed to operational risk. However, by choosing good covenants (the status of the tenant) and prime locations and properties, this can be minimised. Within each main broad category (office, retail and industrial/logistics), there is a degree of demand flexibility in terms of specific business function or type so that if one type of occupier fails then it can be replaced by another firm.

Trade Related Properties

These are linked to a specialised real estate asset but unlike traditional real estate, the returns are more directly dependent on the operation of the business carried out within the building. Investors' expected returns, say from a hotel, may be based on the tenant's performance through a contract and therefore the business component of the future income flows is critical. However, in choosing to invest they are also doing so with regard to both the covenant and skill of the operator and the property and its location. They are real estate assets where there is heightened operational risk, and specialist skills are required to manage them. As with traditional real estate investments, the exit or terminal value at the end of the contract is the building itself on eventual resale.

Social Infrastructure

As an asset, class infrastructure assets are drawn together by the collective characteristic that they have a very predictable underlying revenue stream that is often public sector backed. It is typically agreed at the outset on a long-term contract and often with built-in inflation protection. They may be time limited. From an investor's perspective, the emphasis is on investing in an asset where revenue is subject to predictable demand and is not reliant on short-term economic cycles. As an investment class, its potential is driven less by operator skill but by long-term economic growth, technological progress and climate change. By comparison with traditional property and other forms of alternative assets, risk can be relatively low and returns predictable over the economic life of the asset.

Alternative Assets, Investor Operating Models and Operational Real Estate

Given the greater importance of operators there are different approaches to owning trade related real estate assets. They can be leased or subject to management agreements with the former being closer to the characteristics of traditional real estate. From an investment perspective, we can distinguish between passive and active investment. If we consider the case of a hotel, for example, the owner can enter into the following alternative contractual arrangements:

Passive: Traditional Long Lease

A hotel can be let on a traditional lease with rent reviews at varying periods of time. The variety of types of leases is infinite but of course a lease with a known rental income stream is considered to be secure. In this arrangement, the investor is concerned with covenant strength and the strength of the underlying business to cover the rent. The investor does not retain any operational risk and therefore does not benefit from any enhanced profits generated.

Active: Performance-Based Lease

These leases vary considerably but the common feature is that all or part of the rent is based on an agreed percentage of turnover or profit. With these leases, the investor is dependent on the successful trading of the hotels and retains some of the operational risk. These leases are commonly known as a hybrid or turnover leases. As noted above there is also an increased use of turnover rents within the retail sector.

Franchise

Under this arrangement, the franchisor licenses its brand with its knowhow, associated products/services and intellectual property.

Management Contract

The investor employs the operator to operate and manage the property on their behalf. The investor is responsible for all operating costs and repairing liabilities and therefore retains the operational risk for the property. The investor benefits from enhanced profits generated, but in return has greater risk.

Owner/Operator

Under this fully integrated model, the owner is the operator.

This spectrum of investor operating models illustrates that there is a continuum between passive and operational real estate (ORE) investment. Four of these models can be regarded as ORE and they are not confined to hotels or even more generally to trade related/operational entities within specialised buildings. On the other hand, all these specific models are not applicable to every type of asset. In general ORE models of investment encompass arrangements in which the return to owners is based on the financial performance of the asset. Investors letting traditional real estate can also enter ORE type arrangements and it is common for example within the serviced office sector.

Overview

To summarise ORE is about being receiving returns based on the income streams of the business occupying a property rather than the traditional rent and lease arrangement. It is not confined to alternative investments. It may involve active management of the asset and it is ultimately backed by the value of the property (even if only as land).

There are advantages and disadvantages of ORE versus the traditional model. A traditional lease provides a safe certain income stream with the business expertise and risks clearly with the tenant. The disadvantage is that income has a bond like characteristic between rent reviews and the investor does not benefit from profits generated from the use of its property as with the ORE model. The ORE model is also more appropriate where there is an absence of comparable evidence to agree an appropriate rent or the asset will require frequent upgrading or the returns are based on the expertise of the operator.

There are implications for the investment value of these assets. A valuation and assessment of an ORE asset are in part based on the performance of the private business and part on the property (exit value) using a discounted cash flow framework. In contrast with traditional real estate, the market value is based on net income that is capitalised at an appropriate yield to reflect inherent risks and opportunities.

PropTech, AI and the Commercial Real Estate Industry

The long-term context to real estate investment is changes in information communication and technologies, notably the arrival of first the personal computer and then the internet. It has influenced every aspect of the operation of the real estate market from the way transactions happen to the use and location of buildings, with implications for management and investment. These changes have embraced the paperless office, the ability to work from home and online retail sales.

At the heart of these recent advances is the internet and mobile phones that have transformed every aspect of human lives. In particular, the availability of information online has rewritten knowledge transfer, supported a move to cashless transactions and introduced the remote control of business devices and activities. Closely linked to these developments has been the arrival of online payment systems and internet banking, including lending. It has also facilitated the 'sharing economy' that encompasses owners renting out something they are not using, such as a house, exemplified by the activities of Airbnb.

This section examines the timeline and detail of innovations regarding the operation of real estate markets and considers the (potential) consequences for investment. Baum usefully identifies three stages in this historic continuum of the application of technological change that he refers to as PropTech 1.0, 2.0 and 3.0. These steps are now reviewed as a platform for considering the impact of how information technologies will continue to shape the real estate market. It draws heavily on Baum's framework.

PropTech 1.0

From the early 1980s, innovations were stimulated by a demand for databases to enable the greater performance measurement of commercial real estate by investors to compare the sector with shares and bonds. These databases heralded in a period of statistical analysis and specialist consultancies offering advice. This wave of technological innovation began in the early part of that decade and continued to the millennium.

The first significant real estate database initiative occurred in the United States, and then was quickly taken up in the UK in the early/middle of the decade. In the United States, the National Council of Real Estate Investment Fiduciaries (NCREIF) was established in 1982 to establish a property return index dating back to 1978. It was the first to measure investment performance of commercial real estate. It is based on individual property valuation data provided by the members of the organisation on a quarterly basis. The basic index over the years has been expanded so that there are now separate indices for regions and use sectors.

The equivalent database in the UK, the Investment Property Databank (IPD), was formed in 1985 with a time series originally backdated to 1981. From this base, the essential model of data collection and analysis has been extended by incorporating more institutional contributors that has enabled it to disaggregate results to encompass different UK real estate sectors and regions. Indices are now reported on an annual, quarterly and monthly basis. The model has also been exported to Australia, and then to countries across Europe and Asia, and more recently South America.

As noted above the establishment of these databases reflected a thirst for real estate research. Prior to their establishment individual real estate agencies had started generating their own piecemeal data on local market such as prime rents and yields. Many of the large agencies set up their own research departments in the early 1980s to analyse the data. 1982 saw the founding of Property Market Analysis (PMA), the first specialist standalone real estate research consultancy in London. Over the next two decades, financial institutions also began to set up their own research departments.

Despite these developments, information on the real estate sector remained limited. It was for example difficult to find details on individual transactions and lettings of particular properties. Individual agents saw this information as giving them market power. CoStar was set up in 1987 in the United States to provide this information in a computerised form. There were equivalent initiatives in the UK such as the Scottish Property Network. In the absence of the internet, data was transferred physically to customers and updated regularly using and circulating discs. These could be inputted into personal computers (PCs).

In the housing market, there were parallel initiatives. Mortgage banks (building societies) began trawling their transactions data to produce price indices broken down by buyer type, house type and region. Where there were (paper) public land registers operators stepped into to upgrade the information and create computerised databases.

The rise of these databases not only reflected a demand but also the improvements in computing power associated with the arrival and development of personal computers (PCs) as a standard feature of an office desk. Portfolio management systems became computer and technology based and software advances went hand in hand with the technology. It also stimulated change in traditional skills such as valuation. Argus was established in the United States in the mid-1980s offering software that mechanised the valuation process. About the same time, in 1984, Yardi was set up selling software to support the management of real estate. Both

Argus and Yardi, as well as CoStar, PMA and IPD (now part of MSCI), have become multinational companies.

PropTech 2.0

The key to the next stage was the use of information technologies in real estate via access to online applications. Whereas the focus of PropTech 1.0 was the PC, PropTech 2.0 was stimulated by the connectivity provided by the internet, particularly the arrival and roll out of broadband to domestic customers. It has been supported by the availability of wi-fi and 4G mobile phones.

The databases initiated in PropTech 1 could now be delivered online. It reduced the cost of both data collection (as some of the raw information was now online) and distribution and permitted data to be updated in real time rather than waiting for the latest disc to arrive. It made the use of the data more attractive because of its immediacy and lowered the purchase cost, and hence encouraged take up.

The internet has been used to market and list properties for sale and rent. This began with the residential sector as estate agencies combined to create listing services of properties on the market. No longer did prospective house buyers/renters have to search through adverts in newspapers and then ask for detailed particulars. All this information was readily available online and in some cases videos. Households were able also to look up the details of recent transactions nearby online. One consequence has been that estate agency business models evolved.

Similar initiatives have happened in the commercial and industrial real estate sectors. Firms can search potential locations and properties to decide where to locate. Investors can similarly identify potential purchases in this way and developers can find a range of detailed information on the characteristics of potential sites. This can be linked in with the real estate market databases noted above.

New databases continue to evolve, for example, 'Property Data' was established in the UK in 2000 and provides information on individual commercial and residential real estate transactions. Very often raw databases are now supplemented with add-ons such as immediate online computer-generated valuations on properties for sale as well as the provision of details on comparable properties.

These developments have transformed the operation of real estate markets by the provision of information making it far more efficient. It has also changed the real estate professions both in terms of the number of staff needed and the way they work. Basic market information is no longer exclusively stored in the brain of a specialist property consultant.

As the nature of market processes is changing so there is also the potential to revise or rethink even the nature of some real estate transactions. An example in the UK is IPSX, the first dedicated real estate stock exchange that enables asset owners to raise capital and for investors to invest in listed companies that own just one individual real estate asset. It effectively means that an investor can buy a share in a single property. IPSX received formal government recognition as an exchange in 2019, and the first single property REIT was launched on it in June 2021.

Technological change has not just influenced the operation of real estate markets but also the use of real estate as set out in Chapter 11. Broadband internet connections heralded the rise of online retail sales creating ecommerce. The long-term consequences are a fall in the demand for shops. The resultant surplus of shops has led to reduced rental and capital values. At the same time warehousing has expanded and the distribution process reformulated. Consequently, smaller warehouses have been built while existing industrial units have been switched to parcel storage for distribution.

The innovations of PropTech 2 in a sense began in PropTech 1 but were then accelerated and transformed using the internet, new software and the enhanced power of devices of PCs, tablets and smart phones. It arguably sums to an enduring revolution for real estate in Western economies that will eventually roll out to developing countries. On the one hand, it has created a much more efficient and transparent market that enhances real estate's attractiveness as an investment. But on the other hand, technological change has raised many questions about the returns from real estate investments. Retail investments are going through a substantial upheaval and many individual assets have fallen in value. Even though distribution warehousing is experiencing significant growth in demand, continuing technological change using artificial intelligence to date has also brought obsolescence to existing stock that is unattractive to investors.

PropTech 3.0

We now consider the role of technological change in the future, in particular the possibilities created by new 'blockchain' technology. Databases created by a blockchain, or a distributed ledger, differ from established ones by not having a central management core. So far, the databases discussed in this chapter have a core manager that inputs and holds the information. Customers currently access the data online from this central point that also controls entry. If there are technical problems at the centre, then data may not be available.

In a blockchain, data is in a distributed network as illustrated by Fig. 12.1 with many users who can input information that is verified in a ledger or log. Data is in effect shared in a ledger and once verified by interested individuals an agreed record is available to all parties. There are no intermediaries.

The process by which this is achieved can be seen as first an entry or transaction is agreed between two parties, say A and B. The entry is a potential block and is then communicated or transmitted to other parties, say C to F, and if these agree the entry is added to the blockchain. This blockchain can be visualised as a cluster of nodes, each representing a block that is an electronic file.

Clearly for the system to work the information must take a digital form but once the blockchain is formed it provides a trusted source of information for all parties. To achieve this goal, it requires clear protocols for how entries are committed to

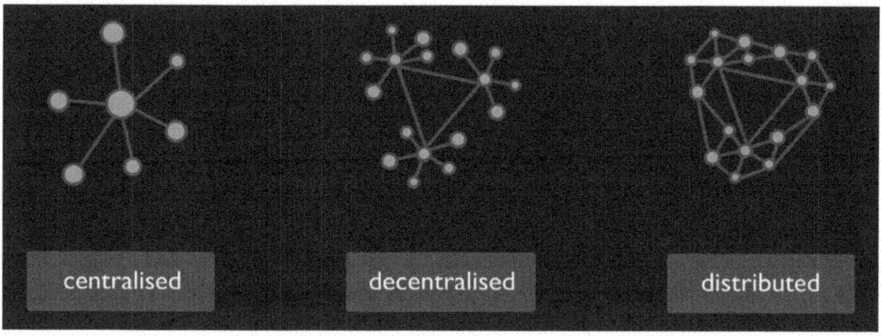

Fig. 12.1 Centralised, decentralised and distributed nodal systems (*Source* Mishcon de Reya [2020])

and synchronised on the ledger, that also ensures real-time oversight. The success of the blockchain of a distributed set of nodes depends only on the integrity of the data transfer within the system.

Baum provides a useful overall description of a blockchain as,

> A distributed ledger (also called shared ledger) is a consensus of replicated, shared, and synchronized digital data spread across multiple sites, countries, or institutions. There is no central administrator or middleman and no centralised data storage. Blockchain is: (i) a technology and a business practice built on peer-to- peer transactions; plus (ii) a packet of information (a block) with the ability to create an historical and permanent ledger of transaction details. (Baum 2017, p. 65)

No one single member of the network can change the information in the database. Changes can only occur by a consensus. Transactions or entries in the blockchain can only be undertaken with an encrypted 'key'. Each one is like a password with a string of characters unique to the account. It is a form of encrypted signature. In a public blockchain, there is also a 'public key' that can be used by anyone to view the information in the blockchain but not the identities of those who have provided inputs. A blockchain can be a private closed system with access prescribed to specific users.

Ultimately a blockchain can include a set of smart contracts or digital protocols that may verify, facilitate or enforce agreements. By applying mathematical algorithms elements of a contract can be made partly or fully self-executing when specific conditions are met. No one party controls the contract, yet all parties can trust it. It removes the need for paper and the certainties created by it take away the opportunity to forge facts as all the parties in the chain need to agree. It has the potential for example to avoid land disputes. It also prevents statements from being altered after they have been recorded, because all parties will be alerted to changes.

The seminal paper on blockchain was published in 2008 and to date their use has been confined to the creation of bitcoins and bitcoin transactions. There has been much speculation that it could be used within the real estate sector. Given that real estate transactions are slow and expensive it is postulated that blockchain technology could not only speed up the process but also reduce costs. It has also been suggested that it could speed up the construction process and change the nature of building ownership by making shared ownership easier. These are considered in turn.

In Sweden the land registry, the Lantmäteriet has been trialling a blockchain designed to track documents during the sale of a property since 2016. The buyer and seller, brokers and banks all take part as members of the blockchain and keep track of a sale digitally. It is now viewed as an operational system. The Land Registry in England has also explored the potential of blockchain and used a prototype to show proof of the concept: the study demonstrated that a real transaction that had taken 22 weeks to complete took less than 10 min with its blockchain.

These initiatives suggest that traditional registers could be replaced by a blockchain based alternative that will operate more cheaply, quicker and be more efficient. Following this argument, it would also make sense to introduce a blockchain approach to land registration in developing countries where there is no complete system of formal land titles at present because of customary or informal approaches to land ownership. It would also enable an incremental solution towards eventual full formal land registration.

The increased transparency inherent in blockchains is particularly attractive in countries with an informal land system where there are often land ownership disputes. It may also reduce some disreputable market behaviours in Western countries such as gazumping. However, while blockchains have been shown to be able to replace traditional land registration there can be legal obstacles to their operation. As it uses digital signatures these are not legally valid for property transfers in Sweden at the time of writing so providing a barrier to its introduction.

There are also the issues of public/professional reluctance to acceptance and the availability of expertise to apply blockchains. Successful implementation of blockchains will replace some professional skills but will require new ones. These skills are likely to be particularly in short supply in developing countries. Digital data are also major constraint.

A real estate transaction in a Western economy can involve a suite of actors starting with an estate agent through a lawyer undertaking the conveyancing, public authorities collecting taxes and recording it to bank providing finance. Using a blockchain it is argued that it would not be necessary to employ a lawyer to access the necessary blocks of information. Nevertheless, it is doubtful that say the individual house buyer will be competent to undertake the task and will therefore require professional expertise. It also requires the relevant information to be digitised. It is possible to imagine a time in the future where the necessary information is held in digital libraries that provide histories of land ownership, planning constraints and proposals, building records and valuation details etc. But it is some time away.

The potential uses of blockchains are not confined to land registration as detailed in Baum's *Tokenisation: The Future of Real Estate Investment?* This section draws on his analysis. Building construction can be enhanced by a blockchain whereby it traces the various stages of the process assessing performance, and with smart contracts used to automatically pay for work completed. In this way, increased efficiency and transparency could contribute to a reduction in the construction costs of real estate. The same approach could be applied to the management of large buildings.

Besides improving the real estate transaction and construction processes, blockchain has the potential to revolutionise real estate investment through partitioning individual properties into tokens. In other words, it can create co-ownership or partial ownership of the legal interests of a real estate asset. Registered token holders within a blockchain can vote on decisions through a smart contract about maintenance, lettings and refurbishment. Overall then tokenisation could open up real estate investment with individual tokens costing far less than a whole building with transaction costs low.

These tokens are akin to bitcoins and tokenisation can be seen as the digital fractionalisation of real estate assets. But in practice, there are constraints on the number of owners of a property in many countries, so tokenisation is more likely of a real estate company, REIT or some other form of co-ownership vehicle such as a partnership or trust (see Chapter 5). Fractionalisaton in this way means that each token is secure and subject the internal rules of the blockchain. A key issue is the transferability of these tokens if an investor wants to sell.

Potentially transaction fees are low because of the transparent rules of the blockchain but in many countries most of the cost of transfer of assets is tax. Liquidity depends on a market mechanism and sufficient demand, and the latter is unproven. It may take many years for market acceptance of the technology and there are concerns about the specific risk of investing in individual properties. Furthermore, there is the potential for 'insider dealing' if there is information available to some real estate professionals that a major tenant is looking for alternative accommodation.

There is almost certainly a need for a manager of the blockchain and the transfer of tokens. It leads to a supplementary question of whether this form of fractionalisation is an improvement on existing forms of co-ownership or shares available via the IPSX exchange noted earlier. The pricing of tokens on transfer is still subject to constraints on liquidity. The take up of blockchains is likely to be driven by economics not just the technology.

So far, the discussion has been about asset digital tokens but there is the possibility of user digital tokens replacing lease arrangements. Similarly, there can be debt digital tokens with the smart contract in the blockchain potentially providing greater clarity to the securitisation of debt and speeding up payments. The technology could also be used for the facilitation of crowd funding of real estate investment, with tokens enabling a clear link to a share in returns. The range of potential applications raises questions about regulation and differences between countries.

The issues considered regarding the digitalisation of land registration are part of a wider problem of regulation of this new technology by governments. To what extent should the new technology be policed by existing laws, or should new legislation be enacted to address a new digital world? There is the additional dimension that digitalisation enables global activities that are not confined by national boundaries. There are many challenges to the adoption of this technology.

Summary

The chapter has examined some of the challenges and opportunities arising from both longer-term trends and short to medium term pragmatic decisions arising from the GFC. At the time of writing many of the challenges highlighted have not been resolved, but all offer opportunities in terms of making the future less uncertain.

The changing role of technological change on real estate markets can be differentiated into three stages as follows:

- PropTech 1.0 from 1980s saw significant developments in real estate databases that transformed the volume of information available.
- PropTech 2.0 saw the widespread embrace of the opportunities now available by the internet, and by bringing data readily available online reformulating market processes.
- Proptech 3.0 centres on the future potential role of blockchains and smart contracts.

Technological change has brought consequences for the use of real estate. Online retail sales creating ecommerce are rethinking shopping and reducing the demand for retail units. On the other hand, demand for distribution warehouses has increased while their forms have been subject to constant revision. The outcome of technological change has contributed to a much more efficient market but also generated turmoil for retail investments and rapid change for distribution warehouses that has left considerable obsolescence.

PropTech 3.0 offers the possibilities of new 'blockchain' technology. The technology is little more than a decade old but there have been many uses within the real estate sector. A blockchain is a decentralised ledger where data is shared and jointly confirmed by encrypted keys to ensure its integrity. In the system, no one can change any information without every member's agreement. The blockchain may encompass a set of smart contracts or digital protocols that may verify, facilitate or enforce agreements.

The immediate potential for the use of blockchain within the real estate sector stems from the slow processes involved in the registration of transactions. It has been shown to work much more efficiently than the current paper-based approach. Although the blockchain approach to land registration in developing countries would be beneficial, there are legal and practical obstacles to the replacement of current land registration systems.

The use of blockchains could also contribute to a reduction in the construction and management costs of real estate and could also be applied to create digital fractionalisation of real estate assets through a co-ownership vehicle such as a single property REIT. This could reduce transaction costs but there are a range of issues about investing in single real estate assets including specific risk and insider trading. It is unclear whether fractionalisation or this form makes economic sense irrespective of the technological advances.

The application of the new technology may be constrained by government regulation, and variations between countries, with the additional dimension that digitalisation activities cross national boundaries.

The chapter has also considered changes in the pension world. Until recently contributory retirement plans have been linked to paying a pension based on the employee's final salary and their years of membership known as DB schemes. Increasingly they have been replaced by a DC approach whereby members receive a pension based on the sums that have been paid in, and how these contributions are invested. With DC schemes, employers have no obligation beyond the contributions that they pay into the scheme. DC scheme members shoulder the investment risk in terms of their pension on retirement.

The move towards DC from DB changes the nature of decisions. As DB schemes mature, they become more risk averse, reflecting the need to reliably pay out pensions month after month. This risk aversion tends to involve selling (riskier) equity type assets and buying (safer) bond type investments including secure income producing commercial real estate. New DC funds may have a strong inflow of capital, consequently, the matching of assets to liabilities is no longer the same and the trend in DC schemes is to diversify into real estate through more liquid indirect property.

The GFC had a range of short-term negative implications for investors in real estate, but it also led to a reappraisal of investment behaviour. Some property funds simply found ways of increasing the proportion of liquid assets as defensive mechanism. The GFC exposed the inadequacy of real estate forecasting as simply extrapolating market sentiment. It also unearthed the scale of gearing of real estate investors and the associated risks. The UK industry sought ways of addressing and managing these risks and protect real estate investment from severe economic downturns. It was accepted that the flow of credit to the commercial real estate sector should be moderated.

One solution is using sustainable valuations by banks when deciding on a commercial real estate loan. They are not widely used in the UK, but long-term valuations are used in Germany. It can be seen as being the average value of the property through the market cycle. Their practical application is still not agreed as there are several ways to define sustainable valuations, each with different attractions. There are also business challenges to introducing each of these more cautious approaches to valuation.

While there have been moves to fix the real estate investment risks revealed by the GFC there remains the issue of irrational behaviour not withstanding a belief in the efficient market hypothesis. However, the conditions for the EMH do not apply to the real estate market querying the basis and power of rational behaviour.

The empirical evidence as shown in the lead up to the GFC is that there can be serious departures from rational behaviour.

Market actors arguably do not properly assess the probabilities of outcomes because decisions are made by reference to behavioural judgements linked to *representative thinking*, *availability* and *anchoring*. The result can be a simplistic perspective that ignores extreme events and the creation of overconfidence with resultant over trading. There may also be a reluctance to alter views despite changing facts.

Real estate decisions are set within cultural or professional values and customs that frame their options. It is a complex system, and it is important to establish the inter-related connections. Overall, it is essential to identify and incorporate the impact of behaviour into the understanding of the market, especially regarding real estate cycles.

Property indices can be either appraisal-based (market price) or transaction-based approaches. There are challenges in constructing and using both types of indices. Appraisal or valuation-based real estate indices are the most common. Indices are constructed by valuing the estimated market prices for a sample of individual properties owned by a set of property funds on a regular basis. These valuations are aggregated into one measure.

While transaction indices are common in the residential market there only a few recent examples for commercial real estate in the UK and the United States. There are different ways of statistically estimating these indices, but a repeat sales approach is becoming the most accepted. Both appraisal and transactions-based indices have drawbacks. Smoothing is the primary concern of appraisal-based indices but there are other issues including representativeness.

In general, the real estate profession prefers appraisal-based to transactions indices. Transactions-based measures suffer from lack of transparency and being based on a small, biased proportion of the market that has high turnover. Market analysts generally see transactions indices as only supplementing the evidence from appraisal indices.

Overall, the chapter has demonstrated that traditional real estate investment models are beginning to be questioned. Technological change is to some extent generating a rethink in the way property is used and paid for, including the replacement of the use of leases. Alternative real estate assets are also being considered as a way of generating greater returns and improving diversification from the long-established sectors.

Alternative assets are wide ranging, but two types can be distinguished: operational entities or trade related properties and social infrastructure. They are specialist more complex real estate investments with poor liquidity and weak information on performance. A key element for success of trade related assets is the ability of the operator, known as operational risk. Traditional prime real estate assets also have some operational risk, but it is limited to temporary voids caused by business failure. Social infrastructure assets have the benefit of revenues defined by a long-term public sector contract with less dependence on operator skill.

Given the greater importance of operators, there are different approaches to owning trade related real estate assets. They can be leased or subject to management agreements with the former being closer to the characteristics of traditional real estate. The use of standard leases is passive investment whereas a management agreement can be seen as an active approach. Performance based leases, franchises and the owner/operator model are also active investment methods. These active approaches can be viewed as *operational real estate* (ORE) no matter what sort of real estate, and the return to owners is based on the financial performance of the asset.

There are advantages and disadvantages of ORE versus the traditional model. A traditional lease provides a safe certain income stream but does not benefit from profits generated from the use of its property. The ORE model is also more appropriate where there is no specific real estate market, or the asset requires frequent capital expenditure, or the returns are based on the expertise of the operator. A valuation and assessment of an ORE asset require a discounted cash flow framework.

Learning Outcomes

Having completed this chapter, the reader should be able to:

- Note that impact of technological change on real estate markets can be differentiated into three stages known as PropTech 1.0, 2.0 and 3.0.
- Understand that PropTech 1.0 began in the 1980s with the establishment of real estate databases that transformed the volume of information available, and stimulated performance measurement.
- Appreciate that PropTech 2.0 represented the greater development and availability of databases enhanced using the internet. In doing so, the operation of real estate markets has been rethought and made the market more transparent and efficient.
- Realise that technological developments have also resulted in fundamental changes to the use of real estate. Online retail sales are revolutionising shopping with a resultant surplus of retail units and centres.
- Be aware of the possibilities of new 'blockchain' technology. The technology is little more than a decade old but there have been many proposed uses within the real estate sector.
- Understand the basics of a blockchain as a decentralised ledger where data is shared and jointly confirmed by encrypted keys to ensure its integrity.
- Realise that the immediate potential for the use of blockchain within the real estate sector stems from the slow processes involved in the registration of transactions.
- Recognise that a blockchain approach to land registration in developing countries would be beneficial. Nevertheless, there are legal and practical obstacles to the replacement of current land registration systems.

- Grasp that there are other potential uses of blockchains including improving the efficiency and transparency of the construction industry.
- Recognise that blockchain technology could also be applied to create digital fractionalisation of real estate assets through a co-ownership vehicle such as a single property REIT.
- Appreciate that while digital fractionalisation has the capacity to reduce transaction costs there are a range of economic barriers to investing in single real estate assets including specific risk and insider trading.
- Recognise that DB pension schemes are being replaced by DC plans and understand why.
- Be aware that the shift from DB to DC schemes has also meant that pension plans are switching from direct to indirect real estate investment.
- Appreciate that the GFC heralded a rethinking of approaches to real estate investment and forecasting. In particular, note that investors recognised that the risk associated with high gearing needed to be reduced.
- Understand the arguments for the use of sustainable valuations by banks when deciding on a commercial real estate loan and recognise that there are difficulties in their introduction in the UK.
- Grasp that the issue of irrational behaviour is an important influence on real estate markets that can bring overconfidence and resultant over trading.
- Recognise that it is important to identify and incorporate the impact of behaviour into the understanding of the market, especially regarding real estate cycles.
- Distinguish between appraisal-based (market price) and transaction-based property indices.
- Comprehend the different ways the two types of indices are constructed.
- Note the significance of smoothing in interpreting a time series based on an appraisal-based index.
- Note that transactions-based indices suffer from being based on a small proportion of the market that has high turnover.
- Understand the attraction of alternative real estate assets compared to long-established sectors.
- Appreciate the relative merits of investing in trade related and infrastructure assets.
- Comprehend that a key element for the success of trade related assets is the ability of the operator.
- Recognise the advantages and disadvantages of different passive and active approaches to owning and managing real estate assets: traditional leases, performance-based leases, franchises management contracts and the owner/operator model are also active investment methods.
- Note that active (ORE) approaches can be applied to all types of real estate, and the return to owners is based on the financial performance of the asset.
- Understand the advantages and disadvantages of ORE versus the traditional real estate model.

Reading

Baum, A. (2017) *PropTech 3.0: The Future of Real Estate*, Said Business School, Oxford University, Oxford.

Baum, A. (2020) *Tokenisation: The Future of Real Estate Investment?* Said Business School, Oxford University, Oxford.

Broadbent, J., Palumbo, M. and Woodman, E. (2006) *The Shift from Defined Benefit to Defined Contribution Pension Plans—Implications for Asset Allocation and Risk Management.* Working Group on Institutional Investors, Global Savings and Asset Allocation (Committee on the Global Financial System).

CREFC, Commercial Real Estate Finance Council Europe and Investment Property Forum (2017) *Long-Term Value Methodologies and Real Estate Lending*. Property Industry Alliance Long-term Value Working Group, London.

Crosby, N. (2018) *Long-Term Sustainable Real Estate Appraisals/Valuations—How far have we got in the UK*. Paper presented to Annual European Real Estate Society Conference, Reading, UK, June.

Gibson, M. (2019). *How Will UK Pensions Reform Affect Real Estate Investment*? CBRE, London.

Investment Property Forum (2014) *A Vision for Real Estate Finance in the UK*. Investment Property Forum, London.

Investment Property Forum (2019) *The Size and Structure of the UK Property Market—End 2018 Update*. Investment Property Forum, London.

Jones, C., Cowe, S. and Trevillion, E. (2018) *Property Boom and Banking Bust: The Role of Commercial Lending in the Bankruptcy of Banks*. Wiley-Blackwell, Chichester.

Mansley, N., Lizieri, C., Wang, Z., Crosby, N. and Devaney, S. (2020). *Long-Term Value Methodologies in Commercial Real Estate Lending*. Investment Property Forum, London.

Mishcon de Reya (2020) *Toward a Distributed Leger of Residential Title Deeds in the UK*. Mishcon de Reya, London.

NAO, National Audit Office (2021) *Pensions Landscape Advice Note*. NAO, London. https://resources.nao.org.uk/pensions_landscape/risks-associated-with-dc-schemes.html. Accessed July 2021.

Richardson, M., Hopkinson, M., Ryan, S., Dunse, N., Jones, C. and White, M. (2021) *Operational Real Estate Risk and Reward*. Investment Property Forum, London.

Shiller, R. J. (2005) *Irrational Exuberance,* 2nd Edition. Broadway Books, New York.

Spence, M. and Libre, J. (2018) *Real Estate Investment in UK Defined Contribution Pension Schemes*. Investment Property Forum Report May 2018. IPF, London.

Trevillion, E. (2021) Using system dynamics modelling to understand behaviour in UK commercial property markets. *Journal of European Real Estate Research,* Vol. ahead-of-print No. ahead-of-print. https://doi.org/10.1108/JERER-01-2021-0007

Trevillion, E., Gardner, A., Cowe, S. and Jones, C. (2020) Current practices in benchmarking real estate investment performance. *Journal of Real Estate Portfolio Management*, 26, 2, 118–131.

Part IV

Future Research and Dissertations

13 Concluding Thoughts and Areas for Future Research

The subject of the book is investment in the real estate sector, a not insignificant part of the wider investment community, and the benefits it offers investors compared with other asset classes. The primary aim has been to provide an overview of real estate investment mainly for students of the subject. However, it also provides a useful refresher for property professionals, providing them with a different, and sometimes new view of how the property market really works. It mainly concerns itself with the commercial property market. However, it recognises that in some countries there are large investors in the residential sector and an increasing interest in it in others such as the UK. Institutional investment in residential markets is really only just beginning to establish itself in the UK.

It was noted at the start of this book that its inspiration came from updating Will Fraser's text 'Principles of Property Investment and Pricing'. Much has changed in the property market since that popular textbook was published at the beginning of the 1990s, and this new book reflects these changes; the growing globalisation of real estate investment, information availability and benchmarking, the rethinking of pensions, the rise of sustainability issues and technological change over the last 30 years. It offers a contemporary reflection on real estate investment practices and tackles the complexity of property markets progressively through the book. It sets out the state of our knowledge about the fundamentals of real estate investment.

A natural conclusion of this progressive analysis is to consider areas which would benefit from future research. There is inevitably more research needed to understand the dynamics of property markets and the implications for investment. There is a strong case to improve data to chart how markets operate. There are continuing insights that will arise from the inevitable change brought about by political events, the climate crisis, the pandemic, technological and urban change and behavioural responses.

Real estate markets are constantly subject to change as the book chapters exemplify. Change inevitably offers opportunities and challenges to investors. The years since the millennium have been dominated by the economic boom in the first

C. A. Jones and E. Trevillion, *Real Estate Investment* ,
https://doi.org/10.1007/978-3-031-00968-6_13

half of the subsequent decade, the global financial crisis and then its continuing aftermath. This is the essential backdrop to our considerations here. Although Chapters 11 and 12 examined some of the consequences of a changing global landscape, we try to identify specific research areas that we think might benefit from more detailed research.

We noted in Chapter 12 that the motivations for changing the way real estate investments are undertaken, and the way that markets operate have often been shaped and stimulated by external macroeconomic forces and facilitated by technological advances. We also noted that speculative market expansions, such as those seen in global property markets in the first decade of the new millennium, have often been associated with popular perceptions that the future is brighter or less un-certain than it was in the past. The term *new era* has periodically been used to describe these times. Shiller in his 2005 book, *Irrational Exuberance*, notes that by many measures the world has indeed been growing into a new and better era. Whether this is true or not needs to play a major part in our examination of future behaviour which is not hidebound by historical models, economic or otherwise. So, research should not only examine the complexity of property market systems but also examine where changing geopolitics will change our perception of the future direction of property markets.

Shiller also notes that the most salient characteristic of popular new era thinking is that it is not continuously in evidence but occurs in pulses. These pulses will be driven by new views of how things work, by novel research as well as by changes in global dynamics.

Along with an examination of possible research areas of interest, given that the book is mainly aimed at students, this final part also offers potential dissertation topics for final year undergraduate and Master's students.

Future Research Areas

Long-Term Consequences of BREXIT

We noted in Chapter 9 that economic integration has meant that property cycles can almost simultaneously occur in distant cities in different parts of the world. Countries integrated into international capital will be destined to suffer from common 'boom and bust' scenarios, but they will inevitably be mediated by local factors.

There are still wide disparities in property related practices worldwide, and these differences segregate property markets and inhibit the ease by which market players can operate in different national markets. New alliances reinforced the apparent benefits of free trade and the acceptance that this economic approach had the potential for providing greater market efficiency compared to strict command economies. However, despite this major change in attitude over the last 60 or so years, the benefits of economic openness have been under increasing scrutiny in

Western countries, giving rise to nationalism and populist politics. In this context, the chapter briefly examined the implications of the UK's BREXIT deal. At the time of writing, it appears that there has not been as severe an impact on the demand for commercial property space as first expected despite no formal agreement, for example, on the trade of financial services to the EU.

There is still uncertainty around the long-term consequences of the deal and the extent to which new business can be generated from the rest of the world to replace that lost to the EU. In this context, we believe that there is much scope for examining the long-term consequences of the BREXIT deal on the UK property market especially with regard to fund management and risk.

To What Extent Has the GFC Impacted on the Investment Process in the UK?

In Chapter 12, we examined some of the challenges and opportunities which have arisen because of changes in UK and global property markets over the last 10 to 20 years. Some of these challenges and opportunities have spun out of the global financial crisis and the need to re-examine risk assessment and valuations.

The increase in property investors' perceptions of risk following the GFC, stimulated a debate in the UK and beyond about the role of valuations in bank funding of investment purchases. It raised questions about what constituted fair value and the potential need to consider the use of sustainable valuations by banks when deciding on whether to agree a loan. This could be applied when assessing the loan-to-value (LTV) ratio for commercial property, and there has been a recognition that long-term sustainable valuations might help in mitigating risk when advancing loans.

We noted that sustainable valuations are not widely used in UK markets, but the approach underpins values applied in Germany's Pfandbrief commercial bond market. With this in mind, we believe that there is still scope for a wider examination of the extent to which the GFC has impacted on the investment process including the scale of debt and the use of sustainable valuations outside of Germany.

The Use of Behavioural Economics to Develop and Model New Forecasting Techniques

Chapter 12 also examined the impact of behaviour in real estate markets. Part of the challenge has resulted from the continuing belief in the application of the efficient market hypothesis (EMH) to property markets and the extent which investor behaviour impacts on market behaviour overall.

Behavioural theory (as manifest in behavioural finance) suggests that individuals do not do a good job at evaluating probabilities and making rational choices. Anomalies can be both important and widespread leading to substantial and systematic effects that are not transient but persist. Behavioural explanations of market anomalies can be seen as bubbles, momentum and systematic mispricing. Market actors arguably often do not properly assess the probability of outcomes instead they use mental shortcuts in their reasoning and so can arrive at biased conclusions.

The chapter noted that recognising behaviour as an important element in real estate market systems suggests that behaviour economics ought to be applied more widely to understand market dynamics. Economic systems such as the real estate market are imbued by cultural values and underpinned by social and psychological customs that influence the way in which people understand their options and make their choices. It is in this context that we believe that there is huge scope for research into these aspects of market dynamics and the use of more inductive systems thinking in forecasting market trends.

The Application of Blockchain Techniques to Land Registration and the Scope for Fractionalisation of Real Estate

Our examination of challenges and opportunities in Chapter 12 included a look at PropTech, AI and the commercial real estate industry. Changes in information communication and technology, notably the arrival of the first personal computer and then the internet, have influenced every aspect of the operation of the real estate market from the way transactions happen to the use and location of buildings, with implications for management and investment. These changes have embraced the paperless office, the ability to work from home and online retail sales. In particular, the availability of information online has re-written knowledge transfer, supported and moved cashless transactions and introduced the remote control of business devices and activities. Closely linked to these developments has been the arrival of online payment systems and internet banking, including lending. It has also facilitated the sharing economy.

Databases created by a blockchain, or a distributed ledger, differ from established ones by not having a central management course. In a blockchain, data is in a distributed network with many users who can input information that is verified in a ledger or a log. Data is in effect shared in a ledger and is verified by individuals as an agreed record. It is available to all parties; there are no intermediaries.

The application of blockchain techniques is still in its infancy and there is huge scope for research into their application across property markets, particularly in the context of land registration and the scope for fractionisation of real estate. The Swedish land registry has been trialling a blockchain designed to track documents during the sale of property since 2006. The land registry in England has also explored the potential use of blockchain and used the prototype to show proof of the concept. These initiatives suggested the traditional register could be replaced by a blockchain-based alternative that will operate more cheaply, quicker and be more efficient. But more research is required in this regard.

Blockchain has also the potential to revolutionise real estate investment through partitioning individual properties into tokens. In other words, it can create a co-ownership or partial ownership of the legal interest of a real estate asset but as discussed in Chapter 12 there are barriers to the viability of this form of application.

The Development of Maturity/Transparency Criteria More Appropriate for Developing Countries

The concept of market maturity is a useful one when assessing the relative development of markets worldwide and with it their investment potential and associated risk. A property market may take a traditional and simple form in which the real estate sector is poorly developed and lacks an identifiable separate market for users' and investors' interests. Alternatively, it may be highly mature with a sophisticated and well-established real estate profession providing the essential requisites for use and investment real estate markets.

However, there are wide disparities in property related practices worldwide. These differences segregate property markets and inhibit the ease by which market players can operate in different national markets. In this context, in addition to so-called mature markets, Chapter 9 defined emerging, transitional and frontier market. The term transitional markets is used to define markets moving from a command economy to economic neoliberalism, and related initially to Central and Eastern European countries emerging from Soviet style economies. Frontier markets are characterised by low levels of per capita income, property investment and market transparency.

It is fair to say that the starting point for the market maturity concept is developed countries and the approach does not sit easily as a measure of the relative state of property markets in developing countries. In this context, it is important to recognise the distinction between formal and informal mechanisms in the operation of land and property markets, including residential markets.

All of this still begs the question that although market maturity may be a good conceptual framework for decision-making, what data should be used to establish a hierarchy of markets in developing countries. There is scope for more understanding and research in this regard to widen definitions of maturity because maturity perceptions influence inward investment.

The Impact of Operational Leases on Future Real Estate Investment

Chapter 12 explored the use of operational real estate (ORE) models of investment. These encompass arrangements in which the return to owners is based on the financial performance of the asset. ORE is about receiving returns based on the income streams of the business occupying a property rather than the traditional rent and lease arrangement. It is not confined to alternative investments. It may involve active management of the asset, and it is ultimately backed by the value of the property (even if only as land).

There are advantages and disadvantages of ORE versus the traditional model. A traditional lease provides a safe, certain, income stream with the business expertise and risks clearly with the tenant. The disadvantage is that income has a bond like characteristic between rent reviews and the investor does not benefit from profits generated from the use of its property as with the ORE model. The ORE model is also more appropriate where there is an absence of comparable evidence to agree an appropriate rent, or the asset will require frequent upgrading, or the returns are based on the expertise of the operator.

There are implications for the investment value of these assets. A valuation and assessment of an ORE asset is in part based on the performance of the private business and part on the property (exit value) using a discounted cash flow framework. In contrast with traditional real estate, the market value is based on net income that is capitalised at an appropriate yield to reflect inherent risks and opportunities. In this context, there is scope for much more research to assess the opportunities and challenges resulting from the use of operational leases on future real estate investment not only in terms of market dynamics but also on the impact of (different?) valuations on perception and with it investment trends.

The Ability of Institutional Residential Investment to Provide Affordable Housing

Historically, large investors have viewed the characteristics of residential investment as less favourable than commercial property and globally most residential investment has been owned by small individual investors, although there are large scale investors in Europe and the United States. In Britain, the majority of residential landlords are private individuals and couples. This ownership structure is a longstanding position going back more than a century. A sudden rise in the UK's private rented sector since the millennium has reinforced this occurence.

However, in recent years, there has also been an increasing movement towards investors building custom built large blocks to rent in cities, following the model in the United States, and supported by subsidies from central government. This phenomenon is known collectively as 'Build to Rent' (BTR). The aim is to introduce mass produced rental housing for middle market tenants. These developments are, generally speaking, not aimed at the lower end of the market but increasingly opportunities are being examined for encompassing affordable rents into larger BTR schemes.

The investors in BTR are focused on the potential long-term cash flow potential from the net rental stream that offers better returns than government bonds. It is envisaged that there is a long-term demand for such flats as owner occupation is increasingly more difficult to access and there is a consequent growth of long-term renters. Long-term tenants will be promoted by high management standards, services and de facto security of tenure. These schemes are not restricted to flatted development but are now also encompassing a range of housing types including low density developments. In addition, these schemes can and do encompass affordable units which utilise the same services of tenants as mid-market tenancies.

These schemes are still on a small scale across the UK. The long-term success of these schemes may bring an opportunity to not only include more affordable units in BTR schemes. Ultimately, it may also extend the principles of BTR to solely affordable estates to help improve the lack of supply using institutional money. While financial institutions are already looking at these options, there is scope for more academic research with the ultimate aim to provide affordable homes with private money.

Development and Expansion of the Transaction-Based Measures of Economic Activity

The choice of a real estate index is not straightforward; indices vary both in the construction methodologies used and the breadth and representativeness of their market coverage. They can be differentiated by the techniques used to collect data and compile the series, either appraisal based (market price) or transaction-based approaches. There are challenges in constructing and using both types of indices, however.

The commonly used benchmarks for market comparison and benchmarking in the unlisted sector of the UK are based on data provided by MSCI/IPD using appraisal-based methods. These are the most commonly used type in the commercial property market as information on transaction prices is scarce. However, they have their drawbacks. The principal concerns with appraisal base industry indices are around valuation smoothing as well as with temporal and spatial aggregation within the appraisal process. Valuations tend to smooth out market movements in a real estate cycle by, for example, underestimating price falls in a downturn. Aggregate indices also hide spatial variations, say between cities. As a result, these indices produced statistics that do not provide investors with an accurate quantification of market risk. It is also questionable whether appraisal-based indices accurately reflect the scale of market movements, particularly when placed under extreme conditions.

Notwithstanding these concerns the appraisal based MSCI/IPD index remains the index of choice when constructing market benchmarks in the UK.

In this context, Chapter 12 explored the use of transaction-based indices. These are common in the residential market where more information on property transaction prices is available. They can be constructed by averaging transaction prices in a given time period, using statistical modelling which assumes the property values depend on the sum of the properties' individual attributes. An alternative approach is the repeat sales method where construction of this type of index is based on calculating the price change that occurs when properties in a database are sold more than once in a specific time period.

These types of indices are in their relative infancy. Like appraisal-based indices though there are concerns with their use particularly with regard to opacity and in how they are calculated. Repeat sales indices in particular suffer from issues of representativeness and spatial coverage.

Generally speaking, there is no enthusiasm in the United Kingdom for using transaction-based indices as benchmarks although they are seen as useful analytical tools and can give more immediate market responses than appraisal-based indices especially at times when market prices are changing rapidly. In this context, there is interest in using transaction-based indices as an early warning system and there is a case for more work to make them more user friendly and better able to quantify risk and return measures. Addressing practical issues should not mask the opportunities that they may offer especially during periods when asset prices are changing rapidly.

Potential Dissertation Topics

The foregoing section has outlined broad areas of research that really would require significant academic or industry support and funding to achieve realistic results. In this section, we address more limited research that could be undertaken as final year undergraduate or postgraduate research dissertations. In this context, it is suggested that it is best to undertake dissertation topics that explain the past whether it is market trends, the impact of events or public policies or the emergence of real estate forms. The following topics are simply exemplars.

- ***Investment in Different Property Sectors*:** Residential, Retailing, Offices, Hotels, Alternative sectors. Studies can examine the differential impact of specific changes resulting from property cycles, legislation, planning, taxation, technologies, cities/regions and the pandemic for individual sectors. The academic base for such research is set out in Chapters 10 through 12 and Chapter 4 for residential use. These studies could focus on the implications for locations, obsolescence and property forms, and the use of operational leases/management.
- ***The Net-Zero Green Agenda*:** Subjects could include the existence of green real estate premiums, investment attitudes towards multi-use developments, urban form, walkable neighbourhoods and real estate markets/development, the adoption of cycling facilities in office blocks or the adoption of ESG by investment funds and developers. Dissertations could cover changes over time and the impact of planning policies in individual cities or countries. Research, in particular, could look at to what extent green public policies have impinged and influenced change in real estate markets and investment decisions. These studies would extend the analysis set out in Chapters 10 and 11.
- ***Country specific research or comparisons*:** Projects might want to compare the performance between markets or across economic regions. This might include the maturity of a specific country, including transparency, foreign investment,

(informal) land registration frameworks and tenure. The development and structure of REITs in different markets would be interesting. Country studies might include tourism and real estate investment, development and investment in second/holiday homes, the consequences of changing demographic structures, e.g. ageing or young populations or house prices and affordability.

Many of these studies could be of countries in Africa, Asia and South America, particularly in relation to maturity as discussed in Chapter 9 or tourism and holiday accommodation. Comparisons across countries may relate to a particular sector of real estate and relate to market characteristics, investment behaviour and development activity. Comparisons could also focus on the real estate impacts of differential taxation treatment or public policy as considered in Chapter 10.

- ***Spatial Economy and Cities***: Changes driven by technology and public policy, with consequences for the spatial economy of cities and real estate markets, can provide a fruitful basis for dissertation studies. Such studies can focus on historical change and highlight both policy and community issues. The role of distance or accessibility to particular types of urban locations can provide perspective on the spatial patterns of real estate values. Topics might include regeneration consequences for real estate markets, online sales and consequences for distribution or the impact of proximity to green space or other urban features on real estate values

The classification of these dissertation topics is to a degree arbitrary and can be overlapping. Students can construct a research project that draws on these topics to address their particular interests. It is important to choose a topic that a student is interested in.

The best dissertations combine a literature review and independent research based on data collection. A key to a successful topic is data availability. Typically, a dissertation is based on a combination of reviewing secondary data and the collection of primary data from interviews or a questionnaire survey. A survey could be undertaken in person, or via email or via the internet. In this context, students are increasingly undertaking internet surveys but there can be problems with constraining samples to a defined community, whether it be households/businesses in a particular area or a professional group. Access via a Facebook page of a community may be one solution. An alternative is to ask a key player in a group to distribute a survey. Yet another way of gaining email addresses to distribute a survey is snowball sampling, namely asking contacts to recommend others.

Final Thoughts

A theme that has continued throughout the chapters in this book is the observation that business or commercial property has a dual function. It is an important factor of production. Without factories, offices, shops and leisure facilities the productive activities of business would not be possible. However, over the last two hundred years, commercial property has been transformed from a 'social institution' to a financial asset and its value now reflects both its importance as a factor of production and its value as an investment medium.

This process has happened not least because of the increasing involvement of financial institutions in the investment process. The dynamic of the commercial property market has changed significantly over this period but none more so than in the last 30 or so years as practices change and markets expend. This is true of both parts of the duality with new investment vehicles being developed as occupier uses change. The residential sector has also developed as a significant investment vehicle.

We noted at the beginning of the book that inevitably, because business property is such an important factor of production, its performance is closely linked to the overall performance of a nation's economy. In different ways, this is true of both the occupier (rental) and investment markets. This dual susceptibility was amply demonstrated in the aftermath of the GFC when a double whammy of poor economic performance and the lack of available credit significantly affected the performance of both the investment and occupier markets. It is also now a global phenomenon.

This duality of commercial property as a consumption and investment good results in complex relationships between the occupier, investment and development sectors, and it is this complexity that continues to offer a rich vein for study. In recent year this complexity has increased with new considerations around climate change and governance.

There is only so much one book can achieve but hopefully the book offers a contemporary reflection on real estate investment practices and processes which will prove of use to students and practitioners alike.

Glossary

***Active management*:** A fund where investments are purchased and sold on a regular basis according to perceived investment opportunities.

***All risk yield*:** This is a term used by UK valuers when using a traditional method of valuation.

***APUT*:** An authorised property unit trust is a means by which UK personal investors can access and invest in the property market.

***Asset management*:** The administration of individual assets within a portfolio.

***Balanced fund*:** A fund investing across the investment spectrum, latterly taken to imply in proportions reflecting the market.

***BASEL Accords*:** These international banking regulations originated in the late 1980s. They focus on monitoring the capital adequacy of financial institutions to deal with risks, particularly associated with an unexpected loss in their loan portfolio. The fourth revision of the Accords, Basel IV, is due to take effect in 2023.

***Benchmarking*:** Benchmarks provide the basis on which performance is monitored and judged. They can also be used to determine strategic asset allocations and form the basis of, and characterise, investment mandates.

***Beta (β)*:** **ß** is a measure of an asset's market risk, namely its volatility relative to the market as a whole. If beta is one then the asset has the same risk and expected return as the market. If beta is>1, then the returns on the asset will outperform the market in a 'bull' phase (as prices rise) but underperform in a 'bear' phase (as prices fall). If beta is <1, then the return from the asset is less volatile than that of the market.

***Capitalisation Rate*:** It is the same an 'equivalent yield', namely the internal rate of return (IRR) of a property's cash flow assuming a rise to estimated rental value at the next rent review but with no change in yield and ignoring further rental growth. It is a term used in the United States and other countries.

***Direct property investment*:** The ownership of a physical real estate asset. It includes investments of land and buildings for owner-occupation and those purchased as a pure investment with the intention to let the occupation right to another party.

C. A. Jones and E. Trevillion, *Real Estate Investment* ,
https://doi.org/10.1007/978-3-031-00968-6

***Discounted cash flow (DCF)*:** The DCF framework explicitly outlines how investors exchange their present capital for future income and capital. The present value of the income streams generated by an investment is the sum of the present values of the individual cash flows in each period into the future. These cash flows vary dependent on the nature of the individual asset.

***Efficient market*:** An efficient market is one in which prices fully reflect information affecting the worth of investments. If markets are efficient, then all information is already incorporated into prices, and there are no undervalued or overvalued securities available.

***Equivalent yield*:** The total annual return (IRR) to be received from property's cash flow assuming a rise to estimated rental value at the next rent review, but with no change in yield and ignoring further rental growth. It is a term used in the UK and is equivalent to capitalisation rate.

***Fund of funds*:** An investment vehicle that holds a portfolio of other investment funds.

***Fund management*:** The administration of a pool of capital with the intention of investing the majority of all the capital in a group of assets.

***Fund mandate*:** The mandate of a collective investment vehicle is a statement of its aims, the limits within which it is supposed to invest, and the investment policy it should follow.

***G10*:** It is a group of ten leading world countries that agreed in 1962 to support the lending capacity of the International Monetary Fund. Switzerland was added to the group in 1964 but the name was unchanged.

***G20*:** It is a forum for most of the world's largest economies that was founded in 1999. It comprises nineteen countries and the European Union.

***Gearing*:** Gearing measures the scale of a firm's borrowing of capital to invest. Capital gearing refers to the relationship, or ratio, of a company's debt-to-equity. Income gearing is the ratio of interest payments to income.

***Global Financial Crisis*:** The global financial crisis (GFC) refers to the period of extreme stress in global financial markets and banking systems between mid 2007 and early 2009. Many banks around the world incurred large losses and relied on government support to avoid bankruptcy.

***Indexed fund*:** An indexed fund has a portfolio designed to copy the generation of returns from a market or an index.

***Index-linked bonds or gilts*:** Government bonds on which the interest payments and redemption value are linked to a measure of inflation.

***Indirect property investment*:** Ownership of an asset whose return is backed by property. This type of investment is sometimes referred to as a paper asset. Shares in property companies, REITs, property unit trusts and investment trusts are examples of equity indirect investments. Mortgages and loans are debt based indirect property investment.

***Initial yield*:** The initial income of an investment expressed as a percentage of its price. For real estate it is the initial rent passing net of ground rent as a percentage of the gross capital value at the same date.

Institutional funds: These are generally pension and life assurance funds. They could also represent money managed by financial intermediaries, such as German open-ended funds.

Limited partnership: A partner in a limited partnership has limited liability but normally has a passive role in management. There is also a manager who decides the investment policy of the partnership.

Liquidity: The capacity to transact without causing a significant change in the asset price. Property tends to be considered illiquid, not least because of the time taken for transaction.

Market risk: Market risk is the degree of risk that cannot be diversified away by investing in a portfolio. This market (or systematic) risk is created by general economic conditions that influence the return on all securities or assets to varying degrees.

Open ended funds: A collective investment vehicle where the number of shares or units can be increased or decreased according to cash flow into and out of the fund.

Pooled fund: A fund in which at least two investors pool their capital in an investment account. Groups such as investment clubs, partnerships and trusts use pooled funds to gather resources to invest. Investors can include financial institutions and retail funds (such as unit linked or Property Unit Trusts).

Price: The actual observable exchange price of an asset in the open market

Portfolio management: The administration of assets within a fund.

Property Unit Trust: These trusts pool investors' money to invest in property. The trusts are open-ended funds, so that the number of units in a fund varies with demand. If the net demand for units falls then the trust needs to sell assets to reflect the shrinkage in units (and vice versa).

Property Universe: A term that is used in large property data sets such as that provided by MSCI to describe the number of properties included in a particular data set - most commonly to describe those properties valued at differing frequencies whether monthly, quarterly or annually.

Reversionary yield: the open market rental value net of ground rent as a percentage of the gross capital value, at the same point in time at a rent review or the termination of a lease sometime in the future.

REIT: A real estate investment trust is a listed company which owns and manages (generally) income producing real estate, and by meeting specific investment criteria is eligible to pay dividends gross of tax to shareholders.

Retail funds: Such funds are sold directly to third-party investors, typically on a daily trading basis. In some cases, they are open to institutional investment as well.

Risk premium: The investment return an asset is expected to yield in excess of the risk-free rate of return.

Securitisation: The practice of pooling debt assets (often commercial/residential mortgages) and selling, usually bonds, with interest payments to third-party investors. The interest payments on the securities are backed by the income from the mortgages.

***Segregated fund*:** This term is used interchangeably with the term separate account. It is a portfolio managed for a single investor. These investors could encompass public or private pension funds, insurance companies, charities, sovereign wealth funds, etc.

***Specialist fund*:** A fund dedicated to one country, currency, asset type or investment class.

***Specific risk*:** The risk that can be removed through diversification and which relates to the individual characteristics of an investment. It is the variability in return due to factors unique to the investment.

***Treasury Bills*:** These are short term securities sold by governments that can be redeemed at a date in the future. This date could be for example a week, a month or a year from issue. They are priced at a discount to their final redeemable value with the difference determining the return to the investor.

***Upward only rent reviews*:** A typical lease may have points in time in the future when the rent is due for review. An upward only rent review is the term used to describe a situation in which the rent payable following a review date cannot be reduced (even if market rents have generally fallen since the last review).

***Value*:** Is an estimate of the price that would be achieved if a property were to be sold in the market

***Worth*:** A specific investor's perception of the capital sum which they would be prepared to pay (or accept) for the stream of benefits which they expect to be produced by the investment.

Index

C. A. Jones and E. Trevillion, *Real Estate Investment*, https://doi.org/10.1007/978-3-031-00968-6

The manufacturer's authorised representative in the EU is Springer Nature Customer Service Centre GmbH, Europaplatz 3, 69115 Heidelberg, Germany. If you have any concerns regarding our products, please contact ProductSafety@springernature.com

Printed and bound by CPI Group (UK) Ltd, Croydon, CR0 4YY
17/08/2026
02198394-0001